Historical Directory of Trade Unions

Historical Directory of Trade Unions

ARTHUR MARSH and VICTORIA RYAN

Foreword by Lord Briggs

Volume 2

including unions in

Engineering, Shipbuilding and Minor Metal Trades

Coal Mining and Iron and Steel

Agriculture, Fishing and Chemicals

Gower

Published by
Gower Publishing Company Limited
Aldershot, Hants, England

British Library Cataloguing in Publication Data

Marsh, Arthur Ivor
  Historical directory of trade unions.
  Vol. 2 : Engineering, coal mining, iron and
  steel, agriculture, chemicals
  1. Trade-unions — Great Britain — History
  I. Title   II. Ryan, Victoria
  331.88′0941   HD6664

  ISBN 0–566–02161–7

Typeset in Great Britain by
Activity, Salisbury, Wilts

Printed in Great Britain by
Redwood Burn Limited, Trowbridge, Wiltshire

Contents

Foreword

Lord Briggs
Provost of Worcester College, Oxford

The history of most trade unions is more complicated than the history of most individuals. Even names can and do change. Records are usually incomplete, and key events in the history often cannot be fully elucidated in retrospect. There is as much myth as fact.

With the enormous expansion in the study of labour history, more and more people are turning back to detailed trade union history. We have long passed the stage described by Hugh Clegg in his Preface to *General Union in a Changing Society* (1964) when trade union historians were content 'to provide a record of [a] union's development which would both aim at a reasonable standard of historical scholarship and prove readable for the active and interested members of the union'. Notions of 'reasonable standard' have changed. So, too, has our knowledge of the relationships between institutions and their context. We now have more than one history of some unions: given the diversities of interpretation there should be no closed shop here. It is now recognised that general questions have to be considered which cannot be answered from the experience of one institution taken by itself.

This second volume of the planned four-volume collection of brief biographies of British trade unions past and present should prove as valuable to historians as Joyce Bellamy and John Saville's *Dictionary of Labour Biography* which deals with individuals. In their introduction to the first of their four volumes (1972) Bellamy and Saville pointed out that while they had at first intended to produce a single large volume on the lines of *Who's Who*, 'the scope and range of the Dictionary grew ... and the present plan for more than one volume was finally decided'. Arthur Marsh and Victoria Ryan have obviously faced the same kind of problem; this second volume covers unions in engineering, coal mining, iron and steel, agriculture, fishing and chemicals.

The entries cover both biographical profiles and bibliographical material, and while it is far too soon (as Bellamy and Saville also remarked in their first volume) 'to indicate even in the most general way the historical perspectives which emerge from a study of a large number of biographical entries', I have no doubt that by the time Volume 4 is published such perspectives will begin to develop. Trade unions can be found in many different societies, but there is something peculiarly British – for good or ill – in the clusters which exist in this country. I can recommend this series, therefore, to readers who wish to understand to what extent in the last years of the twentieth century we are tied to the legacies of the past.

Preface

In Volume 1 of this series, published in 1980, we explained the purpose of a *Historical Directory of Trade Unions* of this kind. Our experience over many years in working on the history of particular unions and in industrial relations in specific industries had been punctuated with the aggravation of encountering the names of trade unions of which we had not previously heard, or about which we knew very little. Where were we to go to find out more? Almost invariably the route was a complex one. Very few of the thousands of unions which have existed in this country have left histories of themselves. In some cases nothing is available but a name; many more can be further identified only from scattered references in academic and trade union texts and other sources.

Our object, therefore, has been to identify as many unions as we can and to pass on to the inquirer such sources of information about them as we have been able to find, so far as possible by industry, on the following plan:

Vol. 1   *Non-Manual Unions* (already published)

Vol. 2   (the present volume) *Trade Unions in Engineering, Shipbuilding, Coal Mining, Iron and Steel, Agriculture, Fishing, Chemicals, Pottery and Glass, Boots Shoes and Leather, Vehicle Building and Minor Metal Trades*

Vol. 3   *Trade Unions in Transport, Construction, Furniture, Government* (forthcoming)

Vol. 4   *Trade Unions in Textiles, Printing and Paper, Retail Distribution and Miscellaneous Industries* (forthcoming).

The standard form of each entry is as follows:

1.   Name of union.
2.   Foundation date;
   Name changes (if any) and relevant dates;
   Any amalgamation or transfer of engagements;
   Cessation, winding up or disappearance, with date and reasons.
3.   Characteristics of:
   Membership (type and numbers);

Leadership;
Policy;
Outstanding events.
4. Sources of information:
Books, articles, minutes, etc.;
Location of documentation.

The present volume of the directory is divided into three parts, subdivided by subject area. Introductory passages are provided before the entries for each industry.

Our policy in dealing with problems of industrial and manual/non-manual treatment was described in Volume 1 in the following way. We acknowledge that any division of trade unions into groupings by industry or occupation involves arbitrary treatment of some organisations. Where *general unions* are concerned our practice is to include these under the main headings related to their original purpose and also to refer to them under any other classification in which they have major interests, e.g. the main entry on the Transport and General Workers' Union will be found in Vol. 3, *Transport, Construction,* etc., but references will also be made to the union under engineering in Vol. 2, *Engineering, Iron and Steel, Coal, Agriculture and Chemicals,* and in Vol. 1 there is an entry for its non-manual subsidiary, the Association of Clerical, Technical and Supervisory Staffs.

In designating unions as *manual* or *non-manual* we have recognised that some non-manual unions may consist, in part, of manual workers. Examples are the Post Office Engineering Union and the Union of Post Office Workers, and also the Union of Shop, Distributive and Allied Workers. Such unions have been allocated to volumes primarily on the basis of the nature of the industry in which they operate. Hence the Post Office Engineering Union and the Union of Post Office Workers have been included as non-manual. Where the Union of Shop, Distributive and Allied Workers is concerned, we have applied the origins rule and placed the union in the non-manual category but will also cross reference it in Vol. 4. The complexity of the British trade union movement makes some untidiness inevitable and completely accurate categorisation almost impossible.

We do not pretend that our lists are exhaustive, nor that every possible reference has been noted. We have tried to include every organisation, past or present, which appears to have represented employees in relation to their terms and conditions of work even though 'many of them have left no documentary trace other than an isolated rule book or membership card and perhaps correspondence in the surviving files of third parties' (see Richard Storey and Janet Druker, *Guide to the Modern Records Centre*, University of Warwick Library, 1977, pp. 9–10). We have omitted organisations which we can name but on which we can add no further information at this juncture. Such unions will be noted as an appendix to subsequent volumes if further information becomes available.

In preparing this second volume we have found our task in many respects more difficult than in tackling the first. The problem has been less associated with numbers *per se* (though there are, of course, more manual than non-manual unions to be recorded), than with the comparatively longer time over which manual unions have been developing, with difficulties in identifying precise titles, and with complexities surrounding formation, mergers and terminations.

Over more than one and a half centuries, the 'turnover' of trade unions has been astonishing. The general tendency for numbers to fall, shown in Table 1, conceals a phenomenal rate of birth, merger and death. The 130 organisations relating to the present volume which still existed in 1978 are the residual product of at least 1,500 unions on which we have some information. Unlike most non-manual organisations, even the most elementary details may be lacking where manual unions are concerned. Almost all of the former date from the First World War when records were becoming relatively well organised. Most of the latter were established in the 1890s or had their origins in one or other of those bursts of organisational enthusiasm which occurred periodically from the late eighteenth century onwards. Until 1871, the status of unions was vague. Some registered as friendly societies; many did not. Some were merely informal organisations or clubs centred around particular situations or individuals. Names were often fluid or merely traditional. Even the legitimisation of unions in 1871 and the possibility of registration as such did not prove attractive for some years to many organisations. By the end of the year in which the Trade Union Act was passed only two unions had registered; by the end of 1872 an additional 66 had taken advantage of the Act. It was not until 1892 that the Registrar of Friendly Societies could report that 'the indisposition which was shown by trade unions in the early years of operation of the Act of 1871 has to a large extent ceased to exist'. The Registrar's remark showed a certain optimism. In 1892 only 493 of the 1,233 unions known to the Board of Trade were on the register.

Table 1
Numbers of Trade Unions
Officially Recorded*

	1892	1900	1910	1925	1947	1978
All Trade Unions	1,233	1,323	1,269	1,176	734	462
Mining and Quarrying	72	59	84	110	48 (16)	46 (3)
Metals, Engineering and Shipbuilding	298	280	211	131	99	62
Agriculture and Fishing	11	5	9	13	9	9
Chemical, Glass, Pottery	42	44	33	29	22	11
Boot, Shoe and Leather	44	51	38	26	14	2
Enginemen	34	32	22	†	†	†
	501	471	397	309	192	130

* 1892–1910 inclusive: Board of Trade, *Reports by the Chief Labour Correspondent on Trade Unions* and *Labour Gazettes*. 1925 to date: *Ministry of Labour Gazettes*; Department of Employment, *Directory of Employers' Associations, Trade Unions, Joint Organisations, etc.*

( ) National organisations, discounting local district unions forming part of them and separately registered or certificated.

† 'Enginemen' are not separately listed after the 1914–18 war; the few unions remaining (4 in 1925) are thereafter included under 'Metals, Engineering and Shipbuilding'.

What we know of the early history of manual unions is mainly derived either from histories written from their surviving records, or from the assiduous attention paid by labour correspondents of the Labour Department of the Board of Trade from the late 1880s in establishing dates of formation, amalgamation and disappearance. These, together with the files of unions which are known to have existed between 1892 and 1972, collected at the University of Warwick and kindly made available by Professor George Bain and Robert Price, have formed the basis of many of our entries in this directory. A prime source of supplementation has been contributed by the Certification Office which took over the role of the former Registrar in 1974. The Certification Office records take the following form: in the case of the first 1,500 unions registering under the 1871 Act, basic changes of title or status were recorded, union by union, until just before the First World War when this practice ceased; thereafter, until 1961, a ledger was kept which recorded such changes by title, by approximate trade grouping, and in some cases by location; after 1961 there is a gap until 1964, when typed monthly lists of such changes become available.

These sources can be supplemented from a number of others of an official and unofficial kind. Where registered (or later 'listed') unions are involved, the returns made by them for Great Britain are now located in four centres. The returns of organisations having their head offices in Scotland can be inspected on inquiry at the Office of the Assistant Certification Officer for Scotland, 19 Heriot Row, Edinburgh EH3 6HT. For the rest of the country annual returns and rules made prior to 1959 are now located at the Public Records Office, Kew; those from 1959–74 are to be found at the Public Record Office Repository, Hayes, Middlesex, and are available by arrangement with the Certification Officer; from 1974 onwards, they are at the Certification Office itself, Ormond Yard, Duke of York Street, SW1. We have to thank the Certification Officer, and particularly Mr Ian Drummond and Mr Viergas of his office, for this information and for their assistance in our own inquiries, which have been both long and unremitting.

Where unregistered unions are concerned, it is worth noting that the Board of Trade Labour Department Correspondents included in their notes *both* registered and unregistered organisations, and that this practice was continued in subsequent Industrial Directories of the United Kingdom by the Board of Trade and, after 1916, by the Ministry of Labour. Since 1960 this has been in a loose-leaf 'up-date' form. The compilation of these under the title *Directory of Employers' Associations Trade Directories*, has relied until recently upon direct postal communication with trade unions to elicit the necessary information. They gave no information on termination or merger of a direct kind until the 'up-date' form was adopted. Many of the files associated with the building up of the Directories have not survived. Those which remain and files on current unions are to be found at the Department of Employment, Statistics Division D2, Orphanage Road, Watford, Hertfordshire WD1 1PJ.

Finally, we have been fortunate to have access to the card index of trade unions to be found in the library of the Trades Union Congress in London. This contains notes on the date of origin, demise or amalgamation of some 1,500 organisations compiled between 1960 and 1968, by Miss Doris Crowther with financial assistance from the National Register of Archives. It is unfortunate that Miss Crowther died before her task could be completed, but her work has solved many riddles for us, especially those concerning the period 1910 to 1939.

These sources apart, we have relied heavily, as in the case of the first volume, upon trade union histories for our more detailed information on individual unions. In some areas of union development this produces an embarrassment of riches. Coal mining is a case in point. In other areas no secondary literature seems to exist, e.g. on domestic and heating engineers. We are left with the impression that, given the survival of at least some documentation, work on trade union history can hardly be said to have begun! The following additional notes expanded from our first volume may continue to be of interest to users of this series.

Collections of Trade Union materials

Relatively little trade union material appears to have been lodged in public collections. A catalogue of *Labour Records in Scotland* has been published by the Scottish Labour History Society, compiled and edited by Ian MacDougall (Edinburgh, 1978). This contains information about political movements and organisations in addition to trade unions – friendly societies, co-operative societies, the Independent Labour Party, the Labour Party, etc. The Modern Records Centre at the University of Warwick provides a similar guide to documents in its own possession updated by Information Bulletins issued from time to time (*Guide to the Modern Records Centre*, 1977, and Bulletins since April 1978). Other main trade union collections are to be found at the London School of Economics (Webb Collection); British Library of Political and Economic Science, Nuffield College, Oxford (Cole Collection); South Wales Miners' Library (50 Sketty Road, Swansea); Ruskin College, Oxford; Bishopsgate Institute; Fawcett Library (now at the City of London Polytechnic); Congress House Library (Trades Union Congress); National Library of Scotland; St Edmund Hall, Oxford (Risborough Collection) the Marx Memorial Library (37a Clerkenwell Gardens, London EC1); and the Department of Employment Library (now at Steel House, Tothill Street, London SW1H 9NA), which contains many early as well as more modern trade union documents. In addition, the Manchester Studies Unit, Manchester Polytechnic, includes cotton records; the Working Class Movement Library (111 King's Road, Old Trafford, Manchester), although a private collection belonging to Mr and Mrs Eddie Frow, is open for the use of students, as are the files of the Dictionary of Labour Biography at the University of Hull; and the Brynmor Jones Library at the same university, which contains a variety of material for research into the Labour Movement. Labour periodicals and their locations in libraries, etc., are noted in R. Harrison, G. Wolven and R. Duncan, *The Warwick Guide to British Labour Periodicals*, Harvester Press, 1977.

AIM
VR

Key

Some of the sources of information have been abbreviated in the text to avoid undue repetition. Below are the abbreviated forms followed by the complete references.

Anderson: John Anderson, *Forty Years' Industrial Progress*, Amalgamated Society of Engineers, 1891

Arnot, *History of the Scottish Miners*: R. Page Arnot, *A History of the Scottish Miners*, George Allen and Unwin, London, 1955

Arnot, *The Miners*: R. Page Arnot, *The Miners: A History of the Miners' Federation of Great Britain, 1889–1910*, George Allen and Unwin, London, 1949

Arnot, *South Wales Miners*: R. Page Arnot, *The South Wales Miners, 1898–1914*, George Allen and Unwin, London, 1967

Bain and Price: G. S. Bain and R. J. Price, unpublished data, Social Science Research Council Industrial Relations Unit, Warwick University.

Barou: N. Barou, *British Trade Unions*, Victor Gollancz, 1947

BoT Reports: Board of Trade, Reports of the Labour Department, HMSO, 1896 to 1910

Burgess, *Origins:* Keith Burgess, *The Origins of British Industrial Relations*, Croom Helm, London, 1975

Burgess, 'Trade Union Policy': Keith Burgess, 'Trade Union Policy and the 1852 Lock-out in the British Engineering Industry', *International Review of Social History*, Vol. XVII, 1972

Carr and Taplin: J. C. Carr and W. Taplin, *History of the British Steel Industry*, Blackwell, 1962

Certification Office: Certification Office, Ormond Yard, Duke of York Street, London, SW1

Clegg, Fox and Thompson: H. A. Clegg, A. Fox and A. F. Thompson, *A History of British Trade Unions since 1889*, Oxford University Press, 1964

Cole, *British Trade Unionism Today*: G. D. H. Cole (ed.), *British Trade Unionism Today*, Methuen, 1945

Cole, *British Working-Class Movements*: G. D. H. Cole, *A Short History of the British Working-Class Movement, 1789–1947*, George Allen and Unwin, London, 1948

Cole, *Organised Labour*: G. D. H. Cole, *Organised Labour: an*

Introduction to Trade Unionism, George Allen and Unwin, London, and Labour Publishing Co., 1924

Cole, 'Some Notes on British Trade Unions': G. D. H. Cole, 'Some Notes on British Trade Unions in the Third Quarter of the 19th Century', *International Review of Social History*, Vol. II, 1937

Cole, *Trade Unionism Today*: G. D. H. Cole, *Trade Unionism Today*, Victor Gollancz, 1939

Cummings: D. C. Cummings, *An Historical Survey of the Boilermakers' and Iron and Steel Shipbuilders' Society from August 1834 to August 1904*, R. Robinson, Newcastle upon Tyne, 1904

Evans, *Mabon*: E. W. Evans, *Mabon: A Study in Trade Union Leadership*, University of Wales Press, Cardiff, 1959

Evans, *Miners of South Wales*: E. W. Evans, *The Miners of South Wales*, University of Wales Press, Cardiff, 1961

Fox: A. Fox, *A History of the National Union of Boot and Shoe Operatives, 1874–1957*, Blackwell, 1958

Francis and Smith: Hywel Francis and David Smith, *The Fed: A History of the South Wales Miners in the Twentieth Century*, Lawrence and Wishart, London, 1980

Fyrth and Collins: H. J. Fyrth and H. Collins, *The Foundry Workers: A Trade Union History*, Amalgamated Union of Foundry Workers, 1959

Green, *History of the Agricultural Labourer*: F. E. Green, *A History of the English Agricultural Labourer, 1870–1920*, P. S. King & Son Ltd, London, 1920

Groves, 'The Long Journey Home': R. Groves, 'The Long Journey Home', *Tribune*, 18 February 1949 (Kent and Sussex Agricultural Labourers' Union)

Groves, *Seed Time and Harvest*: R. Groves, *Seed Time and Harvest*, National Union of Agricultural and Allied Workers, 1972

Groves, *Sharpen the Sickle!*: R. Groves, *Sharpen the Sickle! The History of the Farmworkers Union*, Porcupine Press, 1949

Harrison: Royden Harrison (ed.), *The Independent Collier*, Harvester Press, Sussex, 1978

Horn, 'Agricultural Labourers' Trade Unionism': P. Horn, 'Agricultural Labourers' Trade Unionism in Four Midland Counties, 1860–1900', PhD thesis, Leicester University, 1967–8

Horn, *Joseph Arch*: P. Horn, *Joseph Arch*, Roundwood Press, Kineton, 1971

Industrial Directory: 'Industrial Directory of the United Kingdom, 1913 and 1914', HMSO

Jefferys: J. B. Jefferys, *The Story of the Engineers*, Lawrence and Wishart, London, 1946

Kidd: A. T. Kidd, *History of the Tinplate Workers and Sheet Metal Workers and Braziers Societies*, National Union of Sheet Metal Workers and Braziers, 1949

Lloyd: G. I. H. Lloyd, *The Cutlery Trades*, Longmans Green & Co., London, 1913

Machin: Frank Machin, *The Yorkshire Miners*, National Union of Mineworkers, Barnsley, 1958

McLaine, 'The Engineers' Union': William McLaine, 'The Engineers' Union, Book I: the Millwrights and "Old Mechanics"', PhD thesis, London University, 1939

Marsh, *Concise Encyclopedia*: Arthur Marsh, *Concise Encyclopedia of Industrial Relations*, Gower, 1979

Marsh, *Industrial Relations*: Arthur Marsh, *Industrial Relations in Engineering*, Pergamon, 1965

Marsh, *Trade Union Handbook*: Arthur Marsh, *Trade Union Handbook*, Gower, 1979

Marwick: W. H. Marwick, *A Short History of the Scottish Working Class Movement*, Scottish Secretariat, Glasgow, 1948

Miller: G. D. Miller, 'Trade Unionism in the Engineering Industry', in G. D. H. Cole (ed.), *British Trade Unionism Today*, Victor Gollancz, London, 1939

MoL Reports: Reports of the Department of Labour Statistics, Directory of Industrial and other Associations concerned with matters relating to conditions of Employment 1919–1925, HMSO

Mortimer: J. E. Mortimer, *History of the Boilermakers' Society*, Vol. I (1834–1906), George Allen and Unwin, 1973

Mosses: William Mosses, *The History of the United Patternmakers' Association 1872–1922*, United Patternmakers' Association, Co-operative Printing Society, 1922

NUFLAT: National Association of Footwear, Leather and Allied Trades

NUVB, 1934: National Union of Vehicle Builders, *A Hundred Years of Vehicle Building, 1834–1934*, NUVB, 1934

NUVB, 1959: National Union of Vehicle Builders, NUVB, 1959

Owen: Jack Owen, *Ironmen*, National Union of Blastfurnacemen, 1953

Pollard: S. Pollard, *A History of Labour in Sheffield*, Liverpool University Press, 1959

Pugh: Sir Arthur Pugh, *Men of Steel*, Iron and Steel Trades Confederation, 1951

Robinson: T. H. Robinson, 'The Antecedents and Beginnings of the Amalgamated Society of Engineers', BLitt thesis, Oxford University, 1928

Selley: Ernest Selley, *Village Trade Unionism in Two Centuries*, George Allen and Unwin, 1919

Suthers, 'Amalgamated Engineering Union': R. B. Suthers, 'Amalgamated Engineering Union', *Labour Magazine*, Vol. X, No. 10, February 1932

Suthers, 'National Union of Agricultural Workers': R. B. Suthers, 'National Union of Agricultural Workers', *Labour Magazine*, Vol. X, No. 12, April 1932

Warburton, *History of Trade Union Organisation*: W. H. Warburton, *The History of Trade Union Organisation in the North Staffordshire Potteries*, George Allen and Unwin, 1931

Warburton, 'Progress of Labour Organisation': W. H. Warburton, 'The Progress of Labour Organisation in the Pottery Industry of Great Britain', BLitt thesis, Oxford University, 1928

Wearmouth: R. F. Wearmouth, *Some Working Class Movements of the 19th Century*, Epworth Press, London, 1948

Webb, *Story of the Durham Miners*: Sidney Webb, *The Story of the Durham Miners 1662–1921*, Fabian Society, London, 1921

S. and B. Webb, *History of Trade Unionism*: Sidney and Beatrice Webb, *The History of Trade Unionism*, Longmans Green and Co., London, 1919 and 1920

S. and B. Webb, *Industrial Democracy*: Sidney and Beatrice Webb, Longmans Green & Co., London, 1897

Welbourne: E. Welbourne, *The Miners' Unions of Northumberland and Durham*, Cambridge University Press, 1923

Williams, *The Derbyshire Miners*: J. E. Williams, *The Derbyshire Miners: a Study of Industrial and Social History*, George Allen and Unwin, London, 1962

Williams, 'Labour in the Coalfields': J. E. Williams, 'Labour in the Coalfields: a Critical Bibliography', *Bulletin of the Society for the Study of Labour History*, No. 4, 1962

Williams, 'The Miners' Lockout of 1893': J. E. Williams, 'The Miners' Lockout of 1893', *Bulletin of the Society for the Study of Labour History*, Nos. 24–5, 1972

Part One

Engineering

Engineering and Foundry Work

ENGINEERING

The development of trade unionism in engineering has so often been recounted, in whole or in part, as to require no more than a summary in this volume.[1] Broadly speaking it falls into four overlapping phases. The first covers the age of the millwright, 'that itinerant engineer and mechanic of high reputation' who could 'handle the axe, the hammer and the plane with equal skill and precision ... turn, bore or forge ... and set and cut furrows in a millstone with an accuracy equal or superior to that of the miller himself'.[2] Gradually, on the introduction of the steam engine, this universal craftsman was superseded by the 'engineers' economy', the parcelling out of the trade of the millwright among distinct classes of workmen catered for by 'sectional' trade and friendly societies.[3] Such specialisation, mirrored in trade union organisation, took an unconscionable time in dying as, throughout the nineteenth century and since, new skills took the place of the old and multiplied the demand for specialised representation of labour.

By 1851, however, a third phase had begun, rooted in the vision of the newly established Amalgamated Society of Engineers (ASE) of a consolidation of organised labour in the industry into a centralised national organisation of such strength and stability that employers would be 'too wary to resist any just demand', knowing that the union had the power to enforce it.[4] The ASE came rapidly, in numbers, wealth and coverage, to dominate the industry. The elimination of sectional societies with local and national appeal, however, took a long time to achieve. A few still remain in the 1980s.[5] The 1890s witnessed a fourth development. This was the unexpected capacity, in the wake of the Great Dock Strike of 1889, for lower grade workers in the industry, hitherto regarded as unorganisable labourers, to combine in the new general unions. The process was slow but assisted by further continuous erosion of broader engineering skills and by two world wars. This currently accounts for the numerical strength of the Transport and General and the General and Municipal Workers in the engineering field, and especially of the former in automotive production.

Today, the product of these four phases is an industry still dominated in numbers by the 'New Model' of the ASE through its heir, the Amalgamated Union of Engineering Workers with its 1.5 million members, some 1.2 million of these in 'manufacturing engineering' as distinct from maintenance and construction (and an additional 60,000 in foundry work), but sharing the field with about a dozen other manual unions, some general and some small or expanded sectional societies. The TGWU reckoned an engineering and automative membership of about half a million before the redundancies of 1980 and the GMWU of under 200,000. Sectional societies, or amalgamations based upon them, make up the remainder of engineering manual worker trade unionists, perhaps 2.5 million in all in 1979–80. In the brief summary of trade union development in engineering which follows, unions organising foundry workers are, for reasons of historical continuity, included among the main body of engineering organisations, though separately described at pp. 8–9. Separate sections are, however, devoted to shipbuilding (pp. 69–90), vehicle building unions (pp. 91–100), sheet metal workers' organisations (pp. 101–25), lock, chain, spring, nail, bolt, nut, screw, bedstead and fender organisations (pp. 161–78), hammermen, smiths and strikers (pp. 179–86), the latter developing both towards engineering and shipbuilding.

The Development of Trade Unionism

Little is known about trade unionism in engineering in the age of the millwright. 'The itinerant and often individual character of their work', writes Jefferys, 'militated against organisation, but where engine or bridge building was on a scale which led to regular employment in one locality, a *trade policy* emerged alongside the provision of benefits'.[6] Where petitions failed, Friendly Societies of mechanics and millwrights became unlawful combinations to enforce general increases in wages, and no doubt often paid the price as common law conspiracies in restraint of trade. Early references are to the North in the 1780s when a Friendly Society of Mechanics became established particularly in Bolton, Blackburn and Chorley[7] and to London where in 1799 the master millwrights of that city petitioned Parliament to make illegal combinations of their own journeymen,[8] an act which gave rise to the Combination Acts of 1799 and 1800. The trade society concerned is thought to have been the London Fellowship of Millwrights (1795). By 1810 there appear to have been three separate millwrights' societies in London, powerful enough to control entry to jobs and hours of work,[9] one of these, perhaps, the Amicable and Brotherly Society of Journeymen Millwrights (the 'Old Millwrights'), originating in 1801.

In such circumstances and where all-round craftsmen were in short supply, employers had a strong incentive to increase numbers by using more specialised fitters and turners. The refusal of millwrights to work with such 'inferior' workmen was one reason for the slow development of the 'engineers' economy'. Another was the lack of suitable machine tools. Specialisation seems to have developed in the first instance outside London, for in the Capital the millwrights' societies were most entrenched. A Mechanics' Friendly Union was formed in Bradford in 1822, open to model makers, filers, joiners and turners as well as to millwrights, and accepting a shortened period of apprenticeship. This marked the beginning of the age of local 'engineers' unions' the most important of which was the Steam Engine Makers' Society (1824) and the Friendly Society of Mechanics, formed in Manchester in 1826, which later became the Journeymen Steam Engine and Machine Makers Society (the 'Old Mechanics') to which could be added the London Friendly Society of Engineers (the 'Old Engineers', 1833) and many others.

The types of workers catered for by such unions greatly increased in numbers between 1830 and 1850 as more sophisticated machine tools came into use. Many all-round millwrights who felt that they had much to lose fell back on exclusively millwright societies. Such organisations were founded at Manchester in 1836, at Bolton in the following year, at Liverpool in 1842 and at Preston in 1843, acting in rivalry with both local 'engineers' unions' and with those which aspired to be more national in coverage – the Journeymen Steam Engine Makers, the Associated Fraternity of Iron Forgers (the 'Old Smiths', 1830) and the Boilermakers (1834). The JSEM is reputed to have been the first union of engineering workers which ceased to be a mere local society, absorbing the Yorkshire Mechanics in 1837,[10] quickly dominating the trade in the North of England and establishing branches also at Greenock and in London.[11]

The amalgamation movement gained momentum both from the weaknesses shown by divided and competing organisations in the depressed years in the 1830s and 1840s and from the greater success which communication between sectional societies appeared to promise. Joint Committees of engineering operatives were formed between 1844 and 1850 in all principal Lancashire centres and won important victories, in particular the release of 12 arrested JSEM pickets in 1847.[12] In 1850 steps were taken to advance the notion of amalgamation of sectional societies into a 'gigantic' association.[13]

At the centre of the merger which produced the Amalgamated Society of Engineers, Machinists, Smiths, Millwrights and Patternmakers (January 1851) was the JSEM, with its headquarters in Manchester, which exceeded all other trade societies in wealth and contributed more than three-quarters of the original membership of the new organisation. Many JSEM branches consented to the move only with reluctance; some seceded in protest. Only a fraction of the Steam Engine Makers' Society of Liverpool came over and the 'New' Society of Millwrights, the 'Old' Society of Engineers and Machinists of London and the London Smiths did not join until May, June and September 1851 respectively, making a total membership of 10,841. The Steam Engine Makers' Society with almost 2,000 members, remained aloof.

The new amalgamation survived a national employers' lock-out in 1852. Under Allen as General Secretary it flourished. Well-run, moderate, aristocratic and cautious, it could boast of 186 branches by 1861,[14] 377 in 1874 and 509 in 1891, 81 of them outside the UK, and a membership of 71,221.[15] By that time unions catering for the same trades as the ASE were, on a more or less national scale, in membership terms, relatively pygmies – the Steam Engine Makers' Society, still 'independent', could boast about 6,000 in 1892, the United Patternmakers' Association (founded in 1872) 2,500, the National Society of Brassworkers (also founded in 1872) 6,500, the United Journeymen Brassfounders' Association (1866) 2,500, hardly more than one-quarter in total of the strength of the ASE. Outside the unions not in direct competition with the ASE, the Boilermakers, the Friendly Society of Iron Founders (started as the Friendly Iron Moulders' Society in 1809), the Associated Ironmoulders of Scotland (1869), the Shipwrights and many others could be added to an almost endless list of local societies catering for specific classes of engineers. The early reports of the chief Labour correspondent of the Board of Trade lists some 100 unions in engineering with a total membership of about 300,000 in the 1890s.

If it can be held that the ASE had from its inception harboured the intention of organising *all* skilled workers in the engineering industry, of eliminating *all* sectional societies, 'these small and unnecessary ... absurd and irritating institutions', it was evidently frustrated both by the development of 'new model' unions on its own plan and by the progressive differentiation of skills required by the industry. The 'engineers' economy' which had broken the hold of the millwrights by elevating the importance of fitters and turners had also produced patternmakers, founders in different metals, smiths, hammermen, vicemen and myriads of specialised trades, each of which could claim some skill and, where necessary, aspire to

6

represent others as their own crafts were progressively eroded. Many had, by the latter part of the century, begun to take in the semi-skilled. In 1901 the ASE itself made some effort in this direction by opening a new section of membership for such workers as could earn over 75 per cent of the district rate and who had worked for at least two years in the trade.

In parallel to this the movement which was to bring workers who were even less skilled into engineering trade unionism had already begun. It can hardly be wrong to regard this as a consequence both of the 'new unionism' which followed the Great Dock Strike of 1889, the cautious exclusiveness of traditional craft unions, and the continued dilution of skills which had so long characterised the industry. But for the hope generated by the first of the above there would have been little impetus to make the effort to embark on the founding of new unions to cater for the weaker brethren of the labour force; but for the second they could have been absorbed within existing unions; and but for the third new classes of employees would not have been available for organisation.

The process of mechanisation which produced the semi-skilled 'handyman' machine minder was very uneven. The conditions required were those of the mass market which made the purchase of expensive automatic machines worth while and these were mainly to be found in the production of small arms and ammunition, bicycles, motor vehicles and electrical equipment. The first serious development of engineering of this type dates from about the time of the Great Dock Strike itself. In the first instance new general unions for the unskilled recruited for the most part engineering labourers into their ranks along with those in other industries. The Gasworkers and the National Amalgamated Union of Labour in Lancashire, Yorkshire, the North East Coast, Merseyside and Northern Ireland, all traditional engineering centres (see Vol. 3) formed the basis of the engineering membership of the National Union of General and Municipal Workers (NUGMW) when this was formed in 1924 with some 80,000 engineering, shipbuilding and metal industries membership out of a total of 350,000.[16]

In many ways, however, the most interesting of the new unions in its relationship to engineering was the Workers' Union (WU) founded in 1898. Its role in the industry arose, as its historian has pointed out, as much by accident as by design.[17] The union's founders, which included prominent figures from the Amalgamated Society of Engineers itself, clearly anticipated that where engineering was concerned the WU was free to tackle the unskilled but that the ASE itself would successfully open its ranks to the 'new engineers'. The only engineering workers enrolled in the union's earliest years were labourers in Halifax workshops and foundries. But branches of the ASE did little in practice to apply its relaxed membership rule and in Birmingham and Coventry in particular, centres of the mass production trade in such firms as BSA, the WU found its particular destiny with the semi-skilled in the lighter engineering trades. By 1914 50 of the union's largest branches were composed almost exclusively of engineering workers and a further twenty contained at least a high proportion of members in the industry.[18]

What craft exclusiveness had begun was continued by the First World War which boosted the demand for the semi-skilled and made continued dilution inevitable. Semi-skilled engineering workers in ASE membership increased from about 6 per cent to more than 10 per cent between 1914 and

7

1918. But the bulk went into other organisations, and particularly into the Workers' Union which was in any case the more militant of the two and came to dominate the Midland aircraft and motor factories, including the giant Austin works at Longbridge. The amalgamation of the WU into the Transport and General Workers Union in 1926 brought that union an engineering membership in the Midlands which ultimately, under the regional leadership of Jack Jones, later General Secretary, came to exceed that of the Engineers themselves.

The same processes brought considerable influence to the NUGMW and the TGWU in the Confederation of Shipbuilding and Engineering Unions (CSEU). Founded by Robert Knight of the Boilermakers in 1891 as a counter to the establishment of a national Engineering Employers' Federation in the same year, the original Federation of Engineering and Shipbuilding Trades sought to encourage common action between the sectional societies of the day. The ASE refused to join until 1905 and departed again in 1918, preferring to adopt a renewed drive for amalgamation which produced by 1920 the Amalgamated Engineering Union. Until the formation of the CSEU in 1936 the joint working which the Webbs had a quarter of a century before seen as vital to the organisational efficiency of trade unionism in the industry appeared unlikely to be achieved.[19] The Second World War completed the job which the First World War had begun, first through the Engineering Joint Trades Movement in which the AEU participated and finally, in 1947, by its affiliation to the CSEU on conditions which assured its predominance in engineering national negotiations while ensuring that it could not, by weight of membership, completely dominate CSEU policy-making.[20]

In the years which have elapsed since 1947 the importance of national engineering negotiations and procedure have declined, bringing an easier, if sometimes less purposive role for the CSEU in its relations with the Engineering Employers' Federation as its chief bargaining partner. Competition between a declining number of unions has continued at workshop level. The Boilermakers' amalgamation, the coming together of coppersmiths and sheet metal workers' organisations into a single union of Sheet Metal Workers, Coppersmiths and Heating and Domestic Engineers, the concentration of vehicle builders' societies into a single section of the Transport and General Workers' Union and other developments have effectively reduced 34 affiliated manual unions at the time of the AEU's affiliation to 23.[21]

FOUNDRY WORK

The bulk of foundry work has traditionally been associated with the engineering industry rather than with iron and steel, though organised by different unions catering for moulders, founders, coremakers, and from the end of the nineteenth century, for the labourers working with them. Organisations for skilled ironmoulders can be dated at least from the first decade of the nineteenth century in the form of the Friendly Iron Moulders Society (1809). This union became the Friendly Society of Operative Ironmoulders of the United Kingdom in 1837 and the Friendly Society of Iron Founders of England, Ireland and Wales (the main basis of the

Amalgamated Union of Foundry Workers of the post 1939–45 war period) in 1854.

Apart from the FSIF, most of the early nineteenth century organisations on the iron side of the trade, the Friendly Society of United Journeymen, Platers and Moulders, the Fender Union and the Scottish Iron Moulders Friendly Society, all dating from 1829 or earlier, failed to survive. An exception was the Scottish Iron Moulders Friendly Society (1831) which continued as the Associated Iron Workers of Scotland (1869) to take part in the AUFW amalgamation of 1945. Brassfounders also had a continuous history of organisation from the 1820s and earlier in the form of the London Brassfounders Society, among cockfounders in London and Birmingham, brassmoulders in Birmingham and latterly in local societies in Edinburgh (1838), Belfast (1840), and Hull (1848), as well as an early organisation in Manchester (1825).

From the 1850s to the 1880s attempts were made to centralise English and Scottish societies along the 'new model' lines of the Amalgamated Society of Engineers, principally as national federations – the Scottish Operative Brassfounders Trade, Sick and Funeral Association (1856), the United Journeymen Brassfounders Association of Great Britain and Ireland (1866) and the National Society of Amalgamated Brassworkers (1872), the latter also including non-foundry workers. At the same time, as the division of labour extended in foundries, local organisations of non-founders began to extend to cover iron dressers (the Scottish Iron Dressers (1856) and the Iron Dressers Trade Society (1863)) and to coremakers in Manchester (1860), Bradford, Oldham, Liverpool, etc.

The New Unionism period from 1889 to the beginning of the First World War brought more organisations of non-craftsmen and also major attempts to develop national organisation of a more modern kind. Products of the first attempts were the Welsh Ironfounders Union (1889 – later known as the Amalgamated Society of Moulders and Foundry Workers), the Central Iron Moulders Association (1889 – later in 1926 known as the Ironfounding Workers Association, an organisation in light casting in central Scotland which later spread to England), the National Union of Stove Grate Workers (1890), the Amalgamated Society of Plate and Machine Moulders (1890 – later the Amalgamated Moulders and Kindred Industries Trade Union), the London United Brassfounders (1890) and the General Iron Fitters Association (1892). The Amalgamated Society of Coremakers formed in 1902 brought together a number of local societies into a national organisation in the same way as the Scottish Brassmoulders Union had done for its section of the trade in Scotland in 1888.

Foundry unions proper proved more difficult to bring together into a single organisation. A Federation of Moulders and Collateral Trades, formed in 1906, collapsed four years later and it was not until 1920 that an effective amalgamation process began in the form of the National Union of Foundry Workers which ultimately came to dominate the trade as the Amalgamated Union of Foundry Workers (1946). By the end of the 1950s it had in membership some seven eighths of all organised labour in foundry work outside the general unions and the Amalgamated Engineering Union, with which it finally amalgamated in 1968. Today, few independent unions survive, and these small in size: the National Union of Domestic Appliance and General Metal Workers (the successor to the National

9

Union of Stove Grate Workers), with 5,200 members, and the Associated Metalworkers Union with about 6,000.

Notes

1. See Sidney and Beatrice Webb, *History of Trade Unionism*, 1919 edn; J.B. Jefferys, *The Story of the Engineers 1800–1945*, Lawrence & Wishart 1946; OUP 1964; H.A. Clegg, Alan Fox and P. Thompson, *A History of British Trade Unions since 1889*, Vol. 1; Keith Burgess, *The Origins of British Industrial Relations*, Croom Helm, 1975.
2. Sir William Fairburn, *Treatise on Mills and Millwork*, 4th edn, 1878 (1st edn 1861).
3. S. and B. Webb, *op. cit.*, p. 205.
4. *The Operative*, 17 May 1851, quoted in Jefferys, *op. cit.*, p. 34.
5. E.g. the Card Setting Machine Tenters' Society and others.
6. Jefferys, *op. cit.*, p. 10.
7. W. McLaine, *The Engineers' Union*, PhD thesis, University of London, 1939.
8. A. Aspinall, *The Early English Trade Unions*, Batchworth Press, 1949, pp. x and xi.
9. *Life of Sir William Fairbairn, Bart.* ed. W. Pole, 1877, p. 92.
10. Formerly the Mechanics' Friendly Union Institution (1822).
11. McLaine, *op. cit.*
12. Burgess, *op. cit.*, p. 17.
13. The word is that of Wm Newton (1822–76), who with Wm Allen (1813–74) is credited as the moving force behind the amalgamation.
14. *London Trades Council Directory of Trade Unions*.
15. Jefferys, *op. cit.*, p. 93.
16. H.A. Clegg, *General Union*, Blackwell, 1954, pp. 31–2.
17. Richard Hyman, *The Workers' Union*, OUP, 1971, p. 41.
18. *ibid.*, p. 42.
19. S. and B. Webb, *Industrial Democracy*, 1911 edn, pp. 112 and 140.
20. The AEU affiliated on 770,000 members only, a figure much below its actual membership in the industry. The engineering section of the union is still affiliated on this figure.
21. The Boilermakers have now amalgamated with the General and Municipal Workers Union to form the General, Municipal, Boilermakers and Allied Trades Union (1983).

ABERDEEN AND DISTRICT TOOLSMITHS SOCIETY

The Society was formed in 1892 and never had more than 44 members. It joined the **United Operative Masons and Granite Cutters** (see Vol. 3) in 1897.

Source: BoT Reports.

ABERDEEN OPERATIVE BRASSFOUNDERS AND COPPERSMITHS ASSOCIATION

Established in 1867 the Association had 32 members in 1892 and 36 in 1910 (formerly known as the **Aberdeen Operative Brass Founders Trade, Sick and Funeral Society**). It amalgamated with several other sectional organisations in the industry in order to form the **Amalgamated Association of Brassfounders, Turners, Fitters and Coppersmiths.**

Source: BoT Reports.

ABERDEEN OPERATIVE BRASS FOUNDERS TRADE, SICK AND FUNERAL SOCIETY

See **Aberdeen Operative Brassfounders and Coppersmiths Association**

AMALGAMATED ASSOCIATION OF BRASS FOUNDERS, TURNERS, FITTERS AND COPPERSMITHS

The Association was established in 1912 by an amalgamation of small sectional societies, covering a total of 2,600 members. These societies were: the **Aberdeen Operative Brassfounders and Coppersmiths Association; the Belfast Brassfounders Association; the Bury and District Brass Founders and Finishers Society; the Derby and Burton Brass Founders and Finishers Society; the Dundee Operative Brass Founders and Finishers Association; the Greenock, Port Glasgow and District Association of Brass Turners, Finishers and Fitters; the Glasgow and District Associated Brass Turners, Fitters and Finishers Society; the Manchester Brassfounders and Finishers Association; the Nottingham United Brassfounders and Finishers Association;** and the **Oldham Brassfounders Association.** In 1920 the Amalgamated Association merged with the **Amalgamated Engineering Union.**

Sources: BoT Reports; Certification Office.

AMALGAMATED ASSOCIATION OF MACHINE WORKERS

The Association was established in 1888 and had 267 members by 1892. In 1894 it merged with the **United Machine Workers Association** with a membership of 174.

Source: BoT Reports.

11

AMALGAMATED BRASS WORKERS SOCIETY (NATIONAL)

See **National Society of Metal Mechanics** and **United Metal Founders Society**

AMALGAMATED ENGINEERING UNION

The Union was formed on 1 July 1920, on the initiative of the **Amalgamated Society of Engineers** which had made repeated attempts since its inception in 1851 to persuade the many sectional societies in the industry to amalgamate and form one big union for the engineering industry. In September 1918 the ASE invited 22 unions in the engineering industry to a conference to discuss amalgamation proposals which led to 17 of those unions agreeing to ballot their members. Nine societies gained the necessary percentage of votes from their members, as follows: the **Steam Engine Makers Society**; the **United Kingdom Society of Amalgamated Smiths and Strikers**; the **United Machine Workers Association**; the **Amalgamated Association of Brass Founders, Turners, Fitters, Finishers and Coppersmiths**; the **North of England Brass Turners, Fitters and Finishers Society**; the **London United Metal Turners, Fitters and Finishers Society**; the **East of Scotland Brass Founders Society**; the **Amalgamated Society of General Tool Makers, Engineers and Machinists**; and the **Amalgamated Instrument Makers Society**. The new union upon its formation opened its ranks to include all workers, craftsmen and non-craftsmen in the engineering industry, at the same time continuing the craft tradition of highly centralised negotiations based on District Committees. It appointed J.T. Brownlie and Tom Mann of the Amalgamated Society of Engineers as President and General Secretary respectively. The new constitution for which the academic and social theorist G.D.H. Cole was largely responsible, resembled that of the ASE with slight modifications. In place of the delegate meeting, a National Committee consisting of 2 representatives from each Divisional Committee was to meet annually to receive a report from the Executive Committee and to give guidance as to future policy. Only members working at the trade or signing the vacant-book could be elected to the National Committee which ensured close and regular contact between the Executive Committee and leading members of the rank and file, and ensured a link between the Executive Committee and the membership. Shop stewards were recognised as having a direct right to assist in policy-making by representation on District Committees, and quarterly meetings of such lay officials were to be held in each district. The amalgamation resulted in a membership of 450,000 and funds amounting to £3,250,000. The AEU affiliated to the **Confederation of Shipbuilding and Engineering Unions** in 1947. In 1968 with the accession of the **Amalgamated Union of Foundry Workers** the name of the union was changed to the **Amalgamated Union of Engineering and Foundry Workers** and subsequently, in 1970, after amalgamation with the **Draughtsmen and Allied Technicians Association** (see Vol. 1) and the **Constructional Engineering Union** to the **Amalgamated Union of Engineering Workers** (see Vol. 3).

Sources: Marsh, *Concise Encyclopedia;* Marsh, *Industrial Relations;*

Jefferys; Anderson; Cummings; Amalgamated Society of Engineers, Jubilee Souvenir, Co-operative Printing Society, London, 1901; Robinson; Miller; Cole, *British Trade Unionism Today*.

AMALGAMATED HACKLE PIN GRINDERS SICK AND MUTUAL BENEFIT SOCIETY

Established in 1873, the Society ceased to exist in 1874.

Source: Certification Office.

AMALGAMATED INSTRUMENT MAKERS SOCIETY

The Society was established in 1887 as the **Scientific Instrument Makers Trade Society,** and was a founder member of the **Federation of Engineering and Shipbuilding Trades** when that organisation was formed in 1891. It had 664 members in 1900 and grew to 2,400 in 1914. It was one of the 22 societies in the engineering industry which were invited by the **Amalgamated Society of Engineers** in 1918 to discuss proposals for the formation of one union covering the entire engineering industry. In May 1919 it was one of the 17 societies which agreed to ballot its membership for this purpose, and in 1920 it amalgamated with other unions to form the **Amalgamated Engineering Union.**

Sources: Jefferys; BoT Reports.

AMALGAMATED MACHINE AND GENERAL LABOURERS UNION

The Union was formed in 1890 and by 1892 it had 1,800 members. In 1915 with 1,850 members it merged with the **National Union of Gas Workers and General Labourers of Great Britain and Ireland** (see Vol. 3).

Source: Bain and Price.

AMALGAMATED MECHANICS AND GENERAL LABOURERS UNION

Established in 1889, with a membership of 138 in 1892, the Union ceased to exist in 1897 when its membership was 122.

Sources: Bain and Price; BoT Reports.

AMALGAMATED MOULDERS AND KINDRED INDUSTRIES TRADE UNION

See **Amalgamated Society of Plate and Machine Moulders**

AMALGAMATED SCALE, BEAM AND WEIGHING MACHINE MAKERS ASSOCIATION
See **Society of Scale Beam and Weighing Machinists**

AMALGAMATED SEWING MACHINE, CYCLE AND TOOL MAKERS ASSOCIATION
Established in 1890, the Association had a membership of 883 in 1892. It ceased to exist in 1894 when the number of members had dwindled to 120.

Source: Bain and Price.

AMALGAMATED SOCIETY OF BRASS WORKERS
The members of the above organisation had been part of the **National Amalgamated Brass Workers Society** in 1874 but in 1886 they broke away from that body to form the above Society based in London. (In the Board of Trade Reports it is called the **London Society of Amalgamated Brass Workers and Gas Fitters** and later the **London Amalgamated Brass Workers Society**.) In 1892 it had 408 members, but from that date to 1910 the membership fluctuated between 240 in 1901 and 280 in 1910. It had a recorded membership of 640 in 1948 and again in 1952. In 1961 the level of membership was 339. It ceased to exist in 1962.

Sources: BoT Reports; MoL Reports; TUC Reports 1948, 1952, 1961.

AMALGAMATED SOCIETY OF CASTERS
Established at Walsall in 1890 with G. Hammerton as Secretary, the Society was formed in the wake of the 'New Unionism' of that period. It gave protection to iron casters, brass casters, stampers, annealers and all other metal casters, many of whom were described by other workers as 'employers' who were paying their own 'underhands'. One of their rules forbade underhands changing employment without producing a character note, but gave them the right of appeal to the union if dissatisfied with their employer. The Society had 400 members in 1892 which had fallen to 90 in 1894 when it ceased to exist.

Sources: Fyrth and Collins; Clegg, Fox and Thompson.

AMALGAMATED SOCIETY OF COREMAKERS OF GREAT BRITAIN AND IRELAND
Many of the early craft unions were unwilling to accept semi-skilled or unskilled workers into their ranks with the result that they had, like the coremakers, to form their own societies such as those at Liverpool, Bradford and Oldham which were small and locally based, and remained so. For instance, the **Bradford Coremakers Society,** formed in 1867, had only 13 members after 25 years of existence. The oldest and largest was the **Manchester and District Coremakers Society** which had been formed in 1860. In 1901 some 8 local unions were organising workers in the core shops with a total membership of 700, of whom almost half

were in Manchester and the remaining 350 scattered in different parts of Lancashire. Most of these unions were affiliated to the **United Association of Coremakers.** In 1902 they combined to form the ASC, appointing E. Clegg as General Secretary and organiser at a salary of £2 per week. In 1906 the new union was a founder member of the **Federation of Moulders and Collateral Trades.** In 1910 the ASC had about 1,400 members. It provided benefits similar to the various moulders' societies but its policy was very conservative and there were few attempts to better conditions in its first four years of existence. The branches kept their own autonomy as funds were not centralised. The Executive Committee was made up of one representative from each branch and met twice a year. For a subscription of 1s per week the members were entitled to unemployment and sick pay varying from 11s to 1s; dispute and funeral benefits were also payable and so was superannuation, although in 1906 there were only 3 members drawing this benefit. In June 1920, with 4,022 members, it amalgamated with the **Associated Iron Moulders of Scotland** and the **Friendly Society of Ironfounders of England, Ireland and Wales** in order to form the **National Union of Foundry Workers.**

Sources: Fyrth and Collins; Associated Society of Coremakers, Manchester Coremakers Jubilee Souvenir Number, 1910.

AMALGAMATED SOCIETY OF ENGINEERS
See **Amalgamated Society of Engineers, Machinists, Smiths, Millwrights and Pattern-makers**

AMALGAMATED SOCIETY OF ENGINEERS, MACHINISTS, SMITHS, MILLWRIGHTS AND PATTERN-MAKERS
The Society (quickly becoming known by the shorter title of the **Amalgamated Society of Engineers,** or ASE) was formed in 1851 by an amalgamation of several sectional engineering unions, the largest being the **Journeymen Steam Engine, Machine Makers and Millwrights Friendly Society** (the 'Old Mechanics') and the **Smiths Benevolent Sick and Burial Society,** the combined commencing membership being 5,000 rising to 11,000 by the end of the year. For the first month of its inception the ASE was not a true amalgamation, the membership comprising most of the 'Old Mechanics' under a new title. But by June 1851 the **Society of Millwrights** merged, and in July so did the **Society of Engineers and Machinists.** The immediate objectives were that systematic overtime was to be abolished; the number of apprentices was to be restricted to one apprentice to 4 journeymen; piece-work was to be resisted; and there was to be opposition to the entry into the trade of 'illegal men' who had not served their time in the industry. The member wishing to join the Society had to be a 'sober and efficient workman and to be free from any physical defects likely to affect his ability as a workman'. For example men who were forced to wear spectacles were not admitted, and the Bridgwater Branch felt it necessary to consult the Executive Committee before admitting 'a worker who is a little round shouldered'. The successful formation of the new Society was immediately followed by a dispute with the engineering employers. Men employed at a firm called Hibbert and Platt made a series of demands, not

only for the abolition of overtime but also for the exclusion of 'labourers and other illegal men' from the machines, with which demand the employers were forced to comply. On 1 January 1852 the union members refused to work overtime and demanded an end to piecework. The employers promptly retaliated by closing every engineering establishment in Lancashire and London. During the three months which followed the employers repeatedly demanded the withdrawal of all the men's demands, and also insisted that the workers sign a document repudiating their trade union membership. Union funds were becoming exhausted and during April the men resumed work on the employers' terms and signed the document but did not leave the union. A number of men refused to sign and many emigrated. The union ended the struggle with only £700 in hand and a membership of just over 9,000, but it was still in existence. In 1891 the sectional societies still remaining as independent bodies formed the **Federation of Engineering and Shipbuilding Trades** which the ASE refused to join. It did take a leading part in the formation of the **General Federation of Trade Unions** in 1899 when its official, Isaac Mitchell, became the Federation's first General Secretary. In 1905 it affiliated to the Federation of Engineering and Shipbuilding Trades and continued to press for the amalgamation of all unions in the industry, persuading 6 sectional societies to do so. It withdrew from the Federation in 1918. During the First World War the Society agreed for the first time to the entry of women into the industry, and at the end of the war it renewed its efforts to form one union for the entire industry by inviting 22 societies to discuss amalgamation proposals, and in 1919 17 of those societies agreed to ballot their members on the proposal. Nine sectional societies ultimately agreed to establish the **Amalgamated Engineering Union** on 1 July 1920, with J.T. Brownlie and Tom Mann becoming the first President and Secretary respectively of the new Union. During its existence as the ASE, it disaffiliated twice from the TUC, once in 1905, re-affiliating in 1906; again disaffiliating in 1907 and not re-affiliating until 1918.

Sources: *The Times,* December 1851; *ibid.,* April 1852; *Northern Star,* 1851 and 1852 (passim); Report on Trade Societies, Social Science Association, 1860; Jubilee Souvenir History of the ASE, 1901; Royal Commission on Trade Unions, 1867, Qu.734. and Qu.681; Prof. L. Brentano, 'The Growth of a Trades Union', *North British Review,* October 1870; 'The Claims of Labour': a course of lectures, 1886 (lecture given by John Burnett, General Secretary, ASE); S. and B. Webb, *History of Trade Unionism;* Burgess, 'Trade Union Policy'; Jefferys; Clegg, Fox and Thompson; Fyrth and Collins.

AMALGAMATED SOCIETY OF GENERAL TOOL MAKERS, ENGINEERS AND MACHINISTS

Formed in 1882 as the **National Society of General Tool Makers, Engineers and Machinists,** the society was one of the most successful of its kind, having 51 branches and 4,553 members by 1910 and over 21,400 in 1915. It was a founder member of the **Federation of Engineering and Shipbuilding Trades** when this was formed in 1891. In 1920 it merged in the newly formed **Amalgamated Engineering Union.**

16

Sources: Jefferys; BoT Reports; S. and B. Webb, *History of Trade Unionism*; Robinson; R.B. Suthers, 'Amalgamated Engineering Union'.

AMALGAMATED SOCIETY OF MACHINE MAKERS (LINCOLN)
This was a local engineering society formed in 1899 and registered in 1907. Its membership was only 56 in 1910 but rose to 110 in 1914. It merged with the **Amalgamated Wheelwrights, Smiths and Kindred Trades Union** in 1917 (see Vehicle Building section).

Sources: BoT Reports; Certification Office.

AMALGAMATED SOCIETY OF METAL PLANERS, SHAPERS, SLOT-TERS, HORIZONTAL BORERS AND MILLING MACHINE WORKERS
Formed in 1867, this was a sectional society which found itself in competition with many well organised craft societies during a period of revolutionary changes in engineering methods and an expanding range of jobs which led to many inter-union disputes with organisations like the **Amalgamated Society of Engineers** which was fighting for membership against unions like the **United Machine Workers Association** and the **National United Trades Society of Engineers** as well as the Metal Planers, many of these union members working in the same workshops and using the same materials. The Society of Metal Planers was a founder member of the **Federation of Engineering and Shipbuilding Trades** when it was formed in 1891. It merged with the **Amalgamated Society of Engineers** in 1894 with an estimated membership of 1,414.

Sources: Jefferys; Clegg, Fox and Thompson; Mosses; S. and B. Webb, *History of Trade Unionism*.

AMALGAMATED SOCIETY OF METAL WORKERS
Registered in 1877, registration was cancelled in 1895.

Source: Certification Office.

AMALGAMATED SOCIETY OF OPERATIVE ENGINEERS
Established in 1872, the Society went out of existence in 1874.

Source: Certification Office.

AMALGAMATED SOCIETY OF PLATE AND MACHINE MOULDERS
Formed in 1890 to cater for semi-skilled men working as plate and machine moulders, mainly in Lancashire with a head office in Oldham, the Society worked closely with the **Friendly Society of Iron Founders** which stated that it would give 'every encouragement, assistance and moral support to this class of labour'. The Secretary of the Plate and Machine Moulders' Society was Samuel Howard. In 1893 the FSIF kept its pledge of assistance when it

17

ordered its men not to take the place of the Plate and Machine Moulders who were on strike, after an appeal had been made to the FSIF by Howard. In 1906 the Society became a founder member of the **Federation of Moulders and Collateral Trades** with 950 members. Unfortunately the Federation did not bring the trades together in unity as it was set up to do, but became the arena in which unions fought over lines of demarcation. In 1907 the Society was charged with blacklegging on members of the **United Journeymen Brass Founders Association of Great Britain and Ireland** who were striking against the premium bonus system at Vickers works in Barrow-in-Furness. Samuel Howard countered the accusation by pointing out that as his men were pieceworkers they could not refuse the premium bonus. Although the Federation collapsed in 1910 the unions incorporated within it kept in touch, so much so that in 1912 six unions including the Amalgamated Society presented a claim for 1s and 2½ per cent which the employers agreed to, thus marking the beginning of national and united negotiations within the industry. Due to the low wages paid to moulders, recruitment proved to be very difficult, the men regarding even the lowest rate of union contributions to be beyond their means. The advent of the First World War accelerated the development of *machine* moulding. Wherever possible the employers put semi-skilled men in charge of the new machines at less than the craftsmen's rate. In 1918 the Moulders, together with 11 other unions, formed the **National Federation of Foundry Trades**. From 1918 onwards there were repeated attempts by the TUC to bring all the unions catering for foundry workers into one organisation, and approaches were consistently made to the Moulders by the National Union of Foundry Workers to this end, but the Moulders retained their independence until 1966 when the Union merged under the title of the **Amalgamated Moulders and Kindred Industries Trades Union** with the **Amalgamated Union of Foundry Workers** with just over 2,000 members.

Sources: Fyrth and Collins; TUC Report 1966.

AMALGAMATED SOCIETY OF SCALE BEAM AND WEIGHING MACHINE MAKERS
See **National Union of Scalemakers**

AMALGAMATED SOCIETY OF SHUTTLEMAKERS
See **Society of Shuttlemakers**

AMALGAMATED SOCIETY OF TELEGRAPH AND TELEPHONE CONSTRUCTION MEN
See **Electrical, Electronic, Telecommunication and Plumbing Union**

AMALGAMATED SOCIETY OF WOOL-COMB, HACKLE AND GILL MAKERS
One of the longest lasting of the many specialised unions catering for the production of textile machinery and fittings. It was never large. Formed in 1892, it had two branches and 237 members in 1900, and 208 members in

1910. The general decline of the textile trades eventually resulted in its demise. It was dissolved in December 1980 with some 40 members on its books.

Sources: BoT Reports; General Federation of Trade Unions.

AMALGAMATED UNION OF ENGINEERING WORKERS

The Union was established in 1970 by an amalgamation of the **Amalgamated Union of Engineering and Foundry Workers** (AEF), the **Draughtsmen and Allied Technicians Association** (see Vol. 1), and the **Constructional Engineering Union** (see Vol. 3). The instrument of amalgamation allowed for 4 sections: engineering, foundry, technical and supervisory, and construction, each section retaining its own organisation, but coming together in a national conference with a National Executive Council, the ultimate object being to create one union for the engineering industry. At amalgamation the combined membership was almost 1.4 million. A common rule book was drafted in 1972 but has never been wholly implemented, though closer working has latterly been achieved in some respects.

Source: Marsh, *Concise Encyclopedia.*

AMALGAMATED UNION OF ENGINEERING AND FOUNDRY WORKERS

See **Amalgamated Engineering Union** and **Amalgamated Union of Foundry Workers**

AMALGAMATED UNION OF FOUNDRY WORKERS

Ever since the 1880s the most far-seeing among the moulders had campaigned for an industrial union which would unite all grades in the foundries, and from 1 July 1946 there was such a Union covering some 60,000 workers. It had come into being by an amalgamation of the **National Union of Foundry Workers,** the **Ironfounding Workers Association,** and the **United Metal Founders Society.** The general fund of the Union on its inauguration stood close to half a million pounds. The first National Executive Council numbered 5; there were 3 districts of the Union to cover the whole of the United Kingdom and the first General Secretary of the new body was Jim Gardner. The Union published a monthly Journal. Within 9 months over 11,000 more workers had joined the Union including those from foundries like Singers' of Clydebank and Ford's of Dagenham, hitherto unorganised. Of 70,456 members on 29 March 1947, 38,236 were moulders and coremakers; 1,317 were moulders and coremakers away from trade; there were 5,103 dressers; 6,299 machine moulders; 10,038 labourers; 1,473 women workers; 3,871 juniors; 1,439 were still in the armed forces and there were 2,680 retired members. At the 1948 annual delegate meeting the General Secretary reported that the Union represented some 40 per cent of foundry workers, including about 60 per cent of all moulders and 90 per cent of highly skilled moulders. By 1948 the membership was 80,000 and in Scotland there was now virtually only one foundry union. In 1968, with 63,000 members, it became the Foundry Section of the **Amalgamated Union of Engineering and Foundry Workers** (AEF) and of the **Amalgamated Union of Engineering Workers** in 1970. Before merging with the AEF the AUFW was the only large union catering exclusively for foundry workers.

Sources: Fyrth and Collins; Marsh, *Concise Encyclopedia.*

AMALGAMATED UNION OF MACHINE, ENGINE, IRON GRINDERS AND GLAZERS

The Union was formed in 1844. In 1892 it had 309 members. In 1900 it had 433 in 9 branches and in 1910, 703. In 1955, with 146 members, it merged with the **Amalgamated Engineering Union.**

Sources: BoT Reports; Bain and Price.

AMALGAMATED WELDED BOILER MAKERS SOCIETY

Established in 1899 with 146 members, the Society was dissolved in 1900.

Source: Bain and Price.

AMICABLE AND BROTHERLY SOCIETY OF JOURNEYMEN MILLWRIGHTS

Formed in 1801 and nicknamed the 'Old Millwrights', this was a London based organisation of millwrights. These millwrights' organisations were very exclusive. Not only did they dictate to firms whom to employ but they also maintained strict control over the length of the working day and arrangements for meal times and demanded equality of wages at the rate of 7s a day. These terms were conceded by employers since craft techniques made it necessary for them to identify skilled men who had served a seven-year apprenticeship, an almost universal requirement for trade union membership. The millwrights merged with the **Amalgamated Society of Engineers** when that body was formed in 1851.

Sources: Burgess, *Origins;* William McLaine, 'The Engineers Union Booklet: The Millwrights and Old Mechanics', PhD thesis, University of London 1939; Sir William Pole (ed.), *The Life of Sir William Fairburn,* London, 1877; Jefferys; Suthers, 'Amalgamated Engineering Union'; Anderson; Amalgamated Society of Engineers, Jubilee Souvenir, 1901; Robinson; McLaine, 'The Engineers' Union'.

APPRENTICES UNION

In the aftermath of the wave of 'New Unionism' of 1889 and the upsurge of trade union recruitment, craft unions like the **Friendly Society of Ironfounders of England, Ireland and Wales** turned their attention to their young members. In 1890 the South Shields branch of the union formed the Apprentices Union into which the boys paid 1d a week which was accumulated towards their entrance fee. By 1894 the Friendly Society of Ironfounders had 30 apprentice branches with 1,116 current members and 260 who had already transferred to the parent body.

Source: Fyrth and Collins.

ASSOCIATED BLACKSMITHS OF SCOTLAND
See **Federation of Engineering and Shipbuilding Trades of the United Kingdom** and **Associated Blacksmiths and Ironworkers Society**

ASSOCIATED FRATERNITY OF IRON FORGERS
Established in 1830 and usually called 'the Old Smiths', the Fraternity had branches in several parts of the country and competed with metropolitan and other local societies of millwrights, smiths, patternmakers and general engineers. This competition between unions considerably weakened the power of the individual societies to negotiate with employers who played them off one against the other, at times very successfully. In 1836 a London Joint Committee of several of the sectional societies successfully conducted an 8 months' strike for additional overtime money and a reduction in the working week. Again in 1844, the same sort of united action gained a further reduction of hours and moves were begun towards the creation of one national organisation for the engineering industry which culminated in the formation of the **Amalgamated Society of Engineers** in 1851 of which the Iron Forgers became a part.

Source: S. and B. Webb, *History of Trade Unionism.*

ASSOCIATED IRON MOULDERS OF SCOTLAND
The union was formed in 1831 as the **Scottish Iron Moulders Union**. Its forerunner was the **Friendly Iron Moulders Society** which had been set up in 1809 at Bolton-le-Moors, Lancashire. During a slump in trade in 1826, 27 men had been driven out of the foundries and several branches collapsed, among them the Glasgow branch, and the Society lost all its Scottish members. In 1829 a new effort was made by Scottish workers when they formed the **Scottish Iron Moulders Friendly Society**, which was known as the 'Auld Society' but was shortlived. Its functions were taken over in 1831 by the new body, the founder and secretary being James Dunn, a cotton worker, who gave his time and labour to organising several trades in Glasgow and was blacklisted both in Scotland and England for his efforts. He retained his job as secretary of the union for 24 years. The Canal Basin, Eagle and Phoenix Foundries were the first to be organised and within 3 years the union had 556 members, and by 1838 was claiming it had been instrumental in raising wage levels from 12s to 16s per week. It was a trade society with the aims and objects of raising wages, resisting bad employers, restricting the number of apprentices to 1 for every 3 moulders, and the instruction of its members to end the practice of long 'hirings'. Entry fees were high, 30s for Scottish moulders and up to £5 for English or Irish non-union entrants. Superannuation was 3s 6d a week at 60 years of age after 25 years' membership; with £10 funeral benefit for a man and £6

for his wife. Accident benefit came into force in 1838. The country was divided into 6 districts and the government of the society rested in the Glasgow district. It kept a register of non-members and men were fined for blacklegging across the border. The name was changed to the above in 1869. It affiliated to the TUC in 1875. It had almost 7,700 members (and 191 abroad) in 1910 and about the same number at the beginning of the First World War. It amalgamated in 1920 with the **Friendly Society of Iron Founders of England, Ireland and Wales** and the **Amalgamated Society of Coremakers of Great Britain and Ireland** to form the **National Union of Foundry Workers.**

Sources: Fyrth and Collins; Marwick; Clegg, Fox and Thompson.

ASSOCIATED IRON, STEEL AND BRASS DRESSERS OF SCOTLAND

Formed in 1856 as the **Scottish Iron Dressers Society** with 73 members, the Scottish Iron Dressers paid 1s a month subscription and an entrance fee of £1. There were dressers organised in 36 foundries but a mere handful in most of them, and by 1859 the union had only 182 members, the main concentration being in Glasgow. It had no full time officers and other than trade protection it offered its members merely unemployment benefit of 8s or 4s. It sent its first delegate to the TUC in 1875. In 1900 the Scottish Iron Dressers struck for 2 months to prevent their shops being opened to non-union labour, an action which was taken to combat the employer-sponsored National Free Labour Association which was importing blacklegs into the area, and in 1909 had another strike to gain 6½d an hour, in which they were supported by the **Associated Iron Moulders of Scotland** and the **Central Ironmoulders Association of Scotland.** By 1910 it had 8 branches and 1,100 members, rising to 1,348 in 1914. In 1920 efforts were made to secure amalgamation with the **National Union of Foundry Workers,** the Scottish Dressers voting in favour but the National Union of Foundry Workers' members turning down the proposal. Between 1926 and 1932 the union lost the great bulk of its members, retaining only 494. Problems arising out of mechanisation and bonus systems taxed the efforts of their few officials, almost as much work being turned out in their trade as in 1914 but with 25 per cent fewer men. The aftermath of the General Strike of 1926 had had a very demoralising effect on the union. Many men who had drifted into it during the 40 hours' strike in 1919 were lost during this period. The Secretary at this time was Robert M'Fadyen who retained the job for 42 years. By 1931 the union had a cash deficit with an expenditure of £743 and an income of only £395. M'Fadyen reported that 1932 was 'the worst in the Union's history', and with reserves standing at £500 it was in danger of collapse. By cutting down expenses in every way the deficit was reduced to £227. The trade revival of 1933 helped it to survive. By 1945 the membership totalled 1,400 and it amalgamated with the **National Union of Foundry Workers** after that union had revised its rules to give greater autonomy to district committees, and had agreed to appoint a Dresser Organiser. James Finnigan became the first National Dresser Organiser.

Source: Fyrth and Collins.

ASSOCIATED METAL WORKERS SOCIETY
See **Associated Metal Workers Union**

ASSOCIATED METAL WORKERS UNION
Established in 1863 as the **Iron Dressers Trade Society**, the union changed its title to the **Iron and Steel Dressers Trade Society** in 1876 and to the **Iron, Steel and Metal Dressers Trade Society** in 1878. The precise date of formation seems to be in dispute. The Board of Trade gives 1860, Fyrth and Collins, 1863, and the Union itself, 1868. In its initial form it was organised as a type of federation of local societies with headquarters at Salford, subscriptions being 6d per week until 1870 when an additional 1d was added for superannuation benefit. Union branches controlled their own funds and the Executive met only when the General Secretary considered a meeting to be necessary. The Society considered itself to be a very exclusive body. In 1889 nine new branches were formed and in the following year, with some 1,100 members, it helped to found the Federation of Engineering and Shipbuilding Trades. In 1921 the first steps were taken to amalgamate with the **National Union of Foundry Workers** but the NUFW members voted against such a move. Fresh initiatives in 1937 came to nothing, partly due to the conflicting objectives of the NUFW and the **Amalgamated Engineering Union**, the former stating that 'foundry amalgamations should take place before our members be asked to give consideration to a general merger favoured by the AEU.' In 1951 the name was changed to the **Iron, Steel, Metal Dressers and Kindred Trades Society**, and in 1964 to the **Associated Metal Workers Society,** the above title being subsequently adopted. The Union continues to be an independent organisation and currently has some 6,000 members.

Sources: Fyrth and Collins; Certification Office; BoT Reports.

ASSOCIATED PATTERNMAKERS OF SCOTLAND
In the early part of 1896 the Falkirk Trades Council called a meeting of local patternmakers in an effort to organise them. Not many attended the meeting but the few who did decided to form an organisation strictly confined to the Falkirk area, the membership then numbering 69, and the subscription rate being 6d per week. Members of the newly formed Associated Patternmakers were working in light castings for the building trade using mainly wood, plaster of Paris, tin and lead. No effort was made at first to recruit these men into the main patternmakers' union, the **United Kingdom Patternmakers Association**, on the grounds that the UPA membership was engaged purely in the engineering industry and therefore might undercut workers engaged in the light casting trade. However, relations between the Falkirk-based Association and the UPA were always quite cordial, and efforts were made for the Associated Patternmakers to join the UPA in 1906 and again in 1908, but the problem remained of the differences of working in light castings as against engineering. The union had 228 members in 1910. The National Insurance Act of 1912 gave fresh stimulus to yet another effort by the UPA to recruit their Scottish brothers, and in that year by 169 votes to 35 the Scottish organisation agreed to merge with the UPA. It then had a membership of 260 and funds

of £1,142. It had achieved some successes during the 16 years of its independent existence, including increases in wages on more than one occasion, improved conditions for young journeymen in the trade, and a reduction of hours from 57 to 54.

Source: Mosses.

ASSOCIATED SOCIETY OF MOULDERS
(latterly, Associated Society of Moulders and Foundry Workers)

The Union was established in 1889 in Swansea and Landore under the title of the **Welsh Ironfounders Union**. There were very few members of the **Friendly Iron Moulders Society** in the district because the Welsh workers argued that their wages were so low they were unable to pay high union subscriptions. In Swansea the wages then were 28s and 24s for a 54 hour week, down to 18s to 21s for working unlimited hours in Ebbw Vale. The Union subscriptions were 6d a week for which they got strike money and accident pay, legal assistance and funeral benefit, and it soon had 300 members, including brass-moulders in South and West Wales, and as most of its officials were foremen or leading hands it became quite powerful, winning a 30s minimum wage in Swansea and two years later another 3s after taking joint action with the Friendly Iron Moulders Society. Relations were quite good between the two unions, the members of each frequently paying 'acknowledgement money' to the other when they were in a minority in a shop. In 1906 it became affiliated to the **Federation of Moulders and Collateral Trades** with 353 members, the Federation having been newly established to bring greater alliance between the unions in the industry. In 1913 the Union fought two successful strikes to win a minimum wage of 4s a day at Blaenavon and Dowlais foundries. It changed its title to the Associated Society of Moulders and Foundry Workers and in 1937 took part in a conference with 7 other unions with a view to amalgamation with the **National Union of Foundry Workers**, but the talks broke down. Talks were resumed in 1940 when the membership stood at 400. The conditions laid down by unions like the Moulders amongst others were that the strtucture of the NUFW should be overhauled to give greater autonomy to incoming unions and that the whole administration of the NUFW should be democratised. Amalgamation was not achieved until 1966 when the Union with 240 members went into what was then the **Amalgamated Union of Foundry Workers**.

Sources: Fyrth and Collins; TUC Report 1966.

ASSOCIATED SOCIETY OF RANGE STOVE AND ORNAMENTAL WORKERS
See **Scottish Metal Workers Union**

ASSOCIATION OF CARRIAGE STRAIGHTENERS (NOTTINGHAM)

A society in the textile machinery trade, first established in 1881, the Association had 52 members in 1892 and 85 in 1910. It survived until 1939 when, with a membership which had dwindled to 17, it was dissolved.

Sources: Bain and Price; BoT Reports.

ASSOCIATION OF ELECTRICAL WIREMEN

Established in 1901 with 24 members, the Association was dissolved in 1909 with a membership standing at 54.

Sources: Bain and Price; BoT Reports.

ASSOCIATION OF FOREMEN IRON FOUNDERS

Many moulders became foremen. Keen union men would remain members, athough in Scotland they were allowed to resign on getting command of a shop and to keep their benefits by paying an acknowledgment of 10s a year. The Association was formed in the late 1870s, had its own funeral and superannuation fund and a Secretary, and claimed to have 71 members. It met monthly at a Temperance Hotel to read 'instructive and edifying essays'.

Source: Fyrth and Collins.

ASSOCIATION OF INDUSTRIAL ENGINEERING WORKERS (LONDON)

Formed in 1919 with 920 members, the Association lost support over the years until it ceased to exist in 1935 when it had only 2 members.

Source: Bain and Price.

ASSOCIATION OF IRON ORE GRINDERS AND POLISHERS (FALKIRK)

Established in 1893 with 83 members, the Association was dissolved in 1896 when the membership numbered 63.

Source: BoT Reports.

ASSOCIATION OF LICENSED AIRCRAFT ENGINEERS

The Association was set up in 1970 with 920 members. In 1974 the figure was 775. It has recently obtained a certificate of independence.

Source: Certification Office.

ASSOCIATION OF MARINE AND GENERAL ENGINEERS

Formed in 1893 with 12 members, the Association was dissolved in 1906 when it had 21 members.

Source: Bain and Price.

ASSOCIATION OF MASTER ENGINEERS AND IRON AND BRASS FOUNDERS, NORTH STAFFORDSHIRE AREA

Founded in 1872, the Association was dissolved in 1893.

Source: Certification Office.

ASSOCIATION OF OPTICAL WORKERS AND SPECTACLE FRAME MAKERS

The Association had a very limited existence. It was formed in 1893 with 23 members but was dissolved in 1895 when it had 11 members.

Source: Bain and Price.

ASSOCIATION OF PATTERNMAKERS AND ALLIED CRAFTSMEN

Formed in 1872 as the **United Kingdom Patternmakers' Association** the Association came into existence following a strike on the Tyne and Wear in an effort to gain a 9-hour working day. At that time the patternmakers were the worst organised work force in the engineering industry. The trade had been neglected by the general body of trade unionists both in craft and general unions, and when the decision was made to form the UKPA the membership had to face a good deal of hostility from these other unions. The first branch was opened in Sunderland on 11 March 1872 with 23 members, followed by Newcastle with 15 members. The first General Secretary was R.C. Douglas, a local foreman, followed by R. Reay who remained in office until 1884. He became a full time official in 1882 at a salary of £2 per week. The first registered office address was the Cattle Market Inn. Weekly contributions were 8d with a funeral benefit fixed at £13. There was a levy on each member of 1s per year in order to pay for tool insurance. At the end of its first year the union had 6 branches with 173 members and a balance in hand of £98. By 1873 branches had been opened in Leeds, and in 1875 it extended its activities to Lancashire, and had altogether 16 branches and a membership of 418. In 1876 the first statement was made by the Executive Committee on the question of piece and contract work to which it was opposed, and members were advised to 'avoid such work as much as possible'. It was a founder member of the **Federation of Engineering and Shipbuilding Trades of the United Kingdom** when this was formed in 1891. By 1892 it had over 2,500 members. The union is affiliated to the **Confederation of Shipbuilding and Engineering Unions** and the TUC. In 1969 it adopted its present title. It has remained a union entirely confined to craftsmen of this particular skill, retaining its independence after having turned down amalgamation with the newly formed **Amalgamated Engineering Union** in 1920. The organisation of patternmakers is now approximately shared between the two unions.

Sources: Marwick; Mosses; Jefferys; S. and B. Webb, *History of Trade Unionism*; Marsh, *Concise Encyclopedia*

ASSOCIATION OF RADIO AND ELECTRONIC ENGINEERS
The Association was established in 1957 with 32 members but had ceased to function by 1964.

Source: Bain and Price.

ASSOCIATION OF WOMEN WELDERS
Formed in 1916 with 50 members, the Association had 825 members by the end of the First World War when it ceased to exist.

Source: Bain and Price.

BARRHEAD AND DISTRICT BRASS FINISHERS ASSOCIATION
This was yet another of the small locally based unions which struggled to survive from the time of its inception in 1903 until, with a membership of under 30, it was dissolved in 1910.

Source: BoT Reports.

BELFAST BRASSFOUNDERS ASSOCIATION
Established in 1840, the union had 179 members in 1910. Two years later, in 1912, it amalgamated with other sectional societies in the industry in order to form the **Amalgamated Association of Brassfounders, Turners, Fitters and Coppersmiths.**

Source: BoT Reports.

BELFAST HACKLE AND GILL MAKERS TRADE UNION
Formed in the 1880s, this was one of the sectional societies which became a founder member of the **Federation of Engineering and Shipbuilding Trades** in 1891, but continuous strife over demarcation issues weakened the Union and it merged with the **Amalgamated Society of Engineers** in 1915.

Source: Jefferys.

BIRMINGHAM AND DISTRICT COREMAKERS SOCIETY
A local society of coremakers formed in 1894. It had 60 members in 1900 and came together with other similar societies in 1902 to form the **Amalgamated Society of Coremakers of Great Britain and Ireland.**

Sources: BoT Reports; Fyrth and Collins.

BIRMINGHAM OPERATIVE BRASS COCK FINISHERS TRADE, SICK AND DIVIDEND SOCIETY
The Society was first set up in 1845. In 1892 it had a membership of 53. Although the membership was always small the Society continued in

27

existence until 1931 when, with only 19 members, it was dissolved.

Sources: BoT Reports; Certification Office.

BIRMINGHAM SCALE BEAM, STEELYARD, WEIGHING MACHINE AND MILLMAKERS TRADE PROTECTION ASSOCIATION
See **National Union of Scalemakers**

BLACKBURN AND EAST LANCASHIRE ROLLER COVERERS SOCIETY
Although this was a long established society formed in 1853, its membership never reached many more than 100. Registration was cancelled in 1915.

Sources: BoT Reports; Certification Office.

BOLTON AND DISTRICT COREMAKERS SOCIETY
A local society of coremakers formed in 1890, it had 35 members in 1892 and 76 in 1900. In 1902 it amalgamated with other similar societies to form the **Amalgamated Society of Coremakers of Great Britain and Ireland.**

Sources: BoT Reports; Fyrth and Collins.

BOLTON BRASS FOUNDERS SOCIETY
There appears to be only one recorded entry for this Society as having been established in 1892 with 28 members, and registering 30, 36, 43 and 50 members for the years 1893, 1894, 1895 and 1896 respectively. There appears to be no further record of its existence.

Source: BoT Reports.

BOLTON JOURNEYMEN MILLWRIGHTS FRIENDLY SOCIETY
Founded in 1837, this was an exclusively millwright society. The millwrights had the most to lose from the influx of semi-skilled labour which increased the insecurity of employment, especially for men with skills which were becoming obsolescent. It merged with the **Amalgamated Society of Engineers** when that body was formed in 1851.

Sources: AUEW, Rules of the Journeymen Millwrights Friendly Societies, London, 1842; Burgess, *Origins*; Jefferys.

BOLTON OPERATIVE ROLLER MAKERS ASSOCIATION
An Association in the textile machinery and fittings trade, it was formed in 1886. It had 114 members in 1892, 180 in 1900, and had grown to 4 branches and 366 members in 1910. In 1915, with 430 members, it merged with the **Amalgamated Society of Engineers.**

Sources: BoT Reports; Bain and Price.

BRADFORD COREMAKERS SOCIETY
Originally coremaking was done by apprentices as part of their training, but as mass production improved and the work became repetitive, the employers began to have it carried out by labourers or by boys. The craft unions would not accept the coremakers as members and in desperation they began to organise themselves, their societies being small and local in character. They became affiliated to the **United Association of Coremakers**. The Bradford Society had only 13 members 25 years after it was formed in 1867. It amalgamated with the **Amalgamated Society of Coremakers of Great Britain and Ireland** when this was formed in 1902.

Source: Fyrth and Collins.

BRADFORD MACHINE WOOLCOMB MAKERS MUTUAL BENEFIT SOCIETY
The Society was founded in 1872 and was dissolved in 1880.

Source: Certification Office.

BRISTOL BRASSFOUNDERS AND FINISHERS TRADE SOCIETY
This was a small local society formed in 1838, with 106 members in 1900 and 80 members in 1910. It is possible that it became a branch of the **United Journeymen Brassfounders, Turners, Fitters, Finishers and Coppersmiths Association of Great Britain and Ireland** during the First World War.

Sources: BoT Reports; Certification Office.

BRITISH ASSOCIATED TRADE UNION OF ENGINEERS
The Union was formed in 1892 with 31 members but was dissolved in 1901, the membership having dwindled to 20.

Sources: Bain and Price; BoT Reports.

BURY AND DISTRICT BRASS FOUNDERS AND FINISHERS SOCIETY
Formed in 1862, the Society had only a single branch, with 61 members in 1900 and 72 in 1910. In 1912 it amalgamated, together with other local trade societies, to form the **Amalgamated Association of Brass Founders, Turners, Fitters and Coppersmiths.**

Sources: BoT Reports; Certification Office.

BURY AND DISTRICT COREMAKERS SOCIETY
This was a very small local society of coremakers, formed in 1861, which struggled to remain in existence. It was affiliated to the **United Association**

of Coremakers. It had 26 members in 1892, and with 38 members it joined the **Amalgamated Society of Coremakers of Great Britain and Ireland** upon its formation in 1902.

Sources: BoT Reports; Fyrth and Collins.

BURY JOURNEYMEN MILLWRIGHTS FRIENDLY SOCIETY
Founded in 1843, this was another exclusively millwright society. These skilled workers, whose skills were becoming obsolescent due to the introduction of new techniques, had the most to lose from the influx of semi-skilled labour which increased their insecurity. It merged with the **Amalgamated Society of Engineers** upon the formation of that body in 1851.

Sources: AUEW, Rules of the Journeymen Steam Engine, Machine Maker and Millwrights Friendly Society, London, 1845; Burgess, *Origins*; Jefferys.

CARD SETTING MACHINE TENTERS SOCIETY
A sectional society organising skilled men concerned in the setting up and running of the carding machines which by the 1870s had become the usual way of combing or straightening fibres for use in the textile trade. The precise year of its foundation is uncertain, but is traditionally dated from 1872, when the first delegate meeting took place, though the rules of the Society were not registered until the following year, under a title sometimes listed as the **Wire Card Setting Machine Tenters Society**, a name which it retained until about 1918. Its membership has rarely exceeded 300 and at present stands at about 130, all working for a few specialised firms in Yorkshire, though it has traditionally operated in Lancashire also. It was at first a fighting organisation but had by the 1890s taken on the characteristics of a craft union, independent in spirit, and after the turn of the century inclined towards negotiation; though it was often in conflict with employers until better relations were established after the First World War. A notable General Secretary at this time was Tom Forrest (1850–1951) who held that office between 1898 and 1918.

Source: Malcolm Speirs, *One Hundred Years of a Small Trade Union*, Card Setting Machine Tenters Society, 1972.

CARRIAGE STRAIGHTENERS SOCIETY (NOTTINGHAM)
The Society, formed in 1881, had 53 members in a single branch in 1900 and 85 members in 1910. It remained in existence until 1940 when it ceased to function.

Sources: BoT Reports; Certification Office.

CENTRAL IRONMOULDERS ASSOCIATION OF SCOTLAND
See **Ironfounding Workers Association**

CONFEDERATION OF SHIPBUILDING AND ENGINEERING UNIONS

This is a federation of unions in the shipbuilding and engineering industry which was constituted in its present form in 1936, but had its origins in the **Federation of Engineering and Shipbuilding Trades** established in 1891. In June 1977 the Confederation had 23 constituent organisations with an affiliated membership of 2,416,576. After the Second World War it became primarily a medium through which engineering unions could conduct common industry-wide negotiations with the Engineering Employers' Federation and the Shipbuilders and Repairers National Association, to provide for exchange of views between them and to act in a representative capacity in matters concerning national government. In such a role its success in promoting unity between engineering unions and shipbuilding unions was considerable. In part this was made possible by the affiliation to the Confederation of the Amalgamated Engineering Union which had previously preferred to negotiate separately with the engineering employers or to work with other unions on an ad hoc basis in the Engineering Joint Trades Movement. The Amalgamated Engineering Union remained affiliated with a membership of 770,000; the **Transport and General Workers Union** (Vol. 3) is affiliated with 500,000 members in its various engineering trade groups; the **General and Municipal Workers Union** (Vol. 3) is affiliated with 180,000 members; the **Electrical Electronic Telecommunication and Plumbing Union** with 200,000; and the **Amalgamated Society of Boilermakers, Shipwrights, Blacksmiths and Structural Workers** with 120,000. The CSEU has achieved something which over the long history of engineering seemed impossible – that is, a form of constitution and operation which binds together a large number of sovereign unions of varying size and traditions into a workable unit with very little friction. In 1947 it authorised for the first time the establishment of Joint Shop Stewards Works Committees in individual establishments and provided, under Minute 741, additional machinery for inter-union co-operation on strike action, particularly that arising at factory level.

Sources: Marsh, *Industrial Relations*; Mortimer; Fyrth and Collins.

DERBY AND BURTON BRASS FOUNDERS AND FINISHERS SOCIETY

The Society seems to have originated in Derby in 1875. By the end of the nineteenth century it also had a branch at Burton-on-Trent and a total membership of 93. A few years later it had extended its membership to Coventry and broadened its title to **Derby, Burton and Coventry Brass Founders, Turners, Fitters, Electrical and General Brass Finishers and Coppersmiths Society**, and had almost doubled its membership to 185 by 1910. Two years later it came together with other local societies to form the **Amalgamated Association of Brass Founders, Turners, Fitters and Coppersmiths.**

Sources: BoT Reports; Bain and Price.

DERBY, BURTON AND COVENTRY BRASS FOUNDERS, TURNERS, FITTERS, ELECTRICAL AND GENERAL BRASS FINISHERS AND

COPPERSMITHS SOCIETY
See **Derby and Burton Brass Founders and Finishers Society**

DONCASTER BRASS FOUNDERS AND FINISHERS SOCIETY
This was a Society which was very small in number and had a brief existence. It was established in 1900 with 34 members; the number rose to 56 in 1906 but fell to 35 in 1909. It was dissolved in 1910.

Source: BoT Reports.

DUDLEY TELEGRAPH WORKERS SOCIETY
This local Society was established in 1896 with 30 members but was dissolved in 1901 with only 7 members remaining.

Sources: Bain and Price; BoT Reports.

DUMBARTON BRASS FINISHERS SOCIETY
The Society had a very limited existence and a very low membership, having been established in 1895 with 26 members and dissolved in 1900 when the membership had fallen to 17.

Source: BoT Reports.

DUNDEE OPERATIVE BRASS FOUNDERS AND FINISHERS ASSOCIATION
Formed in 1887, the Association had two branches and 143 members in 1900. In the early 1900s one of these branches appears to have been lost and by 1910 membership had fallen to 78. In 1912 the society amalgamated with others to form the **Amalgamated Association of Brass Founders, Turners, Fitters and Coppersmiths.**

Source: BoT Reports.

EAST OF SCOTLAND BRASS FOUNDERS SOCIETY
Dating from 1857, the union was formerly known as the **Edinburgh and Leith Association of Brass Founders.** It had about 650 members in the early years of the twentieth century. The Society became a founder member of the **Federation of Engineering and Shipbuilding Trades** when it was established in 1891, and also of the **Federation of Moulders and Collateral Trades** upon its formation in 1906. In 1918 the East of Scotland Brass Founders was one of the 22 unions invited by the **Amalgamated Society of Engineers** to discuss proposals for the amalgamation and formation of one big union to cover the entire engineering industry, and in May 1919 it was one of the 17 unions which reacted favourably to this proposal and agreed to ballot its members. It merged with the newly formed **Amalgamated Engineering Union** in 1920.

Sources: Jefferys; Fyrth and Collins; BoT Reports.

EASTERN COUNTIES SOCIETY OF ENGINEERS (GRANTHAM)

Formed in 1897 with 20 members, the Society was dissolved in 1904 when the membership had dwindled to 7.

Sources: Bain and Price; BoT Reports.

EDINBURGH AND LEITH ASSOCIATION OF BRASS FOUNDERS

See **East of Scotland Brass Founders Society**

ELECTRICAL AND MECHANICAL INSTRUMENT MAKERS ASSOCIATION

The Association was formed in 1938 with a small membership. It had 150 members in 1974 and currently holds a certificate of independence.

Sources: Bain and Price; Certification Office.

ELECTRICAL, ELECTRONIC, TELECOMMUNICATION AND PLUMBING UNION

In 1889 a small organisation centred on Manchester and known as the **Amalgamated Society of Telegraph and Telephone Construction Men** held its first conference, which included delegates from a London based organisation called the **Union of Electrical Operatives**. At that conference the decision was made to form a new union, the **Electrical Trades Union**, the two organisations agreeing to amalgamate. The Telegraph and Telephone Construction Men had 400 members organised in 6 branches in Manchester, Liverpool, Leeds, Sheffield, Hanley and Dewsbury, holding a cash balance of £222. The Electrical Operatives had 170 members based in one London branch which had a cash balance of £75. The majority of the founder members were electric light wiremen and telegraph and telephone wiremen and linesmen labourers. At the outset there were no sections, all members paying the same contribution of 6d per week and all receiving the same scale of benefit. The only official was R. Steadman who was the part time General Secretary, but in 1891 A.J. Walker became the first full time General Secretary. In the same year the Union conducted its first strike, which was defeated, the Union losing membership as a result. By 1898 the Union had recovered some of its lost ground and had 702 members organised in 18 branches, with reserve funds of £752. In 1907 the Union proposed the abolition of a purely London-based executive and the institution of a National Executive Council with elected representatives from all parts of the country. In 1905 the Union published its journal *The Eltradion*, the name being changed in 1909 to the *Electrical Trades Journal*. In 1906 the Union joined the **Federation of Engineering and Shipbuilding Trades**. By 1910 the membership was relatively low at under 2,000. In 1920, due to a great increase in membership over the war years, it was decided to appoint Walter Citrine as Assistant General Secretary. The Union was calling for nationalisation of the electrical industry in 1935, which was carried into effect in 1947. In 1968 with the merging of the **Plumbing Trades Union** (Vol. 3) the name was changed to the above. It is affiliated to the TUC and has some 400,000 members.

Sources: ETU, *Fifty Years of the Electrical Trades Union*, 1939; Gordon Schaffer, *Sixty Years with the Electrical Trades Union*, ETU, 1949; ETU, *The Story of the Electrical Trades Union*, 1952; Marsh, *Concise Encyclopedia*.

ELECTRICAL TRADES UNION
See **Electrical Electronic Telecommunication and Plumbing Union**

ELECTRICAL WINDERS SOCIETY OF GREAT BRITAIN AND IRE-LAND
This was a London-based organisation formed in 1902. It had 71 members in 1910 and 120 in 1913, and seems to have gone out of existence during the course of the First World War.

Sources: BoT Reports; Industrial Directory, 1914.

ENGINEER BUYERS AND REPRESENTATIVES ASSOCIATION
Established in 1947, the Association remained in existence for 23 years, ceasing to function in 1970 when its membership was 71.

Source: Bain and Price.

ENGINEERING CRAFTSMEN'S GUILD
Formed at the end of the Second World War in 1945 with 59 members, the Guild was dissolved in 1952 when the membership stood at 14.

Source: Bain and Price.

ENGINEERING INSPECTORS ASSOCIATION
Formed in 1956, the Association had 25 members in 1974. It currently holds a certificate of independence.

Sources: Bain and Price; Certification Office.

FALKIRK ASSOCIATED IRON GRINDERS AND POLISHERS SOCI-ETY
A local society formed in 1898 with 12 members, it was dissolved in the following year.

Source: BoT Reports.

FEDERATION OF ENGINEERING AND SHIPBUILDING TRADES OF THE UNITED KINGDOM

The Federation was formed in 1891 by a number of sectional organisations like the **Steam Engine Makers' Society**; the **Associated Blacksmiths of Scotland**; the **United Kingdom Patternmakers Association**; and the **National Society of Amalgamated Brass Workers**, amongst others. These bodies were comprised of workers who at that time did not wish to join the growing **Amalgamated Society of Engineers**, which remained outside the Federation. The attraction of these sectional unions came from their compactness and specialisation on the problems of particular trades. Without the participation of the ASE the Federation was a weak organisation, but it represented the biggest step toward the unity of engineering and shipbuilding workers since 1851. The Federation's main role was in arbitrating in the demarcation disputes which were inevitable with so many unions catering for the same type of worker. The ASE became a member of the Federation in 1905 and in 1910 tabled a resolution at the Federation meeting that 'the time had arrived when the various organisations in each section of kindred trades should combine by amalgamation'. Local amalgamation committees were established in some of the bigger towns, but the advent of war in 1914 delayed the matter. In January 1918 the ASE seceded from the Federation on the grounds that the spirit of sectionalism was too strongly entrenched in it, but the ASE continued to work with the Federation on matters affecting both bodies. In 1921 the Federation represented 35 different societies. It became the **Confederation of Shipbuilding and Engineering Unions** in 1936. The **Amalgamated Engineering Union** affiliated to the Confederation in 1947, having previously preferred to negotiate separately with the engineering employers and to work with other unions on an ad hoc basis. The Confederation is notable for its authorisation of Joint Shop Stewards Works Committees.

Sources: Jefferys; Marsh, *Industrial Relations*; *Journal of the Associated Society of Engineers*, October 1917; Burgess, *Origins*; Barou; S. and B. Webb, *History of Trade Unionism*.

FEDERATION OF MOULDERS AND COLLATERAL TRADES

Against a background of trade depression in 1906 the **Friendly Society of Ironfounders of England, Ireland and Wales**, the **Associated Iron Moulders of Scotland**, the **Central Ironmoulders Association of Scotland**, the **Welsh Ironfounders Union**, the **Amalgamated Society of Plate and Machine Moulders**, the **Amalgamated Society of Coremakers of Great Britain and Ireland**, the **National Union of Stove Grate and General Metal Workers**, the **Journeymen Brassfounders Union**, the **Scottish Brass Moulders Union**, and the **North of England Brass Moulders Society** agreed to form a federation. The FSIF and the ASC had proposed complete amalgamation of all the organisations, but this was defeated by 15 votes to 11. Instead it was agreed to form the Federation with the aims of helping each other in case of attacks on wages and working conditions on the part of the employers, opposition to the 'character note' and the system of payment of premium bonuses, and arbitrating in disputes between unions. The Federation membership upon formation was 38,373. It soon became merely an arena in which the unions fought over lines of demarcation. At the first annual meeting in 1907 the

Journeymen Brassfounders charged the Amalgamated Plate and Machine Moulders with blacklegging on their members who were on strike against the premium bonus system at Vickers of Barrow-in-Furness, to which accusation J. Howard, the Secretary of the Moulders, pointed out that as his men were pieceworkers they could not refuse the premium bonus. This was a typical example of the many problems the Federation had to face and it did not remain long in existence, collapsing in 1910.

Source: Fyrth and Collins.

FOUNDRY LABOURERS UNION OF GREAT BRITAIN AND IRELAND
Formed in 1889, the Union recruited 2,500 members in the first year of its existence. Its headquarters was based in Glasgow. It is reported as having gone out of existence in 1892.

Sources: Fyrth and Collins; Certification Office.

FRIENDLY IRON MOULDERS SOCIETY
See **Friendly Society of Ironfounders of England, Ireland and Wales**

FRIENDLY SOCIETY OF IRONFOUNDERS OF ENGLAND, IRELAND AND WALES (FSIF)
The Society was formed on 6 February 1809 at Bolton-le-Moors, Lancashire, as the **Friendly Iron Moulders Society**, and in June 1809 articles or rules were signed by 23 moulders (of whom 7 witnessed with a 'cross') and were approved by 119 members of the union. It was the earliest craft union in the industry. The aims were said to be for 'mutual relief in case of old age, sickness and infirmity and for the burial of the dead'. It paid 1s per week sick pay, and provided a pension at 60 years of age of 6s per week. Contributions fluctuated with trade, being 2s 3d a month from 1810 to 1812; 1s 3d until 1813; 1s 9d until 1818; 2s until 1827; and then 3s or more. Benefit also fluctuated. Strike benefit came from special levies. Foundation members paid 6s entrance fee, but from 1810 new members paid one guinea. Thereafter they paid 1s a month with 3d for liquor at each branch meeting. Its main objectives were to force the masters to keep to an agreed ratio of boys to skilled men, and to maintain wages by keeping unemployed moulders off the market and moving them on to an area which had job vacancies. In 1837 the first delegate conference was called and the name was changed to the **Friendly Society of Operative Iron Moulders of the United Kingdom of Great Britain and Ireland**. A new set of rules was agreed together with a tighter system of administration, and the Manchester branch became the seat of government to which all branches were accountable, this right passing to the London branch in 1842 which then had 324 members. In 1853 Samuel Parsons became the first full time General Secretary, and in 1854 the name 'moulders' in the title was changed to 'founders'. In 1890 the members voted to grant strike pay for *offensive* and not just *defensive* action. And from that date all delegates to the TUC and elsewhere were elected by general vote and candidates for the offices of General Secretary and Assistant General Secretary were

permitted to issue election addresses. The union began to admit steel moulders and also coremakers, providing they received the moulders' rate, and the membership had reached 15,000 by 1892. It published its own journal from 1880. In 1920 it amalgamated with the **Associated Iron Moulders of Scotland** and the **Amalgamated Society of Coremakers of Great Britain and Ireland** to form the **National Union of Foundry Workers**.

Sources: Fyrth and Collins; S. and B. Webb, *History of Trade Unionism*; Marsh, *Concise Encyclopedia*; Clegg, Fox and Thompson; Carr and Taplin; Pugh.

FRIENDLY SOCIETY OF MECHANICS
Established as early as the 1780s with branches in several northern towns including Bolton, Blackburn and Chorley, the Society merged with the **Amalgamated Society of Engineers** upon its formation in 1851.

Source: Burgess, *Origins*.

FRIENDLY SOCIETY OF OPERATIVE IRON MOULDERS OF THE UNITED KINGDOM OF GREAT BRITAIN AND IRELAND
See **Friendly Society of Ironfounders of England, Ireland and Wales**

FRIENDLY SOCIETY OF UNITED JOURNEYMEN PLATERS AND MOULDERS
The Secretary of this London-based union, formed in the late 1820s, was Samuel Parsons. It included ironmoulders among its membership. It became a part of the **Friendly Iron Moulders Society**.

Source: Fyrth and Collins.

FRIENDLY UNION OF MECHANICS
Formed in 1826 and operating from Manchester, the Union amalgamated in 1837 with the Yorkshire-based **Mechanics Friendly Union Institution** to form the **Journeymen Steam Engine and Machine Makers Friendly Society**, later to be called the **Journeymen Steam Engine and Machine Makers and Millwrights Friendly Society**. There is a suggestion that the Friendly Union may have originated from a branch of the **United Steam Engine Makers Society** formed in Bradford in 1822, which established branches in Lancashire but failed to recruit many members. There is some evidence of an earlier society in Manchester of which the Union was the direct successor, taken from an account book of the Manchester no.1 branch of the Friendly Union. The book starts in April 1824 and 592 names are listed as paying members, and references are made to branches in Leeds, Bolton, Salford and other Lancashire towns. A gap occurs in the accounts before the names of the Friendly Union members are listed in 1828. It was one of the strongest societies formed prior to or just following the repeal of the Combination Acts, 1824–5.

Sources: W. McLaine, 'The Early Trade Union Organisation among Engineering Workers', PhD thesis, University of London, 1939; S. and B. Webb, *History of Trade Unionism*; Select Committee on Artisans and Machinery, 1824; Jefferys; Burgess, *Origins*.

FRIENDLY UNITED SMITHS OF GREAT BRITAIN AND IRELAND

This organisation was in existence in 1841 with Alexander Hutchinson as General Secretary. In 1844 upon his initiative a **United Trades Association** was set up in Lancashire, the object being to improve trade unions generally in Great Britain and Ireland. The union became a member of the newly formed **Amalgamated Society of Engineers** in 1851.

Sources: S. and B. Webb, *History of Trade Unionism*; Jefferys.

GENERAL IRON FITTERS ASSOCIATION

See **Scottish Metal Workers Union**

GLASGOW AND DISTRICT ASSOCIATED BRASS TURNERS, FITTERS AND FINISHERS SOCIETY

The Society was formed in 1910 by members of a branch which seceded from the **West of Scotland Brass Turners, Fitters and Finishers Society**. It had 364 members in that year. The union did not long remain independent, but in 1912 amalgamated with others to form the **Amalgamated Association of Brass Founders, Turners, Fitters and Coppersmiths**.

Source: BoT Reports.

GLASGOW ASSOCIATION OF MACHINE, ENGINE AND IRON GRINDERS

The Association was set up in 1846. In 1892 the membership was 77, and in 1900, 95. It ceased to exist in 1937.

Sources: Bain and Price; BoT Reports.

GLASGOW BOILER AND PIPE COVERERS ASSOCIATION

Formed in 1893 with 50 members, the Association ceased to exist in 1898 when the membership numbered 67.

Sources: Bain and Price; BoT Reports.

GREENOCK, PORT GLASGOW AND DISTRICT ASSOCIATION OF BRASS TURNERS FITTERS AND FINISHERS

Formed in 1896, the Association had 80 members in 1900 and 120 in 1910. In 1912 it amalgamated with other local societies to form the **Amalgamated Association of Brassfounders, Turners, Fitters and Coppersmiths**.

Source: BoT Reports.

HEYWOOD DISTRICT UNION OF MACHINE AND GENERAL LABOURERS

The Union was established in 1895 by 210 members who had seceded from the **Amalgamated Machine and General Labourers' Union**. In 1920 it merged with the **Workers' Union** (see Vol. 3).

Source: Bain and Price.

HULL BRASSFOUNDERS, TURNERS, FITTERS, FINISHERS AND COPPERSMITHS SOCIETY

This was a local society formed in 1848 which had 224 members in 1900 and 193 in 1910. It became a branch of the **United Journeymen Brassfounders, Turners, Fitters, Finishers and Coppersmiths Association of Great Britain and Ireland** in 1916.

Sources: BoT Reports; Certification Office.

INDEPENDENT ORDER OF ENGINEERS AND MACHINISTS, TRADE AND FRIENDLY SOCIETY

Formed in 1872, the Order was founded in protest against the exclusiveness of the **Amalgamated Society of Engineers** and the neglect of the Order's special interests within that organisation, as workmen who were receiving a high standard rate. It ceased to exist in 1893.

Sources: S. and B. Webb, *History of Trade Unionism*; Certification Office.

IRON AND STEEL DRESSERS TRADE SOCIETY

See **Associated Metal Workers Union**

IRON DRESSERS TRADE SOCIETY

See **Associated Metal Workers Union**

IRON SAFE ENGINEERS SOCIETY

The Society was formed in 1874. It had 134 members in 1892, and by 1910 numbers had fallen to under 100. It remained in existence until 1938 when it ceased to function.

Sources: Bain and Price; BoT Reports.

IRON, STEEL, METAL DRESSERS AND KINDRED TRADES SOCIETY

See **Associated Metal Workers Union**

IRON, STEEL AND METAL DRESSERS TRADE SOCIETY
See **Associated Metal Workers' Union**

IRONFOUNDING WORKERS ASSOCIATION
In 1888 in Falkirk some 400 non-unionists came out on strike for increased wages and after 13 weeks, during which there were bitter battles with blackleg labour and a number of blacklegs were prosecuted for using threats and violence, the strikers obtained a 5 per cent wage increase. The strikers concerned were light casting moulders, mainly pieceworkers paying their own helpers or boys. During the course of the strike the men had approached the **Associated Iron Moulders of Scotland** for assistance but this had been refused, and the strikers decided to form their own union. The **Central Ironmoulders Association of Scotland** was formed on 9 April 1889 with 256 members, John Waddell and Daniel Cameron being elected Secretary and President respectively. By the end of 1889 the membership had risen to 740 and branches were formed at Bonnington, Edinburgh, Granton and Glasgow. It was a new type of union with low entry fees of 2s 6d and subscriptions of 6d per week. Its object was to win improvements in wages and conditions. It did not pay friendly benefits other than a funeral benefit of £8 for a member and £4 for his wife. In 1900 it had 7 branches and 3,150 members, and over 6,500 at the beginning of the First World War. In 1906 it ceased to be an entirely Scottish organisation and began recruiting in England, and in 1926 the name was changed to the Ironfounding Workers Association. In 1946 it amalgamated with the **National Union of Foundry Workers** and the **United Metal Founders Society** in order to form the **Amalgamated Union of Foundry Workers** covering 60,000 workers. Three veteran leaders of the IWA, Hugh Murdoch, Archie Logan and Harry Sinclair, became organisers for the newly formed Union.

Sources: Fyrth and Collins; IWA Jubilee Souvenir Booklet, 1939; BoT Reports.

JOURNEYMEN BRASSFOUNDERS UNION
See **Federation of Moulders and Collateral Trades**

JOURNEYMEN STEAM ENGINE AND MACHINE MAKERS FRIENDLY SOCIETY
See **Journeymen Steam Engine, Machine Makers and Millwrights Friendly Society**

JOURNEYMEN STEAM ENGINE, MACHINE MAKERS AND MILLWRIGHTS FRIENDLY SOCIETY
The union was founded on 26 July 1826 as the **Friendly Union of Mechanics**, later to be called the **Journeymen Steam Engine and Machine Makers Friendly Society**. It was known as the 'Old Mechanics'. John White held the first membership card of the Manchester first branch and he became Treasurer of the union. The highest authority was the delegate meeting attended by representatives from every branch. Central organisa-

tion was effected through an 'Acting Branch', which was chosen every second year by vote at the delegate meeting. The subscription was 6d per week. No definite trade policy was set down but the union constantly made demands for shorter hours of work and payment for overtime, protested against 'illegal men' (those who had not served their time), and objected to overburdening the workshops with apprentices. By 1839 it had 3,000 members and a part time Secretary, Robert Robinson of Manchester, was appointed, becoming full-time in 1845 at a salary of £2 per week. The appointment of a full-time Secretary of a trade union was an unusual step at that time. In 1836 the union made a demand for a 10-hour day and additional payment for overtime which was refused. This refusal resulted in a strike lasting 8 months which cost the union £5,000, but the outcome was complete victory. A journal, *The Mechanics Magazine*, was published in 1843 but was withdrawn through lack of funds in 1845. The word 'Millwright' was added to the title in 1841, thus bringing into the union the older skills of the millwrights who were reported as having said in 1824 that 'they would not work with an engineer as they thought it rather a disgrace'. In 1845 the union attacked the employment of labourers on machines, the piecemaster system, and systematic overtime, and during 1846 a simultaneous attempt was made by many of the union branches to enforce these demands. These actions by the branches at Belfast, Rochdale and Newton-le-Willows led to legal proceedings by the employers, and the officers of the Society and 20 of its members were indicted for conspiracy and illegal combination. A national protest movement was organised to free the men and was supported by all the engineering unions and others, strong financial support was given, and the men were freed in June 1847. This success was one of the factors which accelerated the move towards one national engineering union, and the Society was one of the founders of the **Amalgamated Society of Engineers** in 1851.

Sources: Minutes of the Manchester no. 1 branch of the Journeymen Steam Engine and Machine Makers and Millwrights Friendly Society, 1841–8; Verbatim Report of the Trial for Conspiracy in R. *v*. Selsby and Others, Liverpool, 1847; Steam Engine Makers Society (Manchester Public Library, P.2198); Professor Brentano, 'The Growth of a Trades Union', *North British Review*, October 1870; Jubilee Souvenir History of the ASE, 1901; *The Operative*, January 1851; Jefferys; S. and B. Webb, *History of Trade Unionism*; Cole, *British Trade Unionism Today*; AUEW, Rules of the Journeymen Steam Engine, Machine Makers and Millwrights Friendly Society, London, 1845.

LEEDS BRASSFOUNDERS AND FINISHERS SOCIETY
This was a sectional society, established in 1848, which had a recorded membership of 170 in 1900. In 1909 it merged with the **Manchester Brass Founders, Turners, Fitters, and Finishers Association.**

Source: BoT Reports.

LEEDS COREMAKERS SOCIETY
This was a local society of coremakers formed in 1869. It had 32 members

in 1900 and in 1902 amalgamated with other societies to form the **Amalgamated Society of Coremakers of Great Britain and Ireland.**

Sources: BoT Reports; Fyrth and Collins.

LEEDS DISTRICT PATTERNMAKERS MUTUAL AID ASSOCIATION
See **Leeds Patternmakers Association**

LEEDS GRINDERS AND GLAZERS SOCIETY
Formed in 1904 with 33 members, the Society amalgamated with the **Amalgamated Society of Engineers** in 1914, when its membership was 43. It was one of the sectional societies which had helped to form the **Federation of Engineering and Shipbuilding Trades** in 1891.

Source: Jefferys.

LEEDS PATTERNMAKERS ASSOCIATION
The Association was established in July 1865 under the title of the **Leeds District Patternmakers Mutual Aid Association**, with a subscription of 1½d per week, and took the title of Leeds Patternmakers Association in 1872. A voluntary fund was raised to assist the **London Patternmakers Society** Advance of Wages Movement and a sum of £6 18s 11d was collected for this purpose. In May 1866 a code of rules for the Leeds Patternmakers' Sick Society was agreed and in 1867 an out-of-work fund was instituted. Meetings of the union were held in the William IV Inn, Briggate. Members were required to have good abilities as workmen, steady habits, good moral character, and be in receipt of the average district wage level. The union sent a delegate to the 1868 TUC and made a grant of £2 towards the newly formed Parliamentary Committee. It had a very brief existence as an independent organisation and amalgamated with the **United Kingdom Patternmakers Association** in late 1873 or early 1874, with 95 members and funds amounting to £110 3s 11½d.

Sources: Mosses; Certification Office.

LIVERPOOL AND DISTRICT COREMAKERS SOCIETY
This was a local society of coremakers formed in 1889. It had 17 members in 1892, increasing to 48 in 1900. In 1902 it amalgamated with other local societies to form the **Amalgamated Society of Coremakers of Great Britain and Ireland.**

Sources: BoT Reports; Fyrth and Collins.

LIVERPOOL BRASSFOUNDERS SOCIETY
This was a local society formed in 1826. It had 558 members in 1900 and 506 in 1910. It is possible that it became a branch of the **United Journeymen**

42

Brassfounders, Turners, Fitters, Finishers and Coppersmiths Association of Great Britain and Ireland during the First World War.

Sources: BoT Reports; Certification Office.

LIVERPOOL JOURNEYMEN MILLWRIGHTS FRIENDLY SOCIETY

Founded in 1842, this was an exclusively millwright society. These craft workers had the most to lose from the influx of unskilled labour which increased their insecurity, especially for men whose skills were becoming obsolescent. The union merged with the **Amalgamated Society of Engineers** in 1851.

Sources: AUEW, Rules of the Journeymen Millwrights Friendly Societies, London, 1842; Burgess, *Origins*.

LIVERPOOL SHEET METAL WORKERS SOCIETY

Founded in 1890, the Society went out of existence in 1894.

Source: Certification Office.

LIVERPOOL SMITHS SOCIETY

Formed in the 1880s, this was one of the sectional societies which helped to form the **Federation of Engineering and Shipbuilding Trades** in 1891. It amalgamated with the **Amalgamated Society of Engineers** in 1914.

Source: Jefferys.

LIVERPOOL UNITED SOCIETY OF COPPERSMITHS

Established in 1860, the Society was small in number, having an estimated 80 members in 1892 and 125 in 1899. It reached 144 in 1901 which appeared to be its highest level, as it recorded 110 members in 1910. After this date it would seem that it went out of existence.

Source: BoT Reports.

LONDON AMALGAMATED BRASS WORKERS SOCIETY

See **Amalgamated Society of Brass Workers**

LONDON BRASSFOUNDERS SOCIETY

In towns like London there were dozens of small foundries and many of the moulders employed by the small masters were out-workers. Nevertheless, the workers in the industry formed local clubs even before the repeal of the Combination Acts, and by 1820 this particular London Society had 800 members and had drawn up a list of piece-work prices 'to which in future they respectfully inform their employers they mean to adhere'. It also took part in political events, for instance, actively campaigning for the reform of

43

Parliament, and the members formed themselves into a Lodge of the **Grand National Consolidated Trades Union** (see Vol. 3) when it was formed in 1834. There is no further reference to the society under this title, although there were other London Societies with similar titles.

Source: Fyrth and Collins.

LONDON FELLOWSHIP OF MILLWRIGHTS

The fellowship was said to be the name of a confederacy of men formed in 1799. The master millwrights charged the Fellowship with forming a dangerous combination in London and 25 miles around the metropolis in order to enforce a general increase in wages, the prevention of the employment of journeymen who refused to join the confederacy, and for other illegal purposes, and claimed that in support of such combination the men had established a general fund and demanded regular subscriptions. It would seem that the elements of an effective trade union were in operation at the time. No more is known of this organisation, however.

Source: Jefferys.

LONDON FRIENDLY SOCIETY OF ENGINEERS AND MACHINISTS

Formed in 1833 and known as the 'Old Engineers', the Society merged in May 1851 with the newly formed **Amalgamated Society of Engineers**.

Sources: Jefferys; McLaine, 'The Engineers' Union'; ASE Jubilee Souvenir, 1901.

LONDON JOURNEYMEN SCALEMAKERS TRADE PROTECTION AND BENEFIT SOCIETY

See **National Union of Scalemakers**

LONDON MILLWRIGHTS SOCIETIES

By 1810 there were three separate millwrights' societies operating in London, strong enough to insist on certain jobs being carried out under the terms of a 'closed shop' policy; these organisations were also able to dictate the hours of work – 6 a.m. to 6 p.m. in summer time, and light to dark in the winter time. Fixed wages of 7s per day were also demanded and agreed to. At this time the millwrights 'would not work with engineers; they thought it rather a disgrace' disapproving of the new skills of the engineers. The millwrights' societies remained local organisations of a very exclusive nature until 1841 when they merged with the **Journeymen Steam Engine and Machine Makers Friendly Society**, which added the name of 'Millwrights' to its title and enlarged its range of recruitment.

Sources: Jefferys; First Report of the Select Committee on Artisans and Machinery, 1824; McLaine, 'The Engineers' Union'; S. and B. Webb, *History of Trade Unionism*.

LONDON PATTERNMAKERS SOCIETY

The Society was established in 1865 almost contemporaneously with the **Leeds District Patternmakers Mutual Aid Association**. Its first meetings took place at the Elephant Public House in Fenchurch Street, moving subsequently to The Grapes behind Aldgate Church. In its early days the total membership was 150 members who were generally employed in the Thames area. They were a very exclusive and conservative body of foremen, chargemen and other men firmly established in their jobs. They were sufficiently influential to be in opposition to the **Amalgamated Society of Engineers**. In 1879 the employers gave notice of a reduction of 10s per week which the men refused to accept. There was a strike which lasted nearly 9 months, gradually petering out. The funds of the London Society were greatly depleted by the strike and most of the members were out of work. By 1880 there were only 60 members left, and the union was dissolved.

Source: Mosses.

LONDON AND PROVINCIAL COPPERSMITHS AND METAL WORKERS ASSOCIATION

Two dates are given for the formation of the Society in the Board of Trade Reports; the first is 1866 and the second 1846. It had 360 members in 1892, 387 in 1896, 451 in 1899 and 775 in 1910. After this date there appears to be no further record of its existence under this title.

Source: BoT Reports.

LONDON SOCIETY OF AMALGAMATED BRASS WORKERS AND GAS FITTERS

See **Amalgamated Society of Brass Workers**

LONDON SOCIETY OF MILLWRIGHTS

This organisation was founded as long ago as 1795 and met at The Bell Inn, Old Bailey. Like the **Amicable and Brotherly Society of Journeymen Millwrights** (commonly called the 'Old Millwrights'), which was also a London-based body of men, it was a very exclusive society. It dictated to employers whom to employ, maintained strict control over the length of the working day, and demanded equality of wages at the rate of 7s per day. These demands were conceded by the employers because craft techniques made it necessary to identify skilled men who had served a 7-year apprenticeship, the universal requirement for trade union membership in the trade. The millwrights were originally constructors of mill work of every kind, both in wood and iron, but on the introduction of the steam engine they were superseded by specialised workers in particular sections of their trade, and the parcelling out of the work of the millwright and the substitution of 'payment according to merit' in place of the millwrights' standard rate completely disorganised these skilled mechanics. The union merged with the **Amalgamated Society of Engineers** when it was formed in 1851.

Sources: Burgess, *Origins*; S. and B. Webb, *History of Trade Unionism*; Jefferys.

LONDON SOCIETY OF SCALE BEAM AND WEIGHING MACHINE MAKERS

The Society was formed in 1924 by 120 members who had seceded from the **Amalgamated Scale, Beam and Weighing Machine Makers Association**. This small society continued in existence until 1928 when, with 144 members, it rejoined the Amalgamated Association

Source: Bain and Price.

LONDON UNITED BRASS AND GENERAL METAL FOUNDERS SOCIETY

See **United Metal Founders Society**

LONDON UNITED BRASS FINISHERS SOCIETY

See **London United Metal Turners, Fitters and Finishers Society**

LONDON UNITED BRASSFOUNDERS SOCIETY

See **United Metal Founders Society**

LONDON UNITED METAL TURNERS, FITTERS AND FINISHERS SOCIETY

The union was founded in 1837 as the **London United Brass Finishers Society**. It became a founder member of the **Federation of Engineering and Shipbuilding Trades** in 1891. It was never a large society, having 350 members in 1900. In 1918 it was one of the 22 societies invited by the **Amalgamated Society of Engineers** to discuss proposals for amalgamation and the formation of one big union for the engineering industry, and in May 1919 it was one of the 17 unions who reacted favourably to the proposal and agreed to a postal ballot of its members. It merged with the newly formed **Amalgamated Engineering Union** in 1920.

Sources: Jefferys; S. and B. Webb, *History of Trade Unionism*; BoT Reports; Certification Office.

LONG EATON AND DISTRICT AMALGAMATED SOCIETY OF BOBBIN CARRIAGE, COMB, DROPPED BOX AND STEEL BAR MAKERS

The Society was formed in 1903 as a sectional organisation in the textile machinery trade. It had 53 members at that time. There is no trace of it after 1905 when its registration as a trade union was formally cancelled.

Sources: Certification Office; Bain and Price.

MANCHESTER AND DISTRICT COREMAKERS SOCIETY

The Society was a sectional organisation formed in 1860, and was the oldest established and the biggest of the local coremakers' societies. In 1888 it made its first effort at collective bargaining and won a minimum wage of 32s. In 1889, together with the Bolton and Liverpool societies, it became a founder member of the **United Association of Coremakers**, a federated body. It had 270 members in 1900. In 1902 it amalgamated with other local societies to form the **Amalgamated Society of Coremakers of Great Britain and Ireland**.

Sources: BoT Reports; Fyrth and Collins.

MANCHESTER ASSOCIATION OF MACHINE, ELECTRIC AND OTHER WOMEN WORKERS

The Association was first formed in 1889 and the first recorded membership is in 1903 when it stood at 120. It continued in existence until 1932 when, with a membership of 50, it was dissolved.

Source: Bain and Price.

MANCHESTER BRASS FOUNDERS, TURNERS, FITTERS AND FINISHERS ASSOCIATION

This was an early established union, formed in 1825, which had some 700 members in 1900 and almost 1,000 in 1910. In 1912 it amalgamated with several other sectional societies in the industry in order to form the **Amalgamated Association of Brassfounders, Turners, Fitters and Coppersmiths**.

Source: BoT Reports.

MANCHESTER HAND IN HAND MACHINISTS TRADE UNION

Formed in 1884, the Union ceased to exist after 1887.

Source: Certification Office.

MANCHESTER JOURNEYMEN MILLWRIGHTS FRIENDLY SOCIETY

The Society was founded in 1836. Many all-round millwrights had the most to lose from skilled labour substitution which increased the insecurity of employment, especially for men like the millwrights whose skills were becoming obsolete. In order to protect themselves they formed exclusive millwright societies. The rules of the Manchester Society were less strict than other similar societies, particularly those in London, and admission requirements were less rigid, the apprenticeship qualification being only 5 years instead of the traditional 7. Unemployment benefit was also provided, unlike some earlier societies which only provided tramping allowance. In 1851 it merged with the **Amalgamated Society of Engineers**.

Sources: AUEW, Rules of the Journeymen Millwrights Friendly Societies, London, 1842; Burgess, *Origins*.

MARINE AND GENERAL ENGINEERS ASSOCIATION (LONDON)

Formed in 1893 with only 12 members, the Association struggled to remain in existence until 1907 when, with a membership of only 21, it was dissolved.

Sources: BoT Reports; Certification Office.

MATHEMATICAL, OPTICAL AND PHILOSOPHICAL INSTRUMENT MAKERS SOCIETY

Formed in 1865, this seems to have been a local, probably London, society based on a single branch. It had 140 members in 1900 and 335 members in 1910, after which date nothing further seems to be known of its existence.

Source: BoT Reports.

MECHANICS FRIENDLY UNION INSTITUTION

The Union Institution was formed in 1822 and was successful from the start. Membership was open to model makers, filers, joiners and turners as well as millwrights, and its apprenticeship qualification was 5 not 7 years. It was Yorkshire based and was one of the strongest unions formed prior to the repeal of the Combination Acts of 1824–5. In 1837 it amalgamated with the **Friendly Union of Mechanics** in order to form the **Journeymen Steam Engine and Machine Makers Friendly Society**, which in 1851 merged with the **Amalgamated Society of Engineers**.

Sources: Jefferys; S. and B. Webb, *History of Trade Unionism*; Professor L. Brentano, 'The Growth of a Trades Union', *North British Review*, October 1870; McLaine, 'The Engineers' Union'; Burgess. *Origins*; AUEW, Rules of the Mechanics Friendly Union Institution, London.

MECHANICS PROTECTIVE AND FRIENDLY SOCIETY OF THE UNITED KINGDOM OF GREAT BRITAIN AND IRELAND

In 1840 a **United Trades Association** of millwrights, engineers, iron moulders, smiths and mechanics had been formed in Manchester, publishing a newspaper, *The Trades Journal*, to foster unity among and settle disputes between the trades. Unfortunately the Association was shortlived. In 1844 the attempt by employers in the North of England to crush trade unions by the use of the 'quittance paper' or 'character note' led to the formation of a new society. The purpose of the Protective Society was not in any way to rival or compete with the existing trade unions among engineers but rather to act as a defence alliance between the different societies so that, if one trade was attacked, 'the whole of the trades in that shop shall strike'. On 6 January 1845 the battle with the employers on the 'quittance paper' began. The men working at Walker's Foundry, Bury, refused to work overtime until the 'quittance paper' was abolished and the masters tried to retaliate by cutting wages. 350 men struck work. In February the strike spread to other shops and the Protective Society branch in Bury took over the conduct of the strike, which was successful after 8 months. In London a similar Joint Committee (although not connected officially with the Society) had been successful in reducing hours of work in some workshops without strike action. When victory had been won, the Protective Societies, both in London and elsewhere, were dissolved.

Sources: Fyrth and Collins; *Northern Star*, 3 May 1845; Jefferys; S. and B. Webb, *History of Trade Unionism*.

MILITARY AND ORCHESTRAL MUSICAL INSTRUMENT MAKERS TRADE SOCIETY
The Society was founded in 1895 as the **Military Musical Instrument Makers Trade Society**, the above title being adopted after 1926. It had 151 members in 1900 and 136 in 1910. It is affiliated to the TUC with a current membership of 185.

Sources: Certification Office; Marsh, *Concise Encyclopedia*.

MILITARY MUSICAL INSTRUMENT MAKERS TRADE SOCIETY
See.**Military and Orchestral Musical Instrument Makers Trade Society**

MOULDERS AND DRESSERS UNION (WEDNESBURY)
This was a small local union which was formed in 1896 with 32 members in order to fight the repressive measures carried out by employers in that area. It was dissolved in 1902 with only 9 members remaining.

Source: BoT Reports; Fyrth and Collins.

NATIONAL AMALGAMATED BRASS WORKERS SOCIETY
See **National Society of Metal Mechanics**

NATIONAL ASSOCIATION OF TOOLMAKERS
This was a breakaway union formed by members of the **Amalgamated Engineering Union** working in the Austin Morris Division of the Motor Corporation in Birmingham in 1956. Its first General Secretary was Frank Price. In 1963 the Association began to recruit at the Pressed Steel Company, Cowley, and later in Liverpool and elsewhere. The basic complaint of the Association, was related to the concern that the toolmakers trade was diminishing in status under the umbrella of AEU negotiations and to the narrowing of skill differentials. It was unable to obtain recognition from employers and came into serious conflict with the AEU in various disputes particularly at Pressed Steel. The union had ceased to operate by January 1968. The pressures which gave rise to it nevertheless continued to operate and were seen in the formation of an

unofficial Leyland Toolroom Committee in 1977 and in the subsequent activities of this Committee under its Chairman Roy Fraser.

Sources: John Fray, 'The National Association of Toolmakers of Cowley', Dissertation for Labour Studies Diploma, Ruskin College, 1977; Certification Office.

NATIONAL ENGINEERS ASSOCIATION
Formed in 1894, the Association was based in Lancashire. Nothing seems to be known of its history except that its dissolution was notified in January 1965.

Source: Certification Office.

NATIONAL FEDERATION OF FOUNDRY TRADES UNIONS
The Federation, established in 1918, united 12 foundry unions: the **Friendly Society of Iron Founders**, the **Associated Iron Moulders of Scotland**, the **Central Ironmoulders Association of Scotland**, the **Amalgamated Society of Coremakers**, the **Iron and Steel Dressers Trade Society**, the **London Amalgamated Brass Workers**, the **National Stove Grate, Fender, and General Light Metal Workers**, the **Amalgamated Moulders Union**, the **Scottish Iron Dressers Society**, the **London United Brassfounders Society**, the **National Amalgamated Brassworkers Society** and the **Associated Society of Moulders**. With a membership of approximately 50,000, the Federation was empowered not only to regulate joint relations with the employers, but also to arbitrate in all demarcation disputes between the unions. The rules also provided for mutual recognition of cards by all the constituent societies, but in 1929 a member of the **Ironfounding Workers Association** (previously the **Central Ironmoulders Association of Scotland**) started a job in a workshop entirely controlled by the **National Union of Foundry Workers;** he was told his card would not be recognised and he must either change his union or leave the job. The IWA district committee at once retaliated by demanding the dismissal of two NUFW members working in an IWA shop. Episodes like this which happened at periodic intervals appear to have helped in the disintegration of the Federation which seems to have gradually faded into oblivion.

Source: Fyrth and Collins.

NATIONAL REED AND HEALD MAKERS AND REED WIRE POLISHERS UNION
Established in 1943, the Union was dissolved in July 1968 when its membership was 24.

Source: Bain and Price.

NATIONAL SOCIETY OF AMALGAMATED BRASS WORKERS
See **National Society of Metal Mechanics**

NATIONAL SOCIETY OF AMALGAMATED BRASS WORKERS AND METAL MECHANICS
See **National Society of Metal Mechanics**

NATIONAL SOCIETY OF BRASS AND METAL MECHANICS
See **National Society of Metal Mechanics**

NATIONAL SOCIETY OF CYCLE WORKERS
Formed in 1897, with 1,670 members, the Society collapsed in the following year to a membership of 12 and was dissolved in 1899.

Source: BoT Reports.

NATIONAL SOCIETY OF GENERAL TOOL MAKERS, ENGINEERS AND MACHINISTS
See **Amalgamated Society of General Tool Makers, Engineers and Machinists**

NATIONAL SOCIETY OF METAL MECHANICS
Formed in 1872 as the **Amalgamated Brass Workers Society**, the first Secretary being William John Davis who was only 23 years old at the time, the Society organised trades other than moulders. It was beset by such problems as subcontracting, an abundance of small masters, easy entry to the trade, boy labour, and a product range of enormous size and complexity. The name was changed to the **National Amalgamated Brass Workers Society** in 1874. The Society had been launched in Birmingham but soon spread throughout the Midlands, to London and even to Exeter and Sheffield, and by 1885 had nearly 4,000 members. It reached agreement in 1891 with the General Metal Casters Association on regulating the back-garden outwork trade. A price list was agreed and a Joint Conciliation Board set up to deal with disputes, discipline and conditions, and only union members were to be employed. In 1904, as members were recruited from outside the brass industry, the name was changed to the **National Society of Amalgamated Brass Workers and Metal Mechanics**, and again in 1919 to the **National Society of Brass and Metal Mechanics**. Membership reached almost 7,400 by 1910. It is affiliated to the TUC and to the **Confederation of Shipbuilding and Engineering Unions**. The present title was adopted in 1945. When the union was founded the work consisted of brass, elbow joints, buttons, military ornaments, steam fittings, guns and so on. Today the union's members are to be found on car assembly lines, in aero-engineering, scientific instrument making and other metal-based industries. The growth of mass production methods has brought greater co-operation with the general engineering unions, principally in Birmingham and London, but also in the West and North. Current membership is about 50,000.

Sources: Marsh, *Concise Encyclopedia*; Jefferys; Fyrth and Collins; Clegg, Fox and Thompson; BoT Reports; Malcolm Totten, *Founded in*

NATIONAL UNION OF DOMESTIC APPLIANCE AND GENERAL METAL WORKERS

Founded in 1890 as the **National Union of Stove Grate Workers**, the members of the Union originally worked in the stove grate industry in Rotherham and District. By the end of the century it had 1,460 members in 20 branches. Some time during the first few years of the twentieth century, the union widened its scope by a change of name to **National Union of Stove Grate and General Metal Workers**, taking in a further two branches. In 1910 its membership was 1,248. It has resisted all attempts at merger with other organisations, and adopted its present title in the middle 1960s to take account of the broader nature of its members' work outside the traditional 'Yorkshire range'. Though still predominantly a Northern-based union, it now has members in Birmingham, London and Wales, all working in the fitting, foundry and press shops of the domestic appliance industry. Current membership is about 5,200.

Sources: BoT Reports; the Union; Marsh, *Concise Encyclopedia*.

NATIONAL UNION OF FOUNDRY WORKERS

The Union was formed in 1920 by an amalgamation of the **Friendly Society of Iron Founders**, the **Amalgamated Society of Coremakers of Great Britain and Ireland** and the **Associated Iron Moulders of Scotland**. Efforts had been made for some years by the respective leaders of these unions to rectify a situation wherein no fewer than 11 unions of one kind or another catered for moulders or accepted them as members. Five of the 11 unions consisted entirely of moulders, one entirely of coremakers, one accepted moulders along with fitters and grinders in the stove grate industry, and two labourers' unions accepted moulders. A step to closer unity had been taken in 1916 when the FISF affiliated to the **Federation of Engineering and Shipbuilding Trades**. In 1919 the FISF and the AIMS, after a ballot of their respective membership, agreed to amalgamate and form a new union. Further impetus was given to amalgamation by the emergence of the newly formed **Amalgamated Engineering Union**, then still known as the **Amalgamated Society of Engineers**, which announced it had formed a subcommittee to negotiate the inclusion of foundry unions into its new organisation. The General Secretaries of the FSIF, the AIMS and ASC informed the ASE they intended to amalgamate, and on 28 June 1920 the National Union of Foundry Workers came into being merging these three bodies, and the first step towards the formation of one union for the foundry industry had begun. Despite repeated efforts by the Union and the TUC, it was not until 1946 that this was achieved, by the formation of the **Amalgamated Union of Foundry Workers**, covering all foundry industry grades. Even as late as 1944 the TUC had called a meeting of all foundry unions to push amalgamation (the NUFW, **Ironfounding Workers Association**, **National Union of Stove Grate and General Metal Workers,** Amalgamated Moulders, General Iron Fitters and the Iron, Steel and Metal Dressers), but with the exception of the NUFW, they all preferred a system of federation. Nothing daunted, the NUFW invited all foundry unions to another joint conference in June 1945, and the decision was made by the NUFW, the IWA and the United Metal Founders to form the AUFW. The Amalgamated Moulders, the Iron and Steel Dressers, the Stove Grate Workers, the General Iron Fitters and the National Engineering Brass Moulders withdrew, some of these unions being dissatisfied with the representation they would get on the new Executive Committee and others because they did not obtain the majority required by law.

Sources: Fyrth and Collins; Certification Office.

NATIONAL UNION OF LIFT AND CRANE WORKERS
The Union was established in 1921 with 100 members. In 1935, with 250 members, it would appear to have ceased to exist.

Source: Bain and Price.

NATIONAL UNION OF SCALEMAKERS
The oldest recorded union for scalemakers was the **Scale Beam Makers** which appears to have been in existence in 1811. In the latter half of the nineteenth century there are records of the **London Journeymen Scalemakers Trade Protection and Benefit Society**, and the **Birmingham Scale Beam, Steelyard, Weighing Machine and Millmakers Trade Protection Association**. The London Society grew quite wealthy and powerful, and with the passing of the Weights and Measures Act of 1889 obtained a substantial wage increase. It thereupon disbanded the organisation, sharing out the funds held in reserve. It was not until 1909 that a further effort was made to form a union, the **Amalgamated Society of Scale Beam and Weighing Machine Makers** coming into existence after a strike at a firm called Hodgson and Stead. The first 2 branches were established in Liverpool and Sheffield, and one of the founders of the union, Andrew Leslie, became the first General President. Members had to serve a 5-year apprenticeship, promise to serve faithfully, keep the secrets of the trade and not play at card or dice tables. From 1909 to 1914 the hours of work were 53 or 54 per week with wage rates of 34s to 40s. Up to 1918 the Union was mainly concerned with obtaining *local* agreements on wages and conditions, but on 12 December 1918 the first *national* agreement was signed. In 1909 it was the custom to start work very early in the morning, cooking eggs and bacon on the forge during the breakfast break, the custom ending in 1919 when the weekly hours were worked on the one-break system. The Union had 600 members in 1918 when it appointed its first full-time General Secretary, J.P.Wadsworth. There was a split in 1923 between London and Manchester, the London section becoming the **Society of Scale Beam and Weighing Machinists** and Manchester retaining the title of the **Amalgamated Society of Scale Beam and Weighing Machine Makers,** neither society achieving a very high membership. In 1928 the two bodies were brought together under the auspices of the TUC and agreed to amalgamate, with a combined membership of 282, as the **Society of Scale Beam and Weighing Machinists,** the name being changed

again in 1930 to the National Union of Scalemakers. In 1937 the Union obtained a week's paid annual holiday for its members. It became a member of the **Confederation of Shipbuilding and Engineering Trades** in 1947.

Sources: S. and B. Webb, *History of Trade Unionism*; Certification Office; Harry Bending, *Forty Years: National Union of Scalemakers, 1909–1949*, NUS, 1949; Marsh, *Concise Encyclopedia*.

NATIONAL UNION OF STOVE GRATE AND GENERAL METAL WORKERS
(also referred to as National Union of Stove Grate, Fender and General Light Metal Workers)
See **National Union of Domestic Appliance and General Metal Workers**

NATIONAL UNION OF STOVE GRATE WORKERS
See **National Union of Domestic Appliance and General Metal Workers**

NATIONAL UNITED TRADES SOCIETY OF ENGINEERS
Formed in 1889, the Society had members in the North East who worked in the same workshops and on the same materials as members of the **Amalgamated Society of Engineers**, with whom it came into conflict on demarcation issues. The Society also incurred the displeasure of the **Friendly Society of Ironfounders of England, Ireland and Wales** because it was accepting moulders into membership at 6d per week. It became a member of the **Federation of Engineering and Shipbuilding Trades** in 1891 with a membership of 1,750, but its existence was brief. In 1900 it had 167 members and by 1910 only 23. It finally dwindled to 9 members and was dissolved; the Certification Office gives the date as 1912.

Sources: Fyrth and Collins; Jefferys; Certification Office.

NATIONAL WELDERS ASSOCIATION
The Association was formed in 1943 with 40 members but ceased to exist in 1946 when its membership was 25.

Source: Bain and Price.

NEWCASTLE AND DISTRICT BRASSMOULDERS SOCIETY
See **North of England Brass, Aluminium, Bronze and Kindred Alloys Moulders Society**

NORTH OF ENGLAND BRASS, ALUMINIUM, BRONZE AND KINDRED ALLOYS MOULDERS SOCIETY
This was a union claiming to have been formed in 1859. At some time it seems to have been known as the **Newcastle and District Brassmoulders**

Society, but by the 1890s was known as the **North of England Brass Moulders Society**. It had 460 members in 1900 and 565 in 1910. Relations between the ironmoulders and brassmoulders were bedevilled by demarcation disputes during the 1890s. In 1891 the members of the Society struck against moulders in the **Friendly Society of Ironfounders of England, Ireland and Wales** who were working in brass, and the FSIF immediately filled their places with their own men, claiming that they could do the type of work concerned and that they had some 400 brassmoulders within their own ranks. The Newcastle Society replied that they did not object to FSIF members working in loam but refused to accept them working in sand. 'The FSIF might be the oldest union in the world, but theirs was the oldest trade. The bronze age came before the iron age.' The Society affiliated to the **Federation of Engineering and Shipbuilding Trades** in 1891. In 1906, together with 10 principal foundry unions, it helped to form the **Federation of Moulders and Collateral Trades**. In 1940 it had about 400 members. In 1946 proposals were put to the membership to amalgamate with the **National Union of Foundry Workers**, the **United Metal Founders Society** and the **Ironfounding Workers Association** to form the **Amalgamated Union of Foundry Workers**. At that time the necessary majority was not obtained, though the Society did eventually merge with the AUFW in January 1963.

Sources: Fyrth and Collins; BoT Reports.

NORTH OF ENGLAND BRASS MOULDERS SOCIETY

See **North of England Brass, Aluminium, Bronze and Kindred Alloys Moulders Society**

NORTH OF ENGLAND BRASS TURNERS, FITTERS AND FINISHERS SOCIETY

Formed in 1834 at Newcastle upon Tyne, the Society had 621 members at the end of the last century and formally registered as a trade union in 1898. It was never a large organisation and had barely more than 700 members before the First World War. It became a member of the **Federation of Engineering and Shipbuilding Trades** in 1891. In 1920 it merged with the newly formed **Amalgamated Engineering Union**.

Sources: Jefferys; S. and B. Webb, *History of Trade Unionism*; BoT Reports.

NOTTINGHAM UNITED BRASSFOUNDERS AND FINISHERS ASSO-CIATION

Founded in 1863 this was a single branch society which had 85 members in 1900 and 44 in 1910. In 1912 it amalgamated with several other sectional societies in the industry in order to form the **Amalgamated Association of Brassfounders, Turners, Fitters and Coppersmiths**.

Source: BoT Reports.

OLDHAM AND DISTRICT SOCIETY OF COREMAKERS

The Society, formed in 1872, was open to any competent coremaker aged between 18 and 42 years, at an entrance fee ranging from 5s to 12s 6d according to age, and a weekly contribution of 1s 2d. For this it offered support against wage reductions and unemployment pay at 8s for 8 weeks and 4s for a further 8 weeks. Members striking for higher pay were not allowed to claim strike pay, but their jobs would not be replaced by other members. The Society's motto was 'The labourer is worthy of his hire.' It was affiliated to the **United Association of Coremakers**. In 1902, together with other local societies, it amalgamated to form the **Amalgamated Society of Coremakers of Great Britain and Ireland.**

Sources: BoT Reports; Fyrth and Collins.

OLDHAM BRASSFOUNDERS ASSOCIATION

Formed in 1865, the Association had 321 members in three branches in 1910. In 1912 it amalgamated with several other sectional societies in the industry in order to form the **Amalgamated Association of Brassfounders, Turners, Fitters and Coppersmiths.**

Source: BoT Reports.

OPERATIVE IRONMOULDERS ASSOCIATION

Formed in 1869, the Association was called the 'New Society' because it was a breakaway from the **Scottish Iron Moulders Union**. It was open to all members with or without qualifications and was a purely Friendly Society with no trade rules. The split arose because of the number of apprentices allowed to enter the foundries, resulting sometimes in 12 or 15 boys to one journeyman. The older established SIMU had been forced to accept wage cuts and the policy of wages being paid every fortnight instead of every week. The split in the membership virtually destroyed organisation in the light trades and efforts were made by both sides to reunite.Reunion came about in 1875 with 413 members rejoining the SIMU with a cash reserve of £2,443; this was the bulk of the membership.

Source: Fyrth and Collins.

OPERATIVE MECHANICS UNION

The Union was established about 1830. In 1844 the employers of foundry and engineering workers were being urged to resist wage demands and to come together as a Federation to insist upon the use of the 'quittance paper' (which was supposed to show the character of the workman and the reasons for his leaving his job). In reply to this challenge by the employers, the Operative Mechanics, together with the Moulders, Millwrights, Engineers and Smiths, called a meeting in Manchester to which 3,000 rallied and agreed to form a union called the **Mechanics Protective and Friendly Society of the United Kingdom of Great Britain and Ireland**. Thirty branches were very soon formed in the North of England, of which the Operative Mechanics became a part.

Source: Fyrth and Collins.

OPERATIVE ROLLER MAKERS SOCIETY
Formed in 1886, the Society was one of the many specialist organisations engaged in the textile machinery trade. It was one of the founder members of the **Federation of Engineering and Shipbuilding Trades** in 1891, but strife on demarcation issues led to loss of membership. It had only 366 members in 4 branches in 1901. It merged with the **Amalgamated Society of Engineers** in 1915.

Sources: Jefferys; BoT Reports.

OPTICAL WORKERS AND SPECTACLE FRAME MAKERS UNION
Founded in 1894, the Union ceased to exist in 1895.

Source: Bain and Price.

PERTH OPERATIVE BRASS FOUNDERS AND FINISHERS ASSOCIATION
Formed in 1898, this locally based union struggled to remain in existence with a membership that remained steady at 23 until it was dissolved in 1909.

Source: BoT Reports.

PIANOFORTE MAKERS LABOUR PROTECTION UNION (LONDON)
There was some sort of organisation in existence for these craftsmen in 1852 when £100 was contributed by them towards the strike fund of the newly formed **Amalgamated Society of Engineers**, which had been locked out by the engineering employers for refusing to work systematic overtime and demanding the abolition of piecework. The official formation date of the union was 1894, but it would appear to have been dissolved in 1897.

Sources: Jefferys; ASE Half Yearly Report, June 1852; Certification Office; BoT Reports.

PRESTON JOURNEYMEN MILLWRIGHTS FRIENDLY SOCIETY
Founded in 1843, this was an exclusively millwright society, formed in a desperate attempt to protect millwrights from encroachment by the influx of semi-skilled labour due to the introduction of new techniques. It merged with the **Amalgamated Society of Engineers** in 1851.

Sources: AUEW, Rules of the Journeymen Steam Engine, Machine Maker and Millwrights Friendly Society, London, 1845; Burgess, *Origins*.

SCALE BEAM MAKERS
See **National Union of Scalemakers**

SCIENTIFIC INSTRUMENT MAKERS TRADE SOCIETY
See **Amalgamated Instrument Makers Society**

SCOTTISH BRASS MOULDERS UNION
By the 1880s brassmoulders were being threatened by the substitution of stamping and pressing for casting, and in 1888 the local Scottish brassmoulders' societies which were federated in the **Scottish Operative Brassfounders Trade, Sick and Funeral Association** amalgamated and formed the Scottish Brass Moulders Union. It had 516 members in 1900 and 663 in 1910. It affiliated to the TUC in 1903. In 1906 with 10 other unions it became a founder member of the **Federation of Moulders and Collateral Trades**. It had a membership of 1,000 in 1940. In 1944 it merged with the **National Union of Foundry Workers**.

Source: Fyrth and Collins.

SCOTTISH ELECTRICAL WORKERS UNION
Set up in 1923 with 100 members, the Union lasted only until 1925 when it was dissolved, its membership standing at 110.

Source: Bain and Price.

SCOTTISH IRON DRESSERS SOCIETY
See **Associated Iron, Steel and Brass Dressers of Scotland**

SCOTTISH IRON MOULDERS FRIENDLY SOCIETY
A sectional Society formed in 1829 by former members of the **Friendly Iron Moulders Society**, this was a purely Scottish organisation and was known as the 'Auld Society'. It seems to have been shortlived for in the spring of 1831 its functions were taken over by the **Scottish Iron Moulders Union** which later became the **Associated Iron Moulders of Scotland**.

Source: Fyrth and Collins.

SCOTTISH IRON MOULDERS UNION
See **Scottish Iron Moulders Friendly Society** and **Associated Iron Moulders of Scotland**

SCOTTISH METAL WORKERS UNION
The Union was formed in 1892 as the **Associated Society of Range, Stove and Ornamental Workers**. It had 110 members upon its formation, rising to 787 in 1899 and to 963 in 1907. By 1910 the title had been changed to the **General Iron Fitters Association**, the membership at that date being 982 in 4 branches. The union's members mainly comprised stove dressers and fitters working in the Falkirk area. It did eventually gain members working in Glasgow. The secretary during the whole of the period of the First

World War was J. Fraser of New Market Street, Falkirk. It adopted the above title in 1965, and transferred its engagements to the **General and Municipal Workers Union** (see Vol. 3) in 1968.

Sources: BoT Reports; MoL Reports; Fyrth and Collins; TUC Report 1968.

SCOTTISH OPERATIVE BRASSFOUNDERS TRADE, SICK AND FUNERAL ASSOCIATION
Formed in 1856, this was a federation of small local craft societies. Brassfounders were highly craft conscious and excluded the semi-skilled. In 1888 it became merged into the **Scottish Brass Moulders Union**.

Source: Fyrth and Collins.

SCOTTISH STEAM ENGINE MAKERS SOCIETY
Formed in the 1830s under the leadership of William Pattinson, who was a prominent Chartist at that time, the Society merged in 1851 with the newly formed **Amalgamated Society of Engineers.**

Source: Marwick.

SHEFFIELD AND DISTRICT COREMAKERS SOCIETY
The Society, formed in 1892, never achieved a large membership; in 1900 it was 83. The Society affiliated to the **United Association of Coremakers** and in 1902, together with other sectional bodies of coremakers, amalgamated to form the **Amalgamated Society of Coremakers of Great Britain and Ireland.**

Sources: BoT Reports; Fyrth and Collins.

SHEFFIELD FENDER UNION
Formed some time before 1820, the Union was a domestic heating union based in Sheffield which attempted to limit hours and regulate piece rates. Sometimes it employed violent methods such as setting fire to the works of any obstinate employer. It had ceased to exist by 1820.

Source: Fyrth and Collins.

SMITH BENEVOLENT SICK AND BURIAL SOCIETY
See **Amalgamated Society of Engineers**

SOCIETY OF ENGINEERS AND MACHINISTS
See **Amalgamated Society of Engineers, Machinists, Smiths, Millwrights and Pattern-makers**

SOCIETY OF MILLWRIGHTS
See **Amalgamated Society of Engineers, Machinists, Smiths, Millwrights and Pattern-makers**

SOCIETY OF SCALE BEAM AND WEIGHING MACHINISTS
This was a London based union formed in 1923 by workers who had broken away from the **Amalgamated Society of Scale Beam and Weighing Machine Makers**, but who rejoined that Society in 1928.

Source: Harry Bending, *Forty Years: National Union of Scalemakers, 1909–1949*, NUS, 1949.

SOCIETY OF SHUTTLEMAKERS
Founded in 1891 by a small group of shuttlemakers in Lancashire and Yorkshire, the Society was earlier known as the **Amalgamated Society of Shuttlemakers**. It had 10 branches and 277 members in 1900, rising to 331 in 1910. After the Second World War membership increased to 600, which was 90 per cent of all shuttlemakers in Great Britain. With the introduction of the shuttleless loom and the loss of Indian markets, membership has gradually declined over the last decade and now stands at about 100.

Sources: The Union; BoT Reports; Marsh, *Concise Encyclopedia*; Marsh, *Trade Union Handbook*.

SOUTH WALES AND MONMOUTH SMITHS, STRIKERS, FITTERS AND CARPENTERS GENERAL ASSOCIATION
See **South Wales and Monmouth Tradesmen's Association**

SOUTH WALES AND MONMOUTH TRADESMEN'S ASSOCIATION
The Association had a very brief span of existence. It was formed in 1891 as the **South Wales and Monmouth Smiths, Strikers, Fitters and Carpenters General Association** and had 400 members by 1892, but only 25 members when it was dissolved in 1895 under the above title.

Source: BoT Reports.

STEAM ENGINE MAKERS SOCIETY
The first branch of the Society was formed in Liverpool on 2 November 1824; by 1826 when the first delegate meeting was held in Manchester there were 5 branches in existence. It was one of the strongest unions formed prior to the repeal of the Combination Acts 1824–5. It recruited both skilled, semi-skilled and unskilled workers. Unlike the early miners' unions, the Society was never a supporter of Chartism, even going to the length of suspending branches which supported the movement. By 1836 it had 525 members in 14 branches. It refused to amalgamate with the newly formed **Amalgamated Society of Engineers** in 1851. Of all the societies invited to join by the **Journeymen Steam Engine, Machine Makers and**

Millwrights Friendly Society (known as the 'Old Mechanics'), the union was the only one approaching the Old Mechanics in size and had a longer (though less successful) history. The union felt that amalgamation with a much stronger society would mean that it would become powerless and be outvoted, and although various attempts were made by the ASE to overcome these prejudices, the Steam Engine Makers remained as an independent organisation. It was one of the founding unions which formed the **Federation of Engineering and Shipbuilding Trades** in 1891. It then had over 6,000 members, which grew to 17,800 by the beginning of the First World War. In 1920 it was one of the unions, which, after a ballot of its membership, agreed to amalgamate with the ASE in order to form the **Amalgamated Engineering Union**.

Sources: Jefferys; First Report from the Select Committee on Artisans and Machinery, 1824; W. McLaine, 'The Early Trade Union Organisation Among Engineering Workers', unpublished PhD thesis, University of London, 1939; S. and B. Webb, *History of Trade Unionism*; G.D.H. Cole, *Attempts at General Union*, 1818–1834, Macmillan, 1953; *International Review for Social History*, 1939.

STOVE GRATE WORKERS SOCIETY

The Society was formed in 1894 with a very limited membership, having only 35 members by 1892. The number grew to 110 but the union was dissolved in 1897.

Source: BoT Reports.

SUNDERLAND SMITHS SOCIETY

Formed in the 1870s, the Society amalgamated with the **Amalgamated Society of Engineers** in 1893. From its inception strife with other sectional societies on demarcation issues had weakened the union (which had helped form the **Federation of Engineering and Shipbuilding Trades** in 1891), but it later considered the Federation machinery on inter-union poaching of members to be too slow and cumbersome.

Source: Jefferys.

TECHNICAL ENGINEERS ASSOCIATION

Set up in 1919 with 1,679 members, the Association continued in existence until 1928 when, with 1,251 members, it was dissolved.

Source: Bain and Price.

TRACERS ASSOCIATION

Formed in 1920 with 602 members, the Association ceased to exist in 1922 when the membership had fallen to 286.

Source: Bain and Price.

TRADE SOCIETY OF IRON FOUNDRY LABOURERS
Established in 1873, the Society ceased to exist after 1875.

Source: Certification Office.

TRIMMERS, FIREMEN AND FOUNDRY LABOURERS UNION
The Union was established in 1890 and had 60 members in 1892. It had two branches in 1900 but it ceased to exist a year later when the membership numbered 45.

Sources: Bain and Price; BoT Reports.

TYPEWRITER TRADE AND ALLIED WORKERS ASSOCIATION
Formed in 1919 with 500 members, the Association continued in existence until 1928 when, with a membership of 100, it was dissolved.

Source: Bain and Price.

UNION OF ELECTRICAL OPERATIVES
See **Electrical, Electronic, Telecommunication and Plumbing Union**

UNION OF ELECTRICAL WIREMEN (PORTSMOUTH)
The Union was established in 1903 with 25 members. It ceased to exist in 1911 when its membership was 46.

Source: Bain and Price.

UNION OF OPERATIVE CARD MAKERS AND WIRE DRAWERS
This was an early union of hand card makers in the textile trade operating from Halifax which is known to have existed from 1833 to 1834 but probably disappeared after a short strike in the latter year. It seems to have represented the only serious attempt at organisation in the trade until the machine tenters became organised in the **Card Setting Machine Tenters Society** in 1872.

Source: Malcolm Speirs, *One Hundred Years of a Small Trade Union*, Card Setting Machine Tenters Society, 1972.

UNITED ASSOCIATION OF COREMAKERS
The Association was formed in the 1890s in order to bring together for mutual aid and discussion on wages and conditions all the small sectional societies of coremakers, like those at Sheffield, Liverpool and Oldham. These societies, of which there were about 6 or 7, amalgamated in 1902 in order to form the **Amalgamated Society of Coremakers of Great Britain and Ireland**.

Sources: BoT Reports; Fyrth and Collins.

UNITED COPPERSMITHS TRADE PROTECTIVE ASSOCIATION

Formed in Glasgow in 1889 the Association had 496 members in 1892 and 504 in 1893 falling to 200 in 1896. In 1899 it had 250 members. It registered 345 members in 1910, after which date no further information appears to be available as to its existence.

Sources: BoT Reports; MoL Reports.

UNITED JOURNEYMEN BRASSFOUNDERS ASSOCIATION OF GREAT BRITAIN AND IRELAND

See **United Journeymen Brassfounders, Turners, Fitters, Finishers and Coppersmiths Association of Great Britain and Ireland**

UNITED JOURNEYMEN BRASSFOUNDERS, TURNERS, FITTERS, FINISHERS AND COPPERSMITHS ASSOCIATION OF GREAT BRITAIN AND IRELAND

Formed in 1866 as the **United Journeymen Brassfounders Association of Great Britain and Ireland**, the Association was a federation of small English and Irish sectional societies, each administering its own friendly benefits according to its own rules. They united purely for trade purposes with a common dispute fund and an Executive Committee enabled to call strikes if supported by the decision of two-thirds of the members of the branch involved. It affiliated to the TUC in 1875. By 1890 it had 2,161 members and became a founder member of the **Federation of Engineering and Shipbuilding Trades** in 1891. The Association catered for those men who did not wish to join the **Amalgamated Society of Engineers** on the grounds that their interests would be submerged in that organisation. It joined the **Federation of Moulders and Collateral Trades** when it was formed in 1906. Nothing further is known of its existence after 1920 when the organisation appears to have been dissolved.

Sources: Jefferys; Fyrth and Collins; Certification Office.

UNITED KINGDOM PATTERNMAKERS ASSOCIATION

See **Association of Patternmakers and Allied Craftsmen**

UNITED KINGDOM SOCIETY OF AMALGAMATED SMITHS AND STRIKERS

Formed in 1886, the Society had 2,200 members in 1892 and 2,731 in 69 branches in 1910. It was a founder member of the **Federation of Engineering and Shipbuilding Trades** when this was formed in 1891. In 1918 it was one of 22 societies invited by the **Amalgamated Society of Engineers** to discuss amalgamation proposals for the formation of one big union for engineering workers, and in May of that year it was one of 17 unions which agreed to submit amended proposals for a postal ballot of its members. In 1920 with

8 other unions it amalgamated in order to form the **Amalgamated Engineering Union**; it had on amalgamation a little over 14,000 members.

Sources: S. and B. Webb, *History of Trade Unionism*; Jefferys.

UNITED MACHINE WORKERS ASSOCIATION

Founded in Manchester in 1844, the Association had members in the North East working in the same shops and with the same materials as members of the **Amalgamated Society of Engineers** with whom it came into constant conflict. New techniques in marine engineering and shipbuilding led to fierce and persistent competition among sectional societies. In 1891 the union became a founder member of the **Federation of Engineering and Shipbuilding Trades**. It had 54 branches and 3,800 members in 1900 and over 11,000 at the beginning of the First World War, rising to 14,000 in 1915. In 1918 it was one of the 22 societies invited by the ASE to discuss the possibility of amalgamation in order to form one union for the engineering industry, and in 1920, after a favourable postal ballot of its membership, it amalgamated with 8 other unions to form the **Amalgamated Engineering Union**.

Sources: McLaine, 'The Engineers' Union'; S. and B. Webb, *History of Trade Unionism*; Clegg, Fox and Thompson; Jefferys; *Monthly Journal and Report*, June 1920; *ibid.*, July 1920; Certification Office.

UNITED MECHANICAL ENGINEERS SOCIETY

Formed in 1890, the Society was dissolved in 1893.

Source: Certification Office.

UNITED METAL FOUNDERS SOCIETY

Formed in 1890 as the **London United Brass and General Metal Founders Society** with its headquarters at The Angel, Webber St, London, the Society changed its name to the United Metal Founders Society in 1920. A 'vacant book' was kept at the public house where it held its meetings. The Committee was composed of 6 moulders, 2 coremakers, 2 trimmers and 2 firemen. Members received trade protection, unemployment and funeral pay, and a separate sick club was formed in 1903. In 1893, although with less than 150 members, it had established a minimum rate of 8½d an hour for moulders and 6½d for other grades. The hours worked at that time were 54 to 59 a week, with a few 60-hour foundries. In 1891 the Society was one of the sponsors in the formation of the Federal Council of Brass Workers Societies together with the **Amalgamated Brass Workers Society**. It affiliated to the Labour Representation Committee in 1903. There were efforts towards amalgamation with the **Friendly Society of Iron Founders of England, Ireland and Wales** in 1914 but a two-thirds majority was not reached. In 1918 it became a member of the National Federation of Foundry Workers and in 1925 it amalgamated with the newly formed **National Union of Foundry Workers**. The Society was an opponent of the 'premium bonus system' by which each job was timed and any man doing it in less than the stated time was paid a bonus equivalent to his pay for half the time saved.

Source: Fyrth and Collins.

UNITED OPERATIVE SPINDLE AND FLYER MAKERS TRADE AND FRIENDLY SOCIETY

With the exception of the **Card Setting Machine Tenters Society** and the **Amalgamated Society of Wool-comb and Hackle and Gill Makers**, this seems to have been the longest lived of the many unions which formerly made textile machinery and fittings. It was formed in 1856, and in 1860 applied to join the **Amalgamated Society of Engineers** but was refused on the grounds that its members had insufficient skill to qualify. As an independent organisation, therefore, the union developed 13 branches and a membership of almost 1,300 in 1900 and about 1,200 a decade later. Membership declined to fewer than 600 after the Second World War and this was further reduced by the decline in the textile trade. It numbered less than 200 when it eventually merged with the **Amalgamated Engineering Union** in June 1962.

Sources: Jefferys; BoT Reports.

UNITED ORDER OF SMITHS, ENGINEERS AND MACHINISTS

Formed in 1874, the Order ceased to exist after 1881.

Source: Certification Office.

UNITED SOCIETY OF FITTERS AND SMITHS

See **Heating and Domestic Engineers Union**

UNITED SOCIETY OF PATTERN MAKERS

This Society was founded in 1873; registration was withdrawn in 1879.

Source: Certification Office.

UNITED STEAM ENGINE MAKERS SOCIETY

The Society was formed in Bradford in 1822 and established branches in Lancashire but apparently failed to recruit members in sufficient numbers, and therefore ceased to exist.

Sources: Jefferys; McLaine, 'The Early Trade Union Organisation among Engineering Workers', unpublished PhD thesis, University of London, 1939.

UNITED TRADES ASSOCIATION

In 1839 a Joint Committee representing the engineering trades in Bolton urged upon their members the advantages of one concentrated union and in 1840, through the instigation of Alexander Hutchinson, the Secretary of the **Friendly United Smiths of Great Britain and Ireland**, the United Trades Association was established. The membership comprised the 'five trades of mechanism, viz. mechanics, smiths, moulders, engineers and millwrights'. Its object was to extend and improve trade unions generally in Great Britain and Ireland, to foster unity and settle disputes among the trades. The attempt was shortlived. It was not until 1844 that the men of Bolton succeeded in establishing a stronger federation of unions known as the **Mechanics Protective Society of Great Britain and Ireland**. The establishment of this new organisation followed the attempt by employers in Northern England to crush the unions by the use of the 'quittance paper' (a character note or leaving certificate) which the unions resisted, the Bolton-based Society successfully maintaining a 9 months' strike costing £9,000, eventually forcing the employers to abandon the quittance paper. Following the successful outcome of the strike, joint committees of engineering operatives were formed between 1844 and 1850 in all the principal Lancashire towns and the ground was thus prepared for the eventual amalgamation of many sectional societies, leading to the formation of the **Amalgamated Society of Engineers**.

Sources: Jefferys; S. and B. Webb, *History of Trade Unionism*.

UNITED TRIMMERS, FIREMEN AND FOUNDRY LABOURERS SOCIETY

Formed in 1892, the Society was dissolved in 1901.

Source: Certification Office.

WALSALL AND BLOXWICH FORGERS AND FILERS PROTECTION SOCIETY

Formed in 1891, the Society ceased to exist after 1897.

Source: Certification Office.

WELSH IRONFOUNDERS UNION
See **Associated Society of Moulders**

WEST OF SCOTLAND BRASS TURNERS, FITTERS AND FINISHERS SOCIETY

Formed in 1890 it lost almost 200 of its 1,000 members by secession to the **Glasgow and District Associated Brass Turners, Fitters and Finishers Society** in 1910.

Source: BoT Reports.

WIGAN UNITED JOURNEYMEN BRASSFOUNDERS SOCIETY
See **Wigan United Journeymen Brassfounders, Turners, Fitters, Finishers and Coppersmiths Society**

WIGAN UNITED JOURNEYMEN BRASSFOUNDERS, TURNERS, FITTERS, FINISHERS AND COPPERSMITHS SOCIETY
Formed in 1871 as the **Wigan United Journeymen Brassfounders Society**, the union had 70 members in 1900 and 86 members in 1910, concentrated in one branch. It is possible that it became a branch of the **United Journeymen Brassfounders, Turners, Fitters, Finishers and Coppersmiths Association of Great Britain and Ireland** during the First World War.

Sources: BoT Reports; Certification Office.

WILLENHALL IRON CASTERS SOCIETY
A shortlived society formed in 1899 with 53 members but dissolved in the following year.

Source: BoT Reports.

WIRE CARD SETTING MACHINE TENTERS SOCIETY
See **Card Setting Machine Tenters Society**

WOOLWICH WORKERS UNION
The Union was set up in 1903 with 175 members, and continued in existence until 1911 when, with 400 members, it merged with the **Workers Union** (see Vol. 3).

Source: Bain and Price.

YORKSHIRE FRIENDLY SOCIETY OF COREMAKERS (LEEDS)
This was a local society of coremakers formed in 1897. In 1900 it had 27 members and in 1902 came together with other similar societies to form the **Amalgamated Society of Coremakers of Great Britain and Ireland**.

Sources: BoT Reports; Fyrth and Collins.

YORKSHIRE MECHANICS FRIENDLY UNION INSTITUTION
Formed in the early 1830s, in 1838 the union amalgamated with the **Friendly Union of Mechanics** operating from Manchester to form the **Journeymen Steam Engine and Machine Makers Friendly Society**. The union was said to have originated the scheme adopted by the Journeymen Steam Engine and Machine Makers Friendly Society whereby delegate

meetings received accounts from the branches and instructed them on the sums necessary to be remitted under the scheme for equalisation of funds, which enabled branches to fulfil their commitments to members even when their expenditure was heavier than their income from contributions.

Source: Jefferys.

Shipbuilding

It would be difficult even to estimate how many trade unions organised workers in British shipyards over the major part of the nineteenth century. Local societies of shipwrights, caulkers, riggers, mast and block makers, painters and sailmakers (among other trades) were numerous, and often short lived. Even more failed to meet the change from sail to steam and from wood to iron and steel which characterised the development of the industry from the 1870s and the intense inter-craft competition and demarcation disputes to which this gave rise.

The first union to find its feet in the new situation was the United Society of Boilermakers, dating from 1834. As a Society it had achieved a strong position as early as the middle of the nineteenth century and a membership of 2,000 in 52 branches both in shipbuilding and engineering. The Society continued to prosper under the leadership of Robert Knight, whose autocratic but outward-looking conservatism resulted in a broadening of its ranks to accept other types of worker and in an attempt to co-ordinate the many sectional interest groups within the industry through the Federation of Engineering and Shipbuilding Trades (1891). In an expanding industry the Boilermakers were seen by the Webbs as one of the most powerful and best conducted of English trade societies.[1] From a membership of about 30,000 in 1889 it grew to almost 41,000 in 258 branches by 1896 and to almost 50,000 in 293 branches by 1910, comprising nearly all the men, noted the Board of Trade at the time, in the boilermaking and iron shipbuilding trade.[2]

Compared with the Boilermakers, the Shipwrights, confronted by a more fragmented situation and faced with even greater problems of technical change, found adaptation to circumstances proportionately more difficult. An Associated Society of Shipwrights, formed in 1872 had, nevertheless, 18,000 members in 1900, partly as a result of natural growth and partly from amalgamations which continued into the twentieth century, forming the Ship Constructive and Shipwrights Association (later the Ship Constructors and Shipwrights Association). In the process of the union's development the Shipwrights absorbed earlier amalgamations of drillers and, by the early 1960s, when the Boilermakers and Shipwrights came together with the Associated Blacksmiths, Forge and Smithy Workers Society to form the Amalgamated Society of Boilermakers, Blacksmiths, Shipbuilders and Structural Workers (1963), only a handful of independent societies remained in the industry in addition to general and engineering unions organising labourers and marine engineers. Among the last of these to disappear were the Amalgamated Union of Sailmakers (the residuary legatee of at least 15 local societies which had existed three-quarters of a century earlier) in 1971, and the Iron, Steel and Wood Barge Builders and Helpers Association which transferred its engagements to the Transport and General Workers Union in 1972. The process of absorption of shipbuilding unions into other organisations seems to have been completed by the amalgamation of the Amalgamated Society of Boilermakers with the General and Municipal Workers Union in 1982 to form the General, Municipal, Boilermakers and Allied Trades Union.

Notes

1. *Industrial Democracy*, 1898, p.28.

70

2. Board of Trade Commercial Department: *Report of the Labour Correspondent and Statistical Tables on Trade Unions, Fourth Report, Years 1889–1890,* C–6475, p. 194.

ADMIRALTY WORKS DEPARTMENT EMPLOYEES ASSOCIATION

Established in 1899, the first available membership figure is 124 in 1910. The Association had ceased to exist by 1919 when it had 250 members.

Source: BoT Reports.

AMALGAMATED DRILLERS AND HOLE CUTTERS SOCIETY

Established in 1896 with 308 members, the Society was an amalgamation of three local associations. The major partner was the **United Society of Drillers and Hole Cutters of Hartlepool**; minor partners were the **Cleveland Drillers and Hole Cutters Society** and the **Amalgamated Society of Drillers of Stockton-on-Tees**. The Amalgamated Drillers merged with the **Ship Constructive and Shipwrights Association** in 1909 when it had a membership of 661.

Source: BoT Reports.

AMALGAMATED SHIPYARD HELPERS ASSOCIATION

Established in 1888, the Association had 1,900 members in 1892. It ceased to exist in 1907.

Source: BoT Reports.

AMALGAMATED SOCIETY OF ANCHORSMITHS, SHIP TACKLE AND SHACKLE MAKERS

The Society was formed in 1895 with 185 members and was dissolved in 1924 when it had 133 members.

Source: Bain and Price.

AMALGAMATED SOCIETY OF BOILERMAKERS, SHIPWRIGHTS, BLACKSMITHS AND STRUCTURAL WORKERS

The Society came into existence in 1963 as the result of an amalgamation between the **Associated Blacksmiths, Forge and Smithy Workers Society,** the **United Society of Boilermakers, Shipbuilders and Structural Workers** and the **Ship Constructors and Shipwrights Association**. For some years after the amalgamation each body operated as a separate section for trade purposes, full integration taking place in April 1969. In 1971 the Society estimated it had 30,000 in shipbuilding and ship repairing, the bulk of its membership being engaged in the engineering industry. Nevertheless it is better known as a shipbuilding union, in which industry it organises a variety of crafts, workers mainly engaged in the steel trades, such as welders, caulkers, burners, platers, shipwrights, boilermakers, drillers, riveters, blacksmiths, loftsmen and riggers. The Society also organised supervisory staff up to the level of foremen. A forerunner of the Society, the **United Society of Boilermakers and Iron and Steel Ship Builders**, played a prominent part in the foundation of the **Federation of Engineering** and **Shipbuilding Trades of the United Kingdom** in 1891. In 1982, the Amalgamated Society amalgamated with the **General and Municipal Workers Union** (Vol. 3) to form the **General, Municipal Boilermakers and Allied Trades Union** (Vol. 3).

Sources: Mortimer; Cummings; Clegg, Fox and Thompson; S. and B. Webb, *History of Trade Unionism.*

AMALGAMATED SOCIETY OF CHIPPERS, DRILLERS AND SHIP FITTERS OF LONDON AND DISTRICT

Founded in 1885, with 175 members, the Society had 500 members in 1892. It was apparently dissolved in 1894. See also **Amalgamated Society of Iron and Steel Chippers, Ship and General Fitters of London**.

Source: BoT Reports.

AMALGAMATED SOCIETY OF DRILLERS AND HOLE CUTTERS OF THE RIVER WEAR

See **Wear Drillers and Hole Cutters Society**

AMALGAMATED SOCIETY OF DRILLERS OF STOCKTON-ON-TEES

Established in 1888, the Society in 1896 joined with the **United Society of Drillers and Hole Cutters of Hartlepool** and the **Cleveland Drillers and Hole Cutters Society** to form the **Amalgamated Drillers and Hole Cutters Society**. It had at that time 44 members.

Sources: BoT Reports; Certification Office.

AMALGAMATED SOCIETY OF IRON AND STEEL CHIPPERS, SHIP AND GENERAL FITTERS OF LONDON

Formed in 1909, the Society had a single branch of 70 members in 1910. It was dissolved in July 1913. Whether it had any connection with the previous **Amalgamated Society of Chippers, Drillers and Ship Fitters of London and District** is not clear.

Sources: BoT Reports; Certification Office.

AMALGAMATED SOCIETY OF WELDED BOILER MAKERS

There were two unions of this name. The first was founded in July 1895 and dissolved in December 1895, and the second was formed in 1899 in Halifax with 146 members; it was dissolved in August 1900.

Sources: BoT Reports; Certification Office.

AMALGAMATED UNION OF SAILMAKERS
See **Federation of Sailmakers of Great Britain and Ireland**

AMICABLE AND PROVIDENT SOCIETY OF JOURNEYMEN BOILER MAKERS OF GREAT BRITAIN
The Society was formed in 1849 in London as a rival to the existing **United Friendly Boilermakers Society**, the main difference between the two societies being that the Amicable and Provident Society placed greater emphasis on the provision of financial benefits to members who were unemployed or who retired because of old age. In 1852 the Amicable and Provident Society, together with the **Scottish Society of Boilermakers**, and the **United Friendly Boilermakers Society** amalgamated under the title of the **United Society of Boiler Makers and Iron and Steel Shipbuilders**. Both the merging societies were small having between them only about 200 members.

Source: Mortimer.

ASSOCIATED BLACKSMITHS, FORGE AND SMITHY WORKERS SOCIETY
See **Amalgamated Society of Boilermakers, Shipwrights, Blacksmiths and Structural Workers**

ASSOCIATED SOCIETY OF SHIPWRIGHTS
See **Ship Constructive and Shipwrights Association**

ASSOCIATION OF GOVERNMENT LABOURERS (PEMBROKE DOCK)
Formed in 1902 with 257 members, the Association ceased to exist in 1903.

Source: BoT Reports.

ASSOCIATION OF STOREHOUSEMEN (ROYAL VICTORIA YARD)
The Association was set up in 1906 with 29 members and lasted until 1916 when, with a membership of 21, it ceased to exist.

Source: BoT Reports.

BARGE BUILDERS TRADE UNION
See **Iron, Steel and Wood Barge Builders and Helpers Association**. A second union of the same name was established in 1872 and went out of existence in 1912.

Source: Certification Office.

BARROW-IN-FURNESS DRILLERS ASSOCIATION
Formed in 1890, the Association was dissolved in 1892.

Source: Certification Office.

BARROW-IN-FURNESS SHIPWRIGHTS PROVIDENT ASSOCIATION
Established in 1872, the Association went out of existence in 1875.

Source: Certification Office.

BIRMINGHAM BOAT BUILDERS ASSOCIATION
The Association was in existence in the 1870s. In 1872 it expressed hearty sympathy with the agricultural labourers who were on strike at Wellesbourne and who were victimized for being members of the **National Agricultural Labourers Union**. Nothing more is known of the Association.

Source: Horn, *Joseph Arch.*

BOAT BUILDERS TRADE UNION OF THE RIVER THAMES
See **River Thames Boat Builders Trade Union**

BRISTOL OPERATIVE SAILMAKERS ASSOCIATION
See **Federation of Sailmakers of Great Britain and Ireland**

BYKER SOCIETY OF DRILLERS AND HOLE CUTTERS
Founded in 1890 the Society went out of existence in 1892.

Source: Certification Office.

BYKER UNITED ASSOCIATION OF DRILLERS AND HOLE CUTTERS
Formed in 1894 with 54 members the Association lasted a mere two years before being dissolved in 1896. It never had more than 63 members.

Source: BoT Reports.

CANNOCKS QUAY SHIPWRIGHTS ASSOCIATION
Formed in 1875, the Association was dissolved in 1886.

Source: Certification Office.

CARDIFF SAILMAKERS SOCIETY
This was a small local Society formed in 1904. It had under 20 members in

1910. It still existed in 1913 but apparently disappeared or federated by the end of the First World War.

Sources: BoT Reports; Certification Office.

CARDIFF SHIPWRIGHTS ASSOCIATION
The Association was established in 1852. In 1892, with 504 members, it merged with the **Ship Constructive and Shipwrights Association**.

Source: BoT Reports.

CLEVELAND DRILLERS AND HOLE CUTTERS SOCIETY
Formed in 1890, the Society had between 80 and 90 members for the whole of its existence. In 1896 it merged with the **United Society of Drillers and Hole Cutters of Hartlepool** and the **Amalgamated Society of Drillers of Stockton-on-Tees** to form the **Amalgamated Drillers and Hole Cutters Society**. It had 82 members at that time.

Sources: BoT Reports; Certification Office.

CLYDE FEDERATED SHIP RIGGERS ASSOCIATION (GLASGOW)
The Glasgow section of the Federation was established in 1872 and had 290 members in 1892. In 1924, with 123 members, the Federation merged with the **Transport and General Workers Union** (see Vol. 3).

Sources: BoT Reports; Certification Office.

CLYDE FEDERATED SHIP RIGGERS ASSOCIATION (GREENOCK)
The Greenock section of the Federation was formed in 1890 and had 100 members in 1892. It was dissolved in 1903 when the membership totalled 40.

Source: BoT Reports.

DEVONPORT ROYAL DOCKYARD IRON CAULKERS SOCIETY
The Society was formed in 1892 with 33 members. In 1903 with a membership of 50 the name was changed to the **Royal Dockyard Iron and Steel Shipbuilders Society**. In 1915 it merged with the **United Society of Boiler Makers and Iron and Steel Shipbuilders**.

Sources: BoT Reports; Certification Office.

DOCKYARD SHIP RIGGERS ASSOCIATION
The Association had a very brief existence. It was formed in 1892 with 84

members but had ceased to exist by 1899 when the membership had dwindled to 25.

Source: BoT Reports.

DRILLERS UNION (GLASGOW)
Formed in 1890 the Union had 3 branches and 430 members in 1896. On 3 February 1897 it amalgamated with the **Amalgamated Society of Drillers and Hole Cutters.**

Source: BoT Reports

EAST LONDON HELPERS ASSOCIATION (BRANCH NO. 1)
The Association was formed in 1894 with 100 members, but by 1897 this number had fallen to 38 and the organisation ceased to exist.

Source: BoT Reports.

FEDERATION OF SAILMAKERS OF GREAT BRITAIN AND IRELAND
Formed in 1890, the Federation had 11 branches in the 1900s at Belfast, Bristol **(Bristol Operative Sailmakers Association)**, at Cardiff, Goole, Hull, Newport **(Newport, Mon. Sailmakers Society)**, North Shields **(North Shields Sailmakers Friendly Society)**, South Shields **(South Shields Sailmakers Society)**, Sunderland **(Sunderland and Monkwearmouth Sailmakers Federated Trade Society)**, Swansea **(Swansea Sailmakers Society)** and Great Yarmouth **(Great Yarmouth Sailmakers Trade and Benevolent Society)**, with a total membership of about 500. The Federation continued into the 1920s and became the **Amalgamated Union of Sailmakers** which ceased to exist in 1971.

Sources: BoT Reports; MoL Reports.

GREAT YARMOUTH SAILMAKERS TRADE AND BENEVOLENT SOCIETY
See **Federation of Sailmakers of Great Britain and Ireland**

GREAT YARMOUTH SHIPWRIGHTS PROVIDENT UNION
First formed in 1864, the Association had 125 members in 1892. By 1908 the membership had fallen to 100 and the Association was dissolved at about the end of that year.

Source: BoT Reports.

HEBBURN DRILLERS AND CUTTERS ASSOCIATION
Formed in 1889, the Association was dissolved in 1892.

HULL RIGGERS AND HOBBLERS ASSOCIATION
Established in 1892 with 52 members, the Association ceased to exist in 1894 when the membership numbered 23.

Source: BoT Reports.

HYLTON SHIPWRIGHTS ASSOCIATION
A small local sectional society founded in 1846. It had about 140 members in the 1890s and in 1898 merged into the **Wear Shipwrights Benevolent Society**.

Source: Certification Office.

IRON CAULKERS ASSOCIATION
An Admiralty (Portsmouth) Association formed in 1893. It had 36 members in 1896 and in October 1897 amalgamated with the **Steel and Iron Ship Builders, Boiler and Gasometer Makers Trade Union of Great Britain and Ireland**.

Source: Certification Office.

IRON, STEEL AND WOOD BARGE BUILDERS AND HELPERS ASSOCIATION
The Association was first established in 1872 as the **River Thames Barge Builders**. In 1916 the name was changed to the **Barge Builders Trade Union** but it reverted back to its original title in 1918, the name being changed to the above in 1941. The Association merged with the **Transport and General Workers Union** (see Vol. 3) in 1972 when it had 325 members.

Sources: Bain and Price; Marsh, *Concise Encyclopedia*.

LIVERPOOL MAST AND BLOCK MAKERS SOCIETY
A local sectional society formed in 1848. It had no more than 50 members in 1896 and joined the **Associated Society of Shipwrights** in the following year.

Source: BoT Reports.

LIVERPOOL RIGGERS AND MARINERS TRADE SOCIETY
See **Liverpool Riggers Trade and Benefit Society**

LIVERPOOL RIGGERS TRADE AND BENEFIT SOCIETY
Formed in 1872, the Society reached a peak of membership in 1896 when it had almost 250 members. Thereafter it declined to 100 in 1910. At some

date between 1913 and 1919 it became the **Liverpool Riggers and Mariners Trade Society** and was still in existence in 1924. No record has been found of its subsequent history.

Sources: BoT Reports; MoL Reports.

LIVERPOOL SHIPWRIGHTS TRADE AND FRIENDLY ASSOCIATION
Dating from 1844, the Association had 3 branches and some 900 members before the First World War. It merged with the **Ship Constructors and Shipwrights Association** in 1919.

Sources: Certification Office; S. and B. Webb, *History of Trade Unionism*.

LONDON UNITED SOCIETY OF DRILLERS AND HOLE CUTTERS
Formed in 1886, the Society was dissolved in 1888.

Source: Certification Office.

MARINE AND GENERAL ENGINEERS SOCIETY (LONDON)
Founded in 1895, the Society ceased to exist in 1907.

Source: Certification Office.

MAST AND BLOCK MAKERS SOCIETY (LONDON)
The Society is known to have existed in the 1890s, but there is no information about its date of formation, its membership or its subsequent history.

Source: BoT Reports.

MECHANICS ASSISTANTS AND DRY DOCK WORKERS UNION
The 1,300 members who formed the Union in 1913 had all seceded from the **Dock, Wharf, Riverside and General Labourers Union** (see Vol. 3). In 1921, with a membership of 4,500, it merged with the **National Amalgamated Union of Labour** (see Vol. 3).

Source: Bain and Price.

MERSEY OPERATIVE SHIP PAINTERS SOCIETY
This was a shortlived union founded in 1894 and dissolved three years later when its membership was under 40.

Source: BoT Reports.

MERSEY SAILMAKERS BURIAL SOCIETY
Formed in 1875, the Society had over 100 members in the 1890s and about half that number in the early 1900s. In 1895 it joined the **Federation of Sailmakers of Great Britain and Ireland**.

Source: BoT Reports.

MERSEY SHIP JOINERS SOCIETY
This was a small local craft society formed in 1853. It had about 250 members by the end of the century and joined the **Amalgamated Society of Carpenters and Joiners** (see Vol. 3), in 1900.

Source: BoT Reports.

NATIONAL ASSOCIATION OF OPERATIVE BOILER MAKERS AND IRON SHIP BUILDERS
The Association's membership worked exclusively in the Clyde shipyards. It was formed in 1867 under the leadership of William Swan, a former official of the **United Society of Boiler Makers and Iron and Steel Shipbuilders**. The United Society had dismissed Swan for his support of some 800 Clyde members of that union who had been refused payments of dispute benefit when the shipbuilding employers locked out more than 20,000 men for being members of a trade union. Swan encouraged the Clyde membership to withhold part of their contributions to the Society, was discharged, and formed the rival National Association with temporary offices at 18 Cavendish Street, Glasgow. It was said to enjoy the benevolent regard of the Clyde masters. The new union offered generous scales of benefit for a weekly subscription of 7½d. Unemployment benefit was fixed at 8s per week, sickness benefit at 10s per week and superannuation at 5s per week, which rates were impossible to maintain on such a low subscription. The Association did not remain long in existence, support being negligible among Clyde shipyard workers, although its brief existence is said to have done serious damage to the reputation of the United Society in Scotland for some years.

Sources: Mortimer; Cummings; Clegg, Fox and Thompson; Marwick.

NEWCASTLE AND DISTRICT SOCIETY OF DRILLERS AND CUTTERS
Formed in 1888, the Society was dissolved in 1892.

Source: Certification Office.

NEWPORT (MON.) SAILMAKERS SOCIETY
The foundation date of this Society is uncertain. In the early 1890s it became a constituent of the **Federation of Sailmakers of Great Britain and**

Ireland, with 15 members. In 1897 it seceded, but membership declined still further and there were 11 members in 1903. It was dissolved in 1904.

Source: BoT Reports.

NEWPORT (MON.) SHIPWRIGHTS SOCIETY
Established in 1852, the Society never achieved a high level of membership. It had 88 members in 1892. In 1903, with 85 members, it merged with the **Ship Constructive and Shipwrights Association.**

Source: BoT Reports.

NORTH SHIELDS SAILMAKERS FRIENDLY SOCIETY
See **Federation of Sailmakers of Great Britain and Ireland**

ONWARD SOCIETY OF DRILLERS AND HOLE CUTTERS OF STOCKTON-ON-TEES
The Society was formed in 1889 and in 1898 had a membership of 36. In 1899 it merged with the **Amalgamated Drillers and Hole Cutters Society**.

Source: BoT Reports.

PORT OF MILTON AND DISTRICT ASSOCIATED SHIP, BARGE, YACHT AND BOAT BUILDERS, MAST MAKERS, SMITHS, JOINERS, SAIL MAKERS AND SAWYERS TRADE UNION
Formed in 1890, the Union went out of existence in 1893.

Source: Certification Office.

PORTSMOUTH DOCKYARD HAND DRILLERS ASSOCIATION
Formed in 1893, the Association was dissolved in 1900.

Source: Certification Office.

PORTSMOUTH UNITED DRILLERS SOCIETY
There appear to have been two unions of this name. The first had a brief existence between April 1901 and November 1903 and the second between January 1910 and October 1912. It is not known whether or not there was any connection between the two organisations.

Source: Certification Office.

RED LEADERS ASSOCIATION (GLASGOW)
The Association had a very brief existence. It was formed in 1889 and had

153 members in 1892. It was dissolved in 1893.

Source: BoT Reports.

RIVER THAMES BARGE BUILDERS ASSOCIATION

Formed in 1872, the Association had about 100 members at the end of the century. It proved to be the longest lived of the small local sectional societies in the shipbuilding industry; see **Iron and Steel and Wood Barge Builders and Helpers Association**.

Source: BoT Reports.

RIVER THAMES BOAT BUILDERS TRADE UNION

Established in 1890, the Union had 125 members in 1892. With a membership of 65 it merged in 1899 with the **Ship Constructive and Shipwrights Association**.

Source: BoT Reports.

RIVER THAMES SHIP CAULKERS SOCIETY

See **United River Thames Ship Caulkers Society**

RIVER THAMES SHIPWRIGHTS PROTECTIVE AND BENEFIT SOCIETY

This was a small sectional society founded in 1894. It had about 200 members at the outset and cancelled its registration in 1900 on amalgamation with the **Associated Society of Shipwrights**.

Sources: BoT Reports; Certification Office.

RIVER THAMES SHIPWRIGHTS TRADE UNION

Founded in 1873, the Union was dissolved in 1875.

Source: Certification Office.

ROCHESTER AND DISTRICT ASSOCIATION SHIP, BARGE, YACHT AND BOAT BUILDERS, MAST MAKERS, SMITHS, JOINERS, SAIL MAKERS AND SAWYERS TRADE UNION

Established in 1890, the Union had 78 members in 1892. Numbers dwindled to 23 in 1895 and it was dissolved in the following year.

Source: BoT Reports.

ROSE OF TYNE SOCIETY OF DRILLERS AND CUTTERS

Formed in 1889, the Society became a branch of the **Amalgamated Society**

of Drillers and Hole Cutters in 1892. It had about 100 members at that time.

Source: Certification Office.

ROYAL DOCKYARD IRON AND STEEL SHIPBUILDERS SOCIETY
See **Devonport Royal Dockyard Iron Caulkers Society**

ROYAL DOCKYARD WOOD CAULKERS ASSOCIATION
The Association was set up in 1907 with 23 members and ceased to exist in 1911 when it had 31 members.

Source: BoT Reports.

RUNCORN SHIPWRIGHTS ASSOCIATION
Established in 1873, the Association ceased to exist after 1892.

Source: Certification Office.

ST. BEDES SOCIETY OF DRILLERS AND HOLE CUTTERS
Established in 1888, the Society had 128 members in 1890 and was dissolved in 1892.

Sources: BoT Reports; Certification Office.

SCOTTISH SOCIETY OF BOILERMAKERS
The Scottish Society was probably formed at about the same time as the **Society of Friendly Boilermakers** in the 1830s, and the two societies enjoyed quite friendly relations which ended for a time when the Friendly Boilermakers opened their first branch in Greenock. The Scottish Society never achieved a very big membership and in 1852, together with a London-based organisation, the **Amicable and Provident Society of Journeymen Boilermakers of Great Britain**, it merged with the **Society of Friendly Boilermakers** under the title of the **United Society of Boilermakers and Iron and Steel Shipbuilders**.

Source: Mortimer.

SHEERNESS SAILMAKERS SOCIETY
The Society was set up in 1900 with 17 members and the membership remained at this level until in 1910 it merged with the **Federation of Sailmakers of Great Britain and Ireland**.

Source: BoT Reports.

SHEET IRON WORKERS, LIGHT PLATERS AND SHIP RANGE MAKERS SOCIETY
See **Sheet Iron and Light Plate Workers Society**

SHIP CONSTRUCTIVE AND SHIPWRIGHTS ASSOCIATION (later known as the **Ship Constructors and Shipwrights Association**)

By 1871 revolutionary changes in shipbuilding, from wood to iron and from sail to steam, had established the **United Society of Boilermakers and Iron and Steel Shipbuilders**, dating from 1834, as the predominant union in the industry. The old-established shipwrights' societies were forced into second place and in 1882 most of them federated into a single society, which had been formed in 1872 as the **Associated Society of Shipwrights**. The membership grew rapidly, increasing from 4,000 in 1887 to over 18,000 in 1900. Alexander Wilkie became General Secretary in 1882 and remained in this position until his death in 1928. Collective bargaining procedures developed on lines parallel with the Boilermakers, although the Boilermakers were inclined to hold themselves aloof, whereas the Shipwrights were always ready to co-operate with the smaller unions. A weak spot for the societies of shipbuilding craftsmen were the Admiralty dockyards. There were several wage advances for the dockyard workers during this period and an example was set to private industry by the granting of a 48-hour week in 1894. Nevertheless the Lords of the Admiralty consistently refused to recognise the unions. In the dockyards a separate **Ship Constructive Association** was formed and competed with the Shipwrights outside, and there were many local associations formed catering for other shipyard craftsmen, but all lost membership during the 1890s. In 1891 together with 12 other unions the Associated Society formed the **Federation of Engineering and Shipbuilding Trades** which had been set up to deal with the many demarcation disputes taking place at that time. Between 1900 and 1910 the Associated Society absorbed many local organisations in Newport, Gloucester, and on the Wear, and several small national bodies, including the **Ship Constructive Association** which still organised Admiralty shipwrights, the **National Society of Drillers** and the **Amalgamated Society of Drillers and Hole Cutters**, and the title was changed to the Ship Constructive and Shipwrights Association. In January 1963 it amalgamated with the **United Society of Boilermakers, Shipbuilders and Structural Workers** and the **Associated Blacksmiths, Forge and Smithy Workers Society** in order to form the **Amalgamated Society of Boilermakers, Blacksmiths, Shipbuilders and Structural Workers**.

Sources: Royal Commission on Labour, C.-6894-VII, 1893; Clegg, Fox and Thompson; Cummings; Marwick.

SHIP CONSTRUCTIVE ASSOCIATION

Formed by shipwrights working in the Royal Naval Dockyards, the Association competed for members with the **Associated Society of Shipwrights**. The dockyard-based shipwrights association was able to gain several wage advances and negotiated for and gained a 48-hour week in 1894. Nevertheless the Lords of the Admiralty consistently refused to recognise the unions either inside or outside the dockyard. At some time between 1900 and 1910 the Association merged with the Associated Society of Shipwrights.

Source: Cummings.

SHIP CONSTRUCTORS AND SHIPWRIGHTS ASSOCIATION
See **Ship Constructive and Shipwrights Association**

SHIP RIVETERS AND HOLDERS-UP ASSOCIATION
An Association formed in 1895 at Portsmouth, with 30 members. It was dissolved in 1899, when 24 members remained.

Sources: Certification Office; BoT Reports.

SHIPBUILDERS, BOILER AND GASOMETER MAKERS SOCIETY
See **Steel and Iron Shipbuilders, Boiler and Gasometer Makers Trade Union of Great Britain and Ireland**

SHIPBUILDING, SHIP REPAIRING AND ENGINEERING INDUSTRIAL UNION
Formed in 1922 with 670 members, the Union continued in existence until 1933 when, with a membership of 608, it was dissolved.

Source: Certification Office.

SHIPWRIGHTS AND SHIPWRIGHTS IRON WORKERS ASSOCIATION
The Association was established in 1882, and the membership was 528 in 1896. In 1908 the Association with a membership of 300, merged with the **Ship Constructive and Shipwrights Association**.

Source: BoT Reports.

SHIPWRIGHTS PROVIDENT UNION OF THE PORT OF LONDON
An old established shipbuilding union said to have been founded in 1824, operating as a single branch. It seems to have reached a peak of membership in 1892 with 1,400 members and thereafter declined steadily to 570 in 1910. It merged with the **Ship Constructors and Shipwrights Association** about 1913.

Sources: S. and B. Webb, *History of Trade Unionism*; BoT Reports.

SOCIETY OF FRIENDLY BOILERMAKERS
See **United Society of Boilermakers, Shipbuilders and Structural Workers**

SOCIETY OF RIVETERS (CHATHAM)

The Society was formed in 1901 with 116 members but ceased to exist in 1906 when the membership had fallen to 5.

Source: BoT Reports.

SOUTH SHIELDS SAILMAKERS SOCIETY

See **Federation of Sailmakers of Great Britain and Ireland**

SOUTH SHIELDS SHIPWRIGHTS UNITED SOCIETY

A society said to have dated from 1823 or 1824 when it met at the Sun Inn, West Holborn, South Shields. Its first President was William Copeley and its Secretary John Harper. Meetings were· held monthly and every member was required to contribute 1s to the funds of the Society and expend 2d on ale. The Society's fund was required to amount to £800 before any weekly sick benefits were paid. In 1892 the Society had 410 members. It merged with the **Associated Society of Shipwrights**.

Sources: Select Committee on Artisans and Machinery, Vol. IV, June 1825; BoT Reports.

STEEL AND IRON SHIPBUILDERS, BOILER AND GASOMETER MAKERS TRADE UNION OF GREAT BRITAIN AND IRELAND

A Union formed in 1889 as the **Steel and Iron Shipbuilders, Boiler and Gasometer Makers of London and District**, the name being changed to the above in 1895. It had two branches in 1896 and 282 members in the following year. In 1899 it joined the **United Society of Boilermakers and Iron and Steel Ship Builders**.

Source: Certification Office.

STEEL AND IRON SHIPBUILDERS, BOILER AND GASOMETER MAKERS UNION OF LONDON AND DISTRICT

See **Steel and Iron Shipbuilders, Boiler and Gasometer Makers Trade Union of Great Britain and Ireland**

SUNDERLAND AND DISTRICT SOCIETY OF DRILLERS AND CUTTERS

Formed in 1889, the Society merged with the **Wear Drillers and Hole Cutters Society** in 1904. It had 325 members at the end of 1903.

Source: Certification Office.

SUNDERLAND AND MONKWEARMOUTH SAILMAKERS FEDERATED TRADE SOCIETY

See **Federation of Sailmakers of Great Britain and Ireland**

SWANSEA SAILMAKERS SOCIETY
See **Federation of Sailmakers of Great Britain and Ireland**

UNION OF PLATERS HELPERS
Formed in 1877, the Union was composed of a large class of labourers in shipbuilding yards who were usually employed and paid, not by the owners of the yards, but by members of the **United Society of Boilermakers and Iron and Steel Shipbuilders**. The Union complained that the whole force of the Boilermakers Society had been used to destroy its organisation. When this took place is not exactly known.

Source: S. and B. Webb, *History of Trade Unionism.*

UNITED BOILER SCALERS AND STOKE-HOLD LABOURERS SOCIETY
This was a London Society, formed in 1888. It had about 300 members at the end of the century, but membership subsequently declined to about 40 and it was apparently dissolved in 1909.

Source: BoT Reports.

UNITED FRIENDLY BOILERMAKERS SOCIETY
See **United Society of Boilermakers, Shipbuilders and Structural Workers**

UNITED KINGDOM AMALGAMATED SOCIETY OF SHIPWRIGHTS
Formed in 1888, the Society joined the **Associated Society of Shipwrights** in 1891.

Source: Certification Office.

UNITED KINGDOM SHIPMAKERS ASSOCIATION
Formed in 1872, the Association was dissolved in 1874.

Source: Certification Office.

UNITED RIVER THAMES SHIP CAULKERS SOCIETY
Formed in 1794, the Society had 105 members in 1900 and 71 in 1910. It seems to have been in existence about 1924, but thereafter no record of it has been traced.

Sources: BoT Reports; MoL Reports.

UNITED SHIP SCRAPERS PROTECTION LEAGUE
The League was formed in 1889 and had a membership of 76 in 1892 which had dwindled to 34 in 1896. It ceased to exist in 1897.

Source: BoT Reports.

UNITED SOCIETY OF BOILERMAKERS AND IRON AND STEEL SHIPBUILDERS
See **United Society of Boilermakers, Shipbuilders and Structural Workers**

UNITED SOCIETY OF BOILERMAKERS, SHIPBUILDERS AND STRUCTURAL WORKERS
The Society was formed with 14 members at a meeting in Manchester on 20 August 1834 under the name of the **Society of Friendly Boilermakers**. In 1835 William Hughes became the first General Secretary. The motto of the new union was 'To humanity nothing hostile', and lectures were given for the education of the members stressing the value of brotherhood and unity. In 1839 it opened its first branch in London and drew up the first rule book, the constitution being so framed as to make it an exclusive organisation for craftsmen. The entrance fee was 1 guinea, the lower age limit for joining being 18 years and the upper age limit 45 years, these limits being fixed because of the generous benefits given to members during sickness. Contributions were 1s 9d a month of which 3d was set aside for beer consumed at the meetings. Sick pay was paid at the rate of 10s per week for 6 months, 5s for an additional 6 months and 3s 6d for the remaining time of sickness. Members who had been in the Society for 20 years and reached the age of 60 years were paid a pension of 3s 6d per week. In the 1840s the centralisation of branch funds was introduced which stood the members in good stead in times of trade depression. John Roberts, the first full time General Secretary, was appointed in 1845 and the name was changed to the **United Friendly Boilermakers Society**. In 1852, upon the merging of the **Scottish Society of Boilermakers** and the **Amicable and Provident Society of Journeymen Boilermakers of Great Britain** into the Society, the title was changed again to the **United Society of Boilermakers and Iron and Steel Shipbuilders**, covering a total membership of 2,000 in 52 branches. It affiliated to the TUC in 1870. One of the longest serving and best known General Secretaries was Robert Knight who held the position for 29 years. Upon his appointment in 1871 the union was involved with the **Amalgamated Society of Engineers** in a 5 months' strike in the Tyne and Wear area in support of the 9-hour day which was completely successful in its aim. Under Knight's leadership the union continued to grow but its weakness was its narrow craft outlook, being reluctant to recruit members in closely related occupations. This changed when in 1881 it agreed to admit as members the Ironworkers of Dumbarton and Sunderland, called iron shipwrights, and in 1882 holders-up were admitted under special conditions. In 1891, at the instigation of Robert Knight, the Society together with 12 other organisations formed the **Federation of Engineering and Shipbuilding Trades**. In 1963 it amalgamated with the **Associated Blacksmiths, Forge and Smithy Workers** and the **Ship Constructors and Shipwrights Association** and became the **Amalgamated Society of Boilermakers, Blacksmiths, Shipbuilders and Structural Workers**.

Sources: Cummings; Clegg, Fox and Thompson; Marwick; Mortimer; Marsh, *Concise Encyclopedia*; Cole, *Trade Unionism Today*

UNITED SOCIETY OF DRILLERS
See **National Society of Drillers**

UNITED SOCIETY OF DRILLERS AND HOLE CUTTERS OF HART-LEPOOL
This was a Society formed in 1889. It had 148 members in 1892. In 1896 it joined with the **Amalgamated Society of Drillers of Stockton-on-Tees** and the **Cleveland Drillers and Hole Cutters Society** to form the **Amalgamated Drillers and Hole Cutters Society**.

Source: BoT Reports.

UNITED SOCIETY OF HOLDERS-UP
Established in 1880 to organise men who were a branch of the iron shipbuilding and boilermaking trade, it had over 2,000 members in the following year. This number soon fell as lodges broke up and as the members were absorbed into the **United Society of Boilermakers and Iron and Steel Shipbuilders**, and about 1889 the Society became wholly amalgamated with that union.

Source: BoT Reports.

UNITED SOCIETY OF TANK RIVETERS, HOLDERS-UP AND CAULKERS
Formed in 1886, the Society had a membership of 211 in 1892. The name was changed in 1910 to the **United Tank Makers Association**. It ceased to exist in 1937 when the membership figure had fallen to 25.

Source: BoT Reports; Bain and Price.

UNITED TANK MAKERS ASSOCIATION
See **United Society of Tank Riveters, Holders-up and Caulkers**

WALLSEND AND DISTRICT SOCIETY OF DRILLERS AND HOLE CUTTERS
Formed in 1889, the Society was dissolved in 1892.

Source: Certification Office.

WEAR BOAT BUILDERS BENEVOLENT SOCIETY (MONKWEAR-MOUTH)
Founded in 1872, the Society had 50 members in 1895. In 1898 with 44 members it joined the **Ship Constructive and Shipwrights Association**.

Source: BoT Reports.

WEAR DRILLERS AND HOLE CUTTERS SOCIETY
Established in 1875, the Society merged with the **Amalgamated Drillers and Hole Cutters Society** in 1908 when its membership was about 500.

Source: Certification Office.

WEAR SHIPWRIGHTS BENEVOLENT SOCIETY
First established in 1846, the Society had 6 branches in 1896 and 9 branches and 1,500 members at the end of the century. In 1908 it merged with the **Ship Constructive and Shipwrights Association**.

Source: BoT Reports.

Vehicle Building

Sectional societies concerned with the building of coaches, carts and vehicles of various kinds go back at least to the first quarter of the eighteenth century. Coachbuilders, wheelwrights, smiths, painters and other craftsmen formed natural groups for organisation in major centres of population. Francis Place, the London master tailor best known for his activities in repeal of the Combination Acts in 1824, mentions in his manuscript notes on organisations existing in London in 1720 a Coachmakers' Club, apparently the Amicable Society of Coachmakers, established in 1704.[1] Many others no doubt existed at the same time, an impression confirmed by the London Master Tailors who, in denouncing combinations in their own trade early in the eighteenth century, referred to 'other confederacies of the like nature' among coachmakers, smiths, farriers, curriers and 'artificers of divers other arts'.[2]

Later established unions in vehicle building made no serious attempt to argue continuity of organisation from these early trade societies but usually dated themselves from the 1830s. A Loyal Wheelwrights and Blacksmiths Society formed in Bolton in 1830 became the basis for most of the organising efforts of those trades as it spread from one centre to another, while a strike of coachmakers in Liverpool and Manchester in 1834–5 is usually taken as the point at which a shaky collection of trade societies organising such artisans was inspired to back a United Kingdom Society of Coachmakers and translate its efforts into a national context.[3]

The success of the UK Society was considerable. By the end of the century it had 6,500 members and provided a basis for the amalgamation of the smaller organisations around it. Eventually, as the National Union of Vehicle Builders (1919), it had by the end of the Second World War absorbed all its rivals except the Wheelwrights and Coachmakers Operatives (1896), which continued independently until 1947. After that time the contraction of conventional coachbuilding work and the predominance of mass production in the motor vehicle industry rapidly moved the balance of membership of the NUVB into that aspect of the trade, bringing it into direct competition with the Transport and General Workers and the Amalgamated Engineering Union for membership in the plants of major car producers, in most of which it had a minority membership only. Both these unions attempted to attract the NUVB into amalgamation, the TGWU succeeding in 1972 and establishing as a result a Vehicle Building and Automotive Trade Group separately from its other engineering membership interests.

Notes

1. NUVB, *A Hundred Years of Vehicle Building, 1834–1934*, NUVB, 1934, p. 11.
2. F. W. Galton, *The Tailoring Trade*, Longmans, Green & Co., London, 1896, p.3.
3. NUVB, *op. cit.*, p. 12.

AMALGAMATED CARRIAGE AND WAGON SOCIETY
Founded in 1873, the Society ceased to exist after 1875.

Source: Certification Office.

AMALGAMATED SOCIETY OF RAILWAY VEHICLE WAGON BUILDERS, WHEELWRIGHTS, CARPENTERS AND MECHANICS
The Society was established in 1873 as the **Amalgamated Society of Railway Wagon and Carriage Makers, Wheelwrights, Carpenters and Mechanics**. It had a membership of 195 in 1892, of 221 in 1900, and 20 branches with 823 members in 1910. In 1914 it absorbed the **National Amalgamated Society of Railway Wagon and Carriage Builders and Lifters** and changed its name in 1920 to the **Amalgamated Society of Vehicle Builders, Wheelwrights, Carpenters and Mechanics**. Its headquarters were in Wigan. In 1945, with 5,783 members, it merged with the **Amalgamated Engineering Union**.

Sources: Certification Office; BoT Reports.

AMALGAMATED SOCIETY OF RAILWAY WAGON AND CARRIAGE MAKERS, WHEELWRIGHTS, CARPENTERS AND MECHANICS
See **Amalgamated Society of Railway Vehicle Wagon Builders, Wheelwrights, Carpenters and Mechanics**

AMALGAMATED SOCIETY OF VEHICLE BUILDERS, WHEELWRIGHTS, CARPENTERS AND MECHANICS
See **Amalgamated Society of Railway Vehicle Wagon Builders, Wheelwrights, Carpenters and Mechanics**

AMALGAMATED SOCIETY OF WAGON AND CARRIAGE MAKERS, WHEELWRIGHTS AND CARPENTERS
Founded in 1873, the Society had 823 members meeting in 20 branches by 1910. It merged with the **United Kingdom Society of Coachmakers** in 1912.

Sources: BoT Reports; Certification Office.

AMALGAMATED SOCIETY OF WHEELWRIGHTS, SMITHS AND MOTOR BODY MAKERS
See **Amalgamated Wheelwrights, Smiths and Kindred Trades Union**

AMALGAMATED WHEELWRIGHTS AND CARRIAGE MAKERS UNION
Formed in 1891, the Union had about 90 members in 1900 and about 80 when it merged with the larger **Loyal, Free, Industrious Society of**

Wheelwrights and Blacksmiths to form the **Amalgamated Society of Wheelwrights, Smiths and Motor Body Makers** in 1908.

Sources: BoT Reports; Certification Office.

AMALGAMATED WHEELWRIGHTS, SMITHS AND KINDRED TRADES UNION

The Union was formed in Bolton in 1830 under the title **Loyal Wheelwrights and Blacksmiths Society**, a name changed in 1870 to the **Loyal, Free, Industrious Society of Wheelwrights and Blacksmiths**. By 1900 it had 1,540 members in 26 branches. Each of these branches was given a title as well as a number. It exacted fines for such offences as falling asleep during meetings and singing obscene songs during club hours. For over 30 years the Secretary was Mr A. Powell. Upon his resignation in 1900 the Union's first full-time Secretary was appointed. In 1908 the Union amalgamated with the much smaller **Amalgamated Wheelwrights and Carriage Makers Union** to form the **Amalgamated Society of Wheelwrights, Smiths and Motor Body Makers**, from which in December 1921 there was formed the Amalgamated Wheelwrights, Smiths and Kindred Trades Union. This union merged with the **National Union of Vehicle Builders** in 1925.

Sources: NUVB, 1934; NUVB, 1959; BoT Reports; Certification Office.

AMICABLE SOCIETY OF COACHMAKERS
See **National Union of Vehicle Builders**

ASSOCIATION OF VAN, WAGON AND MOTOR BODY BUILDERS (GLASGOW)

This Association was formed in 1870 and had a membership of 87 in 1892. In 1911, when it had 76 members, it ceased to function.

Source: BoT Reports.

BENEVOLENT SOCIETY OF COACHMAKERS

There is no definite recorded date for the formation of this Society, but a strike is recorded as having taken place in 1819 which resulted in its collapse and the conviction of its General Secretary and 20 of its members, who were released on condition that the organisation was dissolved.

Sources: NUVB, 1934; NUVB, 1959.

LINCOLN AMALGAMATED MACHINE MAKERS SOCIETY

Formed in 1899 with 81 members, the union merged with the **Amalgamated Society of Wheelwrights and Smiths** in 1917 when it had a membership of 120.

Sources: BoT Reports; Certification Office.

LIVERPOOL COACHMAKERS SOCIETY
See **National Union of Vehicle Builders**

LONDON AND PROVINCIAL COACH MAKERS TRADE UNION
The Union was formed in 1842 or 1843 as the **London Coachmakers Friendly Society**, and later as the **London Coach Body and Carriage Makers Trade Union** or simply as the **London Coachmakers Union**. Its early meetings were held at The Crown Tavern, Broad Street. No one was admitted as a member unless he had served a 7-year apprenticeship and was under 35 years of age, or alternatively if he was able to prove a 7-year membership of a coachmakers trade society (10 years if the applicant was over 40 years of age, and 15 years if he was over 50). The Society had been founded by 15 coachmakers and membership was confined to body makers, carriage makers and finishers. Fines for non-attendance at union meetings were strictly enforced, and unemployment and other benefits were payable. Membership grew very slowly, being 300 by 1900, 764 in 1910, and only about 600 in 1914. It was an affiliated member of the TUC. In 1908 the name was changed to the above. The **United Kingdom Society of Coachmakers** (a rival organisation) had approached the Union with a view to amalgamation and this was finally achieved in 1919 when the Union, with 1,603 members and funds amounting to £18,900, together with the **Operative Coachmakers and Wheelwrights Federal Labour Union** and the **London Coachsmiths and Vicemen's Trade Society**, amalgamated to form the **National Union of Vehicle Builders**.

Source: NUVB, 1934.

LONDON COACH BODY AND CARRIAGE MAKERS TRADE UNION
See **London and Provincial Coach Makers Trade Union**

LONDON COACHMAKERS FRIENDLY SOCIETY
See **London and Provincial Coach Makers Trade Union**

LONDON COACHMAKERS UNION
See **London and Provincial Coach Makers Trade Union**

LONDON COACHSMITHS AND VICEMENS TRADE SOCIETY
This was a union formed in 1879. It had a single branch and about 50 members in the 1890s and was based upon the Lamb and Flag Hotel, Covent Garden. It had no more than 55 members in 1910 and in 1919 amalgamated with other unions to form the **National Union of Vehicle Builders**.

Sources: BoT Reports; NUVB, 1934.

LONDON SOCIETY OF COACH WHEELWRIGHTS
The Society was formed about 1790. It had fewer than 40 members in the 1890s, falling in the first decade of the twentieth century to half that number. In 1909 it joined the **United Kingdom Society of Coachmakers**. It had 19 members at that time. It was based for much of its life at the White Hart, Windmill Street, Tottenham Court Road.

Source: BoT Reports.

LONDON UNITED SOCIETY OF WHEELWRIGHTS, BLACKSMITHS, PAINTERS AND HAMMERMEN
The Society was founded in 1886 and had 3 branches and rather more than 200 members. It amalgamated in 1901 with the **London Wheelwrights Operatives**, a union of about the same size founded in 1896, to form the **Wheelwrights Operatives Union**, or, more formally, the **London Wheelwrights and Coach Makers Operatives Union**, which had rather more than 700 members in 1910 and 1,170 in 1917.

Sources: BoT Reports; Certification Office.

LONDON WHEELWRIGHTS AND BLACKSMITHS SOCIETY
The Society was formed in London in 1836. It had 46 members in 1896 and in the following year joined the **London Wheelwrights Operatives Union**, a rather larger organisation.

Source: BoT Reports.

LONDON WHEELWRIGHTS AND COACH MAKERS OPERATIVE UNION
See **London United Society of Wheelwrights, Blacksmiths, Painters and Hammermen**

LONDON WHEELWRIGHTS OPERATIVES UNION
See **London United Society of Wheelwrights, Blacksmiths, Painters and Hammermen**

LOYAL, FREE, INDUSTRIOUS SOCIETY OF WHEELWRIGHTS AND BLACKSMITHS
See **Amalgamated Wheelwrights, Smiths and Kindred Trades Union**

LOYAL WHEELWRIGHTS AND BLACKSMITHS SOCIETY
See **Amalgamated Wheelwrights, Smiths and Kindred Trades Union**

MANCHESTER COACH MAKERS SOCIETY
See **National Union of Vehicle Builders**

MANCHESTER INDEPENDENT COACH MAKERS SOCIETY
The Society was formed about 1848 by members of the **United Kingdom Society of Coachmakers** who had seceded from that organisation. The new body retained an independent existence until 1867 when the remaining membership returned to the UKSC. The Manchester Society was always small in number, never having more than 50 members.

Source: NUVB, 1934.

MANCHESTER WAGON AND CARRIAGE MAKERS (RAILWAY) SOCIETY
This was a local organisation based on Manchester. Its history is obscure. There is evidence that it existed in the 1870s, since it was recorded as having been represented at the Trades Union Congress by George Potter of London (*The Beehive*) and as having 653 members. His connection with the Society has not been established. The union is said later to have amalgamated with the **National Union of Vehicle Builders** at some stage in its history.

Source: NUVB, 1959.

NATIONAL AMALGAMATED SOCIETY OF RAILWAY WAGON AND CARRIAGE BUILDERS AND LIFTERS
See **South Wales Amalgamated Society of Railway Wagon and Carriage Builders and Lifters**

NATIONAL SOCIETY OF CYCLE MAKERS
Established in 1897 with 1,670 members, the Society ceased to exist in 1899.

Source: BoT Reports.

NATIONAL UNION OF AIRCRAFT WORKERS
The Union was formed during the Second World War in 1942 with 550 members and lasted until 1946 when, with 441 members, it was dissolved.

Source: Certification Office.

NATIONAL UNION OF VEHICLE BUILDERS
As early as the beginning of the eighteenth century trade societies of coachmakers, wheelwrights and others began to be formed, like the

Amicable Society of Coachmakers which was established about 1704. Such was the development that it was reported in 1720 that masters in London were complaining that various workmen, including coachmakers, were daring to form these associations. Much later, in 1819, a coachmakers' strike took place during which the General Secretary of the local body and 20 members were arrested. The NUVB was first formed in 1834 as the **United Kingdom Society of Coachmakers**. Its formation resulted from a strike called by two separate organisations, the **Liverpool Coachmakers Society** and the **Manchester Coach Makers Society**, which worked together in the ensuing lock-out, and after achieving a successful conclusion felt that there should be one united organisation catering for coachmakers. A joint conference was called in 1848 at Leeds which elected an Executive Committee which met every Friday night at the Old George Inn, Bridgate, Leeds. The average weekly wage of the members at that time was 22s 6d with 24s 9d for a full week's work. In 1850 the membership totalled 1,567 which rose to 5,000 in 1860. By 1875 it had reached 7,251 and fluctuated between 5,000 and 7,000 until the commencement of the First World War. In 1850 the head office was moved from Leeds to Liverpool which had the largest branch at that time (96 members). The union operated an emigration fund from 1852 onwards. In 1856 it held its first delegate conference, and in 1872, with a membership of 6,800, it affiliated to the TUC, and to the Labour Party in 1906. By 1914 the union had over 10,000 members and a cash reserve of £28,000, and it came to an agreement with the **Scottish Vehicle Builders Association** in regard to wages and hours of work. In 1919 the United Kingdom Society, together with the **London and Provincial Coachmakers Society**, the **Operative Coachmakers and Wheelwrights Federal Labour Union** and the **London Coachsmiths and Vicemen's Trade Society** amalgamated in order to form the NUVB, and the decision was made to open the Union for recruitment to all skilled, semi-skilled and unskilled workers engaged in the vehicle building trade. The first copy of the *NUVB Journal* was published in 1919. In 1925 the **Amalgamated Society of Wheelwrights, Smiths and Motor Body Makers** merged with the NUVB, giving it a total membership of 26,000. The Union became a member of the **Confederation of Shipbuilding and Engineering Unions** in 1935. In 1948 the **Wheelwrights and Coachmakers Operatives Union** merged with the NUVB, the total membership then being 50,000. The NUVB merged with the **Transport and General Workers Union** (see Vol. 3) in 1972.

Sources: S. and B. Webb, *History of Trade Unionism*; NUVB 1934 and 1959; Marsh, *Concise Encyclopedia*.

OPERATIVE COACHMAKERS AND WHEELWRIGHTS FEDERAL LABOUR UNION

A union formed in 1894 with its club room at the Horse and Sacks Inn in the Harrow Road, London. It had one branch only and grew to a membership of 150 by 1910. In 1919 it was one of the unions which came together to form the **National Union of Vehicle Builders**.

Source: BoT Reports.

SCOTTISH ASSOCIATION OF OPERATIVE COACHMAKERS
The history of this union is uncertain. The Association was certainly in existence in the period of 1860/1870 because it was affiliated to the TUC in 1874, and attended the 1875 Congress on affiliation of 200 members. It later merged with the **National Union of Vehicle Builders**.

Source: NUVB, 1934.

SCOTTISH OPERATIVE COACH MAKERS ASSOCIATION
Formed in 1892 with 52 members, the Association was dissolved in 1895 when the membership had fallen to 26.

Source: BoT Reports.

SOUTH WALES AMALGAMATED SOCIETY OF RAILWAY WAGON AND CARRIAGE BUILDERS AND LIFTERS
Founded in 1889 and based in Glamorgan, the Society had 5 branches and 186 members by 1900. In 1891 it changed its name to **National Amalgamated Society of Railway Wagon and Carriage Builders and Lifters** and grew to 500 members by 1910. In 1914 it amalgamated with the **Amalgamated Society of Railway Vehicle Wagon Builders, Wheelwrights, Carpenters and Mechanics**.

Source: Certification Office.

UNITED KINGDOM SOCIETY OF COACHMAKERS
See **National Union of Vehicle Builders**

A second UK Society of Coachmakers seems to have existed, also in Liverpool, in 1876. This registered as a trade union in 1877 (the main society did not do so until 1895). It was removed from the register at its own request in 1880. The two societies may, perhaps, have represented different stages in the development of a single organisation.

Source: Certification Office.

WHEELWRIGHTS AND COACHMAKERS OPERATIVES UNION
A Union formed by amalgamation of the **London United Society of Wheelwrights, Blacksmiths, Painters and Hammermen** and the **London Wheelwrights Operatives Union** in 1901; also known as the **Wheelwrights Operatives (London)**. The original amalgamation had 7 branches and some 500 members and grew after ten years to 11 branches and 735 members. It had a membership of about 1,200 when at the end of the First World War it declined to join the further amalgamation which produced the **National Union of Vehicle Builders** (1919). It continued as an independent union until July 1947 (the NUVB gives the date as 1948) and was the 'last appropriate union' with which the NUVB could amalgamate.

Sources: NUVB, 1959; BoT Reports; Certification Office.

WHEELWRIGHTS AND SMITHS SOCIETY
See **Amalgamated Wheelwrights, Smiths and Kindred Trades Union**

WHEELWRIGHTS OPERATIVES UNION (LONDON)
See **Wheelwrights and Coachmakers Operatives Union**

Sheet Metal Workers, Coppersmiths, Braziers, Heating and Domestic Engineers

Being for the most part only indirectly related to the engineering skills of fitting, turning and founding, sheet metal workers were inclined in the nineteenth century to form their own local societies in almost every town in which their trades were practised. Workers in brass, copper or sheet metal tended at first to be separated into different organisations which later came together in response to technical change and the demand for more comprehensive national organisation as distinct from local sectional societies. Two main strands emerged representing the interests of, on the one hand, sheet metal workers and braziers and, on the other hand, heating and domestic engineers. The first led to a highly successful amalgamation of local organisations in 1920 to produce the National Union of Sheet Metal Workers and Braziers, leaving outside only the National Society of Coppersmiths, Braziers and Metal Workers, historically a London society, and the Birmingham and Midland Sheet Metal Workers. These unions were not absorbed into the national organisation until 1959 and 1973 respectively. The domestic engineers, after a complex history of name changes, eventually in 1948 became known as the National Union of Operative Heating and Domestic Engineers and General Metal Workers and remained independent until 1967 when they joined the main national amalgamation. By 1973, therefore, all strands of organisation in the sheet metal working trade became united in a single entity, the National Union of Sheet Metal Workers, Coppersmiths, Heating and Domestic Engineers.

ABERDEEN AND DISTRICT SHEET METAL WORKERS SOCIETY
This was a local sheet metal workers' society formed in 1890 as the **Aberdeen Operative Tin Plate Workers Protecting and Friendly Society** with a membership of 97, which had risen to 206 by 1910. The Society was one of the organisations which having been a constituent union of the **National Amalgamated Tin Plate Workers of Great Britain**, eventually formed the **National Union of Sheet Metal Workers and Braziers** in 1920.

Sources: BoT Reports; Certification Office.

ABERDEEN OPERATIVE TIN PLATE WORKERS PROTECTING AND FRIENDLY SOCIETY
See **Aberdeen and District Sheet Metal Workers Society**

AMALGAMATED SOCIETY OF KITCHEN RANGE, HOT WATER, ART METAL AND OTHER FITTERS CONCERNED WITH THE ABOVE TRADES
See **Heating and Domestic Engineers Union**

AMALGAMATED SOCIETY OF TIN AND IRON PLATE WORKERS AND GAS METER MAKERS
Formed in 1900, this small union of 74 members merged in May 1901 with the **London Society of Sheet Metal Workers, Braziers and Gas Meter Makers**.

Source: Certification Office.

AMALGAMATED SOCIETY OF TIN PLATE WORKERS
See **London Amalgamated Society of Tin Plate Workers**

AMALGAMATED SOCIETY OF WHITESMITHS, DOMESTIC ENGINEERS AND GENERAL PIPE FITTERS
Formed in 1889 as the **General Smiths, Fitters, Bellhangers and Whitesmiths Association**, the union had 169 members in 1892 and 200 in 8 branches in 1900, rising to 300 members in 1907. The name was changed to the above title and in 1908 it amalgamated with the **Birmingham Society of Hot Water and Steam Engineers** and the **United Society of Fitters and Smiths** in order to form the **National Union of Operative Heating and Domestic Engineers and General Iron Workers**.

Source: BoT Reports.

AMALGAMATED STOVE GRATE AND KITCHEN RANGE FITTERS PROTECTION SOCIETY
See **Heating and Domestic Engineers Union**

AMALGAMATED TIN PLATE WORKERS SOCIETY OF BIRMINGHAM, WOLVERHAMPTON AND DISTRICT
See **National Amalgamated Association of Tin Plate Workers of Great Britain**

ASHTON UNDER LYNE AND DISTRICT ASSOCIATION OF BRAZIERS AND SHEET METAL WORKERS
Little is known of this society. It registered as a trade union in August 1911 and may have been associated with the **National Amalgamated Tin Plate Workers of Great Britain**. Whatever the situation, it formed part of the amalgamation which resulted in the **National Union of Sheet Metal Workers and Braziers** in 1920.

Source: Certification Office.

ASSOCIATION OF CORRUGATED IRON ROOFERS, DOOR MAKERS, SASH MAKERS AND GENERAL IRON WORKERS (LONDON)
Established in 1891, the Association had 85 members in 1892. It ceased to exist in 1906 when the membership had dwindled to 20.

Source: BoT Reports.

ASSOCIATION OF GENERAL HEATING AND DOMESTIC ENGINEERS ASSISTANTS
The Association was established in 1914 with 20 members and ended its existence in 1940 with the same number.

Source: Bain and Price.

ASSOCIATION OF WOMEN TIN BOX AND GENERAL WORKERS (MANCHESTER)
Formed in 1915 with 112 members, the Association ceased to exist in 1918 with a membership standing at only 49.

Source: Bain and Price.

BILSTON IRON PLATE TRADE SOCIETY
Formed in 1890, with 104 members in 1892, the Society became a branch of the **National Amalgamated Iron Plate Trade Society** towards the end of the century.

Source: BoT Reports.

BIRMINGHAM AND DISTRICT OPERATIVE ZINC WORKERS SOCIETY
This was a shortlived local sectional society formed in 1898 and dissolved in January 1908. It had 35 members in 1900 but only 16 in 1907.

Source: Certification Office.

BIRMINGHAM AND MIDLAND SHEET METAL WORKERS SOCIETY

Formed about 1870, the Society amalgamated with the **Wolverhampton Tin Plate Workers Society** and others to form what later became the **National Amalgamated Association of Tin Plate Workers**. It seceded from that union in 1909 after a difference of opinion over the payment of dispute money, and adopted the above title. It remained outside the National Union of **Sheet Metal Workers and Braziers** when it was formed in 1920, and remained independent until its amalgamation with the **National Union of Sheet Metal Workers, Coppersmiths, Heating and Domestic Engineers** in 1973. The Society appeared latterly to be the last of the many local sheet metal worker unions which had been formed in the nineteenth century and which had not become part of any national organisation.

Sources: Kidd; Marsh, *Concise Encyclopedia*; Cole, *British Trade Unionism Today*.

BIRMINGHAM IRON PLATE TRADE SOCIETY

The Society was formed in 1874. It had 300 members in 1892 and became one of the branches of the **National Amalgamated Iron Plate Trade Society** towards the end of the century.

Source: BoT Reports.

BIRMINGHAM OPERATIVE TIN PLATE, SHEET METAL WORKERS AND BRAZIERS SOCIETY

See **Birmingham Tin Plate Workers Society**

BIRMINGHAM OPERATIVE TIN PLATE WORKERS SOCIETY

See **Birmingham Tin Plate Workers Society**

BIRMINGHAM SOCIETY OF HOT WATER AND STEAM ENGINEERS

Formed in 1903, the Society had few members and by 1907 numbers were down to 13. In the following year it amalgamated with the **United Society of Fitters and Smiths** and the **Amalgamated Society of Whitesmiths, Domestic Engineers and General Pipefitters** to form the **National Union of Heating and Domestic Engineers, Whitesmiths and General Ironworkers**.

Source: BoT Reports.

BIRMINGHAM TIN PLATE WORKERS SOCIETY

Little is known about this Society, though it was among the most successful of its kind. Kidd records that in 1876 it amalgamated with two other Midland societies to form the **Amalgamated Tin Plate Workers of Birmingham, Wolverhampton and District**, from which emerged the

National Amalgamated Tin Plate Workers of Great Britain and ultimately the National Union of Sheet Metal Workers and Braziers. Board of Trade Reports note a Birmingham Operative Tin Plate Workers Society, formed in 1859, which is evidently the same union; it also records the two other Midland societies separately, sometimes as constituent of the National Amalgamated Tinplate Workers and sometimes not. The Birmingham society is shown as having over 1,000 members in 1892 and more than 1,600 in 1910, under the title, Birmingham Operative Tin Plate, Sheet Metal Workers and Braziers Society.

Sources: Kidd; BoT Reports.

BOLTON SOCIETY OF BRAZIERS AND SHEET METAL WORKERS

This was a sheet metal workers society which registered as a trade union in 1896. There seems to be no record of it before that date. In 1920 it amalgamated with other societies to form the National Union of Sheet Metal Workers and Braziers.

Sources: Kidd; Certification Office.

BOOTLE SHEET METAL WORKERS AND BRAZIERS SOCIETY

No reference has been found to this union other than that it was dissolved in 1926.

Source: Certification Office.

BRADFORD AND DISTRICT SHEET METAL WORKERS SOCIETY

Originally formed in 1850, the Society had no more than 63 members in 1910. It was part of the amalgamation which produced the National Union of Sheet Metal Workers and Braziers in 1920.

Sources: Kidd; BoT Reports.

BRISTOL IRON PLATE TRADE SOCIETY

The Society was founded in 1889 and had a small membership of 35 in 1892. It merged with the National Union of Gasworkers and General Labourers (see Vol.3) with 30 members in 1896.

Source: BoT Reports.

BRISTOL TIN PLATE, SHEET METAL WORKERS AND BRAZIERS SOCIETY

Formed in 1898, the Society remained small, having one branch and 70 members in 1910. It became part of the amalgamation which formed the National Union of Sheet Metal Workers and Braziers in 1920.

Sources: BoT Reports; Certification Office.

CAST IRON HOLLOW-WARE MOULDERS TRADE SOCIETY
Formed in 1890, the Society was dissolved in 1895 when it had 30 members.

Source: Certification Office.

CAST IRON HOLLOW-WARE TINNERS FRIENDLY AND TRADE SOCIETY
This was a Wolverhampton society, formed in 1890. It seldom had more than 50 members and was dissolved in 1902.

Sources: Certification Office; BoT Reports.

CAST IRON HOLLOW-WARE TURNERS ASSOCIATION
This was a Wolverhampton society formed in 1890. The Association had 236 members in 1897 but in 1900 it had no more than 49. It ceased to exist after 1902.

Source: Certification Office

CO-OPERATIVE TIN-PLATE WORKERS OF WOLVERHAMPTON
The rules and regulations of the society date back at least to January 1848 and its meeting place was the Red Cow, Dudley Street, Wolverhampton. It was a rival organisation to the **Wolverhampton Operative Tin-Plate Workers Society.** Several attempts were made to merge the two societies but without success. The Co-operative Society ceased to exist in 1881 through lack of funds and its members joined the Wolverhampton Tin-Plate Workers Society.

Source: Kidd.

CO-OPERATIVE TINPLATE WORKERS SOCIETY (LONDON)
The Society was founded in 1846. Its meeting place was the Craven Head, Drury Lane, London. George Swainstone was its first Secretary. Its objects were stated to be: 'to obtain a just return for our labour and to defend those who may sacrifice their employment in maintaining the same; to assist each other in obtaining employment; to allow a sufficient sum to admit of the respectable interment of a member or a member's wife'. It was apparently a breakaway from the **London Operative Tin-Plate Workers Society.** It re-amalgamated with the same society in 1875 to form the **London Amalgamated Society of Tin Plate Workers,** later the **London Society of Sheet Metal Workers, Braziers and Gas Meter Makers.**

Sources: Kidd; BoT Reports.

CORRUGATED IRON ROOFERS, DOOR MAKERS, SASH MAKERS AND GENERAL IRON WORKERS UNION
The Union was formed in 1892. Its registration was cancelled in 1908.

DUDLEY IRON PLATE TRADE SOCIETY

A local sectional society formed in 1895 which quickly became part of the **National Amalgamated Iron Plate Trade Society.**

DUNDEE AND DISTRICT SOCIETY OF SHEET METAL WORKERS, GASFITTERS AND BRAZIERS

In 1912 the Society was established by 63 members who had seceded from the **Edinburgh Society of Sheet Metal Workers and Gas Meter Makers**. It continued in existence as an independent body until 1920 when it amalgamated with the newly formed **National Union of Sheet Metal Workers and Braziers**.

EAST LONDON OPERATIVE TIN AND IRON PLATE WORKERS SOCIETY

This was an old-established sectional society formed in 1874 with its base in East London. It had 255 members in 1892 and 368 in 1900. In 1901 it merged into the **Amalgamated Society of Tin and Iron Plate Workers and Gas Meter Makers.**

EDINBURGH SOCIETY OF SHEET METAL WORKERS AND GAS METER MAKERS

Founded in 1866, the Society had two branches by 1900 (the second at Leith) and 359 members, which had risen to 402 by 1910. Its title was sometimes written so as to make the two branches distinct, *viz*: **Sheet Metal Workers and Gas Meter Makers of Edinburgh** and **Leith Protecting and Friendly Society.**

EXETER AND DISTRICT SHEET METAL WORKERS SOCIETY

The Society was founded in 1897 with 34 members as the **Exeter and District Tin and Iron Plate Workers and Gas Meter Makers Society**, the shorter title being adopted at a later date. In 1910 it had 91 members and in 1921 it amalgamated with the **General Union of Braziers and Sheet Metal Workers** in order to form the **National Union of Sheet Metal Workers and Braziers** which later became the **National Union of Sheet Metal Workers and Coppersmiths.**

EXETER AND DISTRICT TIN AND IRON PLATE WORKERS AND GAS METER MAKERS SOCIETY
See **Exeter and District Sheet Metal Workers Society**

FRIENDLY SOCIETY OF IRON-PLATE WORKERS
This was formed in 1838. The Society's rules numbered 27 and the admission fee was 5s. Subscriptions were 1s 3d, payable every fourth Wednesday, and members could claim unemployment benefit. 'Any member in or out of employment refusing to make any article for less than what was paid by the shop shall receive such sum as the members deemed proper.' The sum was raised by a levy on each member, and if another member took a striking member's place at work at a reduced rate, that man was excluded and never allowed to enter the Society again. Unemployment benefit was paid on the basis of how large a fund had been accumulated. Admission into the Society was by a ballot among the members. £5 was paid to the widow of a member as funeral benefit. The Society met at the Sign of the Pickled Egg, Pickled Egg Walk, Clerkenwell. Kidd records that it ultimately merged with the **Amalgamated Society of Tin Plate Workers**.

Source: Kidd.

FRIENDLY SOCIETY OF THE UNITED OPERATIVE TIN-PLATE WORKERS OF WOLVERHAMPTON
See **Wolverhampton Operative Tin-Plate Workers Society**

FRIENDLY SOCIETY OF TIN PLATE WORKERS
See **Liverpool Operative Braziers and Sheet Metal Workers Society**

GALVANISED HOLLOW-WARE SHEET METAL WORKERS AND BRAZIERS ASSOCIATION
Formed in 1874, the Association was based on Tipton, Staffordshire. In 1910 it had 4 branches and 558 members. In 1920 it amalgamated with other societies to form the **National Union of Sheet Metal Workers and Braziers**.

Source: Certification Office.

GAS METER MAKERS ASSOCIATION
The Association was in existence in the early 1840s. In 1843 an attempt was made to reduce the price of gas meters in the firm of a Mr Edge, the men submitting that the time allowed for a dozen cases should be 36 hours, and for the wheels 38 hours, while the firm offered 30 hours for the cases and 32 hours for the wheels. A strike ensued during the course of which differences arose as to the way the reserve fund should be used, and the decision was taken that the Association in future should not discuss or question any trade matter. On 16 April 1888 the union merged with the **Amalgamated Society of Tin Plate Workers**.

Source: Kidd.

GAS METER MAKERS ASSOCIATION OF EDINBURGH AND LEITH
See **National Amalgamated Association of Tin Plate Workers of Great Britain**

GENERAL SMITHS, FITTERS, BELLHANGERS AND WHITESMITHS ASSOCIATION
See **Amalgamated Society of Whitesmiths, Domestic Engineers and General Pipe Fitters**

GENERAL UNION OF BELLHANGERS AND GAS FITTERS
Nothing specific is known of the Union other than the fact that it was broken up in 1875.

Source: Certification Office.

GENERAL UNION OF BRAZIERS AND SHEET METAL WORKERS
The inaugural meeting at which a decision was taken to institute formally what was then called the **General Union of Tin-plate Workers** was held at Manchester on 19 October 1861, and was attended by representatives from tin-plate workers' societies from Manchester, Liverpool, Blackburn, Oldham, Bury, Preston, Ashton, Rochdale and Bacup. The Union was formally constituted on 1 January 1862 with a headquarters at Manchester. The first Secretary was T. Dunn of Manchester and the President was J.G. Brown of Liverpool. The object of the Union at that time was to be primarily a clearing house for tramping tin-plate workers looking for work, but it became evident that a much broader organisation was needed. By 1868 the number of affiliated societies had grown to 19. It registered in 1871 with the objects of raising a fund by entrance fees, subscriptions or levies on members, and of paying death benefits, superannuation and unemployment benefits. The Union was open to tin-plate workers who had served the recognised term of apprenticeship on payment of 1s if under 30 years of age, 2s 6d if over 30 and under 40, and 5s if over 40. No member over 40 joining the Union was admitted to sick or superannuation benefits. In 1892 the name was changed to the **General Union of Braziers and Sheet Metal Workers**. In 1893 the first full-time Secretary was appointed, John Wiltshire, who had hitherto been part-time Secretary for some years. In 1897 the Union affiliated to the **Federation of Engineering and Shipbuilding Trades** and in 1900 to the **National Amalgamated Sheet Metal Workers and Braziers Society** after having turned down amalgamation with this society on several previous occasions. In 1909 it first published the joint *Union of Braziers and Sheet Metal Workers Monthly Journal*, and in 1920 it merged with the newly formed **National Union of Sheet Metal Workers and Braziers**.

Source: Kidd.

GENERAL UNION OF TIN-PLATE WORKERS
See **General Union of Braziers and Sheet Metal Workers**

GLASGOW TIN-PLATE WORKERS PROTECTIVE SOCIETY
See **Scottish Tin-Plate and Sheet Metal Workers Friendly and Protective Society**

GOOD INTENT SOCIETY OF GALVANIZERS AND ENAMELLERS
This was a local union formed in 1893 with a membership of 49, rising to 310 in 1897 when it was apparently dissolved.

Source: BoT Reports.

HALESOWEN ASSOCIATION OF TIN PLATE WORKERS AND TRUNK MAKERS
The Association was formed in 1899 with 39 members and ended its existence in 1905 when it had 36 members.

Source: Bain and Price.

HALESOWEN, LYE, STOURBRIDGE AND DISTRICT TIN-PLATE WORKERS AND TRUNK MAKERS SOCIETY
See **Halesowen Association of Tin Plate Workers and Trunk Makers**

HEATING AND DOMESTIC ENGINEERS UNION
This is a union which has had many changes of title. It is said to have originated in 1872 and was registered in 1874 as the **Amalgamated Stove, Grate and Kitchen Range Fitters Protection Society**. It was formed, it is claimed, as a protective measure against the exclusiveness of the **Amalgamated Society of Engineers** and its failure to represent special interests within the engineering industry. In 1887 the Union changed its name to the **Amalgamated Society of Kitchen Range, Hot Water, Art Metal and Other Fitters Concerned with the Above Trades**, no doubt as a result of further amalgamation. In 1898 it became the **United Society of Fitters and Smiths**, at that time having 360 members. In 1908 it formed part of an amalgamation involving the **Amalgamated Society of Whitesmiths, Domestic Engineers and General Pipe Fitters** and the **Birmingham Society of Hot Water and Steam Engineers** to form the **National Union of Operative Heating and Domestic Engineers, White- smiths and General Iron Workers**, with an office in Birmingham and a total membership of a little over 1,000. Another small society, the **Society of Smiths, Fitters, Hot Water and Steam Engineers** merged in 1911. There were two further changes of name, in 1948 to the **National Union of Operative Heating and Domestic Engineers and General Iron Workers** and again in 1956 to the above title (which incorporated the Ventilating Engineers and General Metal Workers). It amalgamated in 1967 with the **National Union of Sheet Metal Workers and Coppersmiths** to form the

National Union of Sheet Metal Workers, Coppersmiths, Heating and Domestic Engineers.

Sources: BoT Reports; Certification Office; Kidd; S. and B. Webb, *History of Trade Unionism.*

HUMANE SOCIETY OF TINPLATE WORKERS
See **Liverpool Operative Braziers and Sheet Metal Workers Society**

IRON PLATE WORKERS SOCIETY
Established in 1890, the Society always had a struggle to maintain its existence. In 1910 it applied to merge with the Tin and Iron Plate Workers Society but this was refused on the grounds that there was too much discrepancy in their wage levels, those of the Iron Plate Workers not being in accordance with the printed wage list of the Tin and Iron Plate Workers. The bigger union had always helped the Iron Plate men both by appointing the Society's Secretary and with financial assistance, and in 1914, after a ballot of its members, the Iron Plate Workers were accepted into the Tin and Iron Plate Workers Society, bringing in 232 members and a cash balance of £310 19s 3d.

Source: Kidd.

LEEDS AND DISTRICT ASSOCIATION OF TIN-PLATE WORKERS
See **Leeds and District Trade and Friendly Society of Sheet Metal Workers**

LEEDS AND DISTRICT TRADE AND FRIENDLY SOCIETY OF SHEET METAL WORKERS
The Society was formed in 1857 under the title of the **Leeds and District Association of Tin-plate Workers**. It had a membership of 91 in 1910. It merged with the **National Union of Sheet Metal Workers and Braziers** in 1920.

Sources: BoT Reports; Certification Office.

LEITH PROTECTING AND FRIENDLY SOCIETY
See **Edinburgh Society of Sheet Metal Workers and Gas Meter Makers**

LIVERPOOL AMALGAMATED HOLLOW-WARE CASTERS AND TURNERS SOCIETY
This was a shortlived union formed in 1895. It had 27 members in 1896 but was dissolved in the following year.

Source: BoT Reports.

LIVERPOOL OPERATIVE BRAZIERS AND SHEET METAL WORKERS SOCIETY

The Society was formed in 1802, and the Articles of Association were recorded in 1811 under the title of the **Humane Society of Tinplate Workers**. The entrance fee was 5s and the Secretary, E. Gorst, received £2 per annum for his services. A committee member was appointed to be the waiter for serving the ale at lodge meetings, which were held at the Sign of the Swan in Thomas Street, Liverpool. Fines were incurred for bad behaviour at the meetings. Members were paid a pension on retirement of 2s 6d per week after 10 years' membership, 3s per week for 15 years' membership, and 3s 6d per week for 20 years' membership and over. Funeral benefits of £2, £3, £4 and £5 were paid. Contributions were 1s 4d a month which included 1s per month for the trade fund, 1d superannuation fund, and 3d for drink. In 1853 the title was changed to the **Friendly Society of Tin Plate Workers** and in 1890 the above title was adopted, thus broadening the base of recruitment. The Society later merged with the **National Amalgamated Tin Plate Workers of Great Britain**.

Sources: Kidd; Certification Office.

LIVERPOOL SHEET METAL WORKERS SOCIETY

A shortlived union founded in 1890 and dissolved in 1894, when it had 18 members only.

Source: BoT Reports.

LIVERPOOL UNITED SOCIETY OF COPPERSMITHS, BRAZIERS, BRASS, IRON AND STEEL PIPE WORKERS

The Society was formed in 1860 and had about 120 members in 1900 and 110 in 1910. It merged with the **National Society of Coppersmiths, Braziers and Metal Workers** in 1914.

Sources: BoT Reports; Certification Office.

LONDON AMALGAMATED SOCIETY OF TIN AND IRON PLATE WORKERS AND GAS METER MAKERS

See **London Society of Sheet Metal Workers, Braziers and Gas Meter Makers**

LONDON AMALGAMATED SOCIETY OF TIN PLATE WORKERS

See **London Society of Sheet Metal Workers, Braziers and Gas Meter Makers**

LONDON AND PROVINCIAL SOCIETY OF COPPERSMITHS

See **National Society of Coppersmiths, Braziers and Metal Workers**

LONDON BRAZIERS AND SHEET METAL WORKERS HAND-IN-HAND SOCIETY

This was a sheet metal workers' society originally founded in 1829 and was also known as the **London Braziers Hand-in-Hand Society**. In 1892 it had 64 members but only 40 in 1910. It seems to have lost members continuously until in 1928, when the membership was 13, it ceased to function.

Sources: BoT Reports; Certification Office.

LONDON BRAZIERS HAND-IN-HAND SOCIETY

See **London Braziers and Sheet Metal Workers Hand-In-Hand Society**

LONDON IRON PLATE TRADE SOCIETY

A shortlived sectional society formed, it appears, in 1892 and dissolved in 1896.

Source: BoT Reports.

LONDON JEWISH TIN PLATE AND SHEET METAL WORKERS UNION

The Union was dissolved in 1917; no further information about it seems to exist.

Source: Certification Office.

LONDON OPERATIVE GAS METER MAKERS ASSOCIATION

The Association was formed in 1861, and its membership consisted of tin plate workers who were or had been employed in the manufacture of gas meters. The entrance fee on joining was 2s 6d, and the subscription was 6d per week. The objects of the organisation were 'to obtain a just return in exchange for the labour of the members, to defend those who might sacrifice their employment in maintaining the same; to assist each other in obtaining employment; to grant a pension to the aged and infirm members as well as to provide a sufficient sum to admit of the respectable interment of a member or a member's wife'. In 1889 it merged with the **London Amalgamated Society of Tin Plate Workers** with funds at that time amounting to £219 12s 9d.

Source: Kidd.

LONDON OPERATIVE TIN-PLATE WORKERS SOCIETY

The Society was formed in 1805 or even earlier, and its motto was 'We Despair Not'. Its earliest available book of rules is dated 1839. The entrance fee on joining was 2s 6d with a weekly subscription of 6d for men just out of their apprenticeship. Fully experienced tin plate workers paid a 5s entrance fee. The position of Secretary was voted on at the annual meeting, and he was allowed £2 per month in payment of his services. Whenever the Society was involved in a strike, all acting committee men engaged in conducting the dispute received an allowance of 7s 6d per day. An annual dinner was held every year in June, each person attending paying 6d. There was a provision within the rules that 'any manufactory employing more than 12 men is requested to appoint a member of the Committee'; the remaining members of the committee were chosen at the lodge meetings. Any member being made unemployed by virtue of refusing to make any article at a lower price than was usually paid by the trade was paid 16s per week if single and 18s per week if married, with an additional 1s per week for each child under 14 years. A funeral allowance of £6 was paid to a member's next of kin, and £5 on the death of a member's wife. An offshoot of the Society was the Tin Plate Workers Pension Society set up in 1828. The Society amalgamated with the **Co-operative Tinplate Workers Society** in order to form the **London Amalgamated Society of Tin Plate Workers** in 1875.

Source: Kidd.

LONDON OPERATIVE ZINC WORKERS SOCIETY
See **Zinc and Copper Roofers and Tin Sheet Metal Workers Society**

LONDON SOCIETY OF SHEET METAL WORKERS, BRAZIERS AND GAS METER MAKERS
The Society was formed in 1875 by an amalgamation between the **London Operative Tin-Plate Workers Society** (which claimed an existence dating back to 1805), and the **Co-operative Tinplate Workers Society**. The joint title adopted at that time was the **London Amalgamated Society of Tin Plate Workers**, the name being changed in 1889 to the **London Amalgamated Society of Tin and Iron Plate Workers and Gas Meter Makers** when the **London Operative Gas Meter Makers Association** merged with it. It had over 1,000 members in 1900, organised in a single London branch. In 1901 John Deans was appointed as the first full-time General Secretary, and in May of that year a small union, the **Amalgamated Society of Tin and Iron Plate Workers and Gas Meter Makers**, joined the Society and it became the London Society as above. It was still organised in a single branch with a membership which had risen to 1,500. In 1920 it amalgamated with other unions in order to form the **National Union of Sheet Metal Workers and Braziers**.

Sources: BoT Reports; Kidd; Certification Office.

LONDON TIN CANISTER AND PRESERVED PROVISION CASE AND GENERAL TINPLATE WORKERS SOCIETY
This very small society, earlier known as the **London Tin Canister and Tin Mens Society**, established in 1881, merged with the **London Society of Sheet Metal Workers, Braziers and Gas Meter Makers** in 1910, when it had 30 members, agreement being reached that the Canister Makers should be entitled to full benefit immediately. They were men of whom it was said:

'they are working in steady jobs at the most suitable firms and are good, financially sound and working trade unionists'.

Sources: Kidd; BoT Reports.

LONDON TIN CANISTER AND TIN MENS SOCIETY
See **London Tin Canister and Preserved Provision Case and General Tinplate Workers Society**

LONDON WOOD AND TIN PACKING CASE MAKERS TRADE SOCIETY
Formed in 1873, the Society went out of existence in 1912.

Source: Certification Office.

LOWESTOFT AND YARMOUTH ASSOCIATION OF TIN PLATE WORKERS
The Association was set up in 1901 with 33 members and ceased to exist in 1909 when its membership was 30.

Source: Bain and Price.

LYE IRON PLATE TRADE SOCIETY
A sectional society based on Lye, Stourbridge, formed in 1890, which had 324 members in 1892. Towards the end of the century it became a branch of the **National Amalgamated Iron Plate Trade Society**.

Source: BoT Reports.

MANCHESTER FRIENDLY SOCIETY OF TIN PLATE WORKERS
The Society was apparently formed as long ago as 1802. In 1819 the Secretary is recorded as being one William Nicholson. Fines were imposed on members for bad behaviour during the course of lodge meetings and subscriptions ranged from 5d to 1s a week, drink being included. 7s a week unemployment benefit was payable for 24 days in every three months, with £9 funeral benefit on the death of a member and £7 on the death of a member's wife. There was a ruling existing that should any member leave his employment in a clandestine or fraudulent manner or leave his work unfinished, he could not receive any benefit from the Society until he had either finished his work or made due recompense to his employer for the same. Like others of its kind, the Society operated a price list for manufactured articles. It amalgamated with other unions in 1920 to form the **National Union of Sheet Metal Workers and Braziers**.

Sources: Kidd; Certification Office.

MANCHESTER SOCIETY OF BRAZIERS AND SHEET METAL WORKERS

Formed in 1890, the Society amalgamated with other unions in 1920 in order to establish the **National Union of Sheet Metal Workers and Braziers.**

Source: Certification Office.

NATIONAL AMALGAMATED ASSOCIATION OF SHEET METAL WORKERS AND BRAZIERS

The Association was established in 1899 as the **National Amalgamated Association of Tin Plate Workers and Braziers**, the name later being changed to the above. It amalgamated with other unions in 1920 in order to form the **National Union of Sheet Metal Workers and Braziers.**

Source: Certification Office.

NATIONAL AMALGAMATED ASSOCIATION OF TIN PLATE WORKERS AND BRAZIERS

See **National Amalgamated Association of Sheet Metal Workers and Braziers**

NATIONAL AMALGAMATED ASSOCIATION OF TIN PLATE WORKERS OF GREAT BRITAIN

The roots of the Association were laid on 3 January 1876 at a conference at the Pack Horse Inn, Dudley Street, Wolverhampton, held by the **Wolverhampton Tin Plate Workers Society** and the **Birmingham Tin Plate Workers Society** where the decision was made to form the **Amalgamated Tin Plate Workers Society of Birmingham, Wolverhampton and District.** The total funds available at the time were £160, and the first Secretary was Edward Davies. Meetings were held quarterly and subscriptions were 1s per member. The Wolverhampton and Birmingham District took it in turns to appoint the Secretary and President every 3 years on a rota basis. In 1889 the Association developed into something more than a semi-district organisation. Invitations were issued to unattached tin-plate workers' societies with the result that Edinburgh, Aberdeen, Liverpool, Cardiff and 2 London societies decided to affiliate. In April 1889 the **United Tin Plate Workers Association** and the **Gas Meter Makers Association of Edinburgh and Leith** joined the new National Association, bringing the total membership to some 1,400. The name was changed to the **National Amalgamated Tin Plate Workers of Great Britain** and the decision was made to affiliate to the TUC. The Executive Committee at this stage consisted of one representative from each society numbering up to 100 members; over 100 and under 300 members had 2 representatives, and over 300 members had 3 representatives. In cases of strikes or lockouts, members were paid 8s per week for 20 weeks. Any tin-plate society could join by paying an entrance deposit of 5s per member. In 1902 J.C. Gordon (1861–1929) was appointed the first full-time General Secretary. In that year the National Amalgamated Association was composed of the following societies: Aberdeen, Birmingham, Bradford, Bristol, Edinburgh, Exeter, Halesowen, the General Union, London, Lowestoft, Norwich, Oldham, and Wolverhampton, and with the affiliation of the Leeds Society at the end of 1902 all the existing tin-plate societies were members of the National Amalgamated Association, membership then being 6,261. The National Amalgamated Association was always an advocate of one national union for all workers in the industry. In 1920 it amalgamated with other societies to form the **National Union of Sheet Metal Workers and Braziers**.

Source: Kidd.

NATIONAL AMALGAMATED IRON PLATE TRADE SOCIETY
This was a Staffordshire union, based on Tipton and whose earliest branch was apparently established in 1874. The Society had 5 branches and 566 members in 1900, having declined from a peak of about 800 two years earlier. In October 1907 it merged with the **Galvanised Hollow-Ware Sheet Metal Workers and Braziers Association**.

Sources: BoT Reports; Certification Office.

NATIONAL AMALGAMATED TIN PLATE WORKERS OF GREAT BRITAIN
See **National Amalgamated Association of Tin Plate Workers of Great Britain**

NATIONAL SOCIETY OF COPPERSMITHS, BRAZIERS AND METAL WORKERS
The Society was founded in 1846 as the **London and Provincial Society of Coppersmiths**. It had 464 members operating in 5 branches in 1900, and 775 members in 1910, at which time it changed its title to the above. It remained sufficiently independent not to become involved in the 1920 amalgamation of unions which produced the **National Union of Sheet Metal Workers and Braziers**. It retained its independent function until July 1959 when the two unions amalgamated to form the **National Union of Sheet Metal Workers and Coppersmiths**. At the date of the amalgamation the Coppersmiths, still based on London, had a membership of about 6,000, while the National Union of Sheet Metal Workers was almost 43,000 strong.

Sources: Kidd; Certification Office; BoT Reports.

NATIONAL UNION OF DOMESTIC APPLIANCE AND GENERAL METAL WORKERS
First known as the **National Union of Stove and Grate Workers** when it was formed in 1890 and later as the **National Union of Stove, Grate, Fender and General Metal Workers**, the Union was established by men who had been refused entry into the craft unions because they were semi-skilled. It had almost 1,500 members by 1900, though later this number fell somewhat. It

organised light castings workers in Yorkshire, the Midlands and Lancashire and some in London. The Union grew out of a strike for higher wages at Rotherham. The strikers called in H. Sanders, a small businessman and local councillor of Walsall where he had organised the gas workers and led several small strikes among the small trades. In 9 weeks the Rotherham strike was won and Sanders agreed to organise the Union, which soon had substantial membership in Yorkshire, the Midlands and London. Sanders' methods were militant and spectacular. During a strike at Belper in 1890 for a 10 per cent advance in piece rates he organised a demonstration through the town, culminating in a funeral of the effigies of 3 blacklegs with the epitaph 'masters they served, men they betrayed, if they go to heaven, who shall be saved'! The **Friendly Society of Ironfounders of England, Ireland and Wales (FSIF)** poured scorn on a union which took men in poor health, as well as 'lads, labourers and window cleaners', and which offered strike, unemployment, accident and superannuation benefits all for 6d a week or 4d for labourers. The Sheffield Trades Council recommended that the two unions amalgamated. In 1905 the **National Union of Stove and Grate Workers** agreed to federate with 10 foundry unions to form the **Federation of Moulders and Collateral Trades** with 500 members and subscriptions at 6d per week. In 1912 it came together with the **Amalgamated Society of Plate and Machine Moulders**, the **Rotherham Grinders**, the **Operative Heating Engineers** and the **General Iron Workers Union** in order jointly to carry through a successful wage claim. In 1918 it helped to form the **National Federation of Foundry Trades Unions**, a great step towards the unity of the unions in the trade at that time. In 1927 there were moves by the TUC to bring together in one organisation all unions in the industry, but the Union refused. It was a member of the Joint Committee of Light Metal Trade Unions, which united the **National Union of Foundry Workers**, the **Ironfounding Workers Association** and the **Amalgamated Moulders and Iron, Steel and Metal Dressers** to the effect that members of any one of these unions might take similar jobs but as dilutees. In 1942, with the IWA, the National Light Castings Ironfounders' Federation and the **National Union of Foundry Workers**, it entered into an agreement allowing women to enter the trade as moulders, laying down a scale of wages for the women. In the mid-1960s the union changed its name to the National Union of Domestic Appliance and General Metal Workers to take account of the work of its members outside the 'Yorkshire' range. It remains a predominantly Northern-based union.

Sources: Fyrth and Collins; Marsh, *Concise Encyclopedia*.

NATIONAL UNION OF OPERATIVE HEATING AND DOMESTIC ENGINEERS AND GENERAL IRON WORKERS
See **Heating and Domestic Engineers Union**

NATIONAL UNION OF OPERATIVE HEATING AND DOMESTIC ENGINEERS, WHITESMITHS AND GENERAL IRON WORKERS
See **Heating and Domestic Engineers Union**

NATIONAL UNION OF SHEET METAL WORKERS AND BRAZIERS
This was a major amalgamation of sheet metal workers' unions which took place in July 1920 and became responsible for the payment of benefits and administration from 1 January 1921. Of the many attempts in the nineteenth century to bring together local and sectional societies in the trade, the most successful had been the **General Union of Braziers and Sheet Metal Workers** and the National Amalgamated Tin-Plate Workers Society (see **National Amalgamated Association of Tin Plate Workers of Great Britain**). Both were loose affiliations of such societies. By the end of the century they jointly and severally represented the bulk of the trade, and both societies took the initiative from time to time to unite into a single national organisation. In the aftermath of the First World War proposals were submitted which eventually succeeded in overcoming the technical problems involved, leaving outside no society of substance except the **Birmingham and Midland Sheet Metal Workers Society**. The societies involved in 1920 were the **Aberdeen and District Sheet Metal Workers Society**, the **Ashton-under-Lyne and District Association of Braziers and Sheet Metal Workers**, the **Birmingham Association of Operative Tin Plate, Sheet Metal Workers and Braziers**, the **Bolton Society of Braziers and Sheet Metal Workers**, the **Belfast Association of Sheet Metal Workers and Gasfitters**, the **Bradford and District Sheet Metal Workers Society**, the **Bristol Tin Plate, Sheet Metal Workers and Braziers Society**, the **Dundee and District Society of Sheet Metal Workers, Gasfitters and Braziers**, the **Edinburgh Society of Sheet Metal Workers and Gas Meter Makers**, the **Exeter and District Tin and Iron Plate Workers and Gas Meter Makers Society**, the **General Union of Braziers and Sheet Metal Workers**, the **Leeds and District Trade and Friendly Society of Sheet Metal Workers**, the **London Association of Tin and Iron Plate Sheet Metal Workers and Gas Meter Makers**, the **National Amalgamated Association of Sheet Metal Workers and Braziers**, the **Oldham Tin Plate Workers Trade Union**, the **Scottish Tin-Plate and Sheet Metal Workers Friendly and Protective Society** and the **Wolverhampton Operative Tin-plate Workers Society**. The first General Secretary of the National Union was J.C. Gordon, who had previously occupied that position with the National Amalgamated Association from 1902. In July 1959 the Union amalgamated with the **National Society of Coppersmiths, Braziers and Metal Workers** to form the **National Union of Sheet Metal Workers and Coppersmiths** to which was added, in April 1967, the **Heating and Domestic Engineers Union**, to form the present **National Union of Sheet Metal Workers, Coppersmiths, Heating and Domestic Engineers**.

Sources: Kidd; Certification Office.

NATIONAL UNION OF SHEET METAL WORKERS AND COPPER-SMITHS
See **National Union of Sheet Metal Workers and Braziers**

NATIONAL UNION OF SHEET METAL WORKERS, COPPER-SMITHS, HEATING AND DOMESTIC ENGINEERS
The basis of the Union was formed in July 1959 by the amalgamation of the

National Union of Sheet Metal Workers and Braziers and the National Society of Coppersmiths, Braziers and Metal Workers under the title of the National Union of Sheet Metal Workers and Coppersmiths. By a further amalgamation in April 1967 of the Heating and Domestic Engineers Union the title was enlarged to the above. In 1972 delegates of the Union voted in favour of amalgamation with the Amalgamated Society of Boilermakers and Shipwrights, Blacksmiths and Structural Workers and with the Birmingham and Midland Sheet Metal Workers Society. The former union did not amalgamate, but the latter did so in 1973.

Sources: Kidd; Marsh, *Concise Encyclopedia.*

NATIONAL UNION OF STOVE AND GRATE WORKERS
See **National Union of Domestic Appliance and General Metal Workers**

NATIONAL UNION OF STOVE, GRATE, FENDER AND GENERAL METAL WORKERS
See **National Union of Domestic Appliance and General Metal Workers**

NATIONAL UNION OF TIN PLATE WORKERS
This was a federation of tin-plate workers' societies in 1821 designed 'to make a stand against the encroachments of the master' and to act as a clearing house for travelling payments. Some 29 local societies and branches seem to have taken part, with a total membership in Great Britain and Ireland of almost 1,000. How long the Union operated beyond the last extant Annual Report of 1824 is not clear.

Source: Kidd.

NEWCASTLE ON TYNE AND DISTRICT OPERATIVE WHITE-SMITHS AND HEATING ENGINEERS SOCIETY
This local Society was established in 1899 with 83 members. In 1904, with 86 members, it merged with the **Amalgamated Association of Whitesmiths, Locksmiths and Bellhangers**, but seceded from this organisation in 1906 and resumed an independent existence under its original title, taking with it 90 members. It had 76 members in 1910. In 1917 the Society merged with the **National Union of Operative Heating and Domestic Engineers, Whitesmiths and General Iron Workers**.

Sources: BoT Reports; Bain and Price.

OLDHAM FRIENDLY SOCIETY OF TIN PLATE WORKERS
See **Oldham Tin Plate Workers Trade Union**

OLDHAM TIN PLATE WORKERS TRADE UNION
The Union would appear to have been formed in 1844 as the **Oldham Friendly Society of Tin Plate Workers**. It had a membership of 223 in

1910, and merged with the **National Union of Sheet Metal Workers and Braziers** in 1921.

Sources: BoT Reports; Certification Office.

OPERATIVE TIN-PLATE WORKERS SOCIETY
See **Liverpool Operative Braziers and Sheet Metal Workers Society**

PROGRESSIVE SHEET METAL WORKERS SOCIETY (COVENTRY)
Formed in 1907, the Society had 114 members in 1910. Nothing further is known of its history except the fact that registration was cancelled in 1921. It would seem possible that it became involved in some way in the amalgamation of several unions which resulted in the formation of the **National Union of Sheet Metal Workers and Braziers**.

Sources: BoT Reports; Certification Office.

RIPLEY AMALGAMATED HOLLOW-WARE, CASTERS AND TURNERS TRADE SOCIETY
The Society was formed in 1895, and its registration was cancelled in 1899.

Source: Certification Office.

SCOTTISH TIN-PLATE AND SHEET METAL WORKERS FRIENDLY AND PROTECTIVE SOCIETY
Formed in 1833 under the title of the **Glasgow Tin-Plate Workers Protective Society**, the Society was composed at that time of 34 tinsmiths, which number had increased to 114 by 1834. It was a protective society paying no cash benefits. The working week of the craftsmen at that time was 66 hours with wages at 14s per week. The name was changed to the **United Tin-plate Workers Protective Society** and later again the word 'Friendly' was added to the title. In 1871 it became the **United Tin-plate Workers Friendly and Protective Society of Glasgow and the West of Scotland** and the union began payment of sickness, unemployment, funeral and strike benefits. By 1891, when the name was changed yet again to the above, the union had a membership of 650, and it had paid out to its members £3,835 in sickness benefit, £3,804 in unemployment benefit, £1,533 in funeral benefit and £1,118 in strike benefit. In 1913 T. Saunders was appointed the first full time General Secretary, and in 1920 the union became part of the newly formed **National Union of Sheet Metal Workers and Braziers**.

Source: Kidd.

SHEET IRON AND LIGHT PLATE WORKERS SOCIETY
The Society was formed in Glasgow in 1900 with 68 members under the title of the **Sheet Iron Workers, Light Platers and Ship Range Makers Society**, the name later being changed to the above. It was a rival to the **General**

Union of Tin-plate Workers and actually poached some of its members, and also endeavoured to prevent members of the General Union being employed in various shipyards. It was reprimanded for its methods at a public enquiry held by the Federation of Engineering and Shipbuilding Trades, but this did not stop its activities. In 1919 it merged with the United Society of Boilermakers with 1,428 members, but seceded from them in 1921, functioning again as an independent union with a membership of 1,376. It continued in existence until 1950 when it merged with the National Union of Sheet Metal Workers and Braziers, the membership then being 958.

Sources: Mortimer; Kidd.

SHEET IRON WORKERS, LIGHT PLATERS AND SHIP RANGE MAKERS SOCIETY
See **Sheet Iron and Light Plate Workers Society**

SHEET METAL WORKERS AND GAS METER MAKERS OF EDINBURGH
See **Edinburgh Society of Sheet Metal Workers and Gas Meter Makers**

SOCIETY OF GENERAL SMITHS, FITTERS, BELLHANGERS AND WHITESMITHS
See **Society of Smiths, Fitters, Hot Water and Steam Engineers**

SOCIETY OF HOT WATER AND GENERAL FITTERS, CHIPPERS AND JOIST CUTTERS
This was an East London sectional society formed in 1894 with 130 members. Its membership reached a peak of 183 in 1898 which had dwindled to 29 in 1906, and the Society ceased to exist in 1907.

Source: BoT Reports.

SOCIETY OF SMITHS, FITTERS, HOT WATER AND STEAM ENGINEERS
Formed in 1890, the Society was then named the **Society of General Smiths, Fitters, Bellhangers and Whitesmiths**, changing its title to the above in 1900. It had over 400 members in 5 branches of the union in 1896. Thereafter membership declined until in 1910 it was less than 50. In 1911 the Society merged with the more successful **National Union of Operative Heating and Domestic Engineers, Whitesmiths and General Iron Workers**.

Source: BoT Reports.

UNITED ORDER OF SMITHS
See **Heating and Domestic Engineers Union**

UNITED SOCIETY OF FITTERS AND SMITHS
See **Heating and Domestic Engineers Union**

UNITED TIN PLATE WORKERS ASSOCIATION
See **National Amalgamated Association of Tin Plate Workers of Great Britain**

UNITED TIN-PLATE WORKERS FRIENDLY AND PROTECTIVE SOCIETY
See **Scottish Tin-Plate and Sheet Metal Workers Friendly and Protective Society**

UNITED TIN-PLATE WORKERS FRIENDLY AND PROTECTIVE SOCIETY OF GLASGOW AND THE WEST OF SCOTLAND
See **Scottish Tin-Plate and Sheet Metal Workers Friendly and Protective Society**

UNITED TIN-PLATE WORKERS AND GAS METER MAKERS SOCIETY OF EDINBURGH AND LEITH
The Society would appear to have been in existence in the 1870s. It merged with the newly formed **National Amalgamated Tin Plate Workers of Great Britain** in 1890.

Source: Kidd.

WOLVERHAMPTON IRON PLATE TRADE SOCIETY
Formed in 1894, with 72 members, the Society shortly afterwards became part of the **National Amalgamated Iron Plate Trade Society**.

Source: BoT Reports.

WOLVERHAMPTON OPERATIVE TIN-PLATE WORKERS SOCIETY
The Society was established in 1802, but the earliest copy of the rules available is dated 13 November 1834. Membership was open to all tin-plate workers who had served a legal apprenticeship, and no one was eligible to join under 21 years of age. The number of Executive Committee members was regulated by the number of shops in which members were employed. As well as the President and Secretary and committee members there was also an Ale Steward whose duty it was to call for liquid refreshments at the order of the President. No member was allowed to read, sleep, swear, lay wagers or use obscene language during lodge meetings. Subscriptions were 5d a week or 1s 1d per month. In 1850/51 the Society endeavoured to secure a uniform price list for the manufacture of tin goods. Some of the masters agreed, others did not, and the union called a strike of all its members, 6 of whom were charged with conspiracy and sent to prison. In 1856 a decision was made to establish a pension fund, men with 10 years'

membership receiving 3s per week, with 15 years, 4s per week, and with 20 years, 5s per week. It was not until 1870 that sickness benefit was paid. In 1874 a new price list was conceded, a 10 per cent advance on the 1850 price list. In 1876 the Society combined with the **Birmingham Tin Plate Workers Society** and the **Co-operative Tin-Plate Workers of Wolverhampton** to form the **Amalgamated Tin-Plate Workers of Birmingham, Wolverhampton and District**, later to be known as the **National Amalgamated Tin Plate Workers of Great Britain**.

Source: Kidd.

WOLVERHAMPTON TIN PLATE WORKERS SOCIETY
See **National Amalgamated Association of Tin Plate Workers of Great Britain**

ZINC AND COPPER ROOFERS AND TIN SHEET METAL WORKERS SOCIETY
Founded in 1876 as the **London Operative Zinc Workers Society** but with a history dating back to 1853, the Society had about 60 members in 1913. It merged in 1918 with the **London Society of Sheet Metal Workers, Braziers and Gas Meter Makers**.

Sources: Certification Office; BoT Reports.

Edge Tool, Cutlery, File and Needle Trades

Trades designated as 'cutlery and edge tool' have been mainly concentrated in Sheffield, although there was an early established Needlemakers' Association formed in 1857 and based in Loughborough, and two years later, in 1859, another Association of Needlemakers formed in Nottingham, neither of these bodies having a very big membership, although both continued to exist as independent organisations until 1910 and 1912 respectively. The town of Stourbridge managed to sustain a Forgemen, Fork Drawers and Spade Finishers Association for 10 years, and an Edge Tool Society, formed in 1890, catering for members working in the Birmingham, Wolverhampton and Wednesbury district, gradually absorbed workers making awl blades and brace bits and also kept an organisation functioning, albeit with a low membership, until as late as 1946, when it transferred its engagements to the National Union of General and Municipal Workers.

A Hand File Cutters Society existed in Manchester from 1889 up to the beginning of the First World War. London workers had only one known organisation, namely a Cutters and Instrument Makers' Society, which they maintained for 12 years from 1883 to 1895, according to records. The Redditch Fish Hook Makers founded a Society in 1872, had a continuous existence for 21 years and the Warrington File Smiths, established in 1871, had a membership level of 200 in 1892, remaining a functioning body until 1903.

But the great bulk of the work force in the cutlery and edge tool trades were engaged in workshops in Sheffield or its vicinity. As early as 1836, according to reports in the local newspaper, *The Sheffield Iris*, representatives of all the cutlery trades were having constant discussions in that year on the need to form a union of all trades, a joint committee being set up of the grinding branches which concerned itself with the working conditions in the workshops in regard to matters like the improvement of the ventilation and the lessening of the mortality rate amongst such workers. Sheffield had by 1786 no fewer than 52 benefit societies in the cutlery and edge tool trades, which concerned not only knives and forks, but also razors, shears and sickles, saws, files and other cutting instruments. Twenty-three unions in these trades still existed in 1903 and 14 in 1925. Of these, only two now remain as independent organisations – the Sheffield Sawmakers Protection Society, said to date from 1797 (and currently with about 250 members) and the Sheffield Wool Shear Workers Trade Union, founded in 1890 as the Sheffield Wool Shear Grinders, Makers, Finishers and Benders Union, now with only 12 members.The hey-day of the sectional societies catering for the crafts involved in the cutlery trade – forging, tempering, grinding and hafting, as well as that of filemaking – began to be undermined by mechanised methods in the 1860s and 1870s and in the following half-century such methods gradually covered the whole field. Many unions were well established, powerful and unwilling to adapt; some, like the Saw Grinders Trade Protection Society which gave rise to the events known as the 'Sheffield outrages' (which resulted in the Royal Commission of 1867), were willing to use forceful methods to retain their control. But there was little apparent inclination to rationalise until after 1900, when the 'whole outlook of the trade was most deplorable and the condition of those engaged in it went from bad to worse' (Amalgamated Spring Knife Workers Association, Secretary's Report, 1914).

Ahead of the field was the Amalgamated Edge Tool Trade and Protection Association (1890) and the Razor Trade Federation (1891) which brought together organisations in those trades, though the latter had limited success. In the precious metal side of the trade, the Amalgamated Society of Gold, Silver and Kindred Trades (1911) brought together 15 independent societies and proved to be very durable indeed (see National Union of Gold, Silver and Allied Trades p.157). In cutlery, the situation was fraught with greater difficulties of membership, employment and financial weakness. 'The once powerful craft societies saw their membership ebbing away while unskilled labourers and helpers, organised in the "New Unions", made up for the weaknesses of small funds per head and lack of skill by large numbers and a militant policy' (Pollard, p. 220 – see Key). The National Amalgamated Union of Labour was the most successful in Sheffield, the Table and Butchers' Blade Grinders being its first important acquisition (1914) followed by the Spring Knife Cutlers in the following year, and by 1916 it included the Scissor Forgers, the Scissor Workboard Hands, the Edge Tool Cutlers, the Edge Tool Forgers, the Machine Knife and Bayonet Workers, the Spade and Shovel Makers, and the Hammer Makers and Edge Tool Forgers, among others.

Other amalgamations took place in 1915, to produce the Cutlery Union and the Sheffield Amalgamated Union of File Trades. The former resisted amalgamation into the General and Municipal Workers Union in 1937–8 but eventually did so in 1957. The latter proved more durable and remained independent until it transferred its engagements to the Transport and General Workers Union in 1970. The trade had long been a difficult one to organise. A filesmiths society dated from at least 1821. By the end of the century there were hand file grinders, forgers, hardeners and cutters competing with societies organising those who made files by machine methods. In 1915 it was the machine file unions which came together; two years later they were joined by two of the older craft societies and became a general union for the trade, though the hand cutters and grinders remained aloof.

AMALGAMATED ASSOCIATION OF NEEDLE MAKERS (NOTTING-HAM)

Formed in 1859, the Association had 20 members in 1897. With only 16 members it ceased to function in 1912.

Source: Bain and Price.

AMALGAMATED EDGE TOOL TRADE, PROTECTION AND DEATH SOCIETY OF BIRMINGHAM AND DISTRICT

See **Edge Tool Trade Society**

AMALGAMATED ENGINEERS TOOL MAKERS' SOCIETY

Established in 1889, the Society was a small local organisation which had 128 members in 1890 but only 28 out of the 500 workers in the trade by 1910. In 1913 membership had declined to 24 and the organisation ceased to function.

Sources: Lloyd; BoT Reports.

AMALGAMATED FORGEMEN, BLACKSMITHS, FORK DRAWERS AND SPADE FINISHERS ASSOCIATION (STOURBRIDGE)

See **Society of Forgemen, Blacksmiths, Fork Drawers and Makers, and Spade Finishers**

AMALGAMATED HAMMERMEN'S TRADE ASSOCIATION

Established in 1888, this Sheffield Association had a membership of 1,554 in 1892 but ceased to function in 1893.

Source: BoT Reports.

AMALGAMATED SCISSORS WORKERS TRADE, SICK AND FUNERAL SOCIETY (SHEFFIELD)

See **Scissors Grinders Trade, Sick and Funeral Society**

AMALGAMATED SOCIETY OF JOINERS, TOOLMAKERS AND FORGERS (SHEFFIELD)

This Society had evidently existed for some years before 1866 when it issued a revised price list, though the Board of Trade gives its year of formation as 1889. In 1890 its membership was about 100, which dropped to 70 by the end of the century and to 30 by 1909. There is no information about its existence after 1912.

Sources: Lloyd; BoT Reports.

AMALGAMATED SOCIETY OF THE RAZOR TRADES (SHEFFIELD)
A union referred to by Pollard as existing in the 1920s. No further reference has been found.

Source: Pollard, p. 299.

AMALGAMATED SPRING KNIFE WORKERS ASSOCIATION
The Association was formed in 1913 by amalgamation between the **Spring Knife Grinders and Finishers Union** and the **Sheffield Operative Spring Knife Cutlers' Union,** covering a combined membership of 790. In 1914 it merged with the **National Amalgamated Union of Labour** (see Vol. 3).

Sources: Lloyd; Pollard.

ASSOCIATION OF ORGANISED TRADES
In 1859 the Sheffield cutlery sectional societies were federated into the above Association, its formation being accelerated by the resentment caused by a libel action against three trade union officials in the town arising out of a dispute in the printing trade. The sympathy aroused caused a general rallying of the trade societies to their assistance. By February 1860, 22 societies had been enrolled representing a membership of 3,556. The officers were Charles Bagshaw, William Dronfield and William Broadhead. The declared objects were 'the establishment and perpetuation of a more intimate connection between all branches of the operative classes, and giving increased efficiency to the operation of trade societies.' The Association did not seek to interfere with the internal management of its constituent societies but was prepared to support them in any approved dispute. The Association ended its existence in 1864 due to lack of support which had dwindled away over the years.

Sources: J.C. Hill, *Trades Combination in Sheffield,* 1860; J.C. Hill, *The Trades of Sheffield,* 1865; Lloyd.

AWL BLADE MAKERS ASSOCIATION
Formed about the 1850s, this was only a small sectional society numbering about 30 men which was dissolved in 1886, the few remaining members entering the **Amalgamated Edge Tool Trade, Protection and Death Society of Birmingham and District.** The awl blade makers trade appears to have originated in Sheffield but was later carried on in Birmingham and still more extensively in Walsall and Bloxwich.

Source: Lloyd.

BAYONET WORKERS TRADE SOCIETY
See **Machine Knife and Bayonet Workers' Union**

BIRMINGHAM AND DISTRICT OPERATIVE FILE SMITHS' ASSO-CIATION

Established in 1889, the Association had 66 members in 1892. It was dissolved in 1905 when the membership had dwindled to 25.

Source: Bain and Price.

BIRMINGHAM, BRISTOL AND SHEFFIELD PLANE MAKERS' ASSO-CIATION

This was a sectional society said to have been formed in 1857 and having by 1900 three branches and 68 members. It later changed its name to **United Operative Plane Makers Trade Society.** It ceased to exist in 1941 with only 8 members remaining.

Sources: BoT Reports; Certification Office; Lloyd.

BONE HAFT AND SCALE CUTTERS SOCIETY

A price list for this Society survives from 1843 but it had an intermittent life span. It ceased to exist, and a new society with the same name was formed in 1889, remaining in existence for five years until it merged with the **Handle and Scale Cutters Association (Sheffield).**

Source: Lloyd.

BRACE BIT MAKERS SOCIETY

This was a small sectional Society formed in the 1870s which had previously been included in the **Amalgamated Society of Joiners, Toolmakers and Forgers,** but which merged into the newly formed **Amalgamated Edge Tool Trade Protection and Death Society of Birmingham and District** in 1890.

Source: Lloyd.

COMMITTEE OF THE ASSOCIATED TRADES

As early as 1836 there seem to have been regular meetings of the representatives of about 20 organised trade societies in the cutlery trade. In 1842 this representative Committee included a file-smith, a razor-smith, a saw-maker, a saw-handle-maker, an edge tool grinder, a saw grind-er, a joiners' tool grinder, a sawback grinder and a razor grinder. The Committee members found themselves fully employed during the starvation crisis of 1842–3. They urged the adoption of a scheme for purchasing land and setting the unemployed to work to maintain themselves by spade husbandry. The table knife hafters had in 1840 found employment in gravel pits and the joiners' tool and brace bit trades had made work for their unemployed in the cultivation of waste land. There was constant discussion among the delegates to the Committee of the need to form a union of all trades, and the Committee of the Central United Grinding Branches was formed which was primarily concerned with improving the ventilation of the workshops and lessening the trade mortality. It represented the grinders in the razor, fork, scissors, penknife, table knife, saw file, joiners' tool, fender, edge tool, and scythe trades. The effort to form a united organisation would appear to have failed at that time.

Sources: Lloyd; *Sheffield Iris,* 1 March 1836; 10 December 1842, 22 April 1843, 14 March 1844, 17 October 1844.

CUTLERY UNION (SHEFFIELD)
The Union was formed in 1914 by an amalgamation of the **Table and Butcher Knife Hafters Trade and Provident Society** and the **Table and Butcher Blade Smithers Association,** covering a total membership of 1,072. In 1938 with 589 members it amalgamated with the **Amalgamated Scissors Workers Trade, Sick and Funeral Society** in order to form the **National Cutlery Union.**

Sources: Certification Office; Pollard; Barou.

EDGE TOOL CUTLERS ASSOCIATION
This was a small society quite prosperous in its day, formed about the 1840/50s. In 1916 it merged with the **National Amalgamated Union of Labour** (see Vol. 3) and with the support of that union achieved a wage increase and a unified price list.

Sources: Pollard; NAUL Report, April 1916.

EDGE TOOL FORGERS SOCIETY (SHEFFIELD)
This organisation was in existence in 1837, the membership being engaged in the hand-forging of axes, plane irons, chisels, bayonets and so on, the heavy work later being carried out by steam hammer. The industry was formerly divided into three branches – forgers, grinders and hardeners – and there was at one time a strong union among the forgers and their strikers, who in 1843 numbered some 400 men. By 1890 the Society had about 100 members out of the 340 men engaged in the trade, and by 1897 this had grown to 250 members. For some years previous to 1896 the union appeared to transact no business, its funds being securely banked. Price lists had been issued in 1836, 1846, 1853, 1864 and 1872, the latter being the final one. In 1899 it merged with the **Amalgamated Edge Tool Trade, Protection and Death Society of Birmingham and District,** which in 1946 transferred its engagements to the **National Union of General and Municipal Workers** (see Vol. 3).

Sources: BoT Reports; Pollard; Lloyd; Barou.

EDGE TOOL GRINDERS SOCIETY
This was one of the oldest Sheffield societies, formed in 1820. In 1860 there were 190 members in the union, some 60 wool-shear-grinders being included in their ranks at that time. The latter ran out of benefit during a prolonged and bitter resistance to a reduction of prices in 1889 and

subsequently, in 1890, established a society of their own. Until 1870 the edge tool grinders were out-workers. In 1890 the Society had 150 members and in 1910 about 120 out of a total of 260 workers. In 1916 it merged with the **National Amalgamated Union of Labour** (see Vol. 3) and by so doing achieved immediate wage increases and a unified price list. It still appeared, however, as an independent union in the Ministry of Labour Directory of 1919.

Sources: Lloyd; Pollard; NAUL Report, April 1916; MoL Reports.

EDGE TOOL TRADE SOCIETY
The Society was formed in 1890 as the **Amalgamated Edge Tool Trade, Protection and Death Society of Birmingham and District** and gradually absorbed into its ranks such small sectional societies as the **Awl Blade Makers Association** and the **Brace Bit Makers Society.** It never achieved a large membership, having only 280 members in 3 branches in 1910. The above title was adopted in 1920. In 1946 with 240 members it transferred its engagements to the **National Union of General and Municipal Workers** (see Vol. 3).

Sources: BoT Reports; Lloyd; Barou; Pollard.

FEDERATION OF SPRING-KNIFE CUTLERS, BLADE-FORGERS AND SCALE AND SPRING FORGERS
Founded in 1831 to enforce the price lists established in that year, this organisation embraced all branches of the spring knife trade except the grinders, being established by the members of these trades 'for the purpose of promoting their respective interests'. The contributions were 1s per member per week and unemployed benefit was fixed at 7s per week per man, with 2s per week for his wife and 1s 6d a week for each child. It did not last long. Yet another society was founded in 1872 and lasted a considerable time, but little is known of it.

Sources: Lloyd; Abstract of Articles of Agreement between the Pen and Pocket Spring Knife Cutters, Sheffield, 1831.

FILE FORGERS-BY-MACHINE TRADE SOCIETY
See **Machine File Forgers Union (Sheffield)**

FILE GRINDERS TRADE SOCIETY (SHEFFIELD)
The file grinders always had their own separate organisation which at times became very powerful in the industry. The above Society would appear to have had a continuous existence from 1847, the early membership previously belonging to the **United File-smiths Society** which is said to have existed as a secret society in as early as 1784. In 1860 it had 240 members and in 1892, 318. By 1910 it had 195 members out of a total of 250 workers in the trade. It was claimed that the secret of its success lay in the Society's ready acceptance of the introduction of machinery into file grinding.

Average earnings just before the First World War were between 30s and 35s per week, and the work was heavy, dirty and exacting. The union was removed from the trade union register in 1973 at its own request.

Sources: BoT Reports; Lloyd; Certification Office.

FILE HARDENERS ASSOCIATION (SHEFFIELD)

Formerly members of the **United File-smiths Society,** the File Hardeners broke away in 1847 to form their own union, due to their dissatisfaction at an agreement reached by the File-smiths with the masters after a prolonged strike. The hardeners were forced to resume work on the same terms on which the strike had begun, whereas the remainder of the membership of the file-smiths' union had gained an increase in wages. The file hardeners' other dissatisfaction was the withdrawal of objection to the introduction of machinery on which they had strong feelings and which was the real basis of their strike. Before they separated from the file-smiths, the hardeners were usually superannuated file cutters, no hardener being admitted to the union unless he had first been a cutter. After the secession, cutters were excluded on account of friction between the branches. After the formation of the union, the members established a regular price list of piecework rates and were allowed to state their own working hours. Earnings averaged between 24s to 27s a week in 1913 when the union had about 110 members, some 50 per cent of the work force. The Association at first remained aloof from the **Sheffield Amalgamated Union of File Trades** when this was formed in 1915, but later joined in 1917.

Sources: Pollard; Lloyd; *Sheffield Independent,* February to October 1866.

FILESMITHS BENEFIT CLUB

See **Hand File Cutters Society (Sheffield)**

HAFT AND SCALE PRESSERS AND CUTTERS SOCIETY (SHEFFIELD)

This was formed in 1889 as a small sectional society. In 1896 it had 140 members and in 1910 it had 110 members. No information is available other than that it merged with the **National Amalgamated Union of Labour** (see Vol. 3) in 1916 and with that union's support was able to achieve a unified price list and a wage rise which it had found difficult to obtain when functioning as an independent body.

Sources: Lloyd; Pollard; BoT Reports.

HAND FILE CUTTERS SOCIETY (SHEFFIELD)

The Society organised by far the largest group of workers in the trade and was a direct descendant of the **Filesmiths Benefit Club** of 1784. It would seem that when the Benefit Club was reorganised in 1830 the File Cutters were established as a distinct branch on 25 April 1831. The objective was that of 'legally maintaining and supporting the price or value of labour of the members, who are journeymen file cutters residing in Sheffield and its vicinity, to be beneficial to secure to them and their families an adequate remuneration for their industrious and laborious effort and thereby greatly to ameliorate their condition in most respects.' The Society had an executive committee of 6 persons, 3 of whom were changed every 6 weeks. Weekly subscriptions were 6d for adult members and 2d for boys, and defaulting members were sued and prosecuted for the recovery of arrears. Strike pay was 7s per week per man, 2s 6d for apprentices, 2s for a wife and 1s 6d for each child. Until 1879 it was closely identified with the **United File-smiths Society,** but from that year on it became explicitly a purely file cutters' organisation. Up to 1890 membership was quite large but dwindled to 110 by 1910. In 1889 branches were set up in Manchester, Wolverhampton, Birmingham and Glasgow, but the Manchester membership broke away to set up their own **Manchester and District Hand File Cutters Society.** The competition of machine methods became too strong for the continued existence of the File Cutters as a separate organisation. In 1924 the remaining membership transferred engagements to the **Sheffield Amalgamated Union of File Trades.**

Sources: BoT Reports; Lloyd; Pollard; Certification Office.

HAND FILE FORGERS AND STRIKERS MUTUAL AID SOCIETY (SHEFFIELD)

The Society was formed in 1879. Its members were formerly members of the **United File-smiths Society** who, due to dissatisfaction at the conduct of their affairs within that society, seceded from it and formed their own organisation. The Forgers' price list dated back to 1873 when it was issued to register the improvement in prices which had then been secured, as compared with the previous price list of 1854 obtained whilst they were still members of the File-smiths. Machine forging of file blanks had been introduced before the File Forgers established a separate organisation and they had to fight a losing battle against the use of steam hammers. In the year of its formation the Society had 200 members, and in 1890 it was even stronger with 300 of the 400 men employed in the trade. In 1910 membership had fallen to 60 out of a workforce of 150, and thereafter the number gradually dwindled. Earnings in the trade were about 25s a week in 1913. It transferred its engagements to the **Sheffield Amalgamated Union of File Trades** in 1917.

Sources: BoT Reports; Lloyd; Pollard.

HANDLE AND SCALE CUTTERS ASSOCIATION (SHEFFIELD)

Formed in 1894, the Association had 74 members in 1897. By the early 1900s its membership had fallen to about 30. It continued in existence until about the end of 1908 when it is assumed to have been dissolved.

Source: BoT Reports.

JOBBING GRINDERS' PROVIDENT ASSOCIATION

The Association was founded in 1859. Although the work was mainly of a miscellaneous nature, job grinding was a distinct trade and at one time had a formal price list similar to those of other trades and included the making of such implements as reaping-knives, chaffcutters, and so on. The Association was disbanded in 1909, its membership having slowly dwindled from the 76 it claimed to have in 1890 to only 5 members.

Sources: Lloyd; BoT Reports.

LONDON CUTLERS AND SURGICAL INSTRUMENT MAKERS SOCIETY

Formed in 1883, the Society went out of existence in 1895.

Source: Certification Office.

LOUGHBOROUGH INDEPENDENT NEEDLE MAKERS' ASSOCIATION

The Association was established in 1857 and had a membership of 21 in 1897. It had a membership of 22 when it was dissolved in 1910.

Source: Bain and Price.

MACHINE FILE CUTTERS UNION (SHEFFIELD)

Established in 1893, the Union admitted women workers. In 1910, out of a total workforce of 500 workers, the membership was less than 100. It amalgamated in October 1915 to form the **Sheffield Amalgamated Union of File Trades.**

Source: Lloyd.

MACHINE FILE FORGERS UNION (SHEFFIELD)

Founded in 1897, the Union had a small membership of about 50 out of the 300 or more workers in the trade. It was not a job which called for the same dexterity and endurance as hand forging and was therefore not highly paid. It joined the **Sheffield Amalgamated Union of File Trades** when this was formed in October 1915.

Source: Lloyd.

MACHINE KNIFE AND BAYONET WORKERS' UNION

This was a small specialised union formed in 1896 with 68 members under the title of the **Bayonet Workers Trade Society,** the name being changed in 1898. It merged with the **National Amalgamated Union of Labour** (see Vol. 3) in 1916 and with the backing of that union was able to achieve a unified price list and a substantial wage increase.

Sources: BoT Reports; Pollard.

MANCHESTER AND DISTRICT HAND FILE CUTTERS SOCIETY

The Society was established in 1889 and had 15 members in 1896. It was set up in opposition to the **Hand File Cutters Society (Sheffield).** By 1910 the Manchester Society had 112 members and would seem to have been still functioning at the time of the First World War, after which time nothing further is known of its existence.

Sources: BoT Reports; Lloyd.

NATIONAL CUTLERY UNION

Formed in 1938 by an amalgamation of the **Amalgamated Scissors Workers Trade, Sick and Funeral Society** and the **Cutlery Union,** the Union transferred its engagements to the **General and Municipal Workers Union** (see Vol. 3) in 1957.

Sources: Barou; Certification Office.

NEEDLE STAMPERS AND FILERS UNION

Founded in 1872, the Union ceased to exist after 1874.

Source: Certification Office.

OPERATIVE MACHINE NEEDLE MAKERS PROTECTION SOCIETY

Registered in 1873, the Society was broken up in the same year.

Source: Certification Office.

OPERATIVE SOCIETY OF SPRING KNIFE CUTLERS

See **Sheffield Operative Spring Knife Cutlers' Union**

PEN AND POCKET BLADE FORGERS AND SMITHERS PROTECTION SOCIETY

This was a Sheffield-based craft union formed in 1872 which was still in existence in 1910 when it had 132 members, after which date no more is known of its history.

Source: BoT Reports.

PEN AND POCKET KNIFE CUTLERS ASSOCIATION

This would appear to have been an organisation which had its own Abstract of Articles of Agreement in 1831. Unfortunately no further information is available about its history.

Source: Pollard.

POCKET KNIFE ANCILLARY WORKERS' ASSOCIATION
This was an old-established sectional society formed in about 1840, which merged with the **National Amalgamated Union of Labour** (see Vol. 3) in 1916.

Source: Pollard.

PROVIDENT SOCIETY OF THE WORKBOARD HANDS OF THE SCISSORS TRADE
The Society was formed as early as 1817. There had been in existence an even earlier established body which had been dissolved some years before. The Society covered the branches of the trade carried on by the filers, borers and putters. On its inception it published a formal declaration in which was stated that 'having considered the sole cause of reduction in the price of labour has been due to disunity, the members of the scissors trade, constituting the three branches of borers, hardeners and filers, and finishers, have organised themselves into a Society which has for its great and lawful object the legally maintaining and supporting of the price list of 1817.' The official price list had been agreed in 1817, and although it remained in use it was not adhered to and was subject to regular reductions imposed by the masters. In 1831 the workers united in a 'Bond of Agreement made for the purpose of mutually benefiting their respective interests in the trade or occupation of scissor smiths.' Contributions were fixed at 1s and 6d per week for men and boys respectively. In 1867 the Society had 190 members out of a workforce of 230, but by 1890 this number had dwindled to 40 out of a workforce of about 200. By the First World War there were some 160 men and 50 women working in the trade but the union's membership was only 60, the trade having been severely curtailed by the advent of foreign, cheaply produced goods. The board hands (the assemblers) were among the worst paid workers in Sheffield. The Society merged with the **National Amalgamated Union of Labour** (see Vol. 3) in 1916, and with the support of that union were enabled to achieve a unified price list and a wage increase.

Sources: Lloyd (p. 310); Pollard; NAUL Annual Report, 1916.

RAZOR BLADE FORGERS TRADE SOCIETY (SHEFFIELD)
There was a trade society for razor forgers as early as 1810 but the Razor Blade Forgers Trade Society was established in 1848. In 1860 the Society had 100 members and in 1890 it had 140 members out of a workforce of 155 adults. By 1910 the membership had fallen to 54 and the trade was threatened by the substitution of drop-forged razor blades in place of the hand-hammered article. The unit of work was what was called 'day work', the number of blades in a work day varying from 18 to 60 according to the size and quality. Part of the trade was double handed in which case the forger provided tools and paid his striker a fixed proportion of the price received. The union struggled to remain in existence until 1925 when it was dissolved with a membership of 68. It may be that at the time of its dissolution the Society was known as the Razor Trade Forgers Protection Society.

Sources: Lloyd; BoT Reports.

RAZOR GRINDERS' PROTECTION SOCIETY

Founded in 1862, the Society had had several predecessors. Its price list dated from 1873 but was itself a revised edition of a list dating back to 1810. The number of adult men engaged in the trade increased from 96 in 1810 to 275 in 1842. The union's membership was 290 in 1865, 260 in 1890 and about 200 in 1910. In 1865, when the union was at the height of its power, there was a dispute over the refusal of a master to dismiss a non-union worker in which the forgers joined forces with the grinders. The masters also united and formed a central fund to support each other in times of strife, but they had to capitulate and pay a fine to the union as the condition precedent to the enrolling of the non-unionist worker to whose engagement the union had objected. Razor grinding was a highly skilled trade and the workers engaged in it earned high wages, but the advent of machine grinding techniques eventually destroyed the union. It had 310 members in 1910 and 200 ten years later. It was still in existence in 1913. It may have joined the **Amalgamated Society of the Razor Trades.**

Sources: G.C. Holland, *The Mortality, Sufferings and Diseases of Grinders,* 1842; Lloyd.

RAZOR HAFTERS TRADE PROTECTION SOCIETY

There was a form of organisation in existence in the trade in 1814, in which year a price list was issued which included the agreed charges for hafting, setting in, whetting, putting in shields, buffing silver rivets and the cutting and pressing of scales. The list also contained the provision that 'all dy'd and mock shall work 14 to the dozen' which indicated the early origin of this method of counting in this branch of the industry. The above Society seems to have been established in 1871 and reorganised in 1892, by which time there were 66 members out of a possible 200. There were still 66 members in 1910, after which date nothing further seems to be known of the union.

Sources: BoT Reports; Lloyd.

RAZOR SCALE PRESSERS PROTECTION SOCIETY (SHEFFIELD AND STANNINGTON)

This trade, becoming differentiated from the hafters during the first half of the nineteenth century, seems to have attained a separate organisation in about 1840. A revised and increased price list was issued in 1876 which suffered a reduction in 1884. The trade was a poor and vanishing one, carried on mainly by a few outworkers.

Source: Lloyd.

RAZOR TRADE FEDERATION
This association of grinders, forgers and hafters, established in 1891, represented an endeavour to bring about amalgamation among the small and inefficient sectional societies. It was hoped it would be the beginning of a new movement to try and terminate their separate existence but it did not attain any very great success in its endeavours.

Source: Lloyd.

RAZOR TRADE FORGERS PROTECTION SOCIETY
See **Razor Blade Forgers Trade Society (Sheffield)**

RAZOR TRADE FORGERS SOCIETY
See **Razor Blade Forgers Trade Society (Sheffield)**

REDDITCH FISH HOOK MAKERS TRADE PROTECTION SOCIETY
Founded in 1872, the Society went out of existence in 1893.

Source: Certification Office.

SAW GRINDERS TRADE PROTECTION SOCIETY
The Society was formed in 1819. Its Secretary was William Broadbent, who was involved in the infamous 'Sheffield Outrages' and who earned the union an evil reputation by the lengths to which he and other members carried the practice of intimidation and outrage. The only price list known relating to the union is dated 1859. The number of workers employed in the trade was always on a small scale; in 1830 the adult grinders numbered 80 and in 1843 they numbered 120. In 1860 there were 220 employed of whom 188 belonged to the union. After the trial of William Broadbent following the 'Sheffield Outrages', the Society found itself in serious difficulty and disrepute, and for about 5 years it amalgamated with the jobbing grinders, but re-established itself as an independent body in 1872. At that time machine grinding was rapidly replacing the hand process of working, having been introduced about 10 years previously. The Society refused to recognise grinders who worked machines only, as these men earned somewhat less than a man who was competent at both hand and machine work. In the days of hand grinding the union exercised an effective control over the labour supply and was able to demand a good living wage. It was said that 'workmen have earned 20s on a Saturday morning before breakfast', and 15s a day was not uncommon in busy times. But after the trade depression of the 1870s and 1880s, by 1890 there were only 55 grinders in the union out of the 120 men employed. In 1910 the number of workers in the industry numbered 150, of whom about half were union members. The Society remained in existence until 1934 when it was dissolved.

Sources: Pollard; Certification Office.

SAW HANDLE TRADES PROTECTION SOCIETY (SHEFFIELD)

The Society was founded in 1890 with 124 members, a previous organisation having been broken up after the 'Sheffield Outrages' of 1867. It was never a strong or important body and in former days derived its influence largely from the grinders. It had some 62 members in 1892, about half its previous strength, and was not able to issue a price list. In 1910 it had 61 members, after which date nothing further is known of the union.

Sources: BoT Reports; Pollard.

SAWMAKERS ASSOCIATION

See **Sheffield Sawmakers Protection Society**

SAW-SMITHS AND MAKERS TRADE PROTECTION SOCIETY

See **Sheffield Sawmakers Protection Society**

SCISSOR WORKBOARD HANDS SOCIETY

See **Provident Society of the Workboard Hands of the Scissors Trade**

SCISSORS FORGERS' TRADE UNION (SHEFFIELD)

By the end of the nineteenth century the hand forged scissors trade was becoming obsolete and the few workers who still lingered in the industry were not likely to be succeeded by a new generation of scissor forgers. The Union was set up in 1864 and by 1890 had 140 members. There had previously been several active societies in this branch of the trade and price lists had been established in 1819, 1844 and 1872, the latter representing an advance of 12 per cent over the 1844 list. A Scissorsmiths Benefit Society had been established as far back as 1791 and its efforts to raise the scale of payment led to criminal proceedings. Not more than 100 workers remained in the trade in the 1890s, most of the work being carried out at this time by steam driven presses. There was probably no more delicate or ingenious branch of the smith's art than the hand forging of the circular bows of a pair of scissors, yet the skill involved could not save this fine old hand trade once mass production had been introduced. The Union merged with the **National Amalgamated Union of Labour** (see Vol. 3) in 1916 and by so doing was able to achieve a unified price list and a substantial wage increase for its few remaining members.

Sources: Lloyd; Barou; Pollard.

SCISSORS GRINDERS TRADE, SICK AND FUNERAL SOCIETY

The scissors grinders' trade was one of the earliest to attain some effective organisation and the combination to maintain prices came as early as 1790, 5 scissor grinders being sent to prison in that year because they came out on strike in order to enforce a wage increase. In subsequent years there were many prosecutions by the masters for the same reason. Price lists were established in 1810, 1825, 1844 and 1873, that of 1825 achieving the highest level. These lists were never strictly adhered to, the standard rates in many cases being replaced by specific prices arranged by individual bargaining or established in a particular firm. Average payments ranged from 10 to 15 per cent below the price lists. The above Society was founded in 1860 when there were 250 men in the trade, of whom 230 became members. In 1890 the adult membership was 150 out of a total of 200 workers. About half the men were outworkers but all paid the 'wheel rent'. Few were datal workers except those engaged by the small master grinders. The Society was later called the **Amalgamated Scissors Workers Trade, Sick and Funeral Society.** In 1938 it amalgamated with the **Cutlery Union (Sheffield)** in order to form the **National Cutlery Union.**

Sources: Lloyd; Barou.

SCOTTISH ASSOCIATION OF PLANE MAKERS
Formed in 1903 with 36 members, the Association ceased to exist in 1907 when its membership was 26.

Source: Bain and Price.

SCYTHE GRINDERS UNION (SHEFFIELD)
Originally there were five separate societies in the scythe and sickle trade – the scythe makers, patent scythe makers, scythe grinders, sickle forgers and sickle grinders – each having its own organisation. In 1860 the scythe makers, patent scythe makers and scythe grinders all had a membership of about 50, while the sickle forgers had 200 members and the sickle grinders about 70. Although small they were very exclusive organisations. The Scythe Grinders Union was founded in 1862, and was one of the first trades to be in a position to abolish 'wheel rent'. Its first recorded membership is in 1910 when it had 44 members. In 1917, with 32 members, it merged with the **National Amalgamated Union of Labour** (see Vol. 3).

Source: Lloyd.

SCYTHE MAKERS' ASSOCIATION
This was one of the early specialised unions formed in the villages around Sheffield. In this case the workers were in small branches and had strong family connections, more formal organisation existing only among scythe grinders and sickle forgers. Nevertheless, by insisting upon strong discipline amongst the village groupings, they were able to command a fairly high rate of pay. There would appear to be no further information available as to the subsequent history of this association or others like it.

Sources: Pollard; Royal Commission on Trade Unions, 1867, Appendix D.

SHEEP SHEAR MAKERS, GRINDERS, FINISHERS AND BENDERS UNION (SHEFFIELD)

This was a union founded in 1904 with 75 members. It was a fellow union of the **Wool Shear Makers, Grinders, Finishers and Benders Society** which had been formed in 1890 and which was still in existence when the above Union was founded. It had 75 members in 1910. No further information would appear to be available as to the existence of the Sheep Shear Makers. It was in existence before the First World War, and may not have survived it.

Sources: Lloyd; BoT Reports.

SHEFFIELD AMALGAMATED UNION OF FILE TRADES

This Union was an amalgamation of small machine file societies in 1915. Two years later it was joined by the **Hand File Forgers and Strikers Mutual Aid Society** and by the **File Hardeners Association,** both traditional craft organisations, and in 1924 by the **Hand File Cutters Society (Sheffield).** It continued in existence until 1970 when it transferred its engagements to the **Transport and General Workers' Union** (Vol. 3). At that time it had about 600 members, half of them women.

Source: Crowther, TUC.

SHEFFIELD AND DISTRICT SPADE AND FORK TRADES AND DEATH SOCIETY

The Society had a very limited existence of 3 years, being established in 1892 and dissolved in 1895.

Source: Certification Office.

SHEFFIELD JOBBING GRINDERS SOCIETY

This was an outworkers' union formed in 1859. It had 100 members in 1906, but only 5 two years later and was dissolved in 1909.

Source: BoT Reports.

SHEFFIELD MECHANICAL TRADES ASSOCIATION

Formed in 1822, this was the earliest recorded federation of trades and combined 15 branches of the cutlery trades in the city of Sheffield. There was no formal permanent association of local societies until after 1850. It is true that delegates of the trades concerned met several times in order to discuss matters like the government's measures against trade unions and the effects of trade depressions, but the only firm result of these activities was the formation of a **United Trades Union** which was set up to defend existing wage levels but which ended its existence in 1847.

Sources: Lloyd; Pollard.

144

SHEFFIELD OPERATIVE SPRING KNIFE CUTLERS' UNION

The spring knife cutlers were considered to be some of the most highly skilled craftsmen. Their association dates back to 1796 under the title of the **Operative Society of Spring Knife Cutlers.** For some years they were a well organised body of men, showing a remarkable fighting spirit in the period of illegality of trade unions before the repeal of the Combination Acts, 1824–5. In later years it was to be described as a 'weak and poverty stricken Society' although it represented the largest single branch in any of the cutlery trades, the number of workers engaged therein being estimated at 1,800 of whom only 400 were organised. In its early existence the members had proposed a tax on earnings to form an unemployment fund and had urged all 'corporate trades' to form combinations of masters and men in order to fix prices, keep up standards of workmanship and enforce a 7 years' apprenticeship, but the rules were reconstituted in 1844 more on the lines of a trade union, the declared objects being to 'secure a fair remuneration for labour, to improve the conditions under which men work, and in every possible way to better the social and moral conditions of its members'. It was a trade in which outworkers were to be found in considerable numbers. Long and irregular hours were worked, and from 1844 to 1846 the Union engaged in numerous disputes to improve wages and conditions which cost the organisation nearly £3,000. By 1890 it had a membership of over 1,500 out of a total workforce of 2,200 men, but this number had fallen to 700 by 1892. In 1913 with 590 members, it amalgamated with the **Spring Knife Grinders and Finishers Union** in order to form the **Amalgamated Spring Knife Workers Association,** which organisation merged with the **National Amalgamated Union of Labour** (see Vol. 3) in 1914.

Sources: Lloyd; Pollard; BoT Reports; James Barber Turner, Address to the Operative Spring Knife Cutlers, Sheffield, 1873.

SHEFFIELD SAW GRINDERS TRADE PROTECTION SOCIETY

Formed in 1800, the Society had 72 members in 1910. The Society apparently went out of existence in 1934.

Source: Certification Office.

SHEFFIELD SAWMAKERS PROTECTION SOCIETY

There was a society named the **Saw-smiths and Makers Trade Protection Society** in existence with rules and regulations governing its membership as far back as 1797. The model which the Saw-smiths chose in drawing up their rules appears to be the same as that of the elite Cutlers' Company, a masters' organisation. They adopted the title of Master and Warden for their chief officers, imposed fines on members who refused to take office, and laid down regulations governing the admission of apprentices. This society later also provided unemployment and superannuation benefits for its members in the manner of a trade union. Price lists were issued in 1814, 1824 and 1844. A controversy took place in 1830 over a proposed reduction in the 1824 list as a consequence of trade depression, and it emerged that the average earnings over a year had been more than £2 per week, which made the Saw-smiths and Makers a fairly highly paid section of the workforce at that time. Whilst such amounts were being earned by them, cutlers in the trade working 14 and 16 hours a day could not secure more than 12s to 16s a week. In 1850 a **Sawmakers Association** was established at a time when there were 208 men and 130 boys working in the trade, nearly all of whom later became members of the Society. In 1860 when it was at the height of its influence the membership was 370. By 1910 this number was 290. The present Sawmakers Society was established in 1911 with a membership of 280, which reached 500 in 1951 but which has since declined to just over 200. It is affiliated to the TUC.

Sources: *Sheffield Iris,* 16 May 1844; Sheffield City Library Archives; BoT Reports; Lloyd; Pollard; Marsh, *Concise Encyclopedia.*

SHEFFIELD SAWMAKERS TRADE PROTECTION SOCIETY
Said to date from 1797, the Society still exists with a membership of 241. Rules date from 18 December 1797 but a document does exist which suggests that there seems to have been a 'Society of Sawmakers' functioning in 1740.

Source: Lloyd.

SHEFFIELD SCISSORS FORGERS' TRADE UNION
See **Scissors Forgers' Trade Union (Sheffield)**

SHEFFIELD SHEEP SHEAR MAKERS, GRINDERS, FINISHERS AND BENDERS UNION
See **Sheep Shear Makers, Grinders, Finishers and Benders Union (Sheffield)**

SHEFFIELD SPADE AND FORK TRADES AND DEATH SOCIETY
Established in 1892, this was a small sectional society which had an existence of only 3 years, being dissolved in 1895.

Source: Pollard.

SHEFFIELD TABLE BLADE FORGERS AND STRIKERS SOCIETY
The exact date of formation of the Society is not known, although it claimed to have been in existence at an early date in the nineteenth century. It had 281 members in 1898, the number declining to 174 by 1910, after which date nothing further is known of its existence.

Source: BoT Reports.

SHEFFIELD WOOL SHEAR WORKERS TRADE UNION
The Union was formed in 1890 as the Sheffield Wool Shear Grinders,

Makers, Finishers and Benders Union. Until 1889 the shear grinders were members of the **Amalgamated Edge Tool Trade, Protection and Death Society of Birmingham and District.** The logic of the new organisation arose because of a change in trade practice whereby machinery was increasingly being used for flying out a blade of solid steel rather than using the old method of welding a steel edge to an iron blade. It adopted its present title in 1914 after being known successively as the Wool Shear Grinders and Benders Society (Sheffield) (1912) and the **Wool Shear Makers, Grinders, Finishers and Benders Society (Sheffield)** (1913). Its membership has rarely exceeded 100. In 1980 it was 32.

Sources: Certification Office; the Union; BoT Reports; Lloyd.

SICKLE FORGERS TRADE SOCIETY
Formed early in the 1840s, the Society had 200 members in 1860. The scythe, sickle and related trades were mainly carried on in the villages south of Sheffield, and although workers engaged therein were small in number, the union represented a strong exclusive organisation for that period. Nothing further is known of the Society.

Sources: Lloyd; Pollard; Royal Commission on Trade Unions, 1867, Appendix D.

SICKLE GRINDERS ASSOCIATION
The sickle grinders had their own organisation in the 1840s. The Association had 70 members in 1860 and although small in number, it represented a strong and exclusive body of men who were able to command a fairly high rate of pay. There would appear to be no further information on the subsequent history of the union.

Source: Pollard.

SOCIETY OF FORGEMEN, BLACKSMITHS, FORK DRAWERS AND MAKERS, AND SPADE FINISHERS (STOURBRIDGE)
Established in 1899 with 104 members, the Society lasted for ten years. It was dissolved in 1909 when it had only 27 remaining members.

Sources: Bain and Price; BoT Reports; Certification Office.

SPADE AND SHOVEL MAKERS TRADE SOCIETY
This was a small society formed in the 1890s which struggled to maintain an independent existence until 1916 when it merged with the **National Amalgamated Union of Labour** (see Vol. 3) and with the backing of that union was able to obtain a unified price list and a wage increase.

Sources: NAUL Report, April 1916; Pollard.

SPRING KNIFE GRINDERS AND FINISHERS UNION (SHEFFIELD)

This Union dated from 1867. In 1892 it had 600 members. In 1913, with a membership of 220, it amalgamated with the **Sheffield Operative Spring Knife Cutlers' Union** to form the **Amalgamated Spring Knife Workers Association** which afterwards merged with the **National Amalgamated Union of Labour** (see Vol. 3) in 1914.

Sources: Pollard; BoT Reports.

SPRING KNIFE TRADE FEDERATION

An attempt was made in 1843 to bring about a federation of the trade societies concerned in the production of pocket cutlery, namely the pen and pocket blade forgers, the pen and pocket blade grinders, and the spring knife cutlers. Although the Federation had some small success in its initial stages, it soon went out of existence.

Source: Lloyd.

STEEL FORK GRINDERS ASSOCIATION

The steel fork trade was dominated by 'little masters' and was subject very much to competition from the manufacturers of silver plated forks. The Association was formally established in 1889 but could well have been in existence at an earlier date. Nothing more is known of its existence after 1894, when it had 86 members.

Sources: Pollard; BoT Reports.

STEEL FORK MAKERS ASSOCIATION

The Association is formally recorded as having been formed in 1889, but could well have been in existence at a much earlier date. It had 100 members in 1892, after which date no further information is available, its existence having been put into jeopardy by the manufacturers of silver plated forks.

Sources: Pollard; BoT Reports.

TABLE AND BUTCHER BLADE SMITHERS ASSOCIATION (SHEFFIELD)

This was one of the small specialist unions in existence in the early part of the nineteenth century in Sheffield. In 1915 it amalgamated with the **Table and Butcher Knife Hafters Trade and Provident Society** in order to form the **Cutlery Union (Sheffield).**

Source: Pollard.

TABLE AND BUTCHER KNIFE HAFTERS TRADE AND PROVIDENT SOCIETY

Formed in 1900 with 524 members, the Society continued in existence until 1915 when, with 900 members, it amalgamated with the **Table and Butcher**

Blade Smithers Association (Sheffield) in order to form the **Cutlery Union (Sheffield)**.

Source: BoT Reports.

TABLE AND BUTCHERS' BLADE GRINDERS' ASSOCIATION (SHEF-FIELD)

The Association was formed in 1890 and had 600 members in 1892. By 1904 the membership had dwindled to 40 and it seemed to have gone out of existence. In 1907 the Association was reorganised and emerged with 224 members, this figure growing slowly but surely until in 1914, with 850 members, it merged with the **National Amalgamated Union of Labour** (see Vol. 3).

Sources: BoT Reports; Pollard.

UNITED FILE-SMITHS SOCIETY

The workers in the file trades were organised even in the eighteenth century, the above organisation being established as a benefit society in 1784. Their activities from 1810 to 1820 involved them in a number of prosecutions under the Combination Laws. In 1843 the file trade employed 2,620 persons, including 700 boys and 100 women. Among the adult workers were included 520 forgers and strikers, 900 cutters, 190 hardeners and 210 grinders, all covered by the United Society. Unlike the other trade societies in Sheffield, the file-smiths succeeded in maintaining their prices during the trade depression of the 1840s, and obtained an advance in 1853 which established the union on such a scale that for many years it was the largest, most prosperous and best managed union in Sheffield. It had 17 District Committees, 11 in Sheffield and 6 in adjacent villages, a branch in Manchester with 100 members and one at Newburn, near Newcastle, with 25 members. In 1857 there were no unemployed on the books, and cash reserves amounted to £5,000. At the head office there was a private room for meetings and an office where any unemployed men attended to answer roll-call. In 1853 their trade funds were so abundant they returned a bonus to their members, and did so again in 1854 when each man received 20s and boys received 6s. In 1856, 6,000 workers were employed in the trade, 3,500 being union members, but at the end of the 1860s there was a 4-month strike against the introduction of machinery. The dispute ended in some sections being granted small advances in wages, and the opposition to the use of machinery was withdrawn. In dissatisfaction at this outcome the hardeners and cutters broke away from the union and formed their own organisations, which considerably weakened the United File-smiths.

Sources: Select Committee on Artisans and Machinery, 1824; *Sheffield Independent,* May 1849; J.C. Hall, *The Trades of Sheffield,* 1865; *Sheffield Independent,* February 1854; *ibid,* February to October 1866; Pollard; Lloyd.

UNITED OPERATIVE PLANE MAKERS TRADE SOCIETY
See **Birmingham, Bristol and Sheffield Plane Makers' Association**

UNITED TRADES UNION
The Union was formed in the aftermath of the setting up of the **Sheffield Mechanical Trades Association** which met mainly to discuss matters like the government's measures against trade unions and the effect of trade depressions, the Union being established principally to defend existing wage levels. Its existence was brief, lasting only one or two years, and it ceased to exist in 1847.

Sources:　Lloyd; Pollard.

WARRINGTON ASSOCIATION OF FILE SMITHS
Established in 1871 and having 200 members in 1892, the Association was dissolved in 1903 when the membership numbered 60.

Source:　Bain and Price.

WOOL SHEAR MAKERS, GRINDERS, FINISHERS AND BENDERS SOCIETY (SHEFFIELD)
See **Sheffield Wool Shear Workers Trade Union**

Goldsmiths, Silversmiths and Watchmakers

At the turn of the last century the Board of Trade was able to identify about 20 unions in the gold, silver and watchmaking trades. Half of these were in London; 7 were related to the cutlery trade in Sheffield; 3 were in Birmingham. Only one union appeared to have a direct link with the eighteenth century – the Gold Beaters Trade Society, which claimed to have been founded in 1777. Seven unions, according to such records as are available, were established between 1847 and 1875; the remainder were creations of the previous 25 years.

By the end of the 1960s, representation in these trades had been reduced to 3 unions only; the London Jewel Case and Jewellery Display Makers Union (founded in 1894), the National Union of Gold, Silver and Allied Trades, and the Society of Goldsmiths, Jewellers and Kindred Trades (1893). Of these only the first continues to exist in 1983, with 24 members. The Goldsmiths and Jewellers were absorbed into the National Union in 1969, and the National Union itself into the Amalgamated Union of Engineering Workers, Technical, Administrative and Supervisory Section, in October 1981.

This latter development therefore brought substantially to an end the existence of separate trade union representation in the gold, silver and jewellery trades which was first consolidated in a centralised form by the amalgamation which produced the National (then the Amalgamated) Union in 1911.

AMALGAMATED SOCIETY OF GOLD, SILVER AND KINDRED TRADES
See **National Union of Gold, Silver and Allied Trades**

BIRMINGHAM JEWELLERY, SILVER, ELECTROPLATE AND ALLIED TRADE UNION
The origin of this union is obscure. Perhaps it was a breakaway from the **Birmingham Silversmiths and Electroplate Operatives Society** which objected to the 1914 amalgamation. There is no sign of its existence before the First World War, but it was extant in 1918. It was dissolved in August 1922.

Sources: MoL Reports; Certification Office.

BIRMINGHAM SILVERSMITHS AND ELECTROPLATE OPERATIVES SOCIETY
This was a local sectional society which amalgamated with the **Amalgamated Society of Gold, Silver and Kindred Trades** in 1911. The date of the formation of the Society is not known.

Source: BoT Reports.

BIRMINGHAM SOCIETY OF OPERATIVE GOLDSMITHS, JEWELLERS AND SILVERSMITHS
The Society was formed in 1872 and had 196 members 20 years later and 115 at the end of the century. It was dissolved in November 1901.

Sources: BoT Reports; Certification Office.

BRITANNIA ASSOCIATION OF METAL WORKERS (BIRMINGHAM)
The Association was established in 1890 and had 70 members in 1892. It struggled on in existence until 1913 when, with a membership of only 43, it was dissolved in June of that year.

Source: BoT Reports.

BRITANNIA-METAL SMITHS SOCIETY (SHEFFIELD)
Formed in 1882, the Society was a sectional body which considered it necessary to regulate entry into the trade, to maintain extensive friendly benefits, to force employers to recruit labour only through the union and support a closed shop, as well as opposing the use of machinery. It was successful in these aims until the introduction of new techniques of mass production destroyed the monopoly of local skills. Until 1890 apprenticeship to the trade was limited to members' sons only and the union insisted on formal indentures. It enjoyed a new lease of life in the 1880s under the leadership of Charles Hobson who took a leading role in the founding of the

Metal Workers Federation in 1904. He became editor of its monthly journal *The Metal Worker*. In 1911 fifteen independent societies (7 in Sheffield, 6 in London and 2 in Birmingham), including the Britannia-Metal Smiths Society, amalgamated to form the **Amalgamated Society of Gold, Silver and Kindred Trades**.

Sources: Pollard; S. and B. Webb, *Industrial Democracy*; *The Metal Worker*, March 1908, May 1909; *Sheffield Independent*, 11 February 1911.

BRITISH DIAMOND WORKERS TRADE UNION
See **London Diamond Workers Trade Union**

COVENTRY WATCH CASE ENGINE TURNERS ASSOCIATION
The Association had a very limited life. It was set up in 1890 and had 12 members in 1892. It ceased to exist in 1895.

Source: Certification Office.

GOLD BEATERS TRADE SOCIETY
The Society was said to date from 1777. It had three branches and 145 members at the end of the nineteenth century but only 46 members ten years later. It was organised from London and was in existence in 1925. Its subsequent history is not known.

Source: BoT Reports.

GOLDSMITHS AND JEWELLERS TRADE ASSOCIATION
Founded in 1874, the London-based Association went out of existence in 1893.

Source: Certification Office.

HEBREW JEWELLERS SOCIETY
Formed in 1897 with 34 members, the Society ceased to exist in 1901 when its membership was 31.

Source: BoT Reports.

INTERNATIONAL WATCH AND CLOCKMAKERS UNION (LONDON)
Formed in 1910 with 35 members, the Union ceased to exist in 1912.

Source: Certification Office.

LIVERPOOL WATCH CASE MAKERS TRADE SOCIETY
Established in 1880, the Society was dissolved in 1890.

Source: Certification Office.

LONDON AMALGAMATED SOCIETY OF CHASERS AND ENGRAVERS
Established in 1891, the Society was dissolved in 1898.

Source: Certification Office.

LONDON DIAMOND WORKERS TRADE UNION
The Union was set up in 1895 with 76 members but seemed to have gone out of existence by 1900 when the membership stood at 44. In 1906 it appears to have been reconstituted with 30 members, and a record of it continues until 1925 when, with 24 members, it finally was dissolved. During the whole of its existence the Union had one female member.

Sources: BoT Reports; Certification Office.

LONDON GENERAL ENGRAVERS AND CARVERS ASSOCIATION
The Association was established in 1906 with a membership of 85 and ceased to exist in 1909 when its membership was 32.

Source: BoT Reports.

LONDON JEWEL CASE AND JEWELLERY DISPLAY MAKERS UNION
The Union was established in 1894 as the **London Jewel Case Makers Trade Protection Society**. In 1977 it had 18 members, making it probably the smallest union in existence in Britain. It recruits only craftsmen in a few firms in the London area. Its highest peak of membership was 72 members in 1949. It is affiliated to the **General Federation of Trade Unions** (Vol. 3) and had 24 members in 1982.

Sources: Certification Office; Marsh, *Concise Encyclopedia*.

LONDON JEWEL CASE MAKERS TRADE PROTECTION SOCIETY
See **London Jewel Case and Jewellery Display Makers Union**

LONDON SILVER PLATE POLISHERS SOCIETY
The Society was established in 1895. Registration was cancelled by request in 1911 when the Society came together with others in the trade to form the

Amalgamated Society of Gold, Silver and Kindred Trades. It had 75 members at that time.

Source: Certification Office.

LONDON SILVER PLATE WORKERS SOCIETY

A single branch union formed in 1885. Twelve years later it reached its maximum membership of 110; it joined the **Amalgamated Society of Gold, Silver and Kindred Trades** in 1911.

Source: BoT Reports.

LONDON SILVER WORKERS SOCIETY

A single branch union established in 1890 as the **London Society of Small Silver Workers** with about 90 members. It reached its peak with a membership of 200 in 1907, and thereafter declined in numbers. It had 73 members when it joined the **Amalgamated Society of Gold, Silver and Kindred Trades** in 1911.

Source: BoT Reports.

LONDON SOCIETY OF GOLD, SILVER AND KINDRED TRADES

See **London Society of Goldsmiths and Jewellers**

LONDON SOCIETY OF GOLDSMITHS AND JEWELLERS

Formed in 1893, the Society changed its name to the **London Society of Gold, Silver and Kindred Trades**. It was dissolved in 1953.

Source: Certification Office.

LONDON SOCIETY OF SILVER PLATE WORKERS

Formed in 1885, the Society had 97 members in 1900. It had about the same number in 1911 when it came together with other associations in the trade to form the **Amalgamated Society of Gold, Silver and Kindred Trades**.

Source: BoT Reports.

LONDON SOCIETY OF SILVER SPOON, FORK FINISHERS AND FILERS

Established in 1874, the Society had 27 members in 1892. By 1912 membership had dwindled to 16 and the organisation was dissolved.

Source: Modern Records Centre, University of Warwick.

LONDON SOCIETY OF SMALL SILVER WORKERS
See **London Silver Workers Society**

NATIONAL AMALGAMATED SOCIETY OF WATCH MAKERS, JEWELLERS AND KINDRED TRADES
Founded in 1894, the Society went out of existence in 1896.

Source: Certification Office.

NATIONAL UNION OF GOLD, SILVER AND ALLIED TRADES
The Union was formed in 1911 as the **Amalgamated Society of Gold, Silver and Kindred Trades** which brought together 15 independent trade societies, 7 of them based on Sheffield, 6 on London and 2 on Birmingham. The present title was adopted in 1914 on amalgamation with the **Birmingham Silversmiths and Electroplate Operatives Society**. The principal societies concerned in the original amalgamation were the **Sheffield Silversmiths Society**, the **Sheffield Hollow-ware Stampers Society**, the **Sheffield Silver and Electroplate Finishers Society**, the **Britannia-Metal Smiths Society (Sheffield)**, the **London Silver Plate Workers Society**, the **London Silver Plate Polishers Society**, the **Sheffield Silver Platers and Gilders Society**, the **Spoon and Fork Filers, Odd Workers and Stampers Society (Sheffield)**, the **Sheffield Hollow-ware Buffers Society** and the **London Silver Workers Society**. In 1969 the Union absorbed the **Society of Goldsmiths, Jewellers and Kindred Trades**. Its membership was about 1,600 when in October 1981 it was merged into the Technical, Administrative and Supervisory Section of the Amalgamated Union of Engineering Workers (see **Association of Engineering and Shipbuilding Draughtsmen** (Vol. 1)).

Sources: Certification Office; Marsh, *Concise Encyclopedia*.

PRESCOT WATCH MAKERS ASSOCIATION
Established in 1889, the Association ceased to exist after 1892.

Source: Certification Office.

SCOTTISH WATCHMAKERS, JEWELLERS AND ALLIED WORKERS UNION
No information has been found on this union except that it was dissolved in August 1923.

Source: Certification Office.

SHEFFIELD HOLLOW-WARE BUFFERS SOCIETY
Formed in 1889 as a single branch organisation, the Society had 110 members in 1910. It had 73 when it joined with other unions in 1911 to form the **Amalgamated Society of Gold, Silver and Kindred Trades**.

Source: BoT Reports.

SHEFFIELD HOLLOW-WARE STAMPERS SOCIETY
The date of commencement of this society is not known, but in 1897 two members were said to have been in membership for over 40 years. The union had 67 members in 1910 and in the following year joined with others to form the **Amalgamated Society of Gold, Silver and Kindred Trades**.

Source: BoT Reports.

SHEFFIELD SILVER AND ELECTROPLATE FINISHERS SOCIETY
Formed in 1873, the Society had 137 members in 1900 and 127 when it merged with others to form the **Amalgamated Society of Gold, Silver and Kindred Trades** in 1911.

Source: BoT Reports.

SHEFFIELD SILVER PLATERS AND GILDERS SOCIETY
Formed in 1896 in a single branch, the Society never had more than 50 members. It joined with other small unions in the trade in 1911 to form the **Amalgamated Society of Gold, Silver and Kindred Trades**.

Source: BoT Reports.

SHEFFIELD SILVERSMITHS SOCIETY
Founded in 1847, the Society came together with others in 1911 to form the **Amalgamated Society of Gold, Silver and Kindred Trades**. It had 555 members at that time.

Source: BoT Reports.

SILVER SPOON AND FORK MAKERS SOCIETY (LONDON)
Formed in 1874, the Society had 24 members in 1900 and 23 in 1910, after which date nothing further is known of its existence.

Source: BoT Reports.

SILVERSMITHS AND ELECTRO-PLATE OPERATIVES MUTUAL AID AND PROTECTION SOCIETY
Dating from 1883, the Society seems to have been a development from a society originally formed in 1872. It was one of the largest of its type in silver and electro-plate with over 900 members. It merged with the **National Union of Gold, Silver and Allied Trades** in 1914.

Source: Certification Office.

SOCIETY OF GOLDSMITHS, JEWELLERS AND KINDRED TRADES
This was a Society deriving from the **London Society of Goldsmiths and Jewellers,** formed in 1893, which had some 630 members in 1910. It transferred its engagements to the **National Union of Gold, Silver and Allied Trades** in July 1969.

Sources: BoT Reports; Marsh, *Concise Encyclopedia.*

SPOON AND FORK FILERS, ODD WORKERS AND STAMPERS SOCIETY (SHEFFIELD)
Formed in 1889, the Society had 64 members when it joined with other small organisations to form the **Amalgamated Society of Gold, Silver and Kindred Trades** in 1911.

Source: BoT Reports.

TOILET LOOKING GLASS FRAME MAKERS, FITTERS AND SIL-VERERS TRADE PROTECTION SOCIETY
Established in 1874, the Society went out of existence in 1895.

Source: Certification Office.

UNION OF BRASS WORKERS
See **Union of Watchmakers, Clock and Casemakers and Brass Workers in General**

UNION OF WATCH, CLOCK AND CLOCK CASE MAKERS
The Union was formed in 1892 with 73 members but had been dissolved by 1895.

Source: BoT Reports.

UNION OF WATCHMAKERS, CLOCK AND CASEMAKERS AND BRASS WORKERS IN GENERAL
The Union was formed in 1892 as the **Union of Brass Workers**, the full title being adopted in 1894 in order to enlarge the scope of recruitment. Registration of the Union was cancelled in 1898.

Source: Certification Office.

UNITED WATCH MAKERS TRADE ASSOCIATION (LIVERPOOL)
Formed in 1873, the Association ceased to exist after 1895.

Source: Certification Office.

WATCHSMITHS FRIENDLY BENEFIT SOCIETY (LONDON)
Formed in 1897 with 30 members, the Society lasted for one year only and was dissolved in 1898.

Source: BoT Reports.

Lock, Chain, Spring, Nail, Bolt, Nut, Screw, Bedstead, Fender and Wire

A common factor among unions associated with locks, chains, springs, nails, nuts, screws, bedsteads and fenders has been one of location. Almost all these trades have been most highly developed in the area of the Black Country and in Birmingham. All have been extremely vulnerable to changes of technology and, to a lesser extent, of fashion. Few unions have survived. As 'sectional societies' only the National Union of Lock and Metal Workers (and its associated Spring Trap Makers), the Screw, Nut, Bolt and Rivet Trade Society and the Walsall Lock and Key Smiths Male and Female Trade Society now remain.

Wire drawing and weaving organisations have suffered the same fate, although the trade has been more evenly distributed over the kingdom in London, Manchester, Sheffield and Birmingham, to name but a few locations. By 1910 developments had effectively reduced their number to three. The largest of these was the Amalgamated Society of Wire Drawers of Great Britain (1890), with 2,678 members. Two smaller organisations catered for specific parts of the trade, the Federal Union of Wire Weavers of the United Kingdom (1872) with 173 members and the Federal Union of Wire Workers of Great Britain and Ireland (1901) with 118 members. Neither of the latter organisations survived the 1920s, leaving only the presently extant Amalgamated Society of Wire Drawers and Kindred Trades as successor to the 1890 Federation which later produced the Amalgamated Society of Wire Drawers.

ABBOTS UNITED CHAIN MAKERS AND CHAIN STRIKERS ASSOCIATION

A Gateshead Association formed in 1882. It had a membership of 73 in 1892. In 1905, with a membership of 72, it merged with the **United Chain Makers and Strikers Union**.

Sources: BoT Reports; Certification Office.

AMALGAMATED HAME AND CLIP ASSOCIATION

See **National Amalgamated Harness and Saddlery Furniture Trades and Metal Workers Association**

AMALGAMATED SOCIETY OF ANVIL AND VICE MAKERS

Established in 1885 at Dudley in Worcestershire as the **National Association of Anvil Makers**, the union had a membership of 100 in 1892 and 300 in 1910. It continued in existence until 1949 when it ceased to function, its membership having fallen to 25.

Sources: BoT Reports; Certification Office.

AMALGAMATED SOCIETY OF BIT AND STIRRUP WORKERS (WALSALL)

Formed in 1900 with 280 members, the Society was shortlived, being dissolved in 1905 with only 80 members remaining.

Source: Certification Office.

AMALGAMATED SOCIETY OF HARNESS MAKERS, BRIDLE CUTTERS, FANCY LEATHER WORKERS AND MILITARY EQUIPMENT MAKERS

See **National Amalgamated Harness and Saddlery Furniture Trades and Metal Workers Association**

AMALGAMATED SOCIETY OF SCREW MAKERS

Formed in 1895 with 101 members, the Society was dissolved in 1899, the membership having dwindled to 35.

Source: BoT Reports.

AMALGAMATED SOCIETY OF WIRE DRAWERS OF GREAT BRITAIN

See **Amalgamated Society of Wire Drawers and Kindred Trades**

AMALGAMATED SOCIETY OF WIRE DRAWERS AND KINDRED TRADES

The Society dates its history from 1840 when three of the unions which later came together first in the **Federated Wire Drawers Association** as independent organisations and later into amalgamation in the **Amalgamated Society of Wire Drawers of Great Britain** were founded. These were the **Birmingham Wire Drawers Society**, the **Halifax (No. 1) Thick Wire Drawers Society** and the **Manchester Wire Drawers Society**. The Society records that the initial object of these organisations was to organise craft-apprentice trained wire drawers. To these original affiliates others were added by 1901, the **Sheffield Wire Drawers Society**, the **Ambergate Wire Drawers Society**, the **Warrington Wire Drawers Society** and the **Middlesborough Wire Drawers Society** in addition to a Halifax (No. 2) union. The Federation had a membership of 1,808 in 1900 and the Amalgamated Society a membership of 2,678 in 1910, that title being changed to the current one in 1904. The union was federated to the **Iron and Steel Trades Confederation** from February 1921 to March 1924 when federation ceased as a result of differences between the two organisations. The union is based on Sheffield, and now has about 8,000 members, and claims to be the only union still in existence in the world catering for wire drawers.

Sources: Marsh, *Concise Encyclopedia*; Marsh, *Trade Union Handbook*; BoT Reports; Pollard; Certification Office; Annual Reports of Amalgamated Society of Wire Drawers.

AMALGAMATED TUBE TRADE SOCIETY

Two dates are given in the Board of Trade Reports for the formation of the Society: the first date is 1876 and the second 1886. The membership in 1892 was 700, rising to 900 in 1896 and to 920 in 1899. By 1903 it was registering 400 members, falling to 100 in 1906 and dwindling to 60 by 1910. It remained a functioning body until the end of the First World War and in 1921, with 929 members, it joined the **British Iron, Steel and Kindred Trades Association.**

Sources: BoT Reports; MoL Reports; Bain and Price.

AMBERGATE WIRE DRAWERS SOCIETY

A Society founded in 1890, when it became affiliated to the **Federated Wire Drawers Association** as an independent organisation. It lost this status when that Association became a full amalgamation. It had 106 members in 1896.

Source: BoT Reports.

ASSOCIATION OF WOMEN WORKERS IN THE BEDSTEAD TRADE

Formed in 1890 with a membership in 1892 of 600, the Association was dissolved in 1901 when the number of members totalled 650.

Source: BoT Reports.

BEDSTEAD ALLIANCE
See **Bedstead Workmens Association**

BEDSTEAD WORKMENS ASSOCIATION
In 1889 the largest strike hitherto recorded in the city of Birmingham led to the formation of the Association. The 10-day strike of 4,000 men for a 15 per cent wage increase was settled by an arbitration award giving an immediate rise of 10 per cent with a further 5 per cent to follow in March 1890. The making of metal bedsteads was a highly competitive trade and an employer, E.J.Smith, evolved a scheme for a close alliance between the union and the associated manufacturers, members of the union agreeing to work only for members of the employers association. In return the union enjoyed the advantages of a closed shop and equal representation on a wages board. Wage rates were linked with prices and a bonus was paid for every increase secured by the cartel. The cartel was called the **Bedstead Alliance.** The Association had 7 branches by 1899 and over 2,500 members. By the late 1950s its membership was about 200 and it was dissolved in 1961.

Sources: Clegg, Fox and Thompson; Report on Strikes and Lockouts of 1889, C-6176, 1890, pp. 130-1.

BIRMINGHAM AMALGAMATED FIRE IRON SOCIETY
The Society was formed in 1900 with 80 members and continued until 1917 when, with 50 members, it ceased to exist.

Source: Bain and Price.

BIRMINGHAM AND DISTRICT FENDER AND FIRE BRASSES MAKERS ASSOCIATION
The Association was set up in 1879. By 1892 it had 156 members, and 216 in 1900, but ceased to exist in 1904 when the membership had dwindled to 60.

Source: BoT Reports.

BIRMINGHAM AND DISTRICT OPERATIVE ZINC WORKERS SOCIETY
The Society was formed in 1898 with 85 members, thereafter the number gradually dwindling until with only 16 members remaining it was dissolved in 1908.

Source: BoT Reports.

BIRMINGHAM ASSOCIATION OF WIRE WEAVERS
The Association dated from 1862. It had 40 members in 1892, and 25 members in 1899. There appears to be no further information available after this date.

Source: Bain and Price.

BIRMINGHAM WIRE DRAWERS SOCIETY

A Society founded in 1840 and having 200 members in 1896; it became affiliated to the **Federated Wire Drawers Association** (1890) as an independent organisation, but lost this status when the Federated Association became a full amalgamation.

Source: BoT Reports.

BOLT, NUT AND RIVET MAKERS ASSOCIATION OF SCOTLAND

Formed in 1890 and having a membership of 256 in 1892, the Association was dissolved in 1896, the number of members having fallen to 130.

Source: Bain and Price.

BROMSGROVE AMALGAMATED UNION OF WROUGHT NAIL MAKERS

The Union was formed in 1892 with 1,236 members but was dissolved in 1895 with only 45 members.

Source: Bain and Price.

BROMSGROVE NAIL FORGERS PROTECTION ASSOCIATION

Established in 1872, the Association ceased to exist after 1879.

Source: Certification Office.

CHAIN MAKERS AND STRIKERS ASSOCIATION

The Association was formed in 1889 as the **United Chain Makers and Chain Strikers Association of Saltney, Pontypridd and Staffordshire.** Towards the end of the century it was organising factories in all these locations, and it quickly became the largest and most influential union in chain making with about 1,000 members in 1900 and 1,250 in 1910. During the first few years of the twentieth century it changed its name to the Chain Makers and Strikers Association, possibly on amalgamation with other Cradley Heath unions, including the **Cradley Heath and District Chain Makers Association**.

Source: BoT Reports.

CHAIN MAKERS PROVIDENTIAL ASSOCIATION

Formed in 1880, the Association was dissolved in 1893.

Source: BoT Reports.

CITY OF NORWICH UNITED WIRE NETTING WEAVERS UNION
Established in 1890, the Union merged with the **Norfolk and Norwich Amalgamated Labour Union** in 1893.

Source: Certification Office.

CRADLEY HEATH AND DISTRICT CHAIN MAKERS ASSOCIATION
The Union was formed in 1892 and had 300 members in 1900. Registration was cancelled in 1905 when it merged with the **Chain Makers and Strikers Association.**

Sources: BoT Reports; Certification Office.

CRADLEY HEATH ASSOCIATION OF WOMEN WORKING IN THE CHAIN, NAIL AND SPIKE MAKING TRADES
The Association was formed in 1903 with 400 members, which had dwindled to 100 by 1904 when it ceased to exist.

Source: Bain and Price.

CROWN TUBE WORKS FITTING SHOP TRADES SOCIETY
The Society was established in 1901, but had ceased to exist by 1903.

Source: Certification Office.

DOWNALL GREEN AND ASHTON IN MAKEFIELD HINGE MAKERS ASSOCIATION
The Association was formed in 1889; it had 100 members in 1892 and 64 in 1900. It was disolved in 1905 when its membership was only 52.

Source: BoT Reports.

DUDLEY AND DISTRICT ASSOCIATION OF FENDER OPERATIVES
First established in 1863, the Association had almost 500 members in 1900. It was dissolved in 1904.

Source: BoT Reports.

DUDLEY RANGE KNOB MAKERS ASSOCIATION
Formed in 1900 with 80 members, the Association ceased to exist in 1909 when it had 50 members.

Source: BoT Reports.

FEDERAL UNION OF WIRE WEAVERS OF THE UNITED KINGDOM
See **National Society of Wire Weavers of Great Britain**

FEDERAL UNION OF WIRE WORKERS OF GREAT BRITAIN AND IRELAND

The Union came into existence in 1901 and was registered in 1903 by the amalgamation of three local sectional societies, the **London Society of Wire Workers**, the **Manchester and District Wire Workers Society** and the **Scottish Wire Workers Society (Glasgow)**. It had 118 members in 1910. Registration was cancelled in 1927.

Sources: BoT Reports; Certification Office.

FEDERATED WIRE DRAWERS ASSOCIATION

See **Amalgamated Society of Wire Drawers and Kindred Trades**

FENDER UNION (SHEFFIELD)

Formed in the 1820s, the Union attempted to limit hours and regulate piece rates and sometimes employed violent methods such as setting fire to the works of an obstinate employer. Its history is obscure.

Source: Pollard.

FINISHERS SOCIETY

Established in 1896, this was a small union catering for finishers employed at the Wednesbury Crown Tube Works. It had 23 members upon formation and J. Martin of Dale Street Terrace was the secretary. The membership had fallen to 17 in 1897 and it was dissolved in 1898.

Source: BoT Reports.

FITTING SHOP TRADE SOCIETY

Formed in 1892, this was one of the unions catering for this section of workers employed at the Wednesbury Crown Tube Works. It had 89 members upon its formation in 1892, 68 in 1896 and 62 in 1899, rising to 103 in 1901, after which date nothing further seems to be known of its existence.

Source: BoT Reports.

FROST, COG AND SCREWMAKERS SOCIETY

Formed in 1906, the Society catered for the making of frost nails (as a protection against horses slipping in frosty weather) as well as the making of cogs and screws. It had a consistent membership of 80 to 90 until it amalgamated with the **Gas Workers, Brick Makers and General Labourers Union** (see Vol. 3) in 1911.

Source: BoT Reports.

HALESOWEN NAILMAKERS SOCIETY
A local society of nailmakers which existed briefly between 1892 and 1894. Since it had 400 members it seems likely that these transferred to some other organisation.

Source: BoT Reports.

HALIFAX (NO. 1) THICK WIRE DRAWERS SOCIETY
A Society founded in 1840 and having 360 members in 1896; becoming affiliated to the **Federated Wire Drawers Association** (1890) as an independent organisation, it lost this status when that Association became a full amalgamation.

Source: BoT Reports.

HALIFAX (NO. 2) SMALL WIRE DRAWERS SOCIETY
A society founded, according to its Secretary in 1896, 'more than 40 years ago', and having 170 members in 1896, in four branches. It became affiliated to the **Federated Wire Drawers Association** (1890) as an independent organisation, but lost this status when that Association became a full amalgamation.

Source: BoT Reports.

HAMMER MAKERS ASSOCIATION
The Association, formed about 1880/90, maintained a continuous independent existence until 1916 when it merged with the **National Amalgamated Union of Labour** (see Vol. 3), and with the support of that union was able to achieve a unified price list and a rise in wages.

Sources: Pollard; NAUL Report, April 1916.

HAMMERED CHAINMAKERS SOCIETY
This was a society formed in 1906 for both men and women working in the trade. It seems likely to have been associated with the **Hammered Chainmakers Society of Cradley Heath** and had 680 members on its inception, 657 of whom were women. In 1909 it joined the **National Federation of Women Workers** (see Vol. 3).

Source: BoT Reports.

HAMMERED CHAINMAKERS SOCIETY OF CRADLEY HEATH
See **Hammered Chainmakers Society**

KEY MAKERS TRADE PROTECTION SOCIETY
The Society was formed in 1894 and registration was cancelled by request in 1903.

Source: Certification Office.

LAMINATED AND COIL SPRING WORKERS UNION
Founded in 1911, the Union organised workers involved in the manufacture and repair of heavy laminated and coil springs for railway and road vehicles. In 1920 it still worked by piece price lists. It agreed to introduce a comprehensive set of rules for coil spring makers, and in 1931 for laminated spring smiths and strikers, spring fitters and vicemen, all of which closely resembled engineering agreements. The members engaged in anvil and vice making continued to work by piece price lists. In 1974 it had 230 members. On 1 January 1977 the Union transferred its engagements to the **Amalgamated Society of Boilermakers, Shipwrights, Blacksmiths and Structural Workers.**

Sources: Pollard; Marsh, *Concise Encyclopedia.*

LONDON SOCIETY OF WIRE WORKERS
The Board of Trade Reports at first gives the date of formation of this Society as 1887 and then appears to revise this to 1871. It had 63 members in 1900 and in the following year joined with the **Manchester and District Wire Workers Society** and the **Scottish Wire Workers Society (Glasgow)** to form the **Federal Union of Wire Workers of Great Britain and Ireland.**

Source: BoT Reports.

LONDON UNITED WIRE ROPE MAKERS AND FITTERS ASSOCIATION
Formed in 1889, the Association was dissolved in 1897, its membership at that time being less than 30.

Source: Certification Office.

MANCHESTER AND DISTRICT WIRE WORKERS SOCIETY
A local sectional society formed in 1892. It had 29 members in 1900, and in the following year joined the **London Society of Wire Workers** and the **Scottish Wire Workers Society (Glasgow)** to form the **Federal Union of Wire Workers of Great Britain and Ireland.**

Source: BoT Reports.

MANCHESTER FRIENDLY WIRE WEAVERS SOCIETY
The Society was formed in 1827. In 1892 it had 68 members and a membership figure of 85 is recorded for 1899, after which time nothing further appears to be known of its existence.

Source: BoT Reports.

MANCHESTER WIRE DRAWERS SOCIETY

A Society formed in 1840. In 1852 it donated £100 towards the strike fund of the newly formed **Amalgamated Society of Engineers** whose members had been locked out by the employers for refusing to work systematic overtime and for demanding the abolition of piece work. The title was changed to the above in 1912. The Society was dissolved in 1936.

Sources: Jefferys; ASE Half-Yearly Report, June 1852; BoT Reports; Certification Office.

MIDDLESBOROUGH WIRE DRAWERS SOCIETY

Formed in 1893, the Society was affiliated to the **Federated Wire Drawers Association** as an independent trade union. It lost that status when the Association became a full amalgamation. It had 120 members in 1920.

Source: BoT Reports.

MILITARY AND SPORTING GUN WORKERS ASSOCIATION

Formed in 1892 with 550 members, the Association continued in existence until 1916 when, with a membership of 49, it ceased to function.

Sources: Bain and Price; BoT Reports.

NATIONAL AMALGAMATED ASSOCIATION OF NUT AND BOLT WORKERS

The Association was established in 1890 under the leadership of Richard Juggins, who became Secretary of the Midland Counties Trade Federation when the National Amalgamated affiliated to this organisation. The union was composed of hand workers who were engaged in a keenly competitive trade. Richard Juggins associated himself with the employers in setting up the South Staffordshire Bolt and Nut Trade Wages Board which negotiated piece price lists and hired auditors to check the employers' books. If an employer was found to be not paying the standard rate, his workers were called out on strike by the Board and paid their wages from a joint account. The Association remained in existence until 1956.

Sources: Clegg, Fox and Thompson; Certification Office.

NATIONAL AMALGAMATED HARNESS AND SADDLERY FURNITURE TRADES AND METAL WORKERS ASSOCIATION

Formed in 1910 with 229 members as the **Amalgamated Hame and Clip Association**, the Association adopted the above title at a later date. In the 1920s it amalgamated with the **Amalgamated Society of Harness Makers, Bridle Cutters, Fancy Leather Workers and Military Equipment Makers** in order to form the **Walsall and District Amalgamated Leather Trade Union** which ceased to exist in 1938.

171

Sources: BoT Reports; Certification Office.

NATIONAL AMALGAMATED LOCK, LATCH AND KEY SMITHS TRADE SOCIETY
See **National Union of Lock and Metal Workers**

NATIONAL AMALGAMATED LOCK MAKER AND METAL WORKERS TRADE SOCIETY
See **National Union of Lock and Metal Workers**

NATIONAL ASSOCIATION OF ANVIL MAKERS
See **Amalgamated Society of Anvil and Vice Makers**

NATIONAL SOCIETY OF AMALGAMATED METAL WIRE AND TUBE WORKERS
Formed in 1896 with 1,500 members, the Society grew steadily, recording 1,645 members in 1899 but falling to 780 in 1903, rising to 1,292 in 1906 and falling again to 350 in 1910. The membership in 1946 totalled 139. It is recorded as having 100 members in 1949 but seems to have gone out of existence in 1950, there being no notice given of any amalgamation with another union.

Sources: BoT Reports; TUC Reports.

NATIONAL SOCIETY OF WIRE WEAVERS OF GREAT BRITAIN
The Society was based in Glasgow and was formed as the **Federal Union of Wire Weavers of the United Kingdom** in 1872, the name being changed to the above in 1910. There were 6 unions in the Federation at the end of the nineteenth century representing Birmingham, London, Manchester, Newcastle, Warrington and Glasgow. The union ceased to exist in 1924 when the membership stood at 74. Registration was cancelled in 1926.

Sources: Certification Office; BoT Reports.

NATIONAL UNION OF LOCK AND METAL WORKERS
The Union was formed in 1889 at Willenhall as the **National Amalgamated Lock, Latch and Key Smiths Trade Society**, the name later being changed to the **National Amalgamated Lock Maker and Metal Workers Trade Society**. It also incorporated the **Spring Trap Makers Society**, the amalgamation being conditional on the agreement that the Spring Trap Makers should not lose their identity. In 1900 the Lock Makers had over 2,000 members and dominated the trade, but the membership gradually fell to 1,568 in 1906, to 815 in 1907 and to 180 in 1910. The name was changed to the National Union of Lock and Metal Workers in 1925. The Union organises the whole of the lock trade and has a membership of some 7,000, having

absorbed within its ranks a number of small sectional societies. It currently holds a certificate of independence.

Sources: BoT Reports; Certification Office.

NEW BLOCK CHAIN MAKERS ASSOCIATION (CRADLEY HEATH)
The Association was formed in 1895 and registered in 1900 and ceased to exist in 1903.

Source: Certification Office.

NEWCASTLE WIRE WEAVERS ASSOCIATION
When this Society was formed is not clear. It seems to have continued for many years with substantially no membership; this stood at 3 in 1899.

Source: BoT Reports.

OAKENGATES NAIL CASTERS ASSOCIATION
The Association was established in 1894 with 50 members. It remained in existence until 1920 when the membership was 310. There is no further record of this organisation.

Source: Bain and Price.

OLD HILL ANCHOR FORGEMENS ASSOCIATION
The Association was established in 1897 with 20 members. Nothing further is known of its history after 1902, when the membership figure was 13.

Source: Bain and Price

SCOTTISH WIRE WORKERS SOCIETY (GLASGOW)
A local sectional society formed in 1896. It had 54 members in 1900 and in the following year joined the **London Society of Wire Workers** and the **Manchester and District Wire Workers Society** to form the **Federal Union of Wire Workers of Great Britain and Ireland**.

Source: BoT Reports.

SCREW, NUT, BOLT AND RIVET TRADE SOCIETY
See **Screw, Nut, Bolt and Rivet Trade Union**

SCREW, NUT, BOLT AND RIVET TRADE UNION
The Union was formed as the **Screw, Nut, Bolt and Rivet Trade Society** in 1914. Its present membership is about 2,000, all of whom are employed by

Guest, Keen and Nettlefold in Birmingham where it recruits all grades of workers. It is affiliated to the TUC.

Sources: Marsh, *Concise Encyclopedia*; Certification Office; Marsh, *Trade Union Handbook*.

SCREWING SHOP DEPARTMENT SOCIETY (WEDNESBURY)
The Society was established in 1896 with a membership of 109 and remained in existence until 1902, when its membership had dwindled to 37 and it was dissolved.

Source: Bain and Price.

SEDGLEY AND GORNAL NAIL FORGERS PROTECTION ASSOCIATION
Formed in 1873, the Association was dissolved in 1874.

Source: Certification Office.

SEDGLEY AND GORNAL NAILERS ASSOCIATION
Formed in 1873 and with a membership of 349 in 1892, the Association ceased to exist in 1894.

Sources: BoT Reports; Certification Office.

SHEFFIELD WIRE DRAWERS SOCIETY
A Society founded in 1848 and having 170 members in 1896. It became affiliated to the **Federated Wire Drawers Association** (1890) as an independent organisation, but lost this status when that Association became a full amalgamation.

Source: BoT Reports.

SOCIETY OF SHOE, RIVET AND WIRE NAIL MAKERS
This was a local Birmingham union dating from 1876. It had about 70 members at the end of the century and 63 in 1910. It seems to have gone out of existence some time before 1964.

Source: BoT Reports.

SPRING HOOK, CHAIN, CART GEAR AND CASE MAKERS SOCIETY
Formed in 1898, the Society joined forces in the same year with the **Walsall Case Hame Makers Society**, the combined membership being 160 which had risen to 214 by 1900. At some date before 1910 the combined

organisation became known as the **Walsall Buckle, Chain, Cart Gear and Case Hame Makers Trade Protection Society**.

Source: BoT Reports.

SPRING TRAP MAKERS SOCIETY
The Society was established in 1890 as the **Wednesfield Spring Trap Makers Society**. It had 126 members in 1900 but by 1908 this number had fallen and it retained only 68 members in 1910. In 1916 it changed its name to the above title. It has had close associations with the **National Union of Lock and Metal Workers** since 1924, but has always retained a separate existence.

Sources: BoT Reports; Marsh, *Concise Encyclopedia*.

SUNDERLAND CHAIN MAKERS AND CHAIN STRIKERS ASSOCIATION
Formed in 1894, the Association was dissolved in 1895.

Source: Certification Office.

UNION OF BLOCK CHAIN MAKERS (CRADLEY HEATH)
Formed in 1888, the Union had 199 members in 1892. It continued to grow steadily from 222 members in 1900 to 260 in 1910. In 1918 it merged with the **United Chainmakers and Strikers Union**.

Sources: Bain and Price; BoT Reports.

UNITED CHAIN MAKERS AND CHAIN STRIKERS ASSOCIATION OF SALTNEY, PONTYPRIDD AND STAFFORDSHIRE
See **Chain Makers and Strikers Association**

UNITED CHAIN MAKERS AND STRIKERS UNION
See **Chain Makers and Strikers Association**

UNITED CUT NAIL MAKERS ASSOCIATION OF GREAT BRITAIN PROTECTION SOCIETY
This was a Birmingham-based organisation dating from 1851, its early title being the United Cut Nail Makers Mutual Assistance and Protection Society, the name being changed to the above in 1910. It had 139 members in 1892 which by 1900 had fallen to 53, but it continued to function until 1939 when its activities were suspended for the duration of the Second World War. In 1946 its recorded membership was 55. It merged with the **Transport and General Workers Union** (see Vol. 3) in 1952.

Sources: BoT Reports; Certification Office; Bain and Price.

UNITED SOCIETY OF OPERATIVE HORSE NAIL MAKERS
Formed in 1872, the Society ceased to exist after 1874.

Source: Certification Office.

WALSALL AND BLOXWICH ASSOCIATION OF BRIDLE BIT FORGERS AND FILERS
Formed in 1891, the Association had 24 members in 1892. It was dissolved at about the end of 1896, though it had had 120 members at the end of the previous year.

Source: BoT Reports.

WALSALL AND DISTRICT AMALGAMATED LEATHER TRADE UNION
The Union was established some time in the 1920s by an amalgamation of the **National Amalgamated Harness and Saddlery Furniture Trades and Metal Workers Association** and the **Amalgamated Society of Harness Makers, Bridle Cutters, Fancy Leather Workers and Military Equipment Makers**. It was dissolved in 1938.

Sources: BoT Reports; Certification Office.

WALSALL BUCKLE, CHAIN, CART GEAR AND CASE HAME MAKERS TRADE PROTECTION SOCIETY
Formed in 1889 as the **Walsall Case Hame Makers Society** and dissolved in 1894, the Society was principally of interest as having been a branch of the Knights of Labor from its inception to 1893. Re-formed in 1896 with 24 members, it joined forces in 1898 with the **Spring Hook, Chain, Cart Gear and Case Makers Society**, making a union of 160 members which number had risen to 214 by 1900. At some date before 1910 the above title was adopted, but nothing further is known of its existence.

Sources: BoT Reports; Henry Pelling, 'The Knights of Labor in Britain, 1880–1901', *Economic History Review*, Vol. 9, No. 2, December 1956.

WALSALL CASE HAME MAKERS SOCIETY
See **Walsall Buckle, Chain, Cart Gear and Case Hame Makers Trade Protection Society**

WALSALL LOCK AND KEY SMITHS MALE AND FEMALE TRADE SOCIETY
Established in 1898, this was originally formed as the **Willenhall, Walsall and District Lock, Key, Bolt and General Hardware Burial and Trade Protection Society**. The Society had 140 members in 1974. It currently holds a certificate of independence.

Sources: Bain and Price; Certification Office.

WAREHOUSEMEN AND PROVERS TRADE SOCIETY
This was a union catering for workpeople at the Wednesbury Crown Tube Works. Upon its establishment in 1896 it had 70 members, and 72 in 1899 with 48 in 1901, after which date nothing further appears to be known of its existence under this title.

Source: BoT Reports.

WARRINGTON WIRE DRAWERS SOCIETY
It is not known when this Society was founded, but it became affiliated in 1890 to the **Federated Wire Drawers Association** as an independent organisation. It lost this status when that association became a full amalgamation. It had 509 members in 1896.

Source: BoT Reports.

WARRINGTON WIRE WEAVERS ASSOCIATION
Formed in 1872, the Association had only 28 members at the end of the century. Nothing further is known of its history.

Source: Certification Office.

WEDNESFIELD SPRING TRAP MAKERS SOCIETY
See **Spring Trap Makers Society**

WILLENHALL AMALGAMATED SOCIETY OF LOCK AND KEY WORKERS
All that is known of the Society is that it was disbanded in 1880.

Source: Certification Office.

WILLENHALL SOCIETY OF IRON CASTERS
Formed in 1899 with 53 members, the Society ceased to exist in 1900.

Source: Bain and Price.

WILLENHALL, WALSALL AND DISTRICT LOCK, KEY, BOLT AND GENERAL HARDWARE BURIAL AND TRADE PROTECTION SOCIETY
See **Walsall Lock and Key Smiths Male and Female Trade Society**

WOLVERHAMPTON LOCK AND KEY SMITHS DEATH AND TRADE ASSOCIATION

Founded in 1872, the Association was dissolved in 1879.

Source: Certification Office.

Hammermen, Smiths and Strikers

At the end of the nineteenth century there were at least 20 sectional societies in Great Britain catering for smiths, hammermen and strikers, dominated in numbers by the Amalgamated Society of Smiths and Strikers with over 4,500 members. In Scotland the Associated Blacksmiths had fewer branches than the Amalgamated Society (51 compared with 69) and a stable membership of about 2,900. Both unions maintained their standing in the trade until they were eventually drawn by amalgamation into larger units. The Amalgamated Society ultimately became part of the merger which in 1920 produced the Amalgamated Engineering Union. The Associated Blacksmiths of Scotland became the Associated Blacksmiths and Ironworkers Society, absorbing the Blacksmiths Union in 1912 and the National Society of Smiths and Hammermen two years later, subsequently changing its name to Associated Blacksmiths, Forge and Smithy Workers Society. Under this title it amalgamated in January 1963 with the United Society of Boilermakers and the Ship Constructors and Shipwrights Association to form the Amalgamated Society of Boilermakers, Blacksmiths, Shipbuilders and Structural Workers.

AMALGAMATED ORDER OF SMITHS, ENGINEMEN AND MECHANICS

All that is known of this Union is that it was disbanded in July 1881.

Source: Certification Office.

AMALGAMATED PROTECTION UNION OF HAMMERMEN, ENGINEMEN, MACHINEMEN'S HELPERS AND GENERAL LABOURERS

Formed in 1890, the Union had over 1,000 members in 1892, but the membership had fallen to 40 in 1896. It ceased to exist after 1899.

Sources: BoT Reports; Certification Office.

AMALGAMATED SOCIETY OF SMITHS AND STRIKERS

Formed in 1886 as the **United Kingdom Society of Amalgamated Smiths and Strikers**, the union was based at Stockton-on-Tees and the largest in the trade. In 1892 it had 52 branches and 2,200 members and by the end of the century 69 branches and 4,500 members. By the First World War it was based in the Manchester area. In 1920 it merged into the **Amalgamated Engineering Union** when it had 14,080 members.

Sources: BoT Reports; Jefferys.

ASSOCIATED BLACKSMITHS, FORGE AND SMITHY WORKERS SOCIETY

See **Associated Blacksmiths and Ironworkers Society**

ASSOCIATED BLACKSMITHS AND IRONWORKERS SOCIETY

There is evidence that this union existed, as the **Associated Society of Blacksmiths** in 1845, when one of its rules declared that 'strikes are an unpremeditated evil on the part of the operatives' thus establishing it as one of the early anti-strike societies, which preferred disputes to be settled by friendly consultation between master and man, and if agreement could not be reached 'the masters and men should part, the men being supplied with the means of existence until they obtain other situations from the funds of the Society'. Despite this, the Board of Trade gives the date of formation of the **Associated Blacksmiths of Scotland**, which was evidently an alternative name for the union, as 1858, or on some occasions, 1857. By the middle 1880s the Society had some 2,000 members, and branches outside Scotland. By the end of the century 51 branches north and south of the Border had a total strength of about 2,900 reaching an early twentieth century peak of 3,849 in 1907. In 1912 the Society took in the **Blacksmiths Union** and in 1914 the **National United Society of Smiths and Hammermen**. By this time, probably between 1907 and 1910, it had changed its name to the Associated Blacksmiths and Ironworkers Society. A further change was made in the early 1920s to the **Associated Blacksmiths, Forge and Smithy Workers Society**. It was under this title that the union, in January 1963 came together with the **United Society of Boilermakers, Shipbuilders and Structural Workers** and the **Shipconstructors and Shipwrights Association** to form the **Amalgamated Society of Boilermakers, Shipwrights, Blacksmiths and Structural Workers.**

Sources: Clegg, Fox and Thompson; Marsh, *Industrial Relations*; Fyrth and Collins; Mortimer; BoT Reports.

ASSOCIATED BLACKSMITHS OF SCOTLAND
See **Associated Blacksmiths and Ironworkers Society**

ASSOCIATED SOCIETY OF BLACKSMITHS
See **Associated Blacksmiths and Ironworkers Society**

ASSOCIATION OF HAMMERMEN, ENGINEMEN, MACHINE MEN, HELPERS AND GENERAL LABOURERS
Also known as the **Amalgamated Protection Union of Hammermen, Enginemen, Machinemen's Helpers and General Labourers**

BARROW HAMMERMEN AND FORGE FURNACEMEN'S SOCIETY
Formed in 1884, the Society went out of existence in 1886.

Source: Certification Office.

BELFAST AMALGAMATED SMITHS AND IRONWORKERS
This union is noted as having broken up in 1874; no other information about it appears to exist.

Source: Certification Office.

BLACKSMITHS UNION
Amalgamation in 1911 of the **Combined Smiths of Great Britain and Ireland** (485 members) and the **Co-operative Society of Smiths** (902 members). The Union was short lived, merging in the following year with the **Associated Blacksmiths and Ironworkers Society.**

Source: BoT Reports.

BRITISH STEEL MILL AND HAMMERMEN'S ASSOCIATION
Formed in 1889, the Association had 155 members in 1892. It had a very limited existence, being dissolved in 1894 when the membership totalled 102.

Source: BoT Reports.

BRITISH UNITED HAMMERMEN AND FORGE HAMMERMEN'S ASSOCIATION

The Association was set up in 1872. By 1892 it had a membership of 564, which gradually dwindled. The Association continued in existence until 1908 when, with 307 members, it was dissolved.

Sources: BoT Reports; Certification Office.

CARDIFF, NEWPORT AND BARRY SMITHS' HAMMERMEN'S SOCIETY

The Society was formed in 1887 and had branches in all three towns, with a total membership of 1,185 in 1900. About 1905 it seems to have changed its name to the **Smiths' Hammermen's Society (South Wales)** when a further branch was added. Exactly what happened to the Society after 1910, when it had 244 members, is not known, though it was still in existence after the First World War.

Source: BoT Reports.

CHATHAM HAMMERMEN'S ASSOCIATION

The Association was set up in 1890 and had 140 members in 1892. In 1917, with 153 members, it merged with the **Workers' Union** (see Vol. 3).

Source: Bain and Price.

COMBINED SMITHS OF GREAT BRITAIN AND IRELAND

Formed in 1898, the Union retained an independent organisation with a membership of between 400 and 500 until 1911, when it amalgamated with the **Co-operative Society of Smiths** in order to form the **Blacksmiths Union** which in October of the following year came together with the **Associated Blacksmiths and Ironworkers Society**. See also **Oldham Smiths Old Society**.

Sources: BoT Reports; Jefferys.

CO-OPERATIVE SOCIETY OF SMITHS

Formed in 1849, the Association reached a peak membership of 1,068, organised in 21 branches, in 1907. In 1899 it lodged a complaint against the **Amalgamated Society of Engineers** for allegedly blacklegging during a strike. The TUC upheld the charge which resulted in the ASE membership voting to discontinue its affiliation to the TUC, the affiliation not being renewed until 1905. In 1911 the Co-operative Smiths amalgamated with the **Combined Smiths of Great Britain and Ireland** to form the **Blacksmiths Union**.

Sources: BoT Reports; Jefferys.

EAST LONDON UNITY OF HAMMERMEN
The Unity was formed by members who had seceded from the **London Unity of Hammermen** in 1887, and who rejoined that union in 1893 to form the **London Amalgamated Hammermen's Benefit Society**.

Source: Certification Office.

GENERAL UNION OF SMITHS, IRONWORKERS AND GAS FITTERS
This Union appears to have been broken up in 1875; no further information is available about its history.

Source: Certification Office.

HAMMERMEN, HELPERS AND GENERAL LABOURERS SOCIETY
Formed in 1892, the Society never had more than 65 members and was dissolved 3 years later.

Source: BoT Reports.

HULL LOYAL SOCIETY OF SMITHS
The Society was established in 1830. It had 13 members in 1892 and 31 at the end of the century. It ceased to exist at about the end of 1910 when the membership numbered 23.

Source: BoT Reports.

LIVERPOOL AND DISTRICT HAMMERMEN'S SOCIETY
Formed in 1874, the Society had a membership of 130 in 1899 but this had dropped to 107 by 1910. It was still in existence about 1912, but seems to have disappeared before or during the First World War.

Source: BoT Reports.

LONDON AMALGAMATED HAMMERMEN'S BENEFIT SOCIETY
See **London and Provincial Hammermen's Association**

LONDON AND PROVINCIAL HAMMERMEN'S ASSOCIATION
The **East London Unity of Hammermen** and the **London Unity of Hammermen** merged in 1893 to form the **London Amalgamated Hammermen's Benefit Society**. The two societies apparently separated again in 1896, the East London taking the name of London and Provincial Hammermen's Association, with 260 members and two branches (one in Poplar and the other outside London), while the London Unity retained the title of London Amalgamated Hammermen's Benefit Society. The

London and Provincial remained independent for one year only; in 1907 it merged into the **National United Society of Smiths and Hammermen**.

Source: BoT Reports.

LONDON UNITY OF HAMMERMEN

A society formed in 1882. Some members appear to have seceded in 1887 to form the **East London Unity of Hammermen**, leaving the London Unity with only 35 members in 1892. In the following year it joined the East London Unity to form the **London Amalgamated Hammermen's Benefit Society**.

Source: BoT Reports.

LOYAL SOCIETY OF SMITHS

A one-branch society formed in 1830 and based on Hull. It never had more than 30 members, and ceased to exist at about the end of 1910.

Source: BoT Reports.

NATIONAL UNITED SOCIETY OF SMITHS AND HAMMERMEN

A union formed in 1889, apparently as the **United Society of Smiths and Hammermen** and based in South East London. It had 22 branches and almost 1,300 members in the early 1900s, but thereafter declined to 720 in 1910 despite the merger with it of the **London and Provincial Hammermen's Association** (1907). For some reason it was removed from the register of trade unions in 1909. It amalgamated with the **Associated Blacksmiths and Ironworkers Society** in 1914.

Sources: BoT Reports; Certification Office.

OLDHAM SMITHS OLD SOCIETY

A one-branch society formed in 1833 which had 30 members in 1900 and merged with the **Combined Smiths of Great Britain and Ireland** in 1901.

Source: BoT Reports.

SMITHS' HAMMERMEN'S SOCIETY (SOUTH WALES)

See **Cardiff, Newport and Barry Smiths' Hammermen's Society**

SPRING SMITHS AND STRIKERS TRADE UNION (SHEFFIELD)

A one-branch Sheffield union formed in 1886. It had 100 members in 1910. No information seems to exist about it after that date, except that the Union was apparently still in existence at the end of the First World War.

Source: BoT Reports.

UNITED HAMMERMEN AND FORGE FURNACEMEN
This union was formed in 1907 with 70 members but the number had dwindled to 35 by 1908 and the union ceased to exist in 1909.

Source: BoT Reports.

UNITED SOCIETY OF SMITHS AND HAMMERMEN
See **National United Society of Smiths and Hammermen**

Part Two

Coal Mining and
Iron and Steel

Coal Mining

At the end of the Second World War four unions in coal mining were affiliated to the Trades Union Congress – the National Union of Mineworkers with a membership of a little over 533,000, two unions of officials and deputies (the Federation of Colliery Deputies Associations of Great Britain with 15,000 members and the National Federation, Colliery Officials and Staffs, with 8,133 members) and a winding enginemen's union, the South Wales (and Mon.) Colliery Winding Enginemen's Association and Provident Trade Union (591 members). Among manual workers, the NUM, recently established from 1 January 1945 as a more centralised form of the old federal Miners Federation of Great Britain (1889), was already the only force to be reckoned with in the industry, a status confirmed in 1947 by nationalisation, which the miners had eagerly sought for many years, and the advent of the National Coal Board. Local independent windingmen's associations, organised into a National Union of Colliery Winding Enginemen and later a Colliery Winders Federation of Great Britain continued to cause the national union irritation for a few years in an attempt to maintain an element of self-determination. But it was evident that they could not succeed against the NUM's determination not to allow traditional craft groupings to remain outside it. Nor would the union tolerate organisations, craft or otherwise, primarily based in other industries but with membership in mining, to act independently of itself. Before nationalisation the Amalgamated Engineering Union, the Electrical Trades Union and the Amalgamated Union of Building Trades Workers, all of whom were concerned in colliery maintenance, concluded agreements providing that members working at collieries should also be members of the NUM and should be consulted where negotiation on craftsmen's wages and conditions were concerned. Members of the Transport and General Workers' Union and of the National Union of General and Municipal Workers in the industry were similarly dealt with, with the additional condition that both unions should henceforward cease recruitment in the industry.

Where non-manual workers are concerned, the NUM has had greater difficulty. In 1982 the National Association of Colliery Overmen, Deputies and Shotfirers and the British Association of Colliery Management (1947) continue to represent the appropriate grades; the fact that both are affiliated to the Trades Union Congress (the latter as late as 1977) reinforces the independence of their status, though both are radically affected by NUM settlements. This is even more so in the case of the only outside union now representing clerks which retains negotiating rights in the industry, the Association of Professional, Executive, Clerical and Computer Staffs (APEX).[1] In substance the Mineworkers dominate employee–management relations in the industry, though with the decline in demand for coal and rationalisation of coal-getting methods its membership is now no more than 249,711, with 18,575 in NACODS and 16,448 in BACM (see Vol. 1).

Phases of Development

The history of trade unionism in coal mining has probably been more thoroughly researched and more frequently written about than that of any other industry, as the notes on pp.198–200 bear witness. Broadly speaking, it falls into four periods. The first, covering the eighteenth century and the first half of the nineteenth, was primarily a period of localised and shortlived protests, leading to no settled or continuous trade union organisation, but ending in the later 1840s with a vigorous, but ultimately ineffective, attempt to co-ordinate such dispersed activity by means of a national organisation, the Miners Association of Great Britain and Ireland (1842–8). There followed a second period in which it seems that the idea of a national organisation was effectively abandoned and during which efforts were concentrated in the establishment of *district* organisations, some of which, during the 40 years which followed, became sufficiently representative and acceptable to the coal owners as to become parties to joint negotiating machinery and the application of sliding scale agreements. A third period began when the continuous fall of prices in the 1880s discredited such agreements and turned attention once again to the need for nationally co-ordinated leadership, which developed, as coal prices eventually began to rise in the summer and autumn of 1888, into the co-operation of eight districts – Yorkshire, Nottinghamshire, Derbyshire, Lancashire, North Wales, Staffordshire, Warwickshire and Leicestershire – in the Miners Federation of Great Britain (1889).[2] This marked the beginnings of industry-wide collective bargaining on the basis of a regional framework of representation in the industry without extinguishing the habits and practice of local autonomy which had become so ingrained in the miners' patterns of thought and behaviour. By the end of the century all county unions except Northumberland and Durham were federated in the MFGB and in 1908 complete federation was achieved. The years 1889 to 1945 were the age of the MFGB. 'How ridiculous is the call of the miners for a nationalised industry whilst still maintaining a coalfield basis for their own organisation,' wrote Ness Edwards, the South Wales Miners Federation agent and historian in 1938.[3] Even more absurd, as some observers saw the situation, was the existence of 22 separate county unions. It was the Second World War which brought a radical change from the old district basis of handling matters and led to the establishment of the NUM in 1945; and it was the election of a Labour government in the same year which established, in 1947, a National Coal Board which formed a natural negotiating partner for the NUM and made the continued existence of this union inevitable as a fourth phase of trade unionism in the industry.

Development to 1848

The social and industrial history of the eighteenth and early nineteenth centuries is punctuated by 'turn-outs' of colliers in every coal-mining area of the period – in Bristol and the Forest of Dean (1727, 1738, 1792, 1812), in Newcastle upon Tyne (1731, 1738, 1769, 1785, 1818), in Northumberland and Durham (1789, 1793, 1818), in Scotland (1764), in Sheffield and South Yorkshire (1792), in Lancashire and Cheshire (1792, 1818, 1819, 1825), in South Wales (1816, 1820, 1822, 1823), and in Worcestershire and Staffordshire (1793, 1798, 1822, 1825).[4] Coal miners were a formidable crew, prone to the 'seditious doctrines of Paine'[5] and the 'interference of the Jacobins'[6] and arrogant to boot as well as violent. 'About Oldham the colliers are universally out ... the masters have not the courage to proceed against them, either for combination or neglect, though the workmen's organised committee sits on stated days at a public house in Manchester, as if on legal business.'[7]

As with the ironworkers of the day, combinations were temporary only. Violent protest was followed by deceptive calm during which organisation seemed to disappear as the coal trade improved, only to be revived as the market failed again and there were wage cuts to be resisted. Strikes almost invariably led to defeat. It is hardly surprising that lack of success, coupled with strong employer organisation and the instability of the trade, not to mention fragmentation of effort between pit and pit, made permanent organisation difficult. How many shortlived combinations came into existence in the industry during this period it is impossible to say, but 21 separate associations of miners have been noted in the early part of the nineteenth century in central Lancashire alone, operating under the guise of friendly societies.[8]

Historians commonly identify developments towards more advanced if still transient forms of organisation from the 1830s, when, for a time, the miners' bargaining position improved. An organisation known as the Colliers of the United Association of Northumberland and Durham had some temporary success during 1831 and 1832, demanding a reduction in hours, the abolition of truck and protection against the arbitrary actions of colliery officials in making pits idle.[9] The union did not survive an attempt by militants to force up prices by restricting output in opposition to the policy of the official leadership,[10] but it did, along with a similar organisation, the Friendly Society of Coal Miners, formed at Bolton in March 1830,[11] show that *district* organisation might be possible and provide a more stable basis for common action if the hot heads could be controlled and a method devised for curtailing the use of non-union workers from other areas as strike-breakers. The colliers' answer to the latter was the development of an industry-wide trade union of miners which could act to counter the greater mobility between coalfields which the railways were making possible – the Miners Association of Great Britain and Ireland, set up at Wakefield in November 1842.[12]

The constitution of the Association was remarkably modern in tone. Its aim was to unite all miners in obtaining the highest possible wages and shorter working hours by restricting output and by creating a legal fund to defend members prosecuted for breach of contract. It had a national Executive Committee, which in 1844 became full time. Its districts managed their own affairs and retained half of subscriptions collected. Supreme authority lay with a national delegate conference which was required to meet at least twice a year. It nevertheless failed. District interests and loyalties could not be reconciled with national leadership. Yorkshire and the East Midlands defied it, and the mass importation of strike-breakers from badly organised areas was not stopped. An official strike in the North East in 1844 collapsed after four months. The credibility of the Association became undermined, and a commercial crisis in 1847 put an end to the experiment. By the following year the Miners Association of Great Britain was no more, and reversion to district miners' unions now appeared to be the only way forward. Ideas of nationally co-ordinated action were not dead, however. A National Association of Miners was formed in 1863 but eschewed industrial action in favour of parliamentary lobbying.[13] Its lack of vigour gave rise to a rival and more militant Amalgamated Association of Miners, but this did not survive the slump of

1874.[14] Failure continued to discredit the practice of national action until the end of the 1880s.

District Organisation

The 1850s, 1860s and 1870s were therefore the heyday of the district associations. Not all succeeded. A Scottish Coal and Iron Miners Association, formed in 1855, was, after a major conflict with the employers, 'little more than an empty shell' by 1859.[15] A tendency for prices to rise between the late fifties and 1873 provided a basis for more permanent organisation. South Yorkshire and West Yorkshire Associations were formed in the late 1850s and a Derbyshire and Nottinghamshire Association during 1863–4. In South Wales, a district union appears to have been formed in 1864. The Northumberland Miners Mutual Confident Association was established in the same year under the moderate leadership of Thomas Burt, and a Durham Miners Association, with William Crawford as agent following similar policies, in 1869. The first permanent district unions to be set up in Scotland date from the boom years of the early 1870s, though only one, the United Miners of Fife and Clackmannan, is said to have had any real authority.[16]

With the growth of district associations came recognition by local coal owners and collective agreements. John Normansell of the South Yorkshire Association was bargaining with employers in 1866 and operating *ad hoc* joint committees to handle disputes.[17] Similar machinery had been developed by Burt in Northumberland by 1871 and by Crawford in Durham in the following year. In West Yorkshire a conciliation board was set up in 1872[18] and in 1873 Scottish miners met the owners to settle wages for the whole of the West of Scotland.[19] Employers had found that collective bargaining legitimised the position of moderate leaders and gave them authority to curb their militant members.

Such ready co-operation came abruptly to an end with the collapse of coal prices in 1874. District associations once more found themselves with their backs to the wall resisting wage reductions. An early loss was the Amalgamated Association. Involved not only in leading strikes, but also in financing them, the Association quickly went bankrupt and was dissolved (1875), advising its members to join the National Association, now renamed the Miners National Union. For the most part, however, associations survived, much attenuated in membership, by dint of accepting district 'ascertainments' on selling price sliding scales and by resort to arbitration. Each coalfield had a different arrangement. In South Wales coalowners evolved, in the words of Clegg, Fox and Thompson, a 'combination of selling price scales and company unionism which was to control industrial relations in the coalfield until the end of the century.'[20] Miners elected representatives to a Sliding Scale Committee which 'negotiated' the basis of the scale, but who could hardly be called 'independent' trade unionists. South Staffordshire accepted a sliding scale in 1874 to save its association from extinction. West Yorkshire eventually went the same way, South Yorkshire jibbed at the employers' terms; in 1881 the remnants of the two unions came together into a single Yorkshire Miners' Association, but with only 3,000 members out of a labour force of 60,000. Durham adopted a scale in 1877 and Northumberland in 1878.

Whichever way the unions went, wage cuts were the result, but at least their organisation survived. Indeed, a few new ones were formed, the Derbyshire Miners Association at the beginning of 1880 and the Nottinghamshire Association in July 1881, both too weak to pursue anything resembling collective bargaining.[21] The Lancashire Miners' Federation was revived in April 1881 and secured recognition by the coal owners on the basis of avoiding large-scale disputes.[22]

There was no permanent recovery of miners' wages during most of the 1880s and collective bargaining remained confined to Northumberland, Durham, Fife and Clackmannan.[23] The English inland coalfields were in a particularly weak position. No district could stand alone against a tide of wage reductions and falling prices as the owners attempted to maintain their total revenues by continuing to increase output.[24] The eventual result was the Miners Federation of Great Britain.

The Miners Federation of Great Britain

This new phase of trade unionism in the industry was ushered in by an improvement in coal prices towards the end of the 1880s from which the inland coalfields benefited especially. A co-ordination of effort was required which the Miners National Union, dominated by Northumberland and Durham and devoted to the harmony approach to industrial relations of Burt and Crawford, and to sliding scales, was unable to provide. It could hardly be transformed, at short order, into a militant, broadly-based body with industrial as well as legislative objectives.[25] By the 1880s it consisted solely of the county associations in Yorkshire, Durham and Northumberland, together with a few scattered groups of lodges elsewhere. The idea of a new national organisation had been raised in Lancashire as early as 1883 and the notion of a federal structure frequently discussed. In the summer of 1888, as the price of coal began to rise, Lancashire called for a national conference on wages, and in September Yorkshire invited representatives of 'all miners now free from sliding scales' to discuss the best means of securing a 10 per cent advance – and of trying to find common ground for action. From this 'recent wage agitation' came the MFGB, the founding conference of which took place in November 1889.

The Federation as originally established included the county associations of Yorkshire, Nottinghamshire, Derbyshire, Lancashire, North Wales, Staffordshire, Warwickshire and Leicestershire. The Scottish miners affiliated in 1894 and South Wales in 1899. Northumberland came in in 1907 and Durham in 1908, thus fulfilling the original vision of the founders of the MFGB to see all colliers' trade unions federated into a single body. By 1909 the membership covered by the Federation was prodigious – over 600,000 compared with 363,000 in 1900 and about 36,000 in 1889. In strictly trade union terms, however, the situation remained complex. In 1910 there were, in all, 74 unions in coal mining, 21 in the Midlands, 17 in Lancashire and Cheshire, 10 each in Wales and Scotland, 5 in Durham, 4 in Yorkshire, two in Cumberland and Northumberland, and one in Cleveland. As far as the MFGB was concerned there were seventeen constituent bodies, two of which were themselves federal, the Midland Counties Federation of Miners (1886) with 7 unions[26] and the Scottish Miners' Federation (1894) with 8.[27]

194

The remainder were either county unions, or unions covering more than one county, or special districts like Bristol. The constituent bodies of the Federation in 1910 could therefore be listed as shown in Table 2, in order of year of foundation:

Table 2 The MFGB

Body	Year formed	Membership
Yorkshire Miners Association	1858	88,271
Northumberland Miners Mutual Confident Association	1864	37,361
Durham Miners Association	1869	121,805
Cleveland Miners and Quarrymen's Association	1872	9,743
Cumberland Miners Association	1872	6,326
Derbyshire Miners Association	1880	37,428
Nottinghamshire Miners Association	1880	31,252
Midland Counties Federation of Miners	1886	38,005
Forest of Dean Miners Association*	1870	3,000
Leicestershire Miners Association	1887	5,491
Bristol Miners Association*	1887	2,167
Somerset Miners Association*	1888	4,310
South Derbyshire Amalgamated Miners Association	1889	3,622
North Wales Miners Association	1891	12,043
Scottish Miners Federation	1894	67,602
Lancashire and Cheshire Miners Federation	1897	57,516
South Wales Miners Federation	1898	137,553

*The South Western Counties Miners Federation from 1894 to 1904.

In origin and intention, the MFGB was an organisation of underground workers and had little concern for colliery craftsmen, such as winding enginemen or mechanics, or for surface workers generally. By the end of the nineteenth century it could claim to have organised most of the latter, but some surface workers and almost all craftsmen remained in separate local unions. In 1910, these unions could be listed as follows (Table 3), together with their membership at that time.

The minority position of these unions at the time can be illustrated by comparing their total strength of less than 40,000, including deputies, with the 600,000 membership of the MFGB. Their gradual decline, either by dissolution, absorption into MFGB affiliates or inclusion in the Federation's Craftsmen's or Power Groups, is a story which seems hardly to have been explored. By 1944 41,000 such workers were within the Federation (see Table 4) although some independent societies continued to exist and some manual workers were in membership of the Amalgamated Engineering Union, the Electrical Trades Union, the Amalgamated Union of Building Trades Workers, the Transport and General Workers and the National Union of General and Municipal Workers.

Table 3 Enginemen and Firemen

Union	Year formed	Membership
Wigan, Bolton and District Colliery Enginemen*	1856	238
Yorkshire Enginemen and Motormen*	1859	938
Northumberland Colliery Enginemen and Firemen	1864	1,104
St Helens Colliery Enginemen	1864	162
Associated Engine Keepers of Fife and Kinross*	1870	368
Durham Co. Colliery Enginemen Boilerminders and Firemen	1872	2,972
West Yorkshire Enginemen and Firemen	1872	654
Shropshire Enginemen*	1875	32
United Engine Keepers of Scotland*	1875	2,400
Farnworth Enginemen Boilermen and Firemen	Before 1878	61
Cumberland County Colliery Enginemen	1892	155
Ashton Engine Winders*	1890	29
North Wales Enginemen*	1890	279
Derbyshire and Notts Enginemen and Firemen	1892	1,430
Chowbent Colliery Enginemen	1893	96
Leigh Enginemen Boilermen and Stokers*	1893	121
Somerset Enginemen and Firemen	1894	150
Wigan and District Enginemen and Boilermen*	1894	167
South Wales and Mon. Colliery Winding Enginemen	1896	572
Accrington Colliery Enginemen and Boilermen*	1900	48
Radcliffe, Bingley and Little Lever Engineers and Boilermen	1900	60
Anthracite Firemen*	1901	59
Mon. and South Wales Colliery Enginemen, Stokers and Craftsmen	1903	9,367
Pendlebury Enginemen and Boilermen*	1906	50
Walkden Enginemen and Boilermen*	1906	56
Burnley Enginemen and Boilermen*	1907	27

The National Union of Mineworkers

In practice, such a situation did little to challenge the supremacy of the MFGB. More important from the point of view of solidarity was the genuinely federal nature of the organisation and the autonomy enjoyed on many matters by the district associations. Anxieties about the disunity which this could imply, the feeling that there were 'too many unions in the industry', gained strength after the abortive general strike of 1926 and the development of the 'Spencer Union' in the Nottinghamshire coalfield shortly afterwards.[28] Such events forced the question of reorganisation into a more thoroughgoing national union into the centre of the stage.

This phase of the history of mining trade unions has been told in some detail by George B. Baldwin.[29] Parochial attitudes and interests were not

Table 3 continued

Skelmersdale Enginemen and Boilermen*	1907	49
Lancashire and Cheshire Colliery Firemen	1910	184
North Wales Boilermen*	1907	82
Total		21,910

Deputies and Overmen		
Durham Deputy Overmen**	1877	1,933
Northumberland Deputies**	1876	1,195
Notts Undermanagers and Deputies**	1893	120
National Deputies (Chesterfield)**	1908	200
North Wales Mining Officials**	1908	127
Total		3,575

Mechanics		
Northumberland Colliery Mechanics	1875	1,305
Durham Colliery Mechanics	1878	4,746
Engineers, Smiths and Carpenters (Ilkeston)	1874	50
Total		6,101

Other Workers		
Durham Cokemen and Labourers	1874	4,072
Yorkshire and Derby Cokemen and Labourers	1908	1,000
Lancashire Cokemen, Labourers and Local Railway Servants	1895	225
Ashton-in-Makerfield Conservative Miners	1910	75
Ilkeston Conservative Miners	1907	98
North Wales Surfacemen	1907	100
South Wales Wage Rate Men	1910	652
Total		6,222

*Further details are given in Vol. 3 since some members of these unions appear to have worked in industries other than mining.
**See Vol. 4.

easily overcome. It was not until the Second World War brought a radical shift away from the traditional district basis for handling the industry's problems that a compromise was arrived at between district autonomy and complete unification. This was not too dissimilar from proposals drawn up seven years earlier by Arthur Horner of the South Wales Miners Federation and Sam Watson of Durham, which now proved acceptable and led to the inauguration of the National Union of Mineworkers on 1 January 1945, a decision logically related to, though not occasioned by, the public ownership of the industry under the National Coal Board, which was not formally accomplished for a further two years.

Table 4   Constituent Associations of the MFGB, 1944

Constituent associations	Area	1944 membership
Bristol Miners Association	Bristol	400
National Union of Cokemen and By-product Workers	Cokemen	3,000
Cumberland Miners' Association	Cumberland	7,500
Derbyshire Miners' Association	Derbyshire	25,000
Durham Miners' Association	Durham	106,472
Kent Miners' Association	Kent	5,100
Lancashire and Cheshire Miners' Federation	Lancashire and Cheshire	40,000
Leicestershire Miners' Association	Leicester	4,000
Pelsall District Miners' Association Cannock Chase Miners, Enginemen and Surfacemen's Association North Staffordshire Miners' Association South Staffordshire and East Worcestershire Amalgamated Miners Association Warwickshire Miners' Association Shropshire Miners' Association Old Hill and Highley and District Miners' Association	Midlands	30,000
Northumberland Miners' Mutual Confident Association	Northumberland	28,561
North Wales and Border Counties Mineworkers' Association	North Wales	7,526
Nottinghamshire and District Miners' Federated Union	Nottingham	30,000
National Union of Scottish Mineworkers: Ayrshire Miners' Union Fife, Clackmannan and Kinross Miners' Association West Lothian Mineworkers' Union Stirling Miners' County Union Lanarkshire Miners County Union Mid. and East Lothian Miners' Association	Scotland	51,000
Somerset Miners' Association	Somerset	2,600

Notes

1. Although this union has negotiating rights, negotiations are in practice conducted by the NUM.
2. From 1932 the Mineworkers Federation of Great Britain.
3. G.D.H. Cole (ed.), *British Trade Unionism Today*, Gollancz, 1939, p. 292.
4. Noted from C.R. Dobson, *Masters and Journeymen*, Croom Helm, 1980 and A. Aspinall, *The Early English Trade Unions*, Batchworth Press, 1949.
5. Aspinall, *op. cit.*, p. 8, 1792.
6. *Ibid.*, p. 279, 1818.
7. *Ibid.*, p. 286, 1818.
8. Raymond Challinor, *The Lancashire and Cheshire Miner*, Frank Graham, 1972, p.20.
9. E. Welbourne, *The Miners' Unions of Northumberland and Durham*, CUP, 1923.
10. *Ibid.*, p. 192.

Table 4 continued

Constituent associations	Area	1944 membership
South Derbyshire Amalgamated Miners' Association	South Derbyshire	5,743
South Wales Miners' Federation	South Wales	100,000
Yorkshire Mine Workers' Asociation	Yorkshire	115,000
Durham Colliery Mechanics' Association		
Durham County Colliery Enginemen, Boilerminders' and Firemen's Association		
Northumberland Colliery Mechanics' Trade Society	Group No. 1 (Craftsmen)	
Northumberland Colliery Winders, Enginemen and Firemen's Association		15,200
Yorkshire Colliery Enginemen and Firemen's Association		
Yorkshire Winding Enginemen's Association*		
Lancashire and Cheshire Colliery Tradesmen and Kindred Workers*		
Lancashire, Cheshire and North Wales Colliery Enginemen's, Boilermen's and Brakesmen's Fedn.*	Group No. 2 (Craftsmen)	12,200
Derbyshire, Notts and Midland Counties Colliery Enginemen, Firemen, Motormen and Electricians' Union*		
Scottish Colliery Enginemen, Boilermen and Tradesmen's Association*		
National Union of Enginemen, Firemen, Mechanics and Electrical Workers (Colliery membership)		
Cumberland Colliery Enginemen, Boilermen and Electrical Workers	Power Group	13,561
Transport and General Workers' Union (Colliery membership)		
Total		602,863

*See note to Table 3.

11. E.W. Evans, *The Miners of South Wales*, UWP, 1961.
12. A.J. Taylor, 'The Miners' Association of Great Britain and Ireland, 1842–1848', *Economica*, Vol. XXII, 1955.
13. Keith Burgess, *The Origins of British Industrial Relations*, Croom Helm, 1975, p. 180, calls this the National Miners' Union.
14. Ness Edwards in Cole, *op. cit.*, p. 285.
15. R. Page Arnot, *A History of the Scottish Miners*, George Allen and Unwin, 1955, pp. 41–5.
16. *Ibid*, p. 55.
17. F. Machin, *The Yorkshire Miners*, NUM, 1958, pp. 340, 349–50.
18. *Ibid.*, pp. 177–9.
19. Page Arnot, *op. cit.*, p. 54.
20. *A History of British Trade Unions since 1889*, OUP, 1964, p. 18.
21. J.E. Williams, *The Derbyshire Miners*, Allen and Unwin, 1962, pp. 156, 280.
22. Challinor, *op. cit.*, p. 181–2.
23. Burgess, *op cit.*, p.199.

24. R. Page Arnot, *The Miners*, George Allen and Unwin, 1949, pp. 67–8.
25. *Ibid.* pp. 82–7, 94–5.
26. Viz. the South Staffordshire and East Worcestershire Amalgamated Association of Miners (1863), the North Stafford Miners' Federation (1869), the Old Hill and Highley District Miners (1883), the Shropshire Miners' Association (1886), the Cannock Chase Miners, Enginemen and Surfacemen's Association (1887), the Pelsall District Miners' Association (1887) and the Warwickshire and Stafford Miners' Trade Union (1885).
27. The Fife, Clackmannan and Kinross Miners' Association (1870), the Ayrshire Miners' Federal Union (1886), the Clackmannanshire Miners' Association (1887), the Mid and East Lothian Miners' Association (1889), the Kirkintilloch and Twechar Miners' Association (formerly the Dumbartonshire Miners) (1893), the Lanarkshire Miners' County Union (1896), the Stirlingshire Miners' County Union (1896) and the Amalgamated Miners and Manual Workers (coal and ironstone miners in West Lothian and Renfrewshire) (1886).
28. See entries on Nottinghamshire Miners Association and Nottinghamshire and District Miners Industrial Union below. The latter was organised by George A. Spencer as an independent union in a highly productive field in which miners could expect to do better outside the Federation. Spencer was persuaded to rejoin in 1937.
29. See 'Structural Reform in the British Miners Union', *Quarterly Journal of Economics*, November 1953, pp. 576–97 and *Beyond Nationalisation*, Harvard and OUP, 1955. Other references of interest are W. Livesey, *The Mining Crisis: Its History and Meaning to all Workers*, London, 1921 and MFGB Conference Reports from that time onwards.

ABERCARNE VALLEY WORKERS ASSOCIATION
Established in 1889 with 35 members, the Association ceased to exist in 1893.

Sources: BoT Reports; Certification Office.

ABERDARE AND MERTHYR MINERS ASSOCIATION
The Association had originated under the auspices of the **Amalgamated Association of Miners** and was reorganised in 1879, although no agent was appointed until 1882. Membership reached 12,000 in 1890–1, nearly one half of the labour force, but fell to 8,000 in 1893. It had no lodges or branches and the contributions of 2d per month were deducted from wages at colliery offices, the clerks involved retaining a small percentage for their services. Strike pay was distributed in the same way. The administration of the union was conducted by monthly meetings of delegates from each pit. The Association eventually became part of the **South Wales Miners Federation**.

Source: Evans, *Miners of South Wales*.

ABERDARE TIMBERMEN, RIPPERS AND ASSISTANTS' SOCIETY
The Society was registered in 1899 and in 1903 became a member of the **South Wales Miners Federation**.

Source: Certification Office.

AIRDRIE MINERS ASSOCIATION
This was a district union in existence in 1850 which became part of the **Scottish Coal and Iron-stone Miners Protective Association** when it was formed in 1855.

Source: Arnot, *History of the Scottish Miners*.

AMALGAMATED ASSOCIATION OF COLLIERY WORKMEN OF SOUTH WALES AND MONMOUTHSHIRE
By the early 1890s it was clear to the leaders of the district unions operating in South Wales that a stronger union was needed. Unless the coal trade boomed it would require hard bargaining to win any concessions from the coal owners and the unions' bargaining powers would remain weak until they became effectively organised. The formation of a new union was suggested and endorsed and the Association was formed in 1893. It was pledged to safeguard the wages of its members either by negotiation or by providing strike pay of 10s per week. 3d of each member's monthly contribution of 8d was allocated to a central fund and a levy of 6d was imposed periodically to provide the nucleus of such a fund. Administration of the fund was placed in the hands of a council on which each district union was represented in proportion to its membership. The new Association was to be a natural development of the existing district unions and was to be

based upon conciliation. But the district unions were reluctant to lose their autonomy and there was a wide difference of opinion on whether or not to abandon the principle of sliding scale payments. The decision was made to form yet another union to be based upon the existing districts alone. Thus the Amalgamated Association ceased to exist and the **Amalgamated Society of the Colliery Workmen of the South Wales Coalfield** was established in December 1894.

Source: Evans, *Miners of South Wales.*

AMALGAMATED ASSOCIATION OF MINERS

Formed in 1869, the Association's membership consisted of miners who had seceded from the **Miners National Union** in dissatisfaction about the Union's policy and leadership, which had refused to support local strikes and would not even support men who had been locked out. Thomas Halliday, the first President of the AAM, proposed to build a militant organisation by means of central control of strike decisions and a national strike fund, neither of which was to be found in the MNU which preferred district autonomy and the payment of voluntary levies. The new Association gained members in the badly organised districts of North and South Wales, Lancashire, the Midlands and the small coalfields in the South West, and by the date of its first national conference in 1870 it had 12,000 members. Its success depended a great deal on its ability to maintain its central fund, but even at the height of the trade boom in 1873 the total cash reserves were little more than £20,000 for 71,224 members. Those boom years were a period of almost continuous strike activity, much of it successful, but which greatly depleted the cash reserves necessary to tide the union over when trade deteriorated. Worsening trade conditions led to wage reductions. The membership became increasingly unable or unwilling to pay subscriptions and levies and dissatisfaction with the leadership led to fragmentation into smaller bodies. At the end of 1873 there was a long drawn out dispute at Burnley caused by the dismissal of union members. It caused a heavy drain on the funds and prevented the Association from opposing extensive wage cuts in 1874. It faced a series of strikes (some unofficial) and lockouts with its funds being gradually exhausted. The final blow came in 1875 when 50,000 miners in South Wales struck after refusing to accept a wage reduction and the coal owners would not negotiate with the union. The end had come and the AAM was wound up bankrupt in August 1875, the remaining members of its organisation joining the MNU.

Sources: Burgess, *Origins*; Cole, *British Trade Unionism Today*; Clegg, Fox and Thompson; Chris Fisher and John Smethurst *in* Harrison; *Wigan Observer*, 4 April 1873; *Western Mail*, 8 August 1873; Cole, 'Some Notes on British Trade Unions'.

AMALGAMATED MINERS (DONCASTER)

This was purely a local mining union which was established in 1908 with 560 members and had nearly doubled that number by 1909, but which ceased to exist in 1910.

Source: BoT Reports.

AMALGAMATED MINERS AND MANUAL WORKERS UNION
See **Mid and West Lothian Labour Federation**

AMALGAMATED NATIONAL UNION OF QUARRYWORKERS AND SETTMAKERS
The Union came into existence in 1914 as the result of an amalgamation of the **National Union of Quarrymen** and the **Settmakers Union of Great Britain and Ireland** covering a combined membership of 5,655 members. In 1934 it merged with the **Transport and General Workers Union** (Vol. 3).

Sources: Bain and Price; MoL Reports.

AMALGAMATED SECTION SCOTCH MINERS AND OILWORKMEN
See **Mid and West Lothian Labour Federation**

AMALGAMATED SOCIETY OF THE COLLIERY WORKMEN OF THE SOUTH WALES COALFIELD
The Society was established in December 1894 in place of the **Amalgamated Association of Colliery Workmen of South Wales and Monmouthshire** which was a loose federation of local district unions. The policy of basing the Society on a central fund and uniform contributions led to wholesale secessions, and the Society was widely criticised as having been set up by the leaders without taking into account the opinions of the members of the various unions, as well as the fact that the Rhondda miners and the anthracite workers refused to support the new body from the start. The organisation remained in existence until 1897 but its membership and influence were negligible.

Sources: Evans, *Miners of South Wales*; *South Wales Daily News*, 14 February 1895.

AMALGAMATED UNION OF QUARRYWORKERS AND SETTMAKERS
The Union was established in the 1880s, its branches being spread thinly over the country from the Channel Islands to Scotland with half its members in North Wales and the Midlands. Its headquarters was at Leicester and it had two full time officers. By 1934, when it amalgamated with the **National Union of General and Municipal Workers** (see Vol. 3) it claimed to have some 8,000 members. It had funds amounting to £50,000 and more, and had property at Leicester and Guernsey.

Source: H.A. Clegg, *General Union*, Basil Blackwell, Oxford, 1954.

ANTHRACITE MINERS ASSOCIATION

Established in 1882 as the **Anthracite Miners Defence Society**, this was the first union to be formed among the anthracite miners. It had over 3,000 members in 1892 when it became the Association. The rules and administrative organisation were identical with the **Cambrian Miners' Association**. It merged with the **South Wales Miners Federation** in 1899 with a membership of just over 6,000.

Sources: Evans, *Miners of South Wales*; Arnot, *The Miners*.

ANTHRACITE MINERS DEFENCE SOCIETY
See **Anthracite Miners Association**

ARDSLEY OAK SURFACEMEN'S UNION

The Union was formed in 1872. It had 77 members in 1892 and 83 in 1896 when John Newsam of Barnsley was the secretary. The Union retained a membership of between 70 and 80 until it was dissolved in 1905.

Source: BoT Reports.

ASHTON, HAYDOCK AND BOLTON MINERS' TRADE UNION

Established in 1882, the Union had 12,460 members in 1893. In 1897, with 9,346 members, it ceased to exist as an independent trade union and became a district association of the **Lancashire and Cheshire Miners' Federation**.

Source: Arnot, *The Miners*.

ASHTON-IN-MAKERFIELD CONSERVATIVE MINERS ASSOCIATION

There is one reference to the Association as having been formed in 1910 with 75 members, and a further reference to its existence in 1913 when J.J. Merry, of Violet Street, Ashton-in-Makerfield, acted as secretary. Nothing further appears to be known of its history.

Sources: BoT Reports; MoL Reports.

ASHTON-UNDER-LYNE MINERS' ASSOCIATION

Established in 1865, the Association had 3,900 members by 1893. In 1897, with a membership standing at 3,625, it ceased to be an independent union and became a branch of the **Lancashire and Cheshire Miners' Federation**.

Source: Arnot, *The Miners*.

ASPULL AND DISTRICT MINERS ASSOCIATION

Established in 1890, the Association had 664 members in 1893. In 1897, with 419 members, it became a district association of the **Lancashire and Cheshire**

Miners' Federation. It remained separately registered as a trade union until 1926.

Source: Arnot, *The Miners*.

ASSOCIATION OF HAULIERS AND WAGEMEN OF SOUTH WALES AND MONMOUTHSHIRE

At the beginning of the 1890s trade union membership in South Wales seems to have been confined to a relatively privileged minority of Welsh-speaking coal face workers who earned considerably more than the growing number of on-cost day wage men. Many of these men were English migrants recruited to the industry from the agricultural areas and it was they who founded the Association in 1893 to protect their interests. Wages in general were comparatively low, averaging no more than 23s weekly for all underground workers during 1892–3, but the wages of on-cost grades like the hauliers were lower still, averaging only 30s a fortnight. In 1893 an unofficial strike of hauliers in pursuit of a 20 per cent wage increase paralysed the entire industry, reflecting growing discontent with the existing sliding scale method of payment which the miners and hauliers alike considered had failed to protect their living standards. The Association continued to maintain an independent existence until 1898 when it merged with the **South Wales Miners' Federation**.

Sources: Burgess, *Origins*; S. and B. Webb, *History of Trade Unionism*; Evans, *Miners of South Wales*.

ASSOCIATION OF PRACTICAL MINERS

The Association was formed in 1864 by miners who had seceded from the **Miners National Union** because of dissatisfaction with the policies being practised by the leadership of the MNU, whose officials refused to be drawn into 'local grievances' and also refused to support local strikes, advising instead that the miners concerned should persuade the owners to accept arbitration and conciliation. The Association of Practical Miners was set up to provide a lead in policy-making and to finance local strikes. It collapsed in 1865 as a result of a long and eventually disastrous strike that had begun in June 1864 in South Staffordshire – a district where previously it had had some of its strongest support. One of the founders of the union was John Catchpole who was to become Secretary of the **Derbyshire and Nottinghamshire Miners Association** when it was formed in 1865.

Sources: Burgess, *Origins*; Williams, *The Derbyshire Miners*.

AUXILIARY UNION OF THE YORKSHIRE MINERS ASSOCIATION

In 1884 the Wombwell branch of the **Yorkshire Miners' Association**, becoming dissatisfied with the administration of the YMA, tried to secede from the main union in protest at the way in which it was being run. The seceding branch contended that the YMA's leadership were disregarding the interests of their members, in that the Association's demand for a wage increase had been turned down by the coal owners and a proposal for the publication of a Yorkshire miners' newspaper had been abandoned. The supporters of the Auxiliary Union were also angered by the reaction of the YMA to an explosion at the Wharncliffe Carlton Colliery. They accused the Association of helping the owners to cover up their negligence by not being thorough enough in their investigations into the cause of the disaster. Whether these accusations were true or not, there is no further record of the activities of this breakaway branch.

Sources: YMA, Circular of the Auxiliary Union of the Yorkshire Miners' Association, 26 July 1884; Robert G. Neville, 'The Yorkshire Miners, 1881–1926', (D. Phil. thesis, University of Leeds, 1974).

AYRSHIRE MINERS FEDERAL UNION
Formed in 1886, the Union was known as the **Ayrshire Miners Union** until 1893 when it was reorganised on the lines of a federation. It was under the leadership of Keir Hardie. In 1896 it had a membership of 2,332 and in 1900 this had increased to 8,294. It joined the **Scottish Miners Federation** and in 1944 amalgamated with other Scottish miners' organisations into the **National Union of Scottish Mineworkers**.

Sources: Arnot, *The Miners*; Alan Campbell and Fred Reid, 'The Independent Collier in Scotland', *in* Harrison; BoT Reports.

AYRSHIRE MINERS UNION
See **Ayrshire Miners Federal Union**

BAILLIESTON MINERS ASSOCIATION
A local union in existence in the 1850s, the Association became part of the **Scottish Coal and Iron-stone Miners Protective Association** when it was formed in 1855.

Sources: Arnot, *History of the Scottish Miners*; Alan Campbell and Fred Reid, 'The Independent Collier in Scotland,' *in* Harrison.

BALLACHULISH QUARRIERS
See **Scottish Slate Quarriers Union**

BAMFURLONG MINERS ASSOCIATION
Formed in 1878, the Association had 1,356 members in 1892 which had fallen to 722 in 1896, the secretary at that time being S. Judd of 19 Bamfurlong, Wigan. This appears to be the only reference to the existence of the Association in any Board of Trade Report.

Source: BoT Reports.

BANK HALL MINERS ASSOCIATION (BURNLEY)
Registered in 1901 the Association continued in existence for 70 years, registration being cancelled in 1971.

Source: Certification Office

BARNSLEY AND DISTRICT QUARRYMEN'S ASSOCIATION
Established in 1895 with 41 members, the Association had 14 members in 1897 and ceased to exist in 1898.

Source: BoT Reports.

BASSENDEN AND ACCRINGTON MINERS ASSOCIATION
Established in 1890, the Association went out of existence in 1894.

Source: Certification Office.

BELLSHILL MINERS ASSOCIATION
Formed in 1890, the Association had 400 members in 1896 when it became a branch of the **Lanarkshire Miners County Union**.

Source: BoT Reports.

BLACKROD MINERS' ASSOCIATION
Established in 1881, the Association had 380 members in 1893. In 1897, with a membership of 308, it ceased to exist as an independent union and became a branch of the **Lancashire and Cheshire Miners' Federation**.

Source: Arnot, *The Miners*.

BLANTYRE MINERS ASSOCIATION
A local association formed by Andrew McAnulty in 1890 as a result of much pioneer work. It never had more than 350 members and seems to have ceased to exist by 1896.

Source: Arnot, *History of the Scottish Miners*.

BOILERMEN AND ENGINE-WINDERS UNION
In August 1921, D.B. Jones led a breakaway section of some 6,000 craftsmen who were members of the **South Wales and Monmouthshire Federation** in order to form the above Union. It was later called the **South Wales and Monmouthshire Colliery Enginemen, Boilermakers and Craftsmen's Association**. It merged again with the SWMF in 1938, Jones becoming a paid official dealing mainly with recruitment into the craftsmen's section of the Federation.

Sources: *Western Mail*, 16 April, 10 August, 20 October 1938; Francis and Smith.

BRISTOL MINERS ASSOCIATION
Formed in 1887, the Association had 3,035 members in 1892. Charles Gill was appointed Corresponding Secretary. In 1945, with 320 members, it became part of the newly formed **National Union of Mineworkers**.

Sources: Arnot, *The Miners*; BoT Reports; Certification Office.

BRYNMALLY MINERS ASSOCIATION
Established in 1894, the Association ceased to exist in 1899.

Source: Certification Office.

BUCKLEY AND MOLD DISTRICT ASSOCIATION OF COAL MINERS
This was a local miners' organisation formed in 1883 and dissolved in 1887.

Source: Certification Office.

BURNLEY AND CHURCH ASSOCIATION OF MINERS
Formed in 1873, the Association was dissolved in 1874.

Source: Certification Office.

CAERPHILLY MINERS ASSOCIATION
Established in 1881, the Association had 1,340 members in 1892. It ceased to exist in 1894.

Source: BoT Reports.

CAMBRIAN MINERS ASSOCIATION
See **Rhondda District Miners Association**

CANNOCK CHASE MINERS, ENGINEMEN'S AND SURFACEMEN'S ASSOCIATION
Founded in 1876 and registered in 1887, the Association eventually formed part of the **Midland Counties Federation of Miners** which in turn became a constituent member of the **Miners Federation of Great Britain**.

Sources: Arnot, *The Miners*; Certification Office.

CHESTERFIELD WORKING MEN'S UNIONIST ASSOCIATION
Established in 1896 with only 13 members, it ceased to exist in 1900.

Source: BoT Reports.

CHOWBENT COLLIERY ENGINEMEN'S ASSOCIATION

The Association was formed in 1893 with 18 members and had 100 in 1900. It remained small and select until it merged with the **Lancashire and Cheshire Miners' Federation**.

Source: BoT Reports.

CLACKMANNAN MINERS ASSOCIATION

Formed in 1887, the Association had 1,155 members in 1900. It merged with the **Fife and Kinross Miners Association** in 1917. James Cook was Secretary of the Association from 1895 and subsequently became Secretary of the new **Fife, Clackmannan and Kinross Miners Association**.

Sources: Arnot, *History of the Scottish Miners*; BoT Reports.

CLELAND MINERS ASSOCIATION

This was a local union in existence round about 1850 which became part of the **Scottish Coal and Iron-stone Miners Protective Association** when it was formed in 1855.

Source: Arnot, *History of the Scottish Miners*.

CLEVELAND MINERS AND QUARRYMEN'S ASSOCIATION

See **North Yorkshire and Cleveland Miners and Quarrymen's Association**

COAL MINERS OF THE WEST RIDING OF YORKSHIRE

This union was established in 1853 by men who attempted to secure a rise in wages commensurate with the rise in the price of coal. Under the leadership of George Brown a strike was called which lasted for 8 weeks but which failed to secure its objective. In addition, the union had used its cash reserves to support disputes at Flockton, Waterloo Main, Altofts and other collieries, all of which had ended in defeat, the men being forced back to work on the coal owners' terms. By 1855 the union had ceased to exist.

Source: Machin.

COAL MINERS' UNION

The Union was established at Middleton, near Leeds, in July 1919. The rules indicate that its main function was to act as a burial club, although rule 5 imposed a fine on any member who was 'found guilty of boasting of his earnings ... to another member in any public house'. Nothing more is known of this organisation.

Sources: Report Book of John Blenkinsop, 1792–1832, Leeds City Libraries, Archives Department, Acc. 1546; Machin.

COALVILLE AND DISTRICT MINERS ASSOCIATION
Established in 1887, the Association had 2,499 members in 1896 and 3,301 members in 1900. It ceased to exist in 1912.

Sources: BoT Reports; Certification Office.

COATBRIDGE MINERS ASSOCIATION
A local union which was in existence in 1850, the Association became part of the **Scottish Coal and Iron-stone Miners Protective Association** when it was formed in 1855.

Source: Arnot, *History of the Scottish Miners*.

COLLIERS OF THE UNITED ASSOCIATION OF NORTHUMBERLAND AND DURHAM
Formed after the repeal of the Combination Acts, 1824/5, the United Association's objectives were the reduction in the working day from between 14 and 18 hours to 12 hours; the abolition of the truck system of payment; and protection against the arbitrary right of colliery officials to make pits idle. In 1825 it published a pamphlet describing the members' grievances, entitled 'A Voice from the Coal Mines', and another in 1826 entitled 'A Candid Appeal to the Coal Owners and Viewers of Collieries on the Tyne and Wear'. The Association called a strike in 1827 over a decision by the coal owners not to pay 'hiring money', but without financial backing the men were forced back to work on the masters' terms, and earnings fell as low as 8s or 10s per week. The union collapsed completely in 1828 after an unofficial strike to restrict output and force up wages and prices was defeated.

Sources: Welbourne; Burgess, *Origins*; Webb, *Story of the Durham Miners*.

COPPALL MINERS' LABOUR AND CHECKWEIGHMEN'S ASSOCIATION
The Association was established in 1902. Nothing further is known of its history.

Source: Certification Office.

CUMBERLAND COUNTY COLLIERY ENGINEMEN, BOILERMEN, FIREMEN AND ELECTRICAL WORKERS ASSOCIATION
This was formed in 1892 as the **Cumberland County Enginemen's Association**, and the name was changed to the above in 1912. The Association ceased to exist in 1928.

Source: Certification Office.

CUMBERLAND COUNTY ENGINEMEN'S ASSOCIATION
See **Cumberland County Colliery Enginemen, Boilermen, Firemen and Electrical Workers Association**

CUMBERLAND IRON ORE MINERS AND KINDRED TRADES ASSOCIATION
First formed in 1888 as the **Cumberland Iron Ore Miners and Quarrymen's Association** (sometimes called the **West Cumberland Workmen's Association**), the union had 850 members in 1896 and 3,400 members in 1900 distributed amongst 9 lodges. It ceased to exist in 1929.

Sources: BoT Reports; Certification Office.

CUMBERLAND IRON ORE MINERS AND QUARRYMEN'S ASSOCIATION
See **Cumberland Iron Ore Miners and Kindred Trades Association**

CUMBERLAND LIMESTONE QUARRYMEN'S UNION
The Union functioned for 25 years, being established in 1901 with 235 members and dissolved in 1926 when its membership was 484.

Source: Bain and Price.

CUMBERLAND MINERS ASSOCIATION
The Association first came into existence in 1872 as the West Cumberland Miners Association, the title being shortened to the above in 1906. Its aims were to obtain legislation for the more efficient management of mines, whereby the health and lives of miners would be preserved; to make the hours of labour in mines not more than eight in 24 and to obtain compensation for accidents where employers were liable; to protect all lodges when unjustly dealt with by their employers, and to provide a weekly allowance for members when driven into an unavoidable strike, or when locked out. There were two classes of membership, one class paying 6d. and the other paying 3d. a week. Strike pay was 10s. weekly to the first class and 5s. to the second. Members losing their job in the interest of the Association were entitled to 20s. a week with a further allowance of 1s. for each child. The membership in 1892 was 4,961, falling to 2,250 in 1896. The secretary at that time was A. Sharp of Senhouse Street, Maryport, who retained that position until the advent of the First World War. It was a constituent union of the **Miners Federation of Great Britain.** The Association became the Cumberland area of the **National Union of Mineworkers** in 1945 with 7,500 members.

Sources: BoT Reports; MoL Reports; Arnot, *The Miners*; George B. Baldwin; 'Structural Reform in the British Miners' Union', *Quarterly Journal of Economics*, November 1953.

DALRY MINERS ASSOCIATION
In existence in 1873 with 720 members and a financial strength of £420, the Association became part of the **National Union of Mineworkers** in 1945.

Sources: S. and B. Webb, *History of Trade Unionism*; Arnot, *The Miners* and *History of the Scottish Miners*.

DALTON AND DISTRICT UNITED WORKMEN'S ASSOCIATION
Set up in 1888, the Association had a membership of 1,011 in 1896 and 1,236 in 1900. It subsequently changed its name to the **Furness Iron Miners and Quarrymen's Union.**

Sources: BoT Reports; Certification Office.

DEN MINERS ASSOCIATION
In existence in 1873 with 330 members and cash in hand of £300, the Association became part of the **National Union of Mineworkers** in 1945.

Sources: S. and B. Webb, *History of Trade Unionism*; Arnot, *History of the Scottish Miners*.

DENBIGHSHIRE AND FLINTSHIRE MINERS ASSOCIATION
Established in 1892, the Association had a membership of 2,885 in 1896 and nearly 5,000 members in 1910. It merged with the **North Wales Miners Association** in 1912.

Sources: BoT Reports; Certification Office.

DERBYSHIRE AND NOTTINGHAMSHIRE ENGINEMEN'S AND FIRE-MEN'S UNION
In 1891 a meeting was held at the Old Angel Hotel, Chesterfield. Among those present were W.H. Lamberton, the Secretary of the **Durham County Colliery Enginemen Boilerminders and Firemen's Association** who later became Secretary of the **National Federation of Enginemen and Boiler Firemen**, T. Weighall, Secretary of the **Northumberland Miners Mutual Confident Association**, and P. Bossom of Stoke on Trent. A call was made to all colliery enginemen and firemen in Derbyshire to form a union, with the result that the **Derbyshire Enginemen's and Firemen's Union** was established in February 1892 with Hosea Marriott as President and Samuel Rowarth as Secretary. It had 48 members upon its formation. Gradually the membership was built up, first in Derbyshire and then bringing in Nottinghamshire members, and by 1911 the Derbyshire and Nottinghamshire Enginemen's and Firemen's Union had 1,400 members in 23 branches. The Union worked very closely with both the **Derbyshire** and **Nottinghamshire Miners Associations** on the understanding that they would not interfere with the Union in the management of its own local affairs or government.

Sources: Arnot, *The Miners*; *Derbyshire Times*, 7 November 1891, 21 October 1911, 2 December 1911.

DERBYSHIRE AND NOTTINGHAMSHIRE MINERS ASSOCIATION

The Association was formed in December 1865 at the George Inn, Southgate, Eckington. Its officers were William Ball and John Catchpole, President and Secretary respectively, and its aims were to seek an advance in wages and a shortening of the hours of labour; the practice of allowing young boys to work in the pits was condemned and the men were urged to join the union and work for a 7-hour day with 7s weekly wage. By July 1866 some 4,000 coal and ironstone miners working at Selston Common had pledged themselves to support the union, and it had some success in persuading one or two of the coal companies to employ checkweighmen to check when tubs of coal should be disallowed because they contained too much dirt. Nevertheless all the employers were anti-union and at the end of 1866 issued notices of dismissal to union members and eviction orders to vacate their homes. The membership at that time was 7,300, of whom 2,800 were in Nottinghamshire, 1,800 working at Staveley, 700 at Clay Cross and the remaining 2,000 scattered in various parts of Derbyshire. Other attempts were also made to crush the Association, the coal masters subscribing £100,000 towards a fighting fund and funding the organisation of a Free Labour Society which held nonunionist meetings at all the collieries. The weakness of the Association's fight against such tactics was largely due to its inadequate funds. The men were forced back to work and had to renounce the union. By the end of January 1867 the membership in North Derbyshire was virtually nil and by June there were only 500 members in the northern part of the county, although the Association, active in South Derbyshire and Nottinghamshire still, had some 1,400 members. But to all intents and purposes the union was crushed by the events of 1866/7, which put an end to further attempts to form an independent organisation for a number of years.

Sources: *Ilkeston Pioneer*, 31 January 1867, 4 July 1867; *Derbyshire Times*, 26 March, 1866; Williams, *The Derbyshire Miners*; Burgess, *Origins*.

DERBYSHIRE COLLIERY MECHANICS ASSOCIATION

Established in 1893 with a membership of 85, the Association was dissolved in 1895 with a membership of only 74.

Source: BoT Reports.

DERBYSHIRE ENGINEMEN'S AND FIREMEN'S UNION

See **Derbyshire and Nottinghamshire Enginemen's and Firemen's Union**

DERBYSHIRE MINERS ASSOCIATION

The precise circumstances of the founding of the new Derbyshire Miners Association are not known. After the collapse of the joint **Derbyshire and Nottinghamshire Miners Association** in 1868, many of the Derby men had joined the **South Yorkshire Miners Association**. From 1876 the dissatisfaction with the policy of the SYMA led to a number of meetings in Derbyshire on the question of secession and a split in the SYMA in 1879 gave the men their opportunity. In 1880, 10,000 Derbyshire miners were enrolled into the Derbyshire Miners Association with headquarters at Chesterfield and with James Haslam as Secretary. Early officers of the union were victimized by the employers and dismissed. In 1882 Haslam was appointed in a full time capacity. The improvement in trade during the 1880s and the wage concessions won by the union led to a great increase in membership and soon there were 28 lodges. The lodges were carefully regulated by the Executive Council. No new lodge could be formed without the sanction of the Executive Council and lodges were not permitted to strike until the facts had been considered by the Council and referred to other lodges for approval. If it was agreed that a lodge should strike, full members (those over 16 years of age) received 8s a week and 1s for each child under 13 not at work; half members received 4s a week. For these benefits members paid an entrance fee of 1s 6d or 9d for half members. Regular contributions were 6d a fortnight for full members and 3d for half members. Upon the formation of the **Miners Federation of Great Britain** in 1889 the Association at first refused to affiliate but changed its mind in 1890 when the Federation was demanding an increase of 10 per cent for its members. Upon affiliation the Association was given a seat on the Executive Council of the Federation. The effect of the Second World War led to increased growth of national negotiations, and the Greene Award, which conceded the principle of a national minimum wage, was perhaps one of the greatest influences in bringing about the creation of a national miners' union. It was not until January 1945, however, that the Derbyshire Association ended its independent existence, which had lasted for 65 years, and became the Derbyshire area of the newly formed **National Union of Mineworkers**.

Sources: *Derbyshire Times*, 21 February 1880; S. and B. Webb, *Industrial Democracy*; George B. Baldwin, 'Structural Reform in the British Miners' Union', *Quarterly Journal of Economics*, Vol. LXVII (1953), p. 595; Williams, *The Derbyshire Miners*; Burgess, *Origins*.

DUDLEY DISTRICT MINERS ASSOCIATION
Formed in 1872, the Association ceased to exist after 1878.

Source: Certification Office.

DUDLEY PORT MINERS UNION ASSOCIATION
Formed in 1874, the Association went out of existence in 1876.

Source: Certification Office.

DURHAM COKEMEN AND LABOURERS' UNION
The Union was formed in 1874 and by 1892 had 2,819 members. In 1916, with 4,134 members, it amalgamated with the **National Cokemen and Surface Workers' Union** in order to form the **National Cokemen and By-product Workers' Union**.

Sources: Bain and Price; BoT Reports; Certification Office.

DURHAM COLLIERY MECHANICS UNION
Formed in 1878, the Union became the Durham Mechanics Group No. 1 Area of the **National Union of Mineworkers** upon the formation of that union.

Sources: Webb, *Story of the Durham Miners*; Certification Office.

DURHAM COUNTY AMALGAMATED SOCIETY OF COLLIERY MECHANICS
See **National Amalgamated Society of Mechanics**

DURHAM COUNTY COLLIERY ENGINEMEN BOILERMINDERS AND FIREMEN'S ASSOCIATION
The Association was formed in 1872 by colliery engineers who had seceded from the **Miners Association of Great Britain and Ireland**. The first secretary was W.H. Lamberton who also became secretary of the **National Federation of Enginemen and Boiler Firemen**, of which the Association had become a member. By 1892 the Association had 1,689 members, and in 1945 it amalgamated with other unions to form the **National Union of Mineworkers**, at which time it had 4,217 members.

Sources: Arnot, *The Miners*; NUM; Certification Office; Webb, *Story of the Durham Miners*; W.R. Garside, *The Durham Miners 1919–60*, George Allen and Unwin, London 1971; Welbourne; BoT Reports.

DURHAM COUNTY COLLIERY WINDING ENGINEMEN'S MUTUAL AID ASSOCIATION
This was a small union, formed in 1892 with 93 members, which had only a brief existence before being dissolved in 1898.

Sources: BoT Reports; Certification Office.

DURHAM DEPUTIES MUTUAL AID ASSOCIATION
Formed in 1877 as the **Durham Deputy Overmen's Mutual Aid Association**, the Association transferred its engagements to the **National Association of Colliery Overmen, Deputies and Shotfirers** (see Vol. 1) at an unspecified date.

Source: Certification Office.

DURHAM DEPUTY OVERMEN'S MUTUAL AID ASSOCIATION
See **Durham Deputies Mutual Aid Association**

DURHAM MINERS ASSOCIATION
After the collapse of the **Miners Association of Great Britain and Ireland** in 1847, regions of Durham and Northumberland lapsed into disorganisation

and it was not until the 1850s that economic recovery created a favourable situation for the re-emergence of trade unionism. The Durham miners participated in the formation of the **Northumberland and Durham Miners Association** in 1863. But a spate of strikes arising from low wages and under-payment began without union approval and included non-unionists. The Association survived only in Northumberland under the moderate leadership of Thomas Burt. The reimposition of the system of the yearly bond delayed the formation of a permanent trade union in Durham until the trade depression of the late 1860s, when wage cuts of the order of 10–32 per cent led to the setting up of the DMA in 1869. The rules of the DMA were designed to curtail the kind of grass roots militancy that had destroyed the earlier unions. Rule 16 prohibited any colliery from striking without the approval of the Central Committee or delegate meeting, and Rule 26 forbade any colliery from striking for a wage increase where the average daily earnings were 5s or more. William Crawford as the official agent of the DMA followed the moderate policies of Thomas Burt. Yet local disputes persisted as they had done in Northumberland until, in June 1870, Crawford took steps to strengthen the authority of the Executive Committee. The county was divided into three districts, each with a full time agent, and a new rule denied support to any pit which struck in an 'unconstitutional manner'. The new arrangements coincided with a boom in trade in the early 1870s and Crawford was able to win substantial concessions for the Durham miners. Early in 1872 the owners agreed to substitute fortnightly agreements in place of the yearly bond and granted a 20 per cent wage increase to underground workers and a 12½ per cent rise to top men. In return the DMA officials promised to prevent 'idleness' in the pits and to minimise the number of local strikes. The employers had formed the Durham Coal Owners Association and in July 1872 the officials of the two associations agreed to participate in a joint committee of 6 representatives from each side, and thus began the principle of collective bargaining. The Association affiliated to the **Miners Federation of Great Britain** in 1892, but in 1893, when the Federation sanctioned a national strike against a 25 per cent reduction in wages, the DMA refused to strike and was expelled. In 1896 there was again a move to affiliate but this was prevented by differences over the question of the 8-hour day. The affiliation eventually took place in 1908 when the membership of the DMA stood at 121,805.

Sources: Webb, *Story of the Durham Miners*; Burgess, *Origins*; John Wilson, *A History of the Durham Miners Association 1870–1904*, J.H. Veitch, Durham, 1907.

EAST CHESHIRE MINERS ASSOCIATION
Formed in 1874, the Association went out of existence in 1884.

Source: Certification Office.

EBBW VALE AND SIRHOWY COLLIERY WORKMEN'S UNION
Established in 1886, the Union had a membership of 3,500 in 1896 which

dropped to 3,250 in 1897. In 1898 the Union became a district of the **South Wales Miners Federation**.

Source: BoT Reports.

ENGINE DRIVERS' UNION OF SOUTH STAFFORDSHIRE AND EAST WORCESTERSHIRE
The Union would appear to have been in existence in 1863, but it seems that by 1875 it had become the South Staffordshire District of the **National Federation of Enginemen and Boiler Firemen**.

Source: G.J. Barnsby, *Social Conditions in the Black Country*, Integrated Publishing Services, Wolverhampton, 1980.

ENGINEERS, SMITHS AND CARPENTERS ASSOCIATION, ILKESTON AND EREWASH VALLEY LODGE
Established in 1874, the Association never had a large membership, the highest number appearing to have been 68 in 1893. At other times it registered at between 50 and 65. It nevertheless appeared to function as an organising body until the advent of the First World War, when it was dissolved with 44 members.

Sources: BoT Reports; MoL Reports.

EXCELSIOR AMALGAMATED ASSOCIATION OF COLLIERY ENGINE TENDERS
Established in 1872, the Association was dissolved in 1875.

Source: Certification Office.

FARNWORTH ENGINEMEN, BOILERMEN AND FIREMEN'S ASSOCIATION
The Association was based on a single branch which had only 42 members in 1892 and 52 members in 1900. Nevertheless it remained a functioning organisation until it was dissolved in 1920.

Sources: BoT Reports; Certification Office.

FIFE, CLACKMANNAN AND KINROSS MINERS ASSOCIATION
The Association was formed in 1870 as a result of a successful strike in June which secured for the men an 8-hour day. It was the first coalfield in Europe to win the 8-hour day, and this outstanding victory was celebrated for the following 75 years by an annual gala day. The leaders of the Association were Richard Penman and Henry Cook, who became President and Secretary respectively. It formed a central fund and by 1872 had 4,046 members and £1,200 in reserve. By 1880 it had a membership of 7,000 out of a labour force of 9,000. In 1876 the coalowners proposed a wage cut of 15

per cent which after the threat of a strike was reduced to 7½ per cent, and in 1877 there was a further effort to enforce a wages cut, this time of 10 per cent. In desperation the Association called a strike and the men were out for 14 weeks. The **Miners National Union**, realising that the Fife and Kinross Association was the only strongly based union in Scotland, imposed a levy on its affiliated organisations and supported the strikers financially all the way through, and the stoppage ended in victory for the Fife and Kinross men. Rules 3 and 4 of the union were aimed at restricting entry into the industry. No lodge could strike without Executive Committee approval or until the employers had offered arbitration or conciliation proposals, while generous benefits appealed to the loyalty of the rank and file members. Any member found working more than 8 hours daily was liable to expulsion. The economic depression of the 1870s destroyed union organisation in many localities and by 1880 only the Fife and Kinross Association survived. In the period of 1887 to 1894, when it had 5,000–6,000 members, it was the only body which could be called an established union. It grew to 18,000 in 1910. It became part of the **Scottish Miners Federation** and its Secretary, John Weir, became Treasurer of the Federation. In 1944 it was amalgamated into the **National Union of Scottish Mineworkers**.

Sources: Burgess, *Origins*; Arnot, *History of the Scottish Miners*; Royal Commission on Labour, C-6795-IV, 1892, Q.13762; Clegg, Fox and Thompson; Marwick; S. and B. Webb, *History of Trade Unionism*; John Wilson, *A History of the Durham Miners Association 1870–1904*, J.H. Veitch, Durham, 1907.

FOREST OF DEAN MINERS ASSOCIATION

The Association was formed in the village of Cinderford in the Forest of Dean in 1870. The members began to agitate for workmen's representation on the local Board of Guardians and demanded that the waste land of the Forest be divided into small patches and sold to workers at moderate prices. In 1871 it called a strike at Parkend Colliery over the appointment of a checkweighman and in support of a demand for increased wages and was successful on both counts. In 1872 the Association merged with the **Amalgamated Association of Miners** and became a district of that union with 2,000 members in 20 lodges. In 1873 it began publication of the *Forest of Dean Examiner* with guaranteed sales of 1,500 per week, but ceased publication in 1877. In 1875 the union ended its association with the AAM due to dissatisfaction with the leadership in regard to a strike which lasted from November 1874 to February 1875. The AAM Executive refused to pay strike pay to the Dean men although they made contributions of over £8,000 to the funds. To the Dean men resistance to wage reductions was of paramount importance and they expected to have full support from the AAM. Instead they were given an appeal to return to work, which they were forced to do, but with the minor victory of a 5 per cent reduction rather than the proposed 10 per cent reduction. The Forest of Dean Association retained its independent existence until 1940 when it merged with the **South Wales Miners Federation**.

Sources: *Forest of Dean Examiner*, 2 August 1873, November 1874;

Cole, 'Some Notes on British Trade Unions'; Chris Fisher and John Smethurst, 'War on the Law of Supply and Demand: the Amalgamated Association of Miners and the Forest of Dean Colliers, 1869–1875', *in* Harrison.

FREE COLLIERS OR BROTHERED MINERS' MOVEMENT
A report is given in 1864 of the 'Brotherhood extending rapidly in the Ancient Kingdom'. James Simpson was its leader. In East Lothian 215 locals formed a lodge of the Free Colliers and in Midlothian 325 men joined the lodge. By the end of 1844 there were 1,122 members in Midlothian and 1,200 in Fife, but the Free Colliers do not seem to have played any effective part in 1867 or 1868. There are brief notes of certain lodge meetings but by the late 1860s there were only remnants remaining in Fife, and there too the union eventually went out of existence.

Source: Arnot, *History of the Scottish Miners*.

FRIENDLY SOCIETY OF COAL MINERS
Formed at Bolton in March 1830, the Society had members in Lancashire, Yorkshire, Staffordshire and Wales and was affiliated to the **National Association of United Trades for the Protection of Labour** (see Vol. 3). Its main aim was to resist wage reductions and to finance workers who struck against such proposed reductions. It was concerned solely with the question of wages and was not interested in providing sickness or accident benefits. The Society's administrative structure was centred around the Lodge Committee of 7 members, who were elected by the branch. In addition it appointed 4 members whose duty it was to investigate any wage disputes, and based on their report, the Lodge Committee would take such action as it deemed advisable. The union's official rules consisted mainly of a table of fines and penalties designed to encourage 'honesty, sobriety, industry and peaceable behaviour'. The Society also had a set of secret rules which advocated restricting entry into the industry and ensuring that no blacklegs would be allowed to replace colliers who had left the colliery or been dismissed. Another rule stipulated that no union member should engage to do more work than he could complete in a day – in other words, it advocated output restrictions. No further mention has been found of the existence of the Society after December 1833. It is assumed to have collapsed after a lockout of union members when it was unable to provide the locked-out men with even the necessities of life because its funds had been depleted by previous strikes, and it had been unable to gain recognition from the coal owners.

Sources: Arnot, *The Miners*; Burgess, *Origins*; Welbourne; Machin.

GARW MINERS ASSOCIATION
Established in 1880, the Association apparently employed a miners' agent from its inception. It had 3,000 members in 1890 out of some 12,000 men employed in the area. In 1891 it merged with the **Miners Federation of Great Britain** and ceased to have an independent existence. No lodges or branches had been developed but contributions of 4d or 6d per month were

paid voluntarily at the pit head. Administration was apparently in the hands of a monthly meeting of delegates from each pit.

Source: Evans, *Miners of South Wales.*

GATESHEAD AND NEWCASTLE DISTRICT QUARRYMEN'S TRADE ASSOCIATION

Both 1840 and 1842 are given as the date of formation of the Association. Until 1899 its title was the **Gateshead Quarrymen's Trade Association**, the above title being adopted in 1900. It had 279 members in 1892, 406 in 1904, 376 in 1907 and 305 in 1910. It had 2 branches in Gateshead and 2 in Newcastle. It was still on record as a functioning body until the end of the First World War, after which date there is no further reference to its existence under this title.

Sources: BoT Reports; MoL Reports.

GATESHEAD QUARRYMEN'S TRADE ASSOCIATION

See **Gateshead and Newcastle District Quarrymen's Trade Association**

GREAT HARWOOD AND CLAYTON LE MOORS MINERS ASSOCIATION

Formed in 1895, the Association was dissolved in 1900.

Source: Certification Office.

HAMILTON MINERS ASSOCIATION

No formation date is recorded for the Association, but it had an estimated membership of 1,200 in 1894 and 200 in 1895. It became a branch of the **Lanarkshire Miners County Union** in 1896.

Source: BoT Reports.

HAULIERS AND WAGEMEN'S UNION OF SOUTH WALES AND MONMOUTHSHIRE

Set up in 1893, the Union had an estimated recorded membership in that year of 3,004, followed by 5,500 in 1894. It was dissolved in 1895.

Source: BoT Reports.

HINDLEY MINERS' IMPROVEMENT BENEFIT SOCIETY

Established in 1878, the Society had 1,392 members in 1893. In 1898, with a membership of 624, it became a branch of the **Lancashire and Cheshire Miners' Federation**.

Sources: Arnot, *The Miners*; BoT Reports.

HOLYTOWN MINERS ASSOCIATION
The Association was a local union formed early in the 1840s, which in 1847 attempted to combat wage reductions of 1s per day by restricting output. These efforts resulted in the masters imposing a 3-month lockout which ended in defeat for the Association. It merged in 1855 with the newly formed **Scottish Coal and Iron-stone Miners Protective Association**. There appears to have been another association of the same name in the 1890s, which became a branch of the **Lanarkshire Miners County Union**.

Sources: Arnot, *The Miners*; BoT Reports.

HOLYTOWN MINERS ASSOCIATION
No formation date is recorded for the Association which was the second union under this title, but it had an estimated membership of 200 both for 1894 and 1895. In 1896 it became a branch of the **Lanarkshire Miners County Union**.

Source: BoT Reports.

ILKESTON CONSERVATIVE MINERS ASSOCIATION
Formed in 1890, the Association ceased to exist after 1901. It seems to have been re-formed in 1907 and had 98 members in 1910.

Source: Certification Office.

KEARSLEY, CLIFTON, PENDLEBURY AND PENDLETON MINERS ASSOCIATION
Established in 1888, the Association amalgamated with the **National Union of Mineworkers** in 1959 and became the Pendlebury branch of the Union.

Source: Certification Office.

KENT MINERS' ASSOCIATION
The first recorded entry of the Association's existence was made in 1915, the secretary at that time being W.H. Varley of Woods Place, Dover, his place being taken in 1919 by H. Hartley of Stonewall Villas, Lydden. In the early 1920s John Elks became secretary, retaining that position until 1948 when Jack Johnson took over the responsibility, Jack Dunn replacing him in 1960. From its inception it was a constituent union of the **Miners Federation of Great Britain**. It is a small coalfield and consequently its membership has never been very big. The Kent Association has always been known for the militancy of its membership, two examples of which took place in 1941 and in 1961. In 1941 1,000 Betteshanger pit men were served summonses by the government for coming out on strike in breach of the wartime emergency regulations on compulsory arbitration. Three officials were sentenced to hard labour and the remainder were fined £1 each with the option of a prison sentence. The men refused both to pay the fines and to return to work until the release of the three men from Canterbury Gaol. After 11 days of mass

demonstrations by the miners and their families, the government capitulated, the fines were waived and the three branch officials released from prison. In 1961, for six days 127 miners staged a stay-down strike in the Betteshanger pit in opposition to the serving of 140 redundancy notices by the National Coal Board. The men's action was successful in that it was agreed to open up another seam at 1900 feet. The Association became the Kent area of the **National Union of Mineworkers** in 1945 with 5,100 members. Three pits only are now being worked, the Chislet pit having been closed in 1969.

Sources: MoL Reports; Malcolm Pitt, *The World on our Backs: the Kent Miners and the 1972 Miners' Strike*, Lawrence & Wishart, London, 1979; Conversation with Jack Dunn, 21 June 1983.

KILMARNOCK MINERS ASSOCIATION
This was the first union formed amongst Scottish miners after the repeal of the Combination Laws in 1824 and was founded by operative colliers from 27 pits around Kilmarnock who met on 25 October 1824. Although the Association did not remain in existence for any length of time it laid the basis for future organisation. The colliers in this area eventually joined the **Miners Association of Great Britain and Ireland** which itself collapsed in 1848.

Source: Arnot, *History of the Scottish Miners*.

KIRKINTILLOCH AND DISTRICT MINERS ASSOCIATION
See **Kirkintilloch and Twechar Miners Association**

KIRKINTILLOCH AND TWECHAR MINERS ASSOCIATION
In 1893 collieries in Dumbartonshire which had been part of a Lanarkshire Miners' County Federation formerly known as the Dumbartonshire Miners formed themselves into this small separate county union, which remained an independent body until it was absorbed with fewer than 1,000 members into the **Lanarkshire Miners County Union** in 1927.

Sources: Arnot, *History of the Scottish Miners*; BoT Reports.

LANARKSHIRE MINERS COUNTY UNION
Formed in 1896 with under 3,000 of the 31,000 workers then occupied in the coalfield, the Lanarkshire Miners became the most successful of the local unions in the area and in 1910, with 33,000 members, it was the largest and most militant organisation in the **Scottish Miners Federation.** William Small was its first general secretary. In 1944 the Union merged into the **National Union of Scottish Mineworkers** (see also Table 4).

Sources: BoT Reports; Arnot, *History of the Scottish Miners*.

LANCASHIRE AND CHESHIRE COLLIERY FIREMEN'S ASSOCIATION

The Association was registered in 1910, but nothing further is known of its history.

Source: Certification Office.

LANCASHIRE AND CHESHIRE MINERS' FEDERATION

Formerly members of the **Miners Association of Great Britain and Ireland**, the Lancashire miners decided to form their own organisation in 1844 under the title of the **Lancashire Miners Federation**. It never sought to impose centralised control, advocating instead a loose federal structure. The Lancashire mining industry was composed of a number of small pits, and as the owners could not afford to have the pits idle for any length of time they were normally ready to come to terms with the men. An analysis of the Wigan coalfield in 1851 showed that nearly 50 per cent of all collieries had an output of less than 100 tons a day and most pits employed less than 25 men. During the trade depression of the 1870s these small local unions had a total membership of not more than 1,000 and most of those were checkweighmen with a small number of better paid hewers. In 1881 the coal owners tried to force the miners to join the employer-sponsored Lancashire and Cheshire Miners Permanent Relief Society as a condition of employment. The result was an unofficial strike by the 50,000 miners in the region which lasted 3 weeks and was settled by local agreements which marked a substantial victory for the miners; wage increases of between 5 and 12½ per cent were common. The Federation began to grow in strength again and appointed Thomas Ashton as General Secretary, securing recognition from the owners on the basis of avoiding large-scale disputes. In 1897 the name was changed in order to include Cheshire and the new Federation incorporated within it the following mining associations: **Standish and District Miners Association; Wigan Miners Association; Ashton-under-Lyne Miners' Association; Skelmersdale District Miners Association; Leigh and District Miners' Association; St Helens District Federation of Miners; Blackrod Miners' Association; Pemberton and District Miners Association; Ashton, Haydock and Bolton Miners' Trade Union; Manchester Miners Association; Aspull and District Miners Association;** and **Oldham and District Miners Association.**

Sources: A.J. Taylor, 'The Wigan Coalfield in 1851', Transcript of the Lancashire and Cheshire History Society; *Miners Advocate*, March 1847; S. and B. Webb, *History of Trade Unionism*; Raymond Challinor and Brian Ripley, *The Miners Association. A Trade Union in the Age of the Chartists*, Lawrence and Wishart, 1968; Burgess, *Origins*; Arnot, *The Miners*.

LANCASHIRE AND OTHER COUNTIES COLLIERY WINDERS FEDERATION

Established in 1893, the Federation was dissolved in 1898.

Source: Certification Office.

223

LANCASHIRE COKEMEN AND LABOURERS AND LOCAL RAILWAY SERVANTS UNION
See **Yorkshire and Derbyshire Cokemen and Labourers Union**

LANCASHIRE COLLIERY FIREMEN'S SOCIETY
The Society, founded in 1893, had a very short existence, being dissolved in 1896.

Source: BoT Reports.

LANCASHIRE DATALLERS' AND SURFACEMEN'S FEDERATED UNION
The Union was registered in 1912, after which date nothing further appears to be known of its existence.

Source: Certification Office.

LANCASHIRE FEDERATIONIST TRADE UNION
Established in 1903 with 60 members, rising to 285 in 1904, and dropping to 82 in 1905, the Union ceased to exist in 1906.

Source: BoT Reports.

LANCASHIRE MINERS FEDERATION
See **Lancashire and Cheshire Miners' Federation**

LARKHALL MINERS MUTUAL PROTECTION ASSOCIATION
Formed in the late 1860s, the Larkhall Association became, during the boom years of economic expansion and the growth of trade unionism in the 1870s, one of the best organised districts in Scotland, expanding its area of jurisdiction to the new pits around Hamilton and Blantyre, and beyond to Carluke and Lesmahagow. Its 2,500 members were organised in 6 branches and their contributions to the Association from April to June 1874 totalled over £2,000. Larkhall was one of the few districts in Lanarkshire where men were allowed to work only on production of a union 'clearance line' and after giving a declaration to work only the restricted darg. Two newcomers to the district were admitted only on payment of 10s each as they had 'no lines'. As wages increased, so did the price of entry to the union; by 1873 it was £2 for any 'neutral man'. With growing financial strength the Association began discussing the possibility of forming co-operative building societies in order to allow the members to buy their own homes; and it floated the idea of raising funds in order to buy coalfields, sink shafts and work the coal for their own benefit. It became part of the **Lanarkshire Miners County Union** in 1896.

Sources: R. Haddow, 'The Miners of Scotland', 19th century, Vol. 24, No. 139, September 1888, p. 360–373; Minutes of Evidence, Royal

Commission on Labour, Vol. 2, QQ.9879, 9998; A.J.Y. Brown, 'Trade Union Policy in the Scottish Coalfields, 1855–1885', *Economic History Review*, 2nd ser. VI, (1953–4); *Glasgow Sentinel*, 25 January 1873; *Glasgow Herald*, 24 March 1874; Alan Campbell, 'Honourable Men and Degraded Slaves: A comparative study of trade unionism in two Lanarkshire mining communities, c. 1830–1874', in Harrison.

LEICESTERSHIRE MINERS ASSOCIATION
The Association was established in 1887. It had nearly 6,000 members in 1906. It became the Leicester area of the **National Union of Mineworkers** upon the formation of that union.

Source: Certification Office.

LEIGH AND DISTRICT MINERS' ASSOCIATION
Established in 1878, the Association had 5,842 members by 1893. In 1897, with a membership standing at 2,400, it ceased to be an independent union and became a district association of the **Lancashire and Cheshire Miners' Federation**.

Source: Arnot, *The Miners*.

LITTLE LEVER, DARCY LEVER, BREIGHTMET, AND GREAT LEVER MINERS ASSOCIATION AND CHECKWEIGH FUND
There is only one reference to the existence of this Association. It is recorded as having been formed in 1887 and having 1,211, 1,600, 1,194 and 1,014 members in the years 1892 to 1896 respectively. The secretary's address is given as The Hare and Hounds Inn, Little Lever, Bolton.

Source: BoT Reports.

LOFTHOUSE MINERS REFUGE UNION
Established in 1881, the Union went out of existence in 1893.

Source: Certification Office.

MANCHESTER MINERS ASSOCIATION
Established in 1886, the Association had 3,897 members in 1893. In 1897, with 3,229 members, it ceased to exist as an independent union and became a branch of the **Lancashire and Cheshire Miners' Federation**.

Source: Arnot, *The Miners*.

MARYHILL MINERS ASSOCIATION
The Association was probably formed in the early 1870s. It had 1,800

members in 1873 and funds in reserve of £3,700. What happened to the Association is not clear. It probably merged with the **Lanarkshire Miners County Union**.

Source: Arnot, *History of the Scottish Miners*.

METHLEY MINERS ASSOCIATION
Formed in 1888, the Association was dissolved in 1890.

Source: Certification Office.

MID AND EAST LOTHIAN MINERS ASSOCIATION
The Association is said to have been in existence in 1873, though the Board of Trade gives its date of formation as 1889. It had a membership of about 2,000 and financial reserves of £1,500. The Secretary was David Moffat who was succeeded by Alexander Cameron. In March 1944, together with the **Fife, Clackmannan and Kinross Miners Association**, the **Stirling and Linlithgow Miners Association**, the **Larkhall, Maryhill** and **Wishaw Miners Associations** and the **Lanarkshire Miners County Union**, the Association ended its independent existence and became part of the **National Union of Scottish Mineworkers**, later becoming the Scottish area of the **National Union of Mineworkers** in 1945.

Sources: S. and B. Webb, *History of Trade Unionism*; Arnot, *History of the Scottish Miners*; BoT Reports.

MID AND WEST LOTHIAN LABOUR FEDERATION
Formed in 1886 under the above title it was also called the **Amalgamated Section Scotch Miners and Oilworkmen**. It became the **Amalgamated Miners and Manual Workers Union** in 1892. Upon its formation it had 1,577 members which had dropped to 674 in 1890 and to 500 in 1892. Its objects were stated to be 'the protection of labour and the establishment of checkweighmen to secure actual weights, and to resist exaction of illegal claims and deductions; to shorten the hours of labour, to obtain better house accommodation, and to raise men generally to a higher social level'. By 1893 it was registering a membership of 3,000, with 2,000 in 1899, 1,500 in 1904 and 3,050 in 1910. Councillor J. Doonan of Bathgate acted as secretary from 1913 to 1925 by which date the title had been changed to the **West Lothian Mineworkers Union**. It became part of the **National Union of Scottish Mineworkers**.

Sources: BoT Reports; MoL Reports, Statistical Tables and Report on Trade Unions, Fourth Report, 1889 and 1890.

MIDLAND COUNTIES FEDERATION OF MINERS
The Federation owned a rule book dating from 1882 but its recorded date of formation is 1886, with S.H. Whitehouse and Enoch Edwards as Secretary and President respectively. Its membership was composed of: the

South Staffordshire and East Worcestershire Amalgamated Miners Association; the **North Staffordshire Miners Association**; the **Old Hill and Highley District Miners Association**; the **Shropshire Miners Association**; the **Cannock Chase Miners, Enginemen's and Surfacemen's Association**; and the **West Bromwich Miners Association**. The Federation later became the third largest constituent part of the **Miners Federation of Great Britain** upon the formation of that body.

Source: Arnot, *The Miners*.

MILNROW MINERS ASSOCIATION
Established in 1890, the Association was dissolved in 1896.

Source: Certification Office.

MINERS ASSOCIATION OF GREAT BRITAIN AND IRELAND
Strongly supported county mining unions existed in the 1830s in Northumberland, Durham, Lancashire and Yorkshire, which helped lay the ground for the formation of the above union in Wakefield on 7 November 1842. The Association claimed to have nearly 5,000 members in 1843, which had increased to 50,000 by the end of the year. Any coal, lead or ironstone miner was entitled to join. The entrance fee was 6d and 1d was charged for a membership card. The weekly subscription was 1d. Half the amount of money collected was retained by the local organisation and half was paid over to the General Treasurer. The rules and regulations set out the sole aim as 'uniting all miners to equalise and diminish the hours of labour and to obtain the highest possible amount of wages for his labour'. David Swallow was the first General Secretary. In 1847 two of its leaders, William Dixon and W.P. Roberts, were the first trade unionists to stand for Parliament. An active Chartist, William Grocott, became General Secretary in 1847. He was sentenced to imprisonment for his political activities in 1848 and this was considered to be one of the factors for contributing to the decline of the Association. It began publication of its own journal, *The Miners' Advocate*, in 1843. The state of the union at the end of 1844 was one of extreme contrasts. Some sections of it were successful, others had been crushed. In trying to formulate and apply a common strategy and wage levels in all coalfields, it overlooked the local factors which had so much influence. It was not until a national market for coal was created that the preconditions for a unified national organisation were established. The basic reason for the end of the Association's existence was the extreme persecution of union members by the coal owners. Its demise was also hastened by the economic crisis of 1847. It had only succeeded in creating sporadic and unco-ordinated strikes which, in a period of unemployment, were always defeated. It ceased to exist in 1848.

Sources: *Derbyshire Courier*, April 1844; *Northern Star*, November 1844, May 1845; S. and B. Webb, *History of Trade Unionism*; Frederick Engels, *Condition of the Working Class in England in 1844*, William Reeves, London, 1888; Richard Fynes, *The Miners of Northumberland and Durham*, S.R. Publishers Reprint, Wakefield, 1971; Royal Commission on

Trade Unions, 1842; A.J. Taylor, 'The Miners Association of Great Britain and Ireland, 1842–8', *Economica*, February 1955; *Miners Advocate*, January 1844; W. Johnson, *The Miners' Grievances*, n.d., Newcastle; Welbourne; Raymond Challinor and Brian Ripley, *The Miners Association. A Trade Union in the Age of the Chartists*, Lawrence and Wishart, 1968; A. Aspinall, *The Early English Trade Unions*, Batchworth Press, London, 1949; John Wilson, *A History of the Durham Miners Association 1870–1904*, J.H. Veitch, Durham, 1907.

MINERS FEDERATION OF GREAT BRITAIN
See **Mineworkers Federation of Great Britain**

MINERS NATIONAL UNION
Formed in 1863 as the **National Association of Coal, Lime and Ironstone Miners of Great Britain**, the Union's objects were 'to consider, provide for, and execute as far as possible, all public and general business relating to the interests of operative miners as regards legislation for the inspection of mines and for compensation for accidents, but not to interfere with local disputes'. Many colliers expected the Union to provide a lead in policy-making but this idea was disowned by its officials who refused to be drawn into local grievances, supporting the view that the miners should persuade the coal owners to accept arbitration and conciliation. In 1868, during the progress of a strike, the Executive Committee made the decision not to support men who had been locked out. The result was the virtual destruction of trade unionism in the less organised districts as expectations of financial assistance during strike action ended instead invariably in defeat and victimisation due to lack of support by the Union. In 1869 a new union, the **Amalgamated Association of Miners**, was formed in direct opposition to the MNU which lost membership as a result, its remaining strength being concentrated in Scotland, the North East coast, Yorkshire and some of the Midland areas. Agitation by the Union over the years culminated in the passing of the Coal Mines Regulation Act of 1872 which stipulated that output of coal had to be paid by weight, and limiting the hours of work by boys underground. These political gains appeared to vindicate the moderate policy of the Union but it continued to lose support, and by 1880 its membership was confined only to Northumberland, Durham and Yorkshire. The Northumberland and Durham Miners' Associations dominated the MNU. Both Associations held a comparatively privileged position and remained loyal to the sliding scale system of wage payment. The Union was formed and remained under the leadership of Alexander Macdonald, who became one of the first miners' MPs. He died in 1881, Thomas Burt of the Northumberland Miners becoming the next President. The Union's affairs were wound up in 1898 when its last affiliated Associations withdrew, leaving Northumberland as the sole remaining district.

Sources: S. and B. Webb, *History of Trade Unionism*; Arnot, *The Miners*; Transactions and Results of the National Association of Coal, Lime and Ironstone Miners' Conference held at Leeds on 9–14 November 1863; Clegg, Fox and Thompson; Burgess, *Origins*; Williams, *The Derbyshire Miners*; R. Fynes, *The Miners of Northumberland and Durham*, S.R.Publishers reprint, Wakefield, 1971; Welbourne; Ness Edwards, *The History of the South Wales Miners*, Labour Publishing Co, 1926.

MINERS OF RHOSLLANERCHUROG

This was a local organisation for coal miners in North Wales formed in 1900 with three branches. It had 983 members in 1900, but was dissolved in the following year.

Source: BoT Reports.

MINERS ORGANISATION OF THE ADWALTON AND DRIGHLINGTON DISTRICT

The Organisation was a union formed in June 1859 under the leadership of John Dixon. The miners employed in these collieries were the most militant in West Yorkshire. The men had had their wages drastically reduced in 1855, and the region had been plagued with disputes concerning clearance papers, without which it was impossible to find work at other collieries. The decision was made to form their own union due to dissatisfaction at the policies carried out by the **West Yorkshire Miners Association** which purported to act for the miners of Adwalton and Drighlington pits. The breakaway union did not remain long in existence, the men rejoining the WYMA in 1866.

Source: Machin.

MINERS PHILANTHROPIC SOCIETY

The Society was a forerunner of the **Miners Association of Great Britain and Ireland**. It met at the Griffin Inn, Wakefield. All colliers were asked to contact the Society to lay the foundations for a national organisation, and a meeting was held on 7 November 1842 in Wakefield. Every pit was asked to appoint delegates, the conference being called 'for the purpose of taking into consideration the distress of coal miners and adopting a petition to Parliament'. The meeting appointed an Executive Committee and it planned to start a journal. At a public meeting held that evening the following resolutions were passed: 'that the present state of wages paid to colliers is not a fair remuneration for their labour'; and 'that it is the opinion of this meeting that we shall never better our condition, social or moral, until we unite for the protection of our labour'. Many colliers joined the Society and it was resolved to hold a delegate conference of all grades of miners, at which the decision was made to form the **Miners Association of Great Britain and Ireland**.

Source: Raymond Challinor and Brian Ripley, *The Miners Association. A Trade Union in the Age of the Chartists*, Lawrence and Wishart, 1968.

MINEWORKERS FEDERATION OF GREAT BRITAIN

The formation of the Federation (named the Miners Federation of Great Britain until 1932) developed from a series of meetings of delegates from the main coalfields which co-ordinated wage claims in 1888 and 1889. The decision to establish a permanent organisation was taken at a conference in Newport in 1889 at which dissatisfaction was expressed at the policy of the **Miners National Union** which abhorred militancy and believed in the principle of the sliding scale. The **Yorkshire Miners' Association** invited all representatives of miners' organisations 'free from sliding scales' to a conference to discuss the best means of securing a 10 per cent wage increase and to find common ground for action. The success of the subsequent campaign, which resulted in an immediate wage increase of 5 per cent with a further 5 per cent to be paid during the summer months, led to the formation of a formal alliance in 1890, with Ben Pickard, the Secretary of the YMA, becoming President of the Federation. By 1892 trade union membership in the industry was approaching 300,000, more than half of whom were in the Federation. Of these Yorkshire provided 55,000; Lancashire and Cheshire 30,000; Nottinghamshire and Derbyshire 35,000 between them; and some 40,000 to 50,000 were spread over the Midlands, Bristol and Somerset, North Wales and parts of Scotland. The **Durham Miners Association** and the **Northumberland Miners Mutual Confident Association** remained outside the Federation with 50,000 and 17,000 respectively, both organisations later affiliating. It was not until 1908 that complete federation was obtained comprising an affiliated membership of 600,000. The basis of organisation lay in the colliery lodges. The Federation had no organisational control over the domestic affairs of its affiliated units. It was not until 1945, after repeated efforts to achieve greater centralisation that agreement was reached to form one organisation to cover all miners, the **National Union of Mineworkers**.

Sources: Cole, *British Trade Unionism Today*; Burgess, *Origins*; Williams, 'Labour in the coalfields'; Alan Fox, 'Industrial Relations in Birmingham and the Black Country, 1860–1914', B. Litt. thesis, Oxford University, 1952; R. Page Arnot, *The Miners: The Years of Struggle*, George Allen and Unwin, 1953; R. Page Arnot, *The Miners in Crisis and War*, George Allen and Unwin, 1961; Williams, *The Derbyshire Miners*; George B. Baldwin, 'Structural Reform in the British Miners' Union', *Quarterly Journal of Economics*, November 1953, pp. 576–96; Report on the Strikes and Lockouts of 1890, C-6476, 1891; Report on Changes in Rates of Wages and Hours of Labour, 1900, Cmnd.688, 1901; S. and B. Webb, *History of Trade Unionism*.

MONMOUTH WESTERN VALLEY MINERS ASSOCIATION
Established in 1897, the Association had a membership of 500. In 1898 it merged with the **South Wales Miners Federation.**

Source: BoT Reports.

MONMOUTHSHIRE DISTRICT MINERS ASSOCIATION
See **Monmouthshire and South Wales District Miners Association**

MONMOUTHSHIRE AND SOUTH WALES COLLIERY ENGINEMEN, STOKERS AND CRAFTSMEN'S ASSOCIATION
Formed in 1889 with 3,141 members in 1899, the Association would appear

to have joined the **South Wales Miners Federation** in 1900 but seceded from that organisation in 1903.

Sources: Certification Office; BoT Reports.

MONMOUTHSHIRE AND SOUTH WALES DISTRICT MINERS ASSOCIATION

The Association was first formed in 1870 under the auspices of the **Amalgamated Association of Miners** and survived that Association's collapse in 1875. Its original title was the **Monmouthshire District Miners Association**, the above title being adopted in 1896. It was an extremely weak organisation, the membership numbering under 2,000. The Association affiliated to the **Miners National Union** in 1887, but withdrew its affiliation in 1889, transferring to the **Mineworkers Federation of Great Britain**. An agent was appointed in 1890 and by 1891 it had some 5,000 members out of a workforce of 25,000, this number falling to 3,500 by 1893. Lodges were set up near each colliery and subscriptions were 6d and 1s per month, with an entrance fee of 1s. Strike pay was at the rate of 10s per week with an additional 1s per week for dependents. The administration of the union's affairs was in the hands of the President, the Secretary and Treasurer who were elected annually, assisted by a District Council of one delegate from each lodge who met on a monthly basis. In 1892 there were 9 separate district associations of miners in the area which together had no more than 25,000 members in a labour force of over 88,000, and their chief function was to administer the workmen's share of the sliding scale agreements. These sliding scale orientated associations were under the leadership of William Abraham, the policy of collective bargaining being almost non-existent in South Wales. But the success of the militant wages policy being conducted by the MFGB led to increasing dissatisfaction with the sliding scale when coal prices began to fall. In 1898 the men rejected Abraham's plea to reach a new sliding scale agreement with the coal owners and decided on strike action. The ensuing stoppage exhausted the funds of the local unions, the men being forced back to work on the employers' terms. This defeat laid the ground for united action, and the creation of the **South Wales Miners Federation** in 1898 with an initial membership of 60,000 marked the beginning of the end of the sliding scale system of payment in Wales.

Sources: Arnot, *South Wales Miners*; Francis and Smith; Certification Office; Evans, *Miners of South Wales*.

MONMOUTHSHIRE COAL MINERS ASSOCIATION

By 1843 the Monmouthshire colliers apparently formed a local union with the above title, although this is not absolutely certain. What little is known of the Association is derived from accounts of a strike which took place against a wage reduction proposed at sale-coal workings near Newport. Starting in January 1843 the strike spread throughout Monmouthshire and eventually affected Glamorgan where sale-coal pits in the Aberdare Valley and elsewhere became idle. After some weeks representatives of the men and employers met and working was gradually resumed with a compromise settlement. It was generally recognised that the strike was the result of a 'confederacy among the Monmouthshire colliers to obtain such wages as they pleased to exact, by acting in concert with other colliers in the neighbourhood'. Meetings were held to discuss policy, marching gangs spread the strike, and blacklegs were initimidated by warnings such as 'Damn you, you must not send your coal down to Newport or else you shall be burned, you and the trams and the coal, to Hell, you damned set of toads that you are.' The only specific mention of a trade union was made with reference to the hardship suffered by the strikers, when it was observed that 'his trade union subscription funds support him for a time, and when those are expended he has only to return to work'. Yet even if the strike involved no formal and permanent organisation, it was certainly one of the deciding factors leading to a revival of interest in trade union organisation, many mining lodges in Wales joining the **Miners Association of Great Britain and Ireland** until the collapse of that union.

Sources: *Merlin*, 4 February 1843, 11 February 1843, 18 March 1843; *Mining Journal*, 23 December 1843; Ness Edwards, *The History of the South Wales Miners*, Labour Publishing Co, 1926.

MOTHERWELL MINERS ASSOCIATION
Although there is no actual recorded date of formation of the Association given, it had an estimated membership of 300 for the years 1894 and 1895. In 1896 it became a branch of the **Lanarkshire Miners County Union.**

Source: BoT Reports.

NATIONAL AMALGAMATED ASSOCIATION OF COLLIERY ENGINEMEN
Founded in 1874, registration of the Association was cancelled in 1895.

Source: Certification Office.

NATIONAL AMALGAMATED SOCIETY OF MECHANICS
The Society was established in 1873 as the **Durham County Amalgamated Society of Colliery Mechanics**, and the name was changed in 1877 to the above. It merged later with the **Durham Miners Association**.

Source: Certification Office.

NATIONAL ASSOCIATION OF COAL, LIME AND IRONSTONE MINERS OF GREAT BRITAIN
See **Miners National Union**

NATIONAL COKEMEN AND BY-PRODUCT WORKERS' UNION
See **National Cokemen and Surface Workers' Union**

NATIONAL COKEMEN AND SURFACE WORKERS' UNION

The Union was formed in 1911 by an amalgamation of the **Yorkshire and Derbyshire Cokemen and Labourers Union** and the **Lancashire Cokemen and Labourers and Local Railway Servants Union** covering 1,225 members. Membership had risen to 2,382 by 1915. In 1916 the Union amalgamated with the **Durham Cokemen and Labourers' Union** in order to form the **National Cokemen and By-product Workers' Union**.

Source: Bain and Price.

NATIONAL FEDERATION OF ENGINEMEN AND BOILER FIREMEN

Formed in 1872, the Federation had 10,000 members in 1913. It later merged with the **Miners Federation of Great Britain**.

Source: Williams, *The Derbyshire Miners*.

NATIONAL UNDERGROUND COLLIERY FIREMEN'S OR SHOT-LIGHTERS' UNDERLOOKERS' ASSOCIATION (STOKE ON TRENT)

The Association was established in 1902 but seems to have disappeared by 1904.

Source: Certification Office.

NATIONAL UNION OF COKEMEN AND BY-PRODUCT WORKERS

The first cokemen's union was formed in 1874 as the **Union of Cokemen**. The above union was set up in 1916 as the result of an amalgamation between the **National Cokemen and Surface Workers' Union** and the **Durham Cokemen and Labourers' Union**. This title was adopted in order to include the fast growing number of by-product workers engaged in the industry. The Union became the cokemen's area of the **National Union of Mineworkers** upon the formation of that union.

Sources: Webb, *Story of the Durham Miners*; Certification Office.

NATIONAL UNION OF MINEWORKERS

In January 1945 the **Mineworkers Federation of Great Britain** became the NUM. At that time the MFGB had one full time official, three staff members and an annual income of about one-tenth of the £140,000 collected by the **Durham Miners Association**, which underlines the fact that the 22 autonomous districts of the MFGB retained their own powerful autonomy at that time. Previously, in 1939, the decision had been made to restructure the Federation on lines more acceptable to the districts incorporated within it, and in 1944 the reorganisation was completed, giving the newly formed NUM a new legal and financial relationship with the affiliated unions, the old district unions becoming administrative areas of the NUM. It is an industrial union negotiating directly with the National Coal Board and includes coalmining staffs, clerical workers and cokemen. Membership has fallen over the years with the contraction of the coalmining industry.

Sources: George B. Baldwin, 'Structural Reform in the British Miners' Union', *Quarterly Journal of Economics*, November 1953, pp. 576–96; Marsh, *Trade Union Handbook*.

NATIONAL UNION OF QUARRYMEN
Formed in 1887, the Union merged with the **Settmakers Union of Great Britain and Ireland** in 1914.

Sources: Certification Office; MoL Reports.

NATIONAL UNION OF SCOTTISH MINEWORKERS
The title was first used in 1914 when the **Scottish Miners Federation** adopted it in that year. The change did not lead to an amalgamation of Scottish miners' unions until 1944 when the six county associations balloted successfully to achieve this. The reconstituted organisation did not last long in this form. In June 1945 it officially became the Scottish Area of the **National Union of Mineworkers**.

Source: Arnot, *History of the Scottish Miners*.

NATIONAL UNION OF SHALE MINERS AND OIL WORKERS
The Union was formed in 1924 by an amalgamation between the **Scottish Shale Miners and Manual Workers Union** and the **Scottish Oil Workers' Union**, and registration was cancelled at the Certification Office in 1966.

Source: Certification Office.

NATIONAL UNION OF WINDING AND GENERAL ENGINEMEN
Founded in 1878 as the **Winding and General Enginemen's and Associated Trades Society**, the name was changed to the above in the early 1900s. In 1948, it merged with the **National Union of Mineworkers** becoming part of the South Wales area of that union.

Sources: Certification Office; Francis and Smith.

NEATH AND DISTRICT COLLIERY ENGINEMEN AND STOKERS
The Association was established in 1896 with a membership of 69 which had increased to 250 by 1899, and in 1900 the Association joined the **South Wales Miners Federation**.

Sources: BoT Reports; Certification Office.

NEATH, SWANSEA AND LLANELLY MINERS' ASSOCIATION
See **South Wales and Monmouthshire Colliery Workmen's Federation**

NEW CONSOLIDATED UNION OF TRADES
Scottish miners joined this organisation in July 1845 for common industrial

action, but in 1848 their attempt at trade union organisation in Scotland was broken by the deliberate policy of the masters to flood the labour market with immigrant labour from Ireland.

Source: Cole, *British Trade Unionism Today*.

NORDEN AND DISTRICT MINERS ASSOCIATION
Formed in 1891, the Association was dissolved in 1896.

Source: Certification Office.

NORTH STAFFORDSHIRE MINERS ASSOCIATION
The Association was formed in 1869, and had 5,487 members in 1892 and 11,265 members in 43 lodges in 1900. It joined the **Midland Counties Federation of Miners** in 1886, and became the North Staffordshire Federation, Midland area, of the **National Union of Mineworkers** upon its formation.

Sources: Certification Office; BoT Reports; Arnot, *The Miners*.

NORTH WALES MINERS ASSOCIATION
Formed in 1891, the Association became a constituent member of the **Miners Federation of Great Britain** and later joined the **National Union of Mineworkers** upon its formation, becoming the North Wales area of that union.

Sources: Cole, *British Trade Unionism Today*; Certification Office.

NORTH WALES QUARRYMEN'S UNION
Formed in 1874 with a peak membership of 6,600 in 1897, the Union had been involved in regular battles over wages and conditions with the major local employer, Lord Penrhyn, since 1865. In 1874 a union committee negotiated with the management over the complex piece rate wages system but in 1885 recognition was withdrawn. After attempts had been made to regain its former negotiating position with no success, in 1896 the Union called a strike of nearly 3,000 Penrhyn workers for higher wages and recognition of the Union, but it was not until 1897 that a settlement was reached although without protection for union members. In 1900 there was a further strike which lasted well into 1901, the Union being supported by brother unions, who recognised the importance to themselves of the outcome of the strike. In 1903 fellow trade unionists and other sympathisers contributed money in order to establish North Wales Quarries Ltd to employ the Penrhyn strikers, and a conciliation board was set up under the chairmanship of John Hodge of the **British Steel Smelters' Association**, who remained in this office until 1913 when the business experiment ended. The North Wales Quarrymen merged with the **Transport and General Workers' Union** (see Vol. 3) with about 8,000 members in 1923, and remained for some time a largely autonomous body within that union. It was the only union which could claim that all its officials were Welsh-speaking.

Sources: Cole, *British Trade Unionism Today*; Pugh; Clegg, Fox and Thompson.

NORTH WALES SURFACEMEN'S UNION

The Union was registered in 1907 but after that date nothing further seems to be known of its existence.

Source: Certification Office.

NORTH YORKSHIRE AND CLEVELAND MINERS AND QUARRY-MEN'S ASSOCIATION

Formed under the above title in 1872, the Association catered for the ironstone miners of the Cleveland district. Its objects were wide-ranging from the usual raising funds for mutual help, compensation in case of accidents, to regulation of the hours of labour and to securing the true weight of the material sent to bank by the miners. It also sought to improve the intellectual, moral and social conditions of its members, to subscribe to hospitals, infirmaries, and assist members who had treatment within those institutions, and expressed solidarity with other associations with the same objects. Entrance fees were fixed from time to time by the executive committee. Its membership increased over the years, standing at 3,930 in 1892, rising to 7,550 in 1900, to 8,940 in 1907, and to 9,743 in 1910. It changed its title to the **Cleveland Miners and Quarrymen's Association** in the early 1900s. G.B. Hobbs, of Ruby Street, Saltburn-by-the-Sea is recorded as holding the position of secretary from 1896 to 1919. The Association became a district of the **National Union of Mineworkers.**

Sources: BoT Reports; MoL Reports; Statistical Tables and Report on Trade Unions, Fourth Report, 1889 and 1890.

NORTHUMBERLAND AND DURHAM MINERS ASSOCIATION

After the collapse of the **Miners Association of Great Britain and Ireland** in 1847, areas like Northumberland and Durham suffered a decline in trade union activity. It was the coal owners' determination to revive the yearly bonding system which had fallen into disuse after 1844 that led to the formation of the Association in 1863. Subscriptions were 1d per member, victimisation benefit was payable, and a rule laid down that no strike should take place without the prior approval of the Executive Committee. The Secretary was Joseph Sheldon. In spite of the rule, almost immediately upon the Association's formation there was a series of strikes arising from the payment of low wages and under-payments which were undertaken without E.C. approval and which included non-unionists. The union died out of existence after only one year due to many internal quarrels and the decision was taken by the Northumberland men to form their own separate union, the **Northumberland Miners Mutual Confident Association**. In Durham any organisation remaining was confined to small local pit clubs covering a membership of about 1,000. It was not until 1869 that a decision was reached to form the **Durham Miners Association**.

Sources: Webb, *Story of the Durham Miners*; R. Fynes, *The Miners of Northumberland and Durham*, S.R. Publishers Reprint, 1971; J. Wilson, *A History of the Durham Miners Association, 1870–1904*, J.H. Veitch, Durham, 1907; G.H. Metcalfe, 'A History of the Durham Miners Association, 1869–1915', typescript study deposited in the library of the NUM (Durham area), Red Hill, Durham; Arnot, *The Miners*; Clegg, Fox and Thompson.

NORTHUMBERLAND COLLIERY ENGINEMEN AND FIREMEN'S ASSOCIATION

Formed in 1864, the Association became part of the **National Union of Mineworkers** in 1945.

Source: BoT Reports.

NORTHUMBERLAND COLLIERY MECHANICS TRADE SOCIETY

The Society was established in 1875 and eventually became part of the **National Union of Mineworkers** in 1945.

Source: BoT Reports.

NORTHUMBERLAND MINERS MUTUAL CONFIDENT ASSOCIATION

The Association was established in 1864 after the failure of the joint **Northumberland and Durham Miners Association** which had itself been formed only one year previously, but which had not been a success largely because of internal quarrels, the decision being taken by the Northumberland men to secede from the joint association and form their own union. The instigator of the move was a young miner named Thomas Burt, and when after a year of office the first Secretary of the new body resigned, Burt was elected Secretary at a salary of 27s 6d per week, a position he held for nearly 50 years. From 1874 until 1910 Burt was also the Northumberland miners' representative in Parliament. When Burt became Secretary the Association had 4,250 members and a cash reserve fund of £23 3s 2d. The policy of the union set a precedent for trade unionism in the North-East, seeking as it did to acquire strength in a relatively small district and to accumulate a reserve fund as a means of curbing local militants. It gradually won acceptance by the owners due to its policy of co-operation although traditions of militancy still survived for some years in villages like West Cramlington, where the men came out on strike 23 times during 22 years, to the disapproval of Burt and the Executive Committee. The Association affiliated to the **Miners Federation of Great Britain**. It became the Northumberland area of the **National Union of Mineworkers** upon the formation of that union.

Sources: Burgess, *Origins*; Arnot, *The Miners*; Clegg, Fox and Thompson; Webb, *Story of the Durham Miners*; R. Fynes, *The Miners of Northumberland and Durham*, S.R. Publishers Reprint, 1971; J. Wilson, *A History of the Durham Miners Association, 1870–1904*, J.H. Veitch,

Durham, 1907; G.H. Metcalfe, 'A History of the Durham Miners Association, 1869–1915', typescript study deposited in the library of the NUM (Durham area) Red Hill, Durham; Thomas Burt, *An Autobiography*, T. Fisher Unwin, 1924; Certification Office.

NOTTINGHAMSHIRE AND DISTRICT MINERS FEDERATED UNION

The Union was established in 1937 by an amalgamation of the **Nottinghamshire Miners Association**, with 9,700 members, and the **Nottinghamshire and District Miners Industrial Union**, with 17,179 members. Since the General Strike of 1926 these two organisations had been in opposition to each other and eventually were brought together in one single union by the insistence of the MFGB. The former General Secretary of the Industrial Union, George Spencer, became the first President, and Val Coleman, a former official of the Nottinghamshire Miners Association was appointed General Secretary. It merged into the **National Union of Mineworkers** upon the formation of that union in 1945.

Sources: Barou; Williams, *The Derbyshire Miners*; Alan R. Griffin, *Mining in the East Midlands 1550–1947*, London, Frank Cass, 1971.

NOTTINGHAMSHIRE AND DISTRICT MINERS INDUSTRIAL UNION (SPENCER UNION)

The Union, established during the General Strike of 1926 under the leadership of George Spencer, had an initial membership of 39. These members had seceded from the **Nottinghamshire Miners Association** in dissatisfaction at the attitude of that union in returning to work against the wishes of the **Miners Federation of Great Britain**, whose members remained on strike while some mining unions returned to work. It gained membership at the expense of the NMA. In 1937 the two unions were persuaded by the MFGB to amalgamate and a new union was formed, the **Nottinghamshire and District Miners Federated Union**.

Sources: Barou; Williams, *The Derbyshire Miners*; Alan R. Griffin, *Mining in the East Midlands, 1550–1947,* London, Frank Cass, 1971.

NOTTINGHAMSHIRE MINERS ASSOCIATION

Formed in 1880 after the collapse of the joint **Derbyshire and Nottinghamshire Miners Association**, the Association was dominated by coal face workers. It had no more than 1,000 members by the end of 1884 and remained virtually powerless to prevent discrimination against checkweighmen while the practice of dismissing union members was widespread. By May 1926 the Association was in dire straits and on the verge of financial ruin, so much so that the **Derbyshire Miners Association** granted it a loan of £10,000. By the end of 1926 after the General Strike coal owners agreed to negotiate only with the **Nottinghamshire and District Miners Industrial Union** which had been set up under the leadership of George Spencer, and the NMA became virtually extinct because of the coal owners' refusal to recognise it or allow it any facilities at the collieries. The 'Spencer Union', as it was called, also had a detrimental effect on the existence of the Derbyshire Miners Association because the employers used the same tactics against this union as they had done with the Nottinghamshire Association. In 1937 the 'Spencer Union' and the Nottinghamshire Miners Association were brought together at the insistence of the Secretary of Mines and with the agreement of the **Mineworkers Federation of Great Britain**, now acting on behalf of the NMA, and a new organisation was created called the **Nottinghamshire and District Miners Federated Union**, with George Spencer as President and Val Coleman, a former official of the NMA, as General Secretary.

Sources: Barou; Williams, *The Derbyshire Miners*; Alan R. Griffin, *Mining in the East Midlands, 1550–1947*, London, Frank Cass, 1971; Burgess, *Origins*.

OLD HILL AND HIGHLEY DISTRICT MINERS ASSOCIATION
Formed in 1883, the Association became part of the **Midland Counties Federation of Miners**, which in turn formed a constituent part of the **Miners Federation of Great Britain** upon the establishment of that organisation.

Source: Arnot, *The Miners*.

OLDHAM AND DISTRICT MINERS ASSOCIATION
The Association was established in 1894 with a membership of 151. In 1897, with 121 members, it became a district association of the **Lancashire and Cheshire Miners' Federation**.

Source: Arnot, *The Miners*.

PELSALL DISTRICT MINERS ASSOCIATION
Formed in 1887, the Association had almost 2,500 members in 1900 and 4,500 in 1910. It joined the **National Union of Mineworkers** as Pelsall district lodge in 1945.

Sources: Certification Office; BoT Reports.

PEMBERTON AND DISTRICT MINERS ASSOCIATION
Established in 1881, the Association had 1,100 members in 1893. In 1897, with 810 members, it ceased to exist as an independent union and became a branch of the **Lancashire and Cheshire Miners' Federation**.

Sources: Arnot, *The Miners*; BoT Reports.

PHILANTHROPIC AMALGAMATED ASSOCIATION OF COLLIERY ENGINE TENDERS
Formed in 1873, the Association ceased to exist after 1876.

Source: Certification Office.

PIONEERS AMALGAMATED ASSOCIATION OF COLLIERY ENGINE TENDERS

Established in 1872, the Association went out of existence in 1875.

Source: Certification Office.

PITMEN'S UNION OF THE TYNE AND WEAR

In 1830, 2 years after the collapse of the **Colliers of the United Association of Northumberland and Durham**, the Pitmen's Union was formed under the leadership of Tommy Ramsey and Tommy Hepburn of Hetton. In February and March 1831 two great meetings were held at Durham and Newcastle with audiences of 20,000 miners attending at each. They resolved to petition Parliament for redress of their grievances; to send a deputation to London; to subscribe 6d per head towards expenses; to elect delegates to form a General Committee; to refuse to buy meat, drink or candles from the colliery 'Tommy Shops'; to decline to sign a yearly bond and to continue to work unbound thereafter. As the coal owners refused these demands, the men ceased work. Under Hepburn's guidance the men stood firm, argued their case and abstained from violence. In June 1831, after some concessions by the owners, the men resumed work. In August 1831 Hepburn was appointed paid organiser. The Union then had funds of £32,581. In 1832 the owners withdrew the concessions they had granted and threatened again to cut wages and to sack men who were union members, importing workmen from other districts to replace them. 8,000 men were refused employment. The funds of the Union were gradually depleted and notwithstanding all the efforts of the union men, the influx of blacklegs continued and at one colliery after another the union members began to fall away and refused to continue paying their contributions. The strike petered out and the Union was dissolved in September 1832.

Source: Webb, *Story of the Durham Miners*.

PLATT BRIDGE MINERS AND CHECKWEIGH ASSOCIATION

There is only one reference to this Association, giving a membership figure of 150 in 1895. There is no record of its formation date but it is reported as having been dissolved in 1896.

Source: BoT Reports.

PONTYPOOL WORKINGMEN'S UNION

The Union was in existence in 1866 and remained purely local in its influence. It is not known whether it was associated in any way with unions in England, nor is any further information available as to its history.

Sources: Evans, 'The Miners of South Wales', *Merlin*, 8 September 1866.

POOR MAN'S FRIEND LODGE MINERS TRADE UNION

Formed in 1887, the Union ceased to exist after 1894.

Source: Certification Office.

PRACTICAL MINERS' ASSOCIATION
The Association had a brief existence between 1864 and 1865. It was a breakaway from the **Miners National Union** which had been accused of not supporting the struggles of local unions. The Practical Miners' leader was John Towers, with Robert Cheesmond and Scott Sangster as Executive Committee members. It won negligible support, mainly from the **South Yorkshire Miners Association**, and remained in existence for a mere 12 months.

Source: Chris Fisher and Pat Spaven, 'Edward Rymer – The Moral Workman' – the dilemma of the radical miner under 'Mac Donaldism', *in* Harrison.

PRIDE OF GOLBORNE LODGE MINERS TRADE UNION
There is only one reference to the existence of the Union. It is recorded as having been established in 1883 with 250 members and had 228, 152, 213 and 185 members in the years 1892 to 1896, D. Byrom of the Railway Hotel, Golborne, acting as secretary in that year.

Source: BoT Reports.

QUARRYMEN'S TRADE ASSOCIATION
Formed in 1878, the Association was dissolved in 1925.

Source: Certification Office.

QUEEN PIT, LEIGH PIT, AND PRINCESS PIT MINERS TRADE UNION AND CHECKWEIGH FUND
The date of establishment is not known, but apparently the Union was reorganised in 1893. The membership ranged from 230 to 311 until 1896 after which date there is no further record of its existence. The members held their meetings at the Wagon and Horses Hotel, Haydock, the secretary being T. Simm.

Source: BoT Reports.

RADCLIFFE AND BINGLEY AND LITTLE LEVER ENGINEERS AND BOILERMEN'S ASSOCIATION
Registered in 1905, the Association was dissolved in 1907.

Source: Certification Office.

RADCLIFFE ENGINEMEN, BOILERMEN AND FIREMEN'S PROVIDENT SOCIETY
Formed in 1891, the Society was numerically never very large, having 54 members in 1892 and 56 members in one branch in 1900. It functioned until 1940 when it ceased to exist.

Sources: BoT Reports; Certification Office.

RENFREW MINERS ASSOCIATION

A local union in existence in 1850, the Association became part of the **Scottish Coal and Iron-stone Miners Protective Association** when it was formed in 1855.

Source: Arnot, *History of the Scottish Miners*.

RHONDDA DISTRICT MINERS ASSOCIATION

Also known as the **Cambrian Miners Association**, the Association was established in 1870–2 when it formed the backbone of the **Amalgamated Association of Miners**. The Rhondda union virtually disappeared after the demise of the AAM but a new agent appointed in 1877 helped revive the organisation. Its membership included both house and steam coal miners until 1888. Throughout its existence the Association was numerically the strongest in the coal field. Membership in 1885 totalled some 12,000 to 14,000 but fell to 10,000 by 1893. No new lodges or branches were set up. Subscriptions were 1½d per month, increased to 2d in 1883, and were deducted from wages at the colliery offices, the clerks retaining a small percentage for their services. The Executive Committee possessed the power to call levies in the event of a strike and strike pay was in fact distributed. Policy decisions were taken by a monthly meeting of representatives from each colliery. The Association merged with the **South Wales Miners Federation**.

Source: Evans, *Miners of South Wales*.

RHONDDA HOUSE COAL MINERS ASSOCIATION

See **South Wales and Monmouthshire Colliery Workmen's Federation**

RHOSDDU MINERS ASSOCIATION

Formed in 1894, the Association ceased to exist in 1900.

Source: Certification Office.

RHYMNEY COLLIERY WORKERS ASSOCIATION

Founded in 1892, the Association was removed from the register in 1894.

Source: Certification Office.

RHYMNEY ENGINEERS ASSOCIATION

The Association was a small sectional union formed in 1904, which achieved a membership of 105 by 1906 and was dissolved in 1907.

Source: BoT Reports.

RHYMNEY VALLEY MINERS ASSOCIATION

The Association was formed in 1893 with a membership of 3,500, which had dropped to 1,917 by 1897. It merged with the **South Wales Miners Federation** in 1898.

Source: BoT Reports.

RISCA COLLIERY WORKERS ASSOCIATION
Formed in 1889, the Association had 84 members in 1892 and went out of existence in the following year.

Source: Certification Office.

ROSSENDALE AND DISTRICT QUARRYMEN'S ASSOCIATION
The Association was established in 1886. In 1892 it had 1,100 members but it ceased to function as an independent organisation in 1897, the membership having fallen to 252.

Sources: BoT Reports; Certification Office.

ST HELENS COLLIERY ENGINEMEN'S TRADE SOCIETY
This was a small society founded in 1864 which had 163 members in 1892. It eventually merged with the **Lancashire and Cheshire Miners' Federation.**

Source: BoT Reports.

ST HELENS DISTRICT FEDERATION OF MINERS
The Federation was formed in 1880 and had a membership of 1,454 in 1893. In 1897, with 1,148 members, it ceased to exist as an independent organisation and became a part of the **Lancashire and Cheshire Miners' Federation**.

Sources: Arnot, *The Miners*; Certification Office.

SCOTTISH CENTRAL MINERS ASSOCIATION
The Association was formed in 1897 and dissolved in 1904. At its peak it had some 5,000 members; nothing more seems to be known about it.

Source: BoT Reports.

SCOTTISH COAL AND IRON MINERS ASSOCIATION
Scottish miners engaged in three mass strikes against wage reductions in 1837, 1842 and 1850. All were unsuccessful, and in 1855 they formed the association. In 1856 30,000 men tried to fight a 20 per cent wage reduction but after a struggle lasting two months they were forced to submit and victimisation destroyed what was left of the union's strength.

Sources: Clegg, Fox and Thompson; Royal Commission on the Organisation and Rules of Trade Unions, Seventh Report, 1868, QQ.15601–3; Arnot, *History of the Scottish Miners*.

SCOTTISH COAL AND IRON-STONE MINERS PROTECTIVE ASSOCIATION
The Association was one of the many efforts made to form one union for all

mining workers and came into being as a result of a conference of several local unions in October 1855, the rules beginning with article 1 as follows: 'That we, the operative coal and ironstone miners, reddsmen and drawers of Scotland, do form ourselves into one General Association, having for its principal object the protection of each other's rights and privileges.' The entrance fee was 1s 6d and subscriptions were 1d a week. Alexander McDonald acted as Secretary. The first activity of the new union was the organisation of protest against the Special Rules under the Coal Mines Act of 1855, which were considered by the miners to be absurd and oppressive. At the end of 1856 the employers demanded a 20 per cent cut in wages and the men went on strike in protest. They were forced into submission by lack of funds after being on strike for three months. The outcome was that the employers began discharging men for being union members, and things were bad for the Association. An effort was made in 1859 to build within the shell of the Association a Scottish Miners Amalgamated Society on the model of the **Amalgamated Society of Engineers** and with a variety of friendly benefits, but this society never came into being. Subscriptions were now 1d per month, which meant the Association had little in the way of resources. It also had little power as each district managed its own affairs. Wages were cut to below 3s a day and eventually there were less than 1,500 miners paying their dues. After 4 years of effort the Association was visibly failing in its work, and went out of existence in 1863.

Sources: Arnot, *History of the Scottish Miners*; Alan Campbell and Fred Reid, 'The Independent Collier in Scotland', *in* Harrison; *Glasgow Sentinel*, 13 October 1855.

SCOTTISH MINERS ASSOCIATION
Established in 1872, the Association was set up to work in conjunction with the **Miners National Union** which covered the English miners. It had been formed in the optimistic mood of a trade revival and was immediately in a position to force up wage levels, in some areas from 3s 6d a day to as much as 9s and even to 10s. There were localised strikes during 1871 and 1872 and the men were able to force a reduction in output from 3 to 4 tons a day, but these favourable conditions did not last for very long, trade depression forcing the masters to try and reduce wages. The Association's members began to voice dissatisfaction with the methods of Alexander MacDonald who had been appointed paid Secretary-Treasurer, and who was a strong advocate of conciliation with the coal owners, his message being 'peace, and let the word "strike" become obsolete'. In 1874 there was an all-out strike from March to the end of July and the union's cash reserves, which had been built up for nearly two years, were all paid out in strike pay. The Association had been formed in an attempt to unite the county unions of the 1870s into one cohesive whole. Macdonald himself had worked in the pits from the age of 8 years, and his objectives as leader of the Association were mainly concentrated on reforms such as the abolition of truck, the curtailment of deductions from wages for tools, lighting and so on, and for improved ventilation and adequate inspection of the mines, and he was to play a major part in the shaping of the Mines Regulation Act of 1872. He became a Member of Parliament in 1874, becoming, with Thomas Burt, one of the first trade unionists to sit in the House of Commons. Although the Association continued in nominal

existence until 1882 it never functioned effectively as a federation. There was a further abortive attempt in 1886 to form a **Scottish Miners National Federation** under the leadership of Keir Hardie, but this remained in existence for only a short period. It adopted a policy of nationalisation of the mines immediately upon its formation.

Sources: Clegg, Fox and Thompson; Alan Campbell and Fred Reid, 'The Independent Collier in Scotland', *in* Harrison; Arnot, *History of the Scottish Miners*; Alan B. Campbell, *The Lanarkshire Miners*, John Donald Publishers Ltd, Edinburgh, 1979.

SCOTTISH MINERS FEDERATION

In 1894 it was suggested by the Executive of the **Miners Federation of Great Britain** that all the Scottish association should form a Scottish Federation and affiliate to the MFGB as a whole. This was quickly achieved and the SMF continued to 1914, when its title was changed to **National Union of Scottish Mineworkers**.

Source: Arnot, *History of the Scottish Miners*.

SCOTTISH MINERS NATIONAL FEDERATION

When Keir Hardie had succeeded in rebuilding the **Ayrshire Miners Union** he pressed beyond this for a broader Scottish organisation of miners, and upon the formation of the Federation in 1886 he became Secretary of the new organisation. It published a journal, *The Miner – a Journal for Underground Workers*, the first number of which in January 1887 contained an article by Thomas Burt, MP, one of the miners' MPs. The new Federation had connected with it local organisations (with an aggregate membership of about 25,000) which were expected to pay ½d per month per member into the funds. The Federation had no power over the internal management of any local organisation nor had it power to proclaim a strike or enforce a levy for the support of men on strike. Its role was to be 'Guide, Counsellor and Friend'. It began its existence with 26 districts and 23,570 members. After one year its membership had fallen to 13,000 in 15 districts due to the disappearance of some of its local organisations. Its policy was a 5-day week and a set minimum wage. It lasted for only two years but when it was dissolved it left behind as a legacy several new county unions.

Sources: Alan Campbell and Fred Reid, 'The Independent Collier in Scotland', *in* Harrison; Arnot, *History of the Scottish Miners*.

SCOTTISH OIL WORKERS' UNION

The Union was formed in 1900 and had 230 members in 1910 which had increased to 1,800 by 1923. In 1924 it amalgamated with the **Scottish Shale Miners and Manual Workers Union** in order to form the **National Union of Shale Miners and Oil Workers**.

Sources: BoT Reports; Certification Office.

SCOTTISH QUARRYMENS UNION
Formed in 1894, the Union had 230 members in 1896 and 346 in 1899. It ceased to exist in 1900.

Source: BoT Reports.

SCOTTISH SHALE MINERS AND MANUAL WORKERS UNION
The Union was formed in 1886 and was organised chiefly by John Wilson of Broxburn, who dominated the union until his death in 1912. It first operated as a district of the **Scottish Miners Federation** but drew apart from that body. It had bitter and protracted conflicts with the oil companies which suffered from American competition at the end of the century. Scottish shale miners held aloof from the main miners' union and in 1924 joined with the **Scottish Oil Workers' Union** (established in 1900) to form the **National Union of Shale Miners and Oil Workers**.

Sources: Arnot, *History of the Scottish Miners*; John Wilson, *Memories of a Labour Leader*, London, T. Fisher Unwin, 1910.

SCOTTISH SLATE QUARRIERS UNION
Established in 1902, the Union was also referred to as the **Ballachulish Quarriers**. Its membership upon formation was 380, rising to a peak of 621 in 1904, and thereafter dropping steadily until in 1910, with 275 members, it joined the **National Union of Gas Workers and General Labourers** (see Vol. 3).

Source: BoT Reports.

SETTMAKERS UNION OF GREAT BRITAIN AND IRELAND
Formed in 1886, the Union achieved a steady growth of membership, having 1,226 members in 1892, 1,968 in 1896 and 2,840 in 1900, the number falling to just over 2,000 by 1910. It merged with the **National Union of Quarrymen** in 1914.

Sources: BoT Reports; Certification Office.

SHOTTS MINERS ASSOCIATION
Although there is no actual date of formation given for the Association, it is recorded as having an estimated membership of 600 for the years 1894 and 1895. It became a branch of the **Lanarkshire Miners County Union** in 1896.

Source: BoT Reports.

SHROPSHIRE MINERS ASSOCIATION
Established in 1886, the Association had 830 members in 1896 and 850 in 1900. It became an area of the **National Union of Mineworkers** when that union was formed.

Source: Certification Office.

SKELMERSDALE AND DISTRICT ENGINEMEN AND BOILERMEN'S TRADE UNION

The Union was registered in 1910 but nothing further seems to be known of its history.

Source: Certification Office.

SKELMERSDALE DISTRICT MINERS ASSOCIATION

Established in 1873, the Association had 1,693 members by 1893. In 1897, with a membership standing at 722, it ceased to be an independent union and became a district association of the **Lancashire and Cheshire Miners' Federation**.

Source: Arnot, *The Miners*.

SMALLBRIDGE AND LITTLEBOROUGH MINERS ASSOCIATION COME AND WELCOME LODGE

Formed in 1892, the Association was dissolved in 1895.

Source: Certification Office.

SOMERSETSHIRE MINERS ASSOCIATION

The date of formation of the Association was 1888. It had 2,000 members in 1892 to 1896, the secretary in that year being S. Whitehouse, of Radstock, Bath. Mr Whitehouse remained secretary until the end of the First World War. By 1910 the membership had more than doubled. In 1944 it had a recorded membership of 2,600. It was a constituent union of the **Miners Federation of Great Britain.** The Association became the West Country area of the **National Union of Mineworkers** when that Union was established in 1945, bringing in 2,600 members.

Sources: BoT Reports; MoL Reports; George B. Baldwin, 'Structural Reform in the British Miners' Union', *Quarterly Journal of Economics*, November 1953.

SOUTH DERBYSHIRE AMALGAMATED MINERS ASSOCIATION

Established in 1889, the Association amalgamated with the **National Union of Mineworkers** in 1945.

Source: Certification Office.

SOUTH DERBYSHIRE AND NORTH LEICESTER MINERS TRADE SOCIETY

Founded in 1873, the Society ceased to exist after 1878.

Source: Certification Office.

SOUTH STAFFORDSHIRE AND EAST WORCESTERSHIRE AMALGAMATED MINERS ASSOCIATION

Formed in 1863, the Association had 1,800 members in 59 lodges in 1900. It joined the **National Union of Mineworkers** and became the South Staffordshire area.

Sources: BoT Reports; Certification Office; Arnot, *The Miners*.

SOUTH WALES AND MONMOUTH COLLIERY WINDING ENGINEMEN'S ASSOCIATION AND PROVIDENT TRADE UNION

The Association was formed in 1896. In 1930 it had 800 members in 6 lodges, and was dissolved in 1949.

Sources: Cole, *British Trade Unionism Today*; Certification Office.

SOUTH WALES AND MONMOUTHSHIRE COLLIERY ENGINEMEN, BOILERMAKERS AND CRAFTSMEN'S ASSOCIATION

See **Boilermen and Engine-winders Union**

SOUTH WALES AND MONMOUTHSHIRE COLLIERY WORKMEN'S FEDERATION

The formation of such a body was first discussed at a delegate conference of miners in 1887 and the Federation was officially set up on 3 January 1888. Its administration was in the hands of a President, Secretary, Treasurer and Committee of 7 members. Their sole function was to convene and advise conferences and to consider disputes referred to them by the districts. The districts were to retain complete autonomy in local affairs and each member was to pay only ½d per month to meet the expenses of the Central Committee. The Federation's membership was quoted as being at least 28,000 but it lacked any real financial strength. Its aims were the introduction of the 8-hour day, support of mining legislation and federation of the workers of the world. In November 1888 the Federation resolved to demand a wage increase outside the terms of the sliding scale agreement following a revival in trade, ultimately signing a new agreement on 15 January 1890. By June of that year membership had fallen and contributions during the year amounted to only £153 and the Federation was too weak to resist a counter attack launched by the colliery owners when high prices gave way to depression. Thus when the coal owners served notice to terminate the agreement with a view to reducing wages in 1891, the men were forced to accept their terms. The steady fall in wage rates between November 1891 and June 1893 which the Federation could do nothing to check led to a re-examination of the sliding scale policy. In 1893 the

Rhondda House Coal Miners Association and the **Neath, Swansea and Llanelly Miners' Association** withdrew their support from the Federation. In 1889 the **Miners Federation of Great Britain** had been formed but the South Wales and Monmouthshire members refused to join because they were pledged to support the sliding scale principle whilst the MFGB was against it. This difference between the two federations prevented their alliance for nearly 10 years. In 1899 the Federation merged with the **Miners Federation of Great Britain**.

Sources: *South Wales Daily News*, 25 October, 1887; Arnot, *South Wales Miners*.

SOUTH WALES AND MONMOUTHSHIRE ENGINEMEN, STOKERS, AND SURFACE CRAFTSMEN'S ASSOCIATION

Established in 1889, the Association had 329 members in 1896 which had increased to 3,141 by 1899. In 1900 it merged with the **South Wales Miners Federation**.

Source: BoT Reports.

SOUTH WALES COLLIERY ENGINEMEN AND SURFACE CRAFTSMEN'S ASSOCIATION

Formed about 1890, the Association had approximately 6,000 members in 1912. This was one of the craftsmen's unions. It merged with the **South Wales Miners Federation** in 1915 after a successful strike by the Federation to force the employers to agree to operate a closed shop. After this agreement was reached the Rhondda collieries decided to treat craftsmen as non-unionists unless they joined the Federation.

Source: Francis and Smith.

SOUTH WALES MINERS ASSOCIATION

The first meeting of the Association was held at Ebbw Vale on 30 January 1864 when 200 members were enrolled. Little is known of its administrative structure except that lodges were set up and the union was divided into 3 districts, namely East and West Monmouthshire and Glamorganshire. Each district employed a miner's agent but this arrangement was rendered valueless by the employers' refusal to negotiate with them. The Association supported the wage claims which were put forward in 1864. One strike was organised at Abercwmboi and involved 400 men who struck for 9 weeks in sympathy with the door-boys' demand for an increase. Many of the union members were blacklisted and eventually forced to emigrate. It has been said by contemporary observers that no general union existed in South Wales between 1865 and 1870. Although weak and purely local, some unions seem to have survived in Monmouthshire and in the Rhondda, the two centres of union activity being Pontypool and Pontypridd.

Sources: C. Wilkins, *The History of the Iron, Steel, Tinplate and other Industries of Wales*, Joseph Williams, Merthyr Tydfil, 1903; Fifth Report of the Commissioners Appointed to Inquire into Trade Unions (1868), Minutes of Evidence; *Merlin*, February 1868; *Bee Hive*, February 1868, March 1868, May 1868, January 1870; Evans, *Miners of South Wales*.

SOUTH WALES MINERS FEDERATION

The Federation was established on 11 October 1898 with William Abraham (Mabon) and William Brace elected as President and Vice President respectively. The new body, like its predecessors the **Amalgamated Association of Colliery Workmen of South Wales and Monmouthshire** and the **Amalgamated Society of the Colliery Workmen of the South Wales Coalfield**, was framed upon a confederal structure. It was composed of 20 districts, each district retaining considerable autonomy over its funds and the conduct of local disputes. During its early years the Federation served notice to terminate contracts at many pits to compel non-unionists to become members, but this pressure did not always prove to be effective and between 1898 and 1904 there were no fewer than 68 stoppages on this issue. In 1902 it was successful in negotiating the abolition of the sliding scale and the employers agreed to accept the establishment of a conciliation board and the inclusion of a minimum wage rate in the new agreement. The Federation was said to be unique in being more than simply a trade union – it was a social institution providing through its local leaders an all-round service of advice and assistance ranging from 'the cradle to the grave'. In 1912 it published 'The Miners' Next Step', which was considered to be a revolutionary, syndicalist and militant document, advocating supreme control to be in the hands of the miners themselves as regards negotiations, with no paid official dominating policy. The average membership during the period of the General Strike and even up to 1935 always remained about half the work force. In 1933 the 20 districts were re-organised into 8 areas, without separate funds, and therefore less independent than was previously the position. In 1937 the Federation and the coal owners signed the South Wales Wage agreement which rationalised wage grades from 150 down to 6 on the principle of equal pay for equal work. Such a system was not established in the rest of the British coalfields until 1956. In 1942 it succeeded in securing the first coalfield-wide closed shop, and in January 1945 it became the South Wales area of the newly formed **National Union of Mineworkers**.

Sources: Evans, *Miners of South Wales*; Cole, *British Trade Unionism Today*; *South Wales Daily News*, 12 October 1898; Annual Report of the Miners' Federation of Great Britain, 1903; S. and B. Webb, *History of Trade Unionism*; D.L. Thomas, *Labour Unions in Wales*, Swansea, 1901; Cole, *British Working-Class Movements*; Ness Edwards, *The History of the South Wales Miners*, London, Labour Publishing Co, 1926; Arnot, *The Miners*; D. Evans, *Labour Strife in the South Wales Coalfield*, Cardiff, 1911; Ness Edwards, *The History of the South Wales Miners' Federation*, Laurence and Wishart, London, 1937; Francis and Smith; Clegg, Fox and Thompson.

SOUTH WALES MINERS INDUSTRIAL UNION

Formed after the General Strike of 1926, the Union claimed to have 121 branches by 1927 but no records are available to check this claim. The hub of its activity was centred around the Taff-Merthyr pit. The union was accused by its rival, the **South Wales Miners Federation** of being a 'Coffin Club' and a company union. In turn it accused the SWMF of being 'Bolshevik'. Nevertheless it registered as a trade union in June 1927. Weekly subscriptions were 6d and a three-fifths majority of the membership had to be in favour before a strike was called. William Gooding was appointed Chairman and W.A. Williams Organising Secretary at salaries of £275 each per year. In dealing with an accusation that the subscription rate was low the Industrial Union claimed that the men employed at collieries under its control were paid higher wages than their Federation counterparts, and that the subscription was low because arbitration ensured that there was no need for the union to set up a strike fund. In 1938 it merged with the South Wales Miners Federation with an estimated membership of 589 men who were allowed into the Federation without fee and on an equal basis, and this ended the existence of the only rival the SWMF had had since 1898.

Sources: Francis and Smith; *The Miners Monthly*, February 1938; Arnot, *South Wales Miners*.

SOUTH WALES WAGE RATE MEN'S ASSOCIATION (ABERDARE)

The Association was registered in 1911, after which date nothing further is known of its existence.

Source: Certification Office.

SOUTH WALES WESTERN DISTRICT MINERS ASSOCIATION

The Association was a colliery organisation founded in 1869 which joined the **South Wales Miners Federation** in 1899 when it had 5,588 members.

Source: BoT Reports.

SOUTH WESTERN COUNTIES MINERS FEDERATION

Two unions came together to form the Federation in 1894 – the **Bristol Miners Association** and the **Somersetshire Miners Association** – covering a total of 11,800, which had dropped to 4,000 in 1896. The Federation ceased to exist in 1904 when it had 5,300 members.

Source: BoT Reports.

SOUTH YORKSHIRE MINERS ASSOCIATION

Like its counterpart, the **West Yorkshire Miners Association**, the Association was established in 1858 after a threat by the coal owners to reduce wages by 15 per cent. Opposition was expressed by the men who held a delegate meeting on 5 April 1858 at the White Bear Inn, Shambles Street,

Barnsley, and the decision was taken to form a union with lodges at every colliery. Strikes were called at several of the collieries and after a meeting with the miners' representatives, the coal owners withdrew the threat of a reduction. In its early years the Association had a very limited membership and hardly any cash reserves and the owners used this weakness to try and impose wage cuts, and after a lockout in 1864 when the union was defeated the decision was taken to reorganise the Association. The Secretary was replaced by John Normansell who was well known for a campaign against the unfair system of weighing coal, advocating its replacement by payment by weight, with an elected representative of the men to act as checkweighman. At the time of his appointment the Association had 2,000 members in 18 lodges, and a cash reserve of £183 11s 4½d. Nine months afterwards there were 2,568 members and the cash balance had increased to £1,655. In the 1870s the strength of the union fluctuated with the state of trade and the men were subject to a series of wage reductions, the members becoming discontented and allowing membership to lapse, and by 1879 it was reported that there were 4 non-union men to every one in the Association. By the end of 1880 only approximately 2,800 out of 60,000 Yorkshire miners were organised, the union was in debt and in an almost powerless position. By 1881 the threat of bankruptcy was imminent and a merger was arrived at with the West Yorkshire Miners to form a joint body, the **Yorkshire Miners' Association**, and the new union came into being in July 1881 with a total membership of approximately 5,000. Ned Cowey, Ben Pickard, and R.Parrott of the West Yorkshire Miners Association became President, Secretary and agent respectively, and John Frith and George Cragg of South Yorkshire became Financial Secretary and Vice-President.

Sources: Machin; Clegg, Fox and Thompson; Burgess, *Origins*; Williams; S. and B. Webb, *History of Trade Unionism*.

STAFFORDSHIRE UNDERGROUND COLLIERY FIREMEN, SHOT-LIGHTERS AND UNDERLOOKERS UNION
This was a very small, short-lived union, being formed in 1901 with 67 members, having 53 and 32 members in the years 1902 and 1903 respectively, and ceasing to exist in 1904.

Source: BoT Reports.

STANDISH AND DISTRICT MINERS ASSOCIATION
Formed in 1862, the Association had 1,007 members in 1893. In 1897, with 851 members, it ceased to be an independent union and became a district Association of the **Lancashire and Cheshire Miners' Federation**.

Source: Arnot, *The Miners*.

STIRLING AND LINLITHGOW MINERS ASSOCIATION
The Association was in existence in 1873, when it had 5,300 members and a cash reserve of £3,729. Its subsequent history is obscure but in 1944 it

became part of the **National Union of Scottish Mineworkers.**

Source: Arnot, *History of the Scottish Miners.*

STIRLING MINERS COUNTY UNION

Formed in 1899, evidently as a result of the break up of the **Stirlingshire, Forth and Clyde Valley Miners Association,** with 342 members, which quickly grew to over 3,000 and stood at 7,500 in 18 branches by 1910. The union amalgamated into the **National Union of Scottish Mineworkers** in 1944.

Sources: BoT Reports; Arnot, *History of the Scottish Mineworkers.*

STIRLINGSHIRE, FORTH AND CLYDE VALLEY MINERS ASSOCIATION

Formed in 1886, the Association had almost 3,000 members in 1894. At the end of 1895 the Association withdrew from the **Scottish Miners Federation,** partly because of a dispute about strike pay, but also because of friction with the Stirling Secretary, Chisholm Robertson. Membership fell to 800 in 1896 under a new secretary, William Webb, and the Association is reported to have been dissolved in 1898.

Sources: BoT Reports; Certification Office; Arnot, *The Scottish Miners.*

THORNHILL COKEMEN'S MUTUAL AID SOCIETY

Formed in 1936 with 44 members, the Society functioned for only 4 years, being dissolved in 1940 with a membership standing at 28.

Source: Bain and Price.

TOWNELEY MINERS ASSOCIATION

The Board of Trade records the Association as having been established in 1888. It had 500 members for the years 1892, 93, 94 and 95, and 320 members in 1896. A. G. Hugill of Dall Street, Burnley, acted as secretary. There is no further record of its existence after this date.

Source: BoT Reports.

TYDESLEY AND ASTLEY MINERS' ASSOCIATION

Registered in 1907, the Association became part of the Lancashire area of the **National Union of Mineworkers.**

Source: Certification Office.

UNION OF COKEMEN

See **National Union of Cokemen and By-product Workers**

UNION OF COLLIERY ENGINEMEN

Formed in 1872, the Union later became a part of the **National Federation of Enginemen and Boiler Firemen** which, as a national organisation, formed part of the **Miners Federation of Great Britain**.

Source: Webb, *Story of the Durham Miners*.

UNITED KINGDOM SETT MAKERS ASSOCIATION

Formed in 1874, the Association was dissolved in 1876.

Source: Certification Office.

UNITED SOCIETIES OF THE COLLIERS' COMMERCIAL AND BENEFIT UNION IN THE STAFFORDSHIRE AND WORCESTERSHIRE COLLIERIES

This organisation was formed in November 1833, but its existence was brief. It was set up to try and deal with the unrest and strikes in particular collieries in these two counties.

Source: Wearmóuth.

WAKEFIELD ASSOCIATION OF COAL-MINERS

There is evidence that this union was formed in 1811 for the 'Articles, Rules, Orders and Regulations' have been preserved. It met at the Three Tuns Inn. It claimed to be a friendly society although it seems to have functioned secretly as a trade union. Rule 19 of the association stated that if any member, after receiving his wages, 'shall in a boasting manner, publish to other people the amount of his earnings ... such member so offending shall forfeit two shillings'. There is no record of its having undertaken any overt trade union activities.

Source: Miners Offices, Barnsley, Yorkshire area of the National Union of Mineworkers.

WARWICKSHIRE AND STAFFORD MINERS TRADE UNION

There is a reference to an organisation of this name in the Home Office Records No. 44 (1836), p. 29, but its officially recorded date of formation was 1886. It had 5,000 members in 1900. The Union merged with the **National Union of Mineworkers** upon its formation, becoming part of the Warwickshire district, Midland area.

Sources: Wearmouth; Certification Office; BoT Reports.

WEST BROMWICH MINERS ASSOCIATION

The Association was a former district of the **Amalgamated Association of Miners** in 1869. It became part of the **Midland Counties Federation of**

Miners which in turn formed a constituent part of the **Miners Federation of Great Britain** upon the establishment of that organisation.

Source: Arnot, *The Miners*.

WEST CUMBERLAND MINERS ASSOCIATION
See **Cumberland Miners Association**

WEST CUMBERLAND WORKMEN'S ASSOCIATION
See **Cumberland Iron Ore Miners and Kindred Trades Association**

WEST LOTHIAN MINEWORKERS UNION
See **Mid and West Lothian Labour Federation**

WEST YORKSHIRE COKE AND BY-PRODUCT WORKERS MUTUAL AID SOCIETY
The Society had a 7-year existence, being formed in 1929 with 201 members and dissolved in 1936 when it had 117 members.

Source: Bain and Price.

WEST YORKSHIRE ENGINEMEN AND FIREMEN'S MUTUAL PROTECTION ASSOCIATION
See **Yorkshire Colliery Enginemen and Firemen's Association**

WEST YORKSHIRE MINERS ASSOCIATION
The Association was formed in 1858 following a decision by the coal owners to cut wages by 15 per cent. Local traditions of militancy were recognised and the government of the Association was a form of federation composed of districts which retained considerable autonomy, including the right to provide strike pay, and having the authority to initiate strikes involving not more than 10 per cent of the membership without the sanction of the Executive Committee. The persistence of local stoppages induced the coal owners to be more receptive to the union's proposals for a joint committee of equal numbers of employers' and workers' representatives, which was set up in June 1873 and by June 1874 had settled 177 complaints at individual collieries. The Association suffered considerably from the trade depression of the 1870s, losing members as a result, which virtually destroyed it as an effective bargaining agent. A succession of wage cuts was negotiated by the joint committee despite a spate of unofficial meetings against the cuts and short-term disputes. Membership of the Association fell drastically and known militants were victimized, and the Executive Committee claimed that the coal owners were refusing to hold interviews with the officials of the union and were illegally dismissing checkweighmen. In October 1880 a sliding scale was agreed to which did

little to ease the situation. Matters were no better in the **South Yorkshire Miners Association** and in April 1881 the two unions merged to form the **Yorkshire Miners' Association**, covering a total membership of less than 6,000. Ben Pickard and Ned Cowey, who had been Secretary and President of the West Yorkshire Association, took over the same positions in the newly formed organisation.

Sources: S. and B. Webb, *History of Trade Unionism*; Burgess, *Origins*; Arnot, *The Miners*; Machin; Williams, 'Labour in the Coalfields'.

WEST YORKSHIRE MINERS (CASTLEFORD)
This was probably a breakaway organisation from the **Yorkshire Miners' Association** which had been formed in 1881 by an amalgamation between the **West Yorkshire Miners Association** and the **South Yorkshire Miners Association**. The Castleford union had 1,150 members upon its inception in 1908 but it had ceased to exist by 1909.

Source: BoT Reports.

WESTERN COUNTIES EXCAVATORS, QUARRYMEN AND GENERAL LABOURERS' UNION
The Union was established as early as 1864. The first recorded membership was 133 in 1892. It ceased to function in 1912 when the membership stood at 108.

Source: Bain and Price.

WESTMINSTER LODGE OF THE NORTH WALES MINERS UNITED ASSOCIATION
The Lodge was set up in 1879 and remained a functioning body until it was dissolved in 1903.

Source: Certification Office.

WIGAN AND DISTRICT LABOUR UNION
Formed in 1892 with 789 members, falling to 472 in 1893, 313 in 1896 and to 217 in 1897, the Union ceased to exist in 1898. The members held meetings at The Big Lamp, Wallgate.

Source: BoT Reports.

WIGAN MINERS ASSOCIATION
Established in 1862, the Association had 5,382 members by 1893. In 1897 it ceased to be an independent union and became a branch of the **Lancashire and Cheshire Miners' Federation**, the membership then numbering 2,000.

Source: Arnot, *The Miners*.

WIGAN MINERS PROVIDENT BENEFIT TRADE SOCIETY
The Society was formed in 1879 and dissolved the same year.

Source: Certification Office.

WIGAN, ST HELENS, CHORLEY AND DISTRICT ENGINEMEN AND BOILERMEN'S PROVIDENT SOCIETY
The Society was dissolved in 1964 but the date of its formation is unknown.

Source: Certification Office.

WINDING AND GENERAL ENGINEMEN'S AND ASSOCIATED TRADES SOCIETY
See **National Union of Winding and General Enginemen**

WISHAW MINERS ASSOCIATION
In existence in 1850 as a local union, in 1873 the Association had 1,500 members and a credit balance of £927. What subsequently happened to the Association is not known until 1944 when it became part of the **National Union of Scottish Mineworkers**.

Source: Arnot, *History of the Scottish Miners*.

YORKSHIRE AND DERBYSHIRE COKEMEN AND LABOURERS UNION
The Union was established with 200 members in 1908. This number had grown to 1,000 by 1911 when it amalgamated with the **Lancashire Cokemen and Labourers and Local Railway Servants Union** in order to form the **National Cokemen and Surface Workers' Union**.

Source: Bain and Price.

YORKSHIRE AND DERBYSHIRE COLLIERY DEPUTIES ASSOCIATION
The Association was formed in 1893 with a very small membership and remained in existence for 4 years, being dissolved in 1897.

Source: BoT Reports.

YORKSHIRE COLLIERY ENGINEMEN AND FIREMEN'S ASSOCIATION
The Association was founded in 1879 as the **West Yorkshire Enginemen and Firemen's Mutual Protection Association**, the name being changed in 1912. It transferred its engagements to the newly formed **National Union of Mineworkers** in 1945.

Source: Certification Office.

YORKSHIRE MINERS' ASSOCIATION

In 1881 there were two separate Yorkshire unions still in existence – the **South Yorkshire Miners Association** and the **West Yorkshire Miners Association** – both organisations on the verge of bankruptcy. After a joint meeting of the two unions agreement was reached on an amalgamation under the title of the YMA, the 98 lodges involved agreeing to the proposal. The new union's headquarters were established in the former SYMA offices at Barnsley. The new body had only some 3,000 members in an area employing 60,000 miners, and consequently had no control over wages and working conditions. Nevertheless it was at that time the biggest of the county unions in the inland districts. One of its first acts was to terminate the local sliding scale agreement and to refuse to allow wages to be dependent on selling prices. In 1889 it became a founder member of the **Miners Federation of Great Britain**, being the most powerful union to do so at that time, its leadership of Ben Pickard, Ned Cowey and James Murray constituting part of the leadership of the MFGB.

Sources: S. and B. Webb, *History of Trade Unionism*; Burgess, *Origins*; Clegg, Fox and Thompson; Machin; Robert G. Neville, *The Yorkshire Miners, 1881–1926,* Oxford Microform Publications Ltd, 1974.

YORKSHIRE QUARRYMEN'S UNION

Established in 1898 with a membership of 52 which had fallen to only 20 in 1899, the Union was dissolved in 1900.

Source: BoT Reports.

Iron and Steel

At the time of its second nationalisation in 1967 15 trade unions were recognised as organising manual workers in the iron and steel industry.[1] Only 3 of these were unique to iron and steel. These were the Iron and Steel Trades Confederation (the ISTC, previously also known for some purposes by its alternative title as the British Iron, Steel and Kindred Trades Association, BISAKTA), an amalgamation of 1917 with a manual membership of about 94,000, the National Union of Blastfurnacemen, Ore Miners, Coke Workers and Kindred Trades, an amalgamation of 1921 with a manual membership of rather more than 19,000, and the British Roll Turners Trade Society, a small sectional society of about 1,000 members founded in 1898. The remaining 12 unions, representing an iron and steel membership of about 56,000, were all 'general' unions or historically craft organisations associated with the engineering or building industries.[2] Of the two general unions, the National Union of General and Municipal Workers and the Transport and General Workers, the former had acquired a considerable foothold in the industry during and after the First World War, particularly in Scotland, the North East, South Yorkshire and the Midlands, where it became a rival to the Blastfurnacemen in some works, while Gasworker Union membership and a take-over of the Welsh Artisan's Union gave it representation in tin-plate in South Wales. The TGWU owed its original stake in the industry to its connections with dockers, particularly in South Wales and Gloucestershire and later in South Yorkshire and elswhere as a result of absorption of the National Winding and General Engineers' Society in 1935. Of the craft unions, that with the earliest established membership was probably the Bricklayers who were concerned in the relining of furnaces. A large growth of craft membership in other unions was mostly associated with technological developments since the late 1950s.

Excepting these latter-day developments of trade unionism in the iron and steel industry, its history is principally a story of a multiplicity of organisations established from the 1860s onwards and their absorption, with the notable exception of the Blastfurnacemen and the less important exception of the Roll Turners, into the ISTC. Compared with engineering, iron was, in trade union terms, a late developer. Eighteenth-century combinations and benefit clubs in the cutlery and file trades, in early steel and tool manufacture in Sheffield, and among lockmakers and scissor grinders, to name only a few examples, were all on the fringes of the manufactured iron industry. None has been found in the industry itself. The Friendly Society of Iron Moulders (known from the mid-1850s as the Friendly Society of Iron Founders), which was formed in Bolton on 6 February 1809, may possibly have attracted some skilled ironworkers, but, like the other examples quoted, could be said to be outside the iron industry proper.[3]

Lack of evidence does not, as Professor Ashton has reminded us, prove that no industrial combinations existed in the iron trade earlier than the nineteenth century.[4] If they did, they were so ephemeral or clandestine that they escaped the notice of William Matthews, a well known Midland ironmaster who could, as late as 1833, declare with confidence that there was no combination of workmen in the industry during the Napoleonic wars.[5] Matthews, if he is to be understood literally, is almost certainly wrong.[6] In 1801, following riots which had been suppressed, Dowlais puddlers petitioned for higher wages and frequent references exist to illustrate industrial action in the years that follow – disturbances, the taking of Luddite oaths, protests against the blowing out of furnaces at the end of the war, strikes of puddlers at Cyfarthfa, Merthyr and Clydach in 1816 and 1817 'though far short of what would justify any ... wish to bring military into the neighbourhood'[7] – all these events were features of the iron industry in the early part of the nineteenth century, though the combinations concerned in them remained nameless and were evidently highly localised outbursts rather than persistent attempts at trade union organisation.

Whatever potential for trade unionism existed in the iron trade remained unfulfilled until the 1860s. Though William Walters, in evidence to the Royal Commission of 1867, claimed that those reported to exist at that time were the third set of trade unions which he had known,[8] he failed to name the organisations concerned, and no record now exists earlier than the Amalgamated Malleable Ironworkers, founded in 1862, and other unions which followed close upon its heels. Though we now see these as the basis of trade unionism in iron and steel as we have come to know it, this was evidently far from obvious at the time. Indeed, it was not until the end of the last century that the industry could be said to have developed a trade union organisation which was at all stable and comprehensive.

The late appearance of continuous organisation in an industry surrounded by developments in active trade unionism remains something of a puzzle. As Ashton has pointed out, there could be little possibility of common action among workers in the charcoal-iron industry, scattered as they were in small groups in different parts of the country.[9] The practicability and likelihood of organisation at the larger ironworks which later grew up were quite a different question. A need for self-protection in circumstances of increasing scale and capital intensity seems natural enough. But works still remained scattered and localised. It was far from easy to link up the interests of workers in North and South Staffordshire, or in West and East Wales, and even more difficult to find common interest between South Wales and the North East Coast, or between the Midlands iron industry and that in Scotland. There was, moreover, much skilled hand labour in the industry and employment conditions differed widely. Acquired skill in short supply might place workers in so strong a bargaining position that organisation seemed unnecessary[10] and some ironmasters at least could claim to be, and be accepted as, benevolent if autocratic.[11] In ironmaking the contract system was widespread, puddlers and mill operators employing their own underhands, a situation which limited the scope for common interest and activity.[12] Fluctuations in the demand for iron, and consequently fitful movements of prices and unemployment, were apt to alternate periods of despair with relative affluence. Despair was easily forgotten as prosperity took hold and thoughts of effective combination were cast aside, while trade depression dissipated such union funds as remained. Finally, variability of demand and shifting technology often served to bring large numbers of raw and industrially unsophisticated workers into the labour force, resulting in an immaturity of approach which made continuous organisation difficult[13] and adaptation to change a serious problem. It is not surprising that even such relatively well based unions as the Malleable Ironworkers could run into difficulties or that, for more than a century, the organisational base of trade unionism remained insecure.

As in other industries, it was skilled workers in iron manufacturing who formed the basis for trade union growth. The Amalgamated Malleable Ironworkers which was established with its headquarters at Gateshead in 1862 was composed almost entirely of puddlers. A second Midlands union, the Associated Ironworkers of Brierley Hill formed in the following year in North Staffordshire, was similarly based but included forgemen, while a third catered for millmen. Together, while the prosperity of the early 1860s held, the three unions were said to organise three-quarters of all iron workers; the Malleable Ironworkers alone claimed to have 6,500 members during this period.[14] The situation did not last. The iron trades strikes of 1864–6, undertaken against a resolute alliance of employers and the worsening of trade, decimated the membership. Only the Malleable Ironworkers seem to have emerged to fight another day and to reform in 1868 as the National Amalgamated Association of Ironworkers, absorbing or replacing, it seems, most if not all the local unions in the industry, including the Brierley Hill executive,[15] and becoming substantially country-wide in organisation.

By 1872, the Amalgamated Ironworkers could claim over 200 branches with 20,000 members in the North of England, North and South Staffordshire, Wales and Scotland. For a decade John Kane, President of the Malleable Ironworkers from 1862 to 1867 and General Secretary of the Amalgamated Association, bestrode the world of iron manufacture like a colossus, his members dominating the puddling processing during the peak of iron prosperity, seeking to control labour supply by emigration, to avoid exhausting trade union funds by strikes,[16] to blunt the edge of aggression by the development of Boards of Conciliation and Arbitration,[17] and to stabilise wages by the use of sliding scales. Puddlers, if we are to believe the Comte de Paris, were moderate if independent and resolute men, not naturally given to confrontation.[18] Kane, it seems, in his own generation struck the mood of the most influential ironworkers and of the more moderate employers and was evidently among the first of the great trade union administrators of the century.

An end had to come to the dominance of the Ironworkers, and the writing was on the wall before the death of Kane in 1876. The union reached its peak of membership in 1873 (35,000). In part the problem was the familiar one of falling demand, but in this case there was little chance of revival. For many purposes iron was being replaced by steel. Traditionally-minded puddlers, the aristocrats of the old régime, were reluctant to believe that steel could ever succeed.[19] How wrong they were was soon apparent. In 1875 there were 7,575 puddling furnaces in England and Wales; in 1886 there were 5,640, of which 1,581 were idle. The Ironworkers retained control of some works which changed from iron to steel, but this only cushioned the union's slow decline. Failure to adapt has often been blamed on Edward Trow, the successor of John Kane. Perhaps he merely had the misfortune to lead the union when the tide was moving against it and when the conservatism of the rank and file precluded the possibility of rapid change. When it proved possible to form a new organisation, the Associated Iron and Steel Workers of Great Britain (1876), with a formally broadened base of membership, it is typical of the Ironworkers that they cautiously maintained the old association in existence in case of failure. And so it remained until 1891 when the new union, with 114 branches and funds standing at over £5,000, felt sufficiently secure to proceed alone.

The Ironworkers' delay in shifting their ground gave other unions their chance in steel and tin-plate and among blastfurnacemen. The Royal Commission on Labour of 1891 recorded that its membership in the iron making districts of South Yorkshire, East Lancashire, West Worcestershire, West Cumberland and the North of England amounted to no more than 9,500 to 10,000 – not even a quarter of the men employed – owing to the number of sectional unions which existed in connection with the trade.[20] The possibility of a new organisation for steel was increased by the fact that the Ironworkers had never become well established in Scotland, where major developments in steel were taking place. The Siemens steel trade, as John Hodge, the General Secretary of the recently formed British Steel Smelters Association[21] (established in Scotland in January 1886) pointed out, was practically a new industry.[22] The men engaged in it were of all kinds – carpenters, joiners, iron founders, ex-policemen, miners – all attracted by the big money which it was said could be earned. Few old puddlers were among them and no long standing traditions of trade unionism stood to be preserved. The new union was not committed to the past. Unlike the Ironworkers it was not traceable to the efforts of any particular individual, and none of its originators possessed previous trade union experience. Hodge himself had never been in a union before and appears to have gleaned little from his father's experience as a former member of the Ironworkers. There had been few smelters in Scotland in the early 1880s.[23] The development of steel increased their number, and also resulted in a dispute at Colvilles about dispensing with third hand melters in 1885. It was from this incident that the union was born.

Once established the union quickly extended to cover all the melters and Siemens plant men in South Wales (1887) and by 1888 had begun to assume a national character with 8 branches in England, 6 in Scotland and 6 in Wales. By 1890 it had 2,700 members, by 1891 had established 5 districts based on Glasgow, Darlington, Preston, Sheffield and Swansea. And by 1896 its membership was 3,400, almost exclusively from men employed on open-hearth furnaces of steel manufacturing works, though in South Wales the membership also included steel bar millmen.[24] Its advantages lay not only in being able to tap a growing source of membership and in being uninhibited by traditional craft considerations (though the membership turned down the amalgamation of the Scottish Millmen in 1892), but also in sharing with employers a dislike of the contract system which failed 'to offer an incentive to anyone but the contractors'.[25] In 1899 it took in some 2,000 former members of the dissolved Tinplaters' Union, lengthening its name to the British Steel Smelters, Mill, Iron, Tinplate and Kindred Trades Association, and ultimately embraced the cause of amalgamation with an enthusiasm which led to its absorbing the iron and steel membership of the National Amalgamated Society of Enginemen, Cranemen, Boilermen, Firemen and Electrical Workers (1893) in 1912. Its air of competent aggressiveness and its general aspirations brought a new flavour to trade unionism in iron and steel, although, after some hesitation and with some differences, it came to share the preference of the ironworkers for close and stable relations with employers.

A further by-product of the aristocratic behaviour of the Ironworkers was the development of trade union organisation among the blastfurnace-men. As a group they suffered from the low status accorded to the labourer among skilled workers and their isolation was increased by developments which made the blastfurnace a separate unit in the economic structure of the industry.[26] Often rough and individualistic, it took them some time to learn that the help they could expect from the Ironworkers was limited and that the problems of organising a national union on their own behalf could not easily be overcome. They were not too proud to ask the assistance of John Kane in organising themselves,[27] though with no apparent results; spasmodic attempts to form an independent national organisation came to nothing.[28] In the end it was a district by district approach which brought success. A Cleveland Association formed in 1878 proved viable and led to an agreement with the Cleveland ironmasters providing for a joint board and a sliding scale. The pattern was repeated in Cumberland which came together with the Cleveland Association to form the National Association of Blastfurnacemen (1887). By 1890 5 district associations had been formed in North and South Staffordshire, Shropshire and the West Riding in addition to the two originals,[29] and there seems to have been membership also in Nottinghamshire, Lincolnshire and in Scotland, to a total of about 8,000 members.[30] All 5 associations,[31] some of which had developed joint committees and sliding scales after the Cleveland pattern, came together in 1892 in a loose federation, the National Federation of Blastfurnacemen, Ore Miners and Kindred Trades. By 1898 there had been success in organising some plants in South Wales and this was followed by organising attempts which gave a further foothold in the East Midlands and the establishment of the Lincolnshire sliding scale in 1909. By 1918 the Federation had, in all its districts, a total membership of 25,200. By that time it had come to function substantially as a national union, which it finally became in 1921.

In South Wales the stimulus which produced the Ironworkers in the Midlands and the North East resulted in a growth of trade union membership both in the Swansea area and in Monmouthshire, East Glamorgan (and in Gloucestershire). Until 1871 it seems that John Kane's union had little competition. In that year, in somewhat doubtful circumstances if Kane's report is accepted, there was in West Wales a desertion to a new local organisation, the Independent Association of Tinplate Makers.[32] This was a strike organisation with no friendly benefits, confined to works within a 15 mile radius of Swansea and with more than a flavour of Welsh nationalism since its members were principally Welsh speaking.[33] In the event the Tinplate Makers seem never to have claimed the allegiance of more than a small fraction of tinplate workers in West Wales[34] and, after some success in negotiation which culminated in the emergence of the 1874 uniform piece price list, it rapidly declined.

One result of the Tinplate Union and of other attempts at breakaways in the Dowlais area was the withdrawal of the Ironworkers from South Wales in 1876.[35] The union itself lasted, latterly without any ability to enforce the price list which it had negotiated and with a small and fitful membership, until the death of its originator, Lewis Afan, in 1887; like other unions in the industry it was the victim of unsettled trade and employment, poverty, weak organisation and leaders 'whose ability lay in oratory and evangelism rather than negotiation and administration'.[36] Coincidental with the demise of one union there grew up another, this time combining the representation of workers of both West and East Wales – the South Wales,

Monmouth and Gloucester Tinplate Workers Union. The new tin-plate workers' union was larger, richer, and better equipped than the old. Prosperity for a time aided its growth. By 1892 it claimed a membership of 10,000 of the 25,000 men employed in the tinplate industry. Six years later it had collapsed. Unemployment resulting from the American McKinley Tariff was one reason.[37] Another was the depression and resentment of the millmen whose production of sheet steel and backplate had grown, but who were accused of too many stoppages and irregularity in paying contributions.[38]

The stage for a takeover by other unions had already been set. The Tinplate Workers Union had never sought to organise outside that industry. From the formation of the Steel Smelters in 1887 John Hodge had set out with some success to organise melters in Wales;[39] in the course of time millmen dissatisfied with the TWU had already joined his union and more did so when the Tinplate Union collapsed. After 1898 some tinhousemen and millmen, especially in the Briton Ferry area, chose to remain with a reconstituted rump of the old union, now known as the Tin and Sheet Millmen's Association. Yet others, particularly the tinhouse-men, joined Ben Tillett's Dockers' Union (formed in 1887) and the remaining workers were recruited either by the Welsh Artisans' Union (founded in 1888–9), by the National Union of Gasworkers and General Labourers who were particularly strong in Llanelly, or by the Amalga-mated Society of Engineers. By 1914 the tinplate industry in South Wales was almost 100 per cent organised,[40] though in many different unions. In the steel works outside tinplate the Steel Smelters organised both melters and millmen substantially without competition, except in the great integrated coal and steel plants at Dowlais, Ebbw Vale, Tredegar, Cyfartha and Blaenavon. Here the South Wales Iron and Steel Workers and Mechanics association was recognised by the employers to represent blastfurnacemen, Bessemer operatives, millmen, forgemen, mechanics, smiths, boilermakers and locomotive drivers. Only at Dowlais were some of the Siemens furnacemen in the Smelters Association, which reckoned the Iron and Steel Workers and Mechanics (established in 1890 to negotiate with the employers of the 6 works for the creation of a sliding scale and local procedure – the first of its kind in Wales) as no union at all.[41] Though disapproved of by other organisations the Iron and Steel Workers and Mechanics continued in existence for 30 years.

By the end of the nineteenth century, therefore, more than 7 unions were organising iron, steel and tinplate workers in South Wales. In England and Scotland the situation was equally complex. In addition to the Steel Smelters, with 12,300 members in 1905, the Associated Iron and Steel Workers of Great Britain, whose membership had continued to decline and stood at 6,500 in 1906, and the Blastfurnacemen's Federation (11,242 members in 1906), there were a number of other organisations, large and small. The National Amalgamation of Engineers, Cranemen, Firemen and Electrical Workers (whose iron and steel members were absorbed into the Steel Smelters in 1912) was formed in 1889 and had some 6,000 members before amalgamation. The Scottish Associated Society of Millmen, formed in Glasgow by John Hodge as an independent venture in 1888 on the supposition that it would amalgamate with the Steel Smelters, was rejected by the membership of that society, and remained as an independent organisation for 31 years on a distinctly Scottish basis, changing its name in

1895 to the Amalgamated Society of Steel and Iron Workers and reaching a peak of some 10,000 members in 1901. The National Steelworkers Associated Engineering and Labour League (1888) operated in the North East and from 1891 in Sheffield. Also based on the North East, the National Amalgamated Enginemen and the Northern United Enginemen, rivals from a split in the ranks of the Amalgamated Enginemen, Cranemen, Boilermakers and Firemen (1889) in 1893, also operated in Scotland. A Rotherham union, the National Amalgamated Enginemen, Cranemen and Hammer Drivers (1895) had similar aspirations to expand outside its own district, and there are said to have been a score or more of local unions organising the same classes of workers.[42] As in South Wales, the Dockers and the Gasworkers recruited wherever they could.

The situation came to a head in 1912. The Steel Smelters, by 1910 the leading union in the industry with a membership of 17,500, had for some years favoured amalgamation and began talks with other organisations, resulting in the absorption of the Enginemen and Cranemen; and stimulated in part by the Hawarden Bridge dispute of 1910, one element of which was an unseemly and destructive squabble between the Smelters and the Iron and Steel Workers, a Trades Union Congress sub-committee took the matter in hand and convened a meeting of all the unions connected with the iron, steel, sheet and tinplate trades. This move took some time to bear fruit. Ultimately it resulted in the formation of the British Iron, Steel and Kindred Trades Association in 1917.

The new organisation was ingenious in form. It also proved to be effective in action. In 1916 a General Committee was created to produce a scheme for amalgamating the trade union forces of 7 organisations – the Associated Iron and Steel Workers of Great Britain, the British Steel Smelters, the Amalgamated Steel and Iron Workers, the Blastfurnacemen's Federation, the National Steel Workers' Union, the Tin and Sheet Millmen's Union and the tinplate section of the Dockers' Union. Amalgamation as such appeared to be almost impossible. There seemed to be little chance of securing the two-thirds majority vote of the total membership of the unions concerned as required by the Trade Union Act 1876. The problem was to secure something less than amalgamation but more than federation. The proposal was that a new organisation be established, the British Iron, Steel and Kindred Trades Association, termed, for the purposes of the scheme, the Central Association. Provision was also made for an Iron and Steel Trades Confederation to which all unions, including the Central Association, were to be affiliated and to which all affiliated bodies were required to pay affiliation fees. Unions were not immediately to give up their separate existences, but the Confederation was to take over all the official and organising staff and be responsible, through a Central Committee composed of General Secretaries, for all purely trade union functions, leaving affiliated bodies to administer their own friendly benefits. Unions were to cease organising membership and would therefore ultimately disappear, the Central Association being the body to which membership was attributed. In practice, therefore, the Confederation was to take over and maintain the existing machinery of negotiation, while the Central Association would handle membership until this should all be attributable to itself, at which point its rationale in bringing individual unions together would disappear.

The Dockers' Union showed little interest in an arrangement which would have implied an ultimate hiving-off of its iron and steel membership. By a narrow majority of 13 votes to 11 a conference of the Executives of the Blastfurnacemen's Federation withdrew from further association with the scheme in March 1916.[43] Of the 5 remaining unions only 3, the Steel Smelters, the Associated Iron and Steel Workers and the National Steel Workers, with a total membership of 52,460, became merged into the Central Association on 1 January 1917. The Amalgamated Steel and Iron Workers and the Tin and Sheet Millmen failed in their initial ballot to obtain a majority in favour of merger, but later did so, the former in 1920 and the latter in 1921.

The creation of BISAKTA/ISTC[44] set the course and balance of trade unionism in the iron and steel industry for half a century or more. In attracting to itself other unions in the industry it became virtually the only organisation to represent production workers; in its relations with the employers it assumed a rationality and stability which gave the industry an untroubled industrial relations history for many years. Such a situation continued virtually unchanged for some time after the steel industry nationalisation took effect in 1967, though by that time the balance of employment in newer mills had turned significantly towards craftsmen, increasing in importance the role of the Engineers and others as seen by the development of a National Craftsmen's Co-ordinating Committee for negotiation with the employers and a Steel Industry Trade Union Consultative Committee of the Trades Union Congress, which was originally formed to examine problems associated with the transfer to public ownership and involving all the principal manual worker unions with membership in the industry. The increasing economic problems of the industry and consequently harder attitudes of the British Steel Corporation brought the first national stoppage in which the Iron and Steel Confederation had ever been involved – between 2 January and 3 April 1980 – and a further severe contraction in the size of the industry.

Notes

1. Of the 52,300 non-manual employees in the new British Steel Corporation over 25,000 were in nationally and locally recognised unions. Of the former, the Iron and Steel Trades Confederation had 11,750, the National Association of Clerical and Supervisory Staffs (TGWU), 3,200, the National Union of Blastfurnacemen, 300, the National Union of General and Municipal Workers, 400, and various craft unions, 2,300 or more. Locally recognised unions were the Clerical and Administrative Workers Union (3,500) and the Association of Scientific, Technical and Managerial Staffs (4,100). To these should be added the Steel Industry Management Association (now amalgamated with the Electrical, Electronic, Telecommunication and Plumbing Union) which was later recognised by the BSC.

2. The Transport and General Workers Union, the National Union of General and Municipal Workers, the Amalgamated Engineering Union, the Amalgamated Society of Boilermakers, Shipwrights, Blacksmiths and Structural Workers, the Amalgamated Union of Foundry Workers, the Electrical Trades Union, the National Union of Operative Heating and Domestic Engineers and General Metal Workers, the United Pattern Makers Association, the Amalgamated

Union of Building Trades Workers, the Amalgamated Society of Woodworkers, the National Society of Painters and Decorators and the Plumbing Trades Union.

3. H.J. Fyrth and H. Collins, *The Foundry Workers*, AUFW, 1959, p. 16.
4. T.S. Ashton, *Iron and Steel in the Industrial Revolution*, Manchester University Press, 1924, p. 208.
5. *S.C. Manufactures, Shipping and Commerce* (1833), Q. 9819.
6. Alan Birch, *Economic History of the British Iron and Steel Industry*, Frank Cass, 1967, pp. 249 ff.
7. A. Aspinall, *The Early English Trade Unions*, Batchworth Press, 1949, pp. 206, 220, 231 and 242.
8. William Walters, Royal Commission Report, 1867.
9. Ashton, *op. cit.*, p. 206.
10. Sir A. Pugh, *Men of Steel*, ISTC, 1951, p. 9.
11. Ashton, *op. cit.*, p. 206.
12. Pugh, *op. cit.*, p. 10.
13. As in West Wales (see W.E. Minchinton, *The British Tinplate Industry*, OUP, 1957, Chapter IV) and in Cleveland (*Royal Commission on Labour*, Group A, Q. 14,978, 14,983–93) in the 1960s and in Scotland in the 1880s (John Hodge, *Workman's Cottage to Windsor Castle*, Sampson Low, 1931, pp. 40–1).
14. *Royal Commission on Labour*, Evidence of John Kane.
15. In 1870, according to Eric Taylor, 'The Origin and Early Years of the Midland Wages Board', *Man and Metal*, April 1972, p.101.
16. *Royal Commission on Labour*, Statement by Mr John Jones, Secretary of the North of England Iron Manufacturers' Association and the Cleveland Iron Masters' Association. Nevertheless the Ironworkers was a purely 'strike society' with no friendly benefits.
17. Kane was involved in the establishment of the Board of Conciliation and arbitration for the Manufactured Iron Trade of the North of England which formed the model for other such joint boards in the industry.
18. Comte de Paris *The Trades Unions of England*, 1869.
19. Hodge, *op. cit.*, p. 41.
20. *Royal Commission on Labour*.
21. It is interesting that the membership of the Association was referred to as 'smelters' rather than 'melters', since it is often regarded as a vulgar error to confuse 'melting', the reduction of ore to liquid metal form for refining or reconversion, with 'smelting', the reduction of ore to liquid metal. Hodge's members were 'melters' rather than 'smelters', a term which might more appropriately be applied to blastfurnacemen.
22. Hodge, *op. cit.*, p. 40.
23. Pugh, *op. cit.*, p. 85, estimates the number at about 500.
24. H.A. Clegg, A. Fox and A.F. Thompson, *A History of British Trade Unions since 1889*, Vol. I, 1889–1910, OUP, 1964, p. 206.
25. Pugh, *op. cit.*, p. 20.
26. *Ibid.*, Chapter IV.
27. Jack Owen, *Ironmen*, National Union of Blastfurnacemen, p. 9.
28. *Ibid.*, pp. 10–11.
29. *Ibid.*, p. 19.
30. *Royal Commission on Labour*, 1891.

31. The Cleveland and Durham Blastfurnacemen and Cokeminers' Association, The Cumberland and Lancaster Blastfurnacemen's Association, The Eastern Midland Blastfurnacemen, Ore Miners and Kindred Trades Association, the Midland (Staffs) Blastfurnacemen, Cokeminer and By-products Workers Association and the South Wales and Monmouthshire District Association of Blastfurnacemen, Quarrymen, Ore Miners and Kindred Trades.
32. Pugh, *op. cit.*, p. 11.
33. J.H. Jones, *The Tinplate Industry*, P.S. King, 1914, pp. 177 ff.
34. Minchinton, *op. cit.*, p. 118.
35. Pugh, *op. cit.*, p. 12.
36. Minchinton, *op. cit.*, p. 119.
37. A protective tariff placing a duty of 2.2 cents per pound on imported tinplate and coming into operation on 1 July 1891. The object of the tariff was to encourage the establishment of an American tinplate industry. As a result imports of tinplate from Great Britain fell from 325,100 tons in 1891, to 223,100 tons in 1895 and to 63,500 tons in 1899. By 1895 there were 10,000 out of work in South Wales tinplate of whom 6,530 had been idle since 1893 and by the end of the century 10,000 workers had left the industry.
38. Jones, *op. cit.*, p. 195.
39. Hodge, *op. cit.*, pp. 118 ff.
40. Minchinton, *op. cit.*, p. 126.
41. J.C. Carr and W. Taplin, *History of the British Steel Industry*, Blackwell, 1962, p. 145.
42. Clegg, Fox and Thompson, *op. cit.*, p. 212.
43. Minutes of the Blastfurnacemen's Federation, Leeds, 31 March 1916.
44. 'BISAKTA' was finally dropped in 1974, leaving the union to be known only as the Iron and Steel Trades Confederation.

AMALGAMATED IRON AND STEEL WORKERS AND MECHANICS OF SOUTH WALES AND MONMOUTHSHIRE

Formed in 1890, the association was a local union for the older works on the northern fringe of the Welsh coalfields. It covered only 6 works, namely Blaenavon, Ebbw Vale, Tredegar, Rhymey, Dowlais and Cyfarthfa, and membership was composed of blastfurnacemen, Bessemer operatives, millmen, forgemen, mechanics, smiths, boilermakers and locomotive drivers. It claimed to have 10,000 members, though it is doubtful whether it ever reached such a figure. Board of Trade Reports give a peak membership of 5,744 in 1892, falling thereafter to about 4,000, until 1909 when, on a new basis, membership is given at about 6,500. It was reported in 1892 that in the two years of its existence it had had only one dispute, which had been settled to the men's satisfaction. The Association had been formed in the first place to negotiate with the employers the terms of a sliding scale and the establishment of machinery to settle local differences, and a joint board consisting of 6 representatives each from the employers' and the workers' sides met every month. Although the masters refused to concede the principle of arbitration failing agreement, there was an implicit understanding between the two parties that in the event of a deadlock in any dispute, they would be willing to refer the matter to an umpire. The basic strength of the Association's membership was in the Merthyr Tydfil area, and it was the only union recognised in that district. It was dissolved in 1920 when it joined the **British Iron, Steel and Kindred Trades Association**.

Sources: BoT Reports; Carr and Taplin; Certification Office; Bain and Price.

AMALGAMATED MALLEABLE IRONWORKERS ASSOCIATION
See **Amalgamated Malleable Ironworkers of Great Britain**

AMALGAMATED MALLEABLE IRONWORKERS OF GREAT BRITAIN

John Kane founded this union in 1862 under the title of the **Amalgamated Malleable Ironworkers** with a membership principally confined at that time to the North of England. Kane was elected President of the union and also editor of the *Sons of Vulcan*, the union journal. (The name was later changed to the *Ironworkers Journal*.) In 1866 the ironmasters proposed cuts in wages ranging from 10 per cent to 60 per cent and the workers in all the trades in the industry came out in a strike lasting for 20 weeks and culminating in defeat for the unions concerned. At that time the Malleable Ironworkers' membership was 6,500 and its annual income amounted to £6,000. After the strike the membership had fallen to 476 and income to £1,000. The funds were not centralized and branches were largely autonomous, central administration costs being met by a branch levy and branches being free to divide their remaining funds among the members instead of building up a reserve. Kane described this method as 'the short and easy way to defeat', and he was proved to be correct because by 1868, with a trade depression at its worst, the union reached crisis point. A new constitution was adopted and 'Great Britain' was added to the name, Kane being appointed General Secretary. The union made a startling recovery, Kane reporting to the annual conference of 1871 that there were 14,000 members in 196 branches, and at the end of 1872 that there were over 200 branches with 20,000 members in the North of England, North and South Staffordshire, Wales and Scotland. For the first time there was a national union for the manufactured iron industry. By 1873 it reached a peak membership of 35,000. Included in this figure were 15,500 iron and tinplate workers in South Wales, and a good number from West Wales, where the union found itself in competition with the **Independent Association of Tinplate Makers**, a local union which had a lower subscription rate and to which many of the Malleable Ironworkers defected. By 1874 membership in South Wales had dwindled to just over 1,000 and the South Wales branches ceased to appear in the Malleable Ironworkers' records. At the time of John Kane's death in 1876 its sphere of influence was shrinking, until by 1878 its membership was less than 5,000. The union remained primarily a puddlers' organisation, and although it offered membership to steel workers in the 1880s, these were mainly confined to millmen. By 1884 the paying membership had dropped to less than 1,200, and the rules were altered to permit the payment of unemployment money, £775 being paid out in 1884 and over £1,000 in 1885. By 1887 the finances were at a very low level and the union was wound up, being replaced by the **Associated Iron and Steel Workers of Great Britain** which was intended to cover the newly emerging steel industry as well as the existing ironworkers.

Sources: Pugh; Carr and Taplin; Nicholas Howard, 'A Note on the Ironworkers Journal, 1869–1916', *Soc. Study Labour History Bulletin*, 13, Autumn 1966; Clegg, Fox and Thompson; Cole, *British Trade Unionism Today*; S. and B. Webb, *History of Trade Unionism*

AMALGAMATED SOCIETY OF STEEL AND IRON WORKERS OF GREAT BRITAIN (SCOTLAND)

Founded in Glasgow in February 1888 as the **Associated Society of Millmen**, the Society was formed with the aid of John Hodge, General Secretary of the **British Steel Smelters Association**, who agreed to be in charge of the funds of the new union. He resigned from this task in 1889 when John Cronin became Secretary of the union. The subscription was 6d per week with an entrance fee of 5s and 229 members enrolled. The Scottish millmen were very successful in recruiting in both steel mills and iron forges in which the contract system was prevalent, but the behaviour of some of the members at a strike at Clydebridge in 1889 led to several arrests and the imprisonment for two months of John Cronin. The union became a member in 1890 of the Board of Conciliation and Arbitration for the Manufactured Steel Trade of the West of Scotland, the first joint board to be established in Scotland. The Scottish ironmasters were not sympathetic to trade unionism and the Society struggled to remain in existence, having only 3,000 members in 1892 out of nearly 6,000 working in the industry, and of these only 1,127 were paid-up members. The name was changed in 1895 to the Amalgamated Society of Steel and Iron Workers in order to include the workers in the wrought iron industry. In 1897 John Cronin became the operatives' secretary on the Manufactured Iron Trade

Conciliation and Arbitration Board, and the Society was able to strengthen its position and widen its scope, establishing a section for the blastfurnacemen and setting up a wages board for them in 1900. In 1901 it absorbed the nut, bolt and tube workers and reached a membership of 10,000, but this figure had fallen to less than 6,000 by 1906. In 1911 it had talks with the **British Steel Smelters, Mill, Iron, Tinplate and Kindred Trades Association** with a view to amalgamation but the proposal was rejected. In 1912 the Society suggested federation rather than outright amalgamation and in 1913 became a member of the newly formed **Iron and Steel Trades Federation**. It refused to join the **British Iron, Steel and Kindred Trades Association** when this was first formed in 1917, but did so in 1920 and was joined by the **Amalgamated Society of Wire Drawers and Kindred Trades** and the **Tin and Sheet Millmen's Association**. For the whole of its existence the Society remained a distinctly Scottish organisation.

Sources: Pugh; Carr and Taplin; Cole, *British Trade Unionism Today*; S. and B. Webb, *History of Trade Unionism*.

ASSOCIATED IRON AND STEEL WORKERS OF GREAT BRITAIN
Following the demise of the **Amalgamated Malleable Ironworkers of Great Britain**, a national conference was called of many of the members of this organisation and the decision was taken to form the Associated Iron and Steel Workers, which was intended to cover both existing ironworkers and those engaged in the newly developed steel industry. The new union, formed in 1887, gradually came to be dominated by the higher paid tonnage rate men, and particularly by the contractors. In 1896 it was the largest and most representative union in the industry, covering both wrought iron and steel workers in the Midlands, the North of England and Cumberland, but it had lost members in South Wales and Scotland. In 1900 the union had over 8,000 members which had fallen to some 6,000 by 1906 due to years of trade depression, and also to the fact that the wrought iron industry was slowly waning in importance, although in certain areas like the Midlands and the North East it still overshadowed steel making. It was the only union represented on the two iron trade conciliation boards, the President and Secretary acting as the Operatives' Vice-Chairman and Secretary on both boards. In 1909 it was involved in a dispute with the **British Steel Smelters Association** at John Summers and Sons' Hawarden Bridge Works at Shotton, which proved to be a decisive episode in the ending of the contract system which had always been opposed by the Steel Smelters. The quarrel between the two unions was referred to the Disputes Committee of the TUC which found for the Associated Iron and Steel Workers, which decision resulted in disaffiliation from the TUC by the Steel Smelters for the next 6 years. The dispute brought to the fore the need for one union to represent the whole industry; in 1912 the TUC convened a meeting to discuss this proposal and in 1913 the **Iron and Steel Trades Federation** was formed as a first step toward amalgamation, with the Associated Iron and Steel Workers as a member, its Secretary, James Cox, becoming Secretary of the Federation. In 1917 with nearly 10,000 members and over £39,000 in funds, it became part of the newly formed **British Iron, Steel and Kindred Trades Association**.

Sources: Pugh; Clegg, Fox and Thompson; Carr and Taplin; Nicholas Howard, 'A Note on the Ironworkers Journal, 1869–1916', *Soc. Study Labour History Bulletin*, 13, Autumn 1966.

ASSOCIATED IRONWORKERS (STAFFORDSHIRE)

Formed in the early 1860s with W. Hobson as Secretary, this union catered mainly for puddlers but included some forgemen. It took a firm stand against all reductions in wages proposed by the masters in times of trade depression. In 1863 Staffordshire workers went on strike for 14 weeks, selecting a few works at a time, and in 1864/5 30,000 North Staffordshire men struck for 21 weeks against a proposed reduction in wages of 10 per cent. In retaliation the ironmasters of the South Staffordshire ironworks locked out their workers until the North Staffordshire men capitulated. After yet another unsuccessful strike against a further 10 per cent reduction in 1868, which lasted for 20 weeks and ended in defeat, the ironworkers union based on Staffordshire finally collapsed. This was the third set of local unions in that area to perish in face of the determined opposition by the ironmasters. The remnants of the Union merged with the **Amalgamated Malleable Ironworkers of Great Britain** in 1868.

Sources: Royal Commission on the Organisation and Rules of Trade Unions, Fifth Report, 1868, pp. 55–6; Carr and Taplin; Pugh.

ASSOCIATED SOCIETY OF MILLMEN

See **Amalgamated Society of Steel and Iron Workers of Great Britain**

BRITISH IRON AND STEEL FURNACE BUILDERS AND REPAIRERS SOCIETY

Formed in 1922 with 200 members, the Society ceased to exist in 1923.

Source: Bain and Price.

BRITISH IRON, STEEL AND KINDRED TRADES ASSOCIATION

See **Iron and Steel Trades Confederation**

BRITISH ROLL TURNERS TRADE SOCIETY

Formed in 1898, the Society has for many years been the smallest of those recognised in the iron and steel industry. It had 219 members in 1910, 723 in 1979 and 376 at the end of 1980. It operates in a small number of branches in Lancashire, the Midlands and South Wales.

Sources: Pugh; Marsh, *Concise Encyclopedia*.

BRITISH STEEL MILL AND HAMMERMEN'S ASSOCIATION
The Association was established in 1889 but it never achieved a very high membership, and lasted only 5 years before being dissolved in 1894.

Source: BoT Reports.

BRITISH STEEL SMELTERS ASSOCIATION
See **British Steel Smelters, Mill, Iron, Tinplate and Kindred Trades Association**

BRITISH STEEL SMELTERS, MILL, IRON, TINPLATE AND KINDRED TRADES ASSOCIATION
Although there were only 500 steel smelters in Scotland in the 1880s, the decision to form a union in 1886 (originally called the **British Steel Smelters Association**) was made following a strike at David Colville and Sons' Motherwell Works in 1885. The strike was against the decision of the firm to dispense with third-hand melters. John Hodge, himself a third-hand melter, was asked to become Secretary of the new union. Steel was a new industry and the Association was not therefore hampered by past traditions. At the first delegate conference held in 1888 it had 750 members in 20 branches, 6 of them in Scotland, 8 in England and 6 in Wales. By 1890 the union membership had grown to 2,700 and by 1891 it was established in 5 additional districts in Glasgow, Darlington, Preston, Sheffield and Swansea. In 1899 the name was changed to the above. The main aims of the Association were to secure the abolition of Sunday work, better regulation of promotion for furnacemen, and the ending of the contract system of payment – a system which had been inherited from the older established iron industry and which failed to offer incentives to anyone but the contractors. John Hodge was a strong supporter of one union for the whole of the industry in order to avoid the constant accusations of poaching and made repeated attempts to bring this about with no success. But the problem of having a number of unions representing different sections of the industry was exacerbated by a clash of interests between the Smelters Association and the **Associated Iron and Steel Workers of Great Britain** at John Summers and Co.'s Hawarden Bridge Works in 1909, the matter being referred to a TUC sub-committee which took the initiative and convened a meeting of all the unions in the industry. There was no immediate result of this move but a dispute at the Consett Works in 1915 led to further discussions on the need for amalgamation, and in 1917 the Smelters, with a membership of 39,507 and funds of £176,157, together with the **Associated Iron and Steel Workers of Great Britain** became members of the **British Iron, Steel and Kindred Trades Association**, which in turn affiliated to the **Iron and Steel Trades Confederation**, John Hodge being elected President of the Confederation and Arthur Pugh appointed Secretary.

Sources: Carr and Taplin; Pugh; Barou; BoT Reports; Clegg, Fox and Thompson; Cole, *British Trade Unionism Today*; Cole, 'Some Notes on British Trade Unions'.

CENTRAL IRON DRESSERS ASSOCIATION OF SCOTLAND
The Association was set up in 1900 with 50 members and was dissolved in 1905 when it had 56 members.

Source: Bain and Price.

CLEVELAND BLASTFURNACEMEN'S ASSOCIATION
See **National Union of Blastfurnacemen, Ore Miners, Coke Workers and Kindred Trades**

CUMBERLAND AND LANCASHIRE DISTRICT OF THE NATIONAL FEDERATION OF BLASTFURNACEMEN
Registered as a trade union in 1905, this local district of the National Federation of Blastfurnacemen amalgamated with others in 1921 to form the **National Union of Blastfurnacemen, Ore Miners, Coke Workers and Kindred Trades**.

Source: Owen.

CUMBERLAND IRON ORE, ENGINEMEN, FIREMEN AND ELECTRICAL WORKERS UNION
The Union's membership was never very large. It was established in 1916 with 20 members and ceased to exist in 1926 when only 10 remained.

Source: Bain and Price

CUMBERLAND IRON ORE MINERS AND KINDRED TRADES ASSOCIATION
Formed in 1888, the Association was dissolved in August 1929.

Source: Certification Office.

DALTON AND DISTRICT UNITED WORKMEN'S ASSOCIATION
The Association was a local iron mining union formed in 1888. It had ten branches in 1900, and about 1,200 members. It subsequently changed its name to the **Furness Iron Miners and Quarrymen's Union**.

Source: BoT Reports.

EAGREMONT AND DISTRICT IRON ORE MINERS ASSOCIATION
This was a local iron ore miners union formed in 1903 with 38 members. In the following year it had 26 members only, and was dissolved in the following year.

Source: BoT Reports.

FURNESS IRON MINERS AND QUARRYMEN'S UNION

The Union was established in 1888 as the **Dalton and District United Workmen's Association**, and had achieved a membership of 1,236 by 1900. In 1944, with only 129 members it transferred its engagements to the **National Union of Blastfurnacemen, Ore Miners, Coke Workers and Kindred Trades**.

Sources: Barou; Bain and Price; Certification Office.

INDEPENDENT ASSOCIATION OF TINPLATE MAKERS

The decision to form the Association was made at a meeting of a few iron and tinplate workers held at the Bird-in-Hand public house, Swansea, in 1871, the chief sponsors of the union being Jenkyn Thomas (Llew or Llewyn) of Aberdulais, and William Lewis (Lewys Afan), who became President and Secretary respectively, both men retaining these positions during the 16 years of its existence. The Association paid no friendly benefits; it was purely a strike organisation. Its influence never extended beyond 15 miles of Swansea. The tinplate workers in this area of West Wales were in an isolated position. Transport was primitive and the workers themselves were predominantly Welsh-speaking so that as well as being separated geographically from the workers in Glamorgan in the East, there was also the linguistic barrier which helped to prevent united action between them. In 1874 a strike was called by the leaders of the Association for an immediate increase in wages, but the masters, as a protective measure against the men's demands, amalgamated in March 1874 to form the Carmarthenshire and Glamorganshire Tinplate Makers' Association covering 31 of the 35 works in the western district. The strikers were locked out of all the works covered by the Tinplate Makers' Association with the further proviso they would not be re-engaged for a further 3 months. The men were defeated and went back to work in July 1874 on the old terms. Nevertheless the Makers' Association, in an effort to avoid further disputes, drew up a scale of wages known as the '1874 List' which remained the standard of tinplate wages for many years afterwards and eventually came to be regarded by the workers as a standard they had achieved by their own efforts. The Independent Association remained in existence with limited functions until 1887, when its chief pioneer and long-standing Secretary, Lewys Afan, died, but it never recovered from its defeat of 1874 and its demise was also hastened by the growth of steel production.

Sources: Pugh; Cole, *British Trade Unionism Today*; Clegg, Fox and Thompson; J.H. Jones, *The Tinplate Industry*, P.S. King and Son, 1914; C. Wilkins, *The History of the Iron, Steel, Tinplate and Other Industries of Wales*, Merthyr Tydfil, Joseph Williams, 1903.

IRON AND STEEL TRADES CONFEDERATION

The Confederation was a trade union operative from January 1917, created to take responsibility for trade questions affecting wages and conditions of work in the iron and steel industry. The Confederation arose out of the need of the government during the First World War to consult the

276

multiplicity of unions then existing in the industry. This resulted in a scheme of amalgamation which is discussed in some detail on p. 267. Briefly, existing members of confederating organisations were transferred to the **British Iron, Steel and Kindred Trades Association** (BISAKTA), the same union ultimately becoming the only affiliate of the ISTC, all members being recruited into it, and the ISTC taking over all the affiliated organisations. This ingenious method avoided problems arising from direct amalgamation and led, in substance, to the basis of an industrial union. The **National Union of Blastfurnacemen, Ore Miners, Coke Workers and Kindred Trades** remained outside the ISTC, and other organisations later came to have substantial membership. As an industrial union ISTC has never, therefore, been completely representative. In 1968 ISTC's manual worker membership in the British Steel Corporation was reckoned at 105,400 out of a total membership in all such unions of 188,200. Its membership in 1979, including non-manual members, was 114,000, but this has now declined as a result of the rapid contraction of the industry, particularly after the national steel strike of 1980.

Sources: Pugh; Carr and Taplin; Clegg, Fox and Thompson; Fyrth and Collins; Cole, *British Trade Unions Today*; Marsh, *Concise Encyclopedia*.

IRON AND STEEL TRADES FEDERATION

In April 1912 the TUC convened a meeting under the chairmanship of Arthur Henderson of all the unions connected with the iron, steel and tinplate trades to consider the question of an amalgamation between them, but a counter proposal suggesting a federation as opposed to an amalgamation was put forward by the **Associated Iron and Steel Workers of Great Britain** and the **Associated Society of Millmen**, and this was accepted. In the event the Federation was established in 1913 representing a total of some 30,000 members of the **Associated Iron and Steel Workers of Great Britain**; the **Amalgamated Society of Steel and Iron Workers of Great Britain; the Tin and Sheet Millmen's Association; the National Steelworkers Associated Engineering and Labour League**; and the tinplate and galvanizing section of the **Dockers' Union** (see Vol. 3). James Cox, Secretary of the Associated Iron and Steel Workers, was appointed Secretary of the Federation. The Federation was eventually superseded by the formation of the **Iron and Steel Trades Confederation** in 1917.

Sources: Carr and Taplin; Pugh.

MIDLAND BLASTFURNACEMEN, COKEMEN AND BY-PRODUCT WORKERS ASSOCIATION

Registered as a trade union in March 1907, the Association was primarily a Staffordshire organisation. It amalgamated with others in 1921 to form the **National Union of Blastfurnacemen, Ore Miners, Coke Workers and Kindred Trades**.

Sources: Certification Office; Owen.

MONMOUTHSHIRE AND SOUTH WALES IRON AND STEEL WORKERS UNION

This was a single branch organisation formed in 1898 with 140 members. It rapidly lost membership and had only 52 in the following year. The Board of Trade Reports claim that it may have ceased to exist at the end of 1900. Certification Office records note that dissolution was notified to the Registrar in March 1903.

Sources: BoT Reports; Certification Office.

NATIONAL AMALGAMATED SOCIETY OF ENGINEMEN, CRANEMEN, BOILERMEN, FIREMEN AND ELECTRICAL WORKERS

Formed in 1893, the Society had 49 branches and 3,785 members by 1910. It merged with the **British Steel Smelters, Mill, Iron, Tinplate and Kindred Trades Association** in 1912.

Source: Certification Office.

NATIONAL ASSOCIATION OF BLASTFURNACEMEN

See **National Union of Blastfurnacemen, Ore Miners, Coke Workers and Kindred Trades**

NATIONAL BLASTFURNACEMEN'S FEDERATION

See **National Union of Blastfurnacemen, Ore Miners, Coke Workers and Kindred Trades**

NATIONAL FEDERATION OF BLASTFURNACEMEN, ORE MINERS AND KINDRED TRADES

See **National Union of Blastfurnacemen, Ore Miners, Coke Workers and Kindred Trades**

NATIONAL IRON ORE MINERS ASSOCIATION

The Association was formed in Cleator Moor in 1907 with 806 members. It had 4 branches in 1910 and ceased to function in 1914 when it had 610 members.

Source: BoT Reports.

NATIONAL STEELWORKERS ASSOCIATED ENGINEERING AND LABOUR LEAGUE

The Association was basically a local union like so many others at this time which overlapped similar organisations and catered for production workers. Formed in Middlesborough in 1888 at the same time as the Scottish Millmen's Association (more formally known as the **Scottish**

278

Associated Society of Millmen), the Association began recruiting in Sheffield where it had some success, doubling its membership from 1,000 to 2,000 between 1895 and 1913. The industry was bedevilled by inter-union discord and in 1912 the TUC convened a meeting of all unions connected with the iron, steel, tinplate and sheet metal trades in order to discuss the possibility of amalgamation, but the proposal was not given a favourable response, a federation meeting with greater acceptance. Accordingly the **Iron and Steel Trades Federation** was formed in 1913 of which the Association became a founder member. In 1917, with 3,153 members and a cash reserve of £3,423, it joined the newly formed **British Iron, Steel and Kindred Trades Association**.

Sources: Carr and Taplin; Pugh; Cole, *Trade Unionism Today.*

NATIONAL UNION OF BLASTFURNACEMEN, ORE MINERS, COKE WORKERS AND KINDRED TRADES

The Union was founded in 1921 as the successor to the **National Blastfurnacemen's Federation** (1892). Blastfurnacemen had originally been admitted to the **Amalgamated Malleable Ironworkers of Great Britain** (1868), but this union's primary concern was for the puddlers, whose high status and earnings made dues high and not easily payable by its lower paid members, including the blastfurnacemen, who formed a separate **Cleveland Blastfurnacemen's Association** in 1878, followed by a Cumberland Association (1887), with the two combining in 1888 to form the **National Association of Blastfurnacemen**. By 1890 5 district associations of blastfurnacemen had been formed in England and in 1892 the National Association became the **National Federation of Blastfurnacemen, Ore Miners and Kindred Trades** covering Cleveland, Durham, Cumberland, Lancashire, North and South Staffordshire and Scotland, with a membership of about 8,000; it later spread to other areas, Derbyshire, Lincolnshire and Northamptonshire (1903), East Midlands and South Wales between 1904 and 1908 and North Lincolnshire in 1909. In 1903 its title was changed to include Ore Miners and Kindred Trades, the Federation having a membership of 25,200 in 1918. Two years earlier a conference of Executives of the Federation had turned down, by 13 votes to 11, a proposal to associate with the **British Iron, Steel and Kindred Trades Association** then being formed by major unions as a basis for an industrial union, and in 1919 it was decided that a ballot vote of the whole membership of the district associations should be taken to decide on a blastfurnacemen's amalgamation. The National Union was formed two years later, its General Secretary being Tom McKenna, President of the Federation since 1915 and Secretary since 1917. The Union has remained resolutely independent since that time and now has a membership of under 14,000.

Sources: Carr and Taplin; Owen; Clegg, Fox and Thompson; Pugh; Cole, *British Trade Unionism Today.*

ORMSBY IRON WORKS PIPE MAKERS ASSOCIATION

Formed in 1889, the Association was dissolved in 1893.

Source: Certification Office.

SCOTTISH ASSOCIATED SOCIETY OF MILLMEN
See **National Steelworkers Associated Engineering and Labour League**

SHEFFIELD AND DISTRICT ORGANISED ROLL TURNERS SOCIETY
The Society appears to have had a brief existence at the end of the First World War and into the 1920s. It was apparently unregistered and no record has been found of its history.

Source: MoL Reports.

SOUTH WALES AND MONMOUTHSHIRE DISTRICT OF THE NATIONAL UNION OF BLASTFURNACEMEN
This was a district of the union, dating from 1908, which, together with others, came together in 1921 to form the **National Union of Blastfurnacemen, Ore Miners, Coke Workers and Kindred Trades.**

Source: Owen.

SOUTH WALES FEDERATION OF IRON AND STEEL WORKERS
Established in 1894 with 135 members, the Federation ceased to exist in 1895.

Source: BoT Reports.

SOUTH WALES FEDERATION OF IRON AND STEEL WORKERS, RAILBANK MEN, MECHANICS, STOKERS, BLASTFURNACEMEN, ENGINE DRIVERS, MASONS, BRICKLAYERS, MOULDERS, BLOCK-LAYERS, NAVVIES, GENERAL LABOURERS AND OTHERS
The Federation was formed in 1894 and dissolved in November 1895.

Source: Certification Office.

SOUTH WALES IRON AND STEEL WORKERS AND MECHANICS
See **Amalgamated Iron and Steel Workers and Mechanics of South Wales and Monmouthshire**

SOUTH WALES, MONMOUTH AND GLOUCESTER TINPLATE WORKERS UNION
In 1886 there was an attempt by the employers in the Eastern district of Wales to impose a 10 per cent wage reduction which led to a strike and

lockout of the Monmouth works in November and December of that year. With a revival of trade in 1887 the Monmouth works were reopened and the men re-engaged. Up to that time there had been no union in this area, but the strike brought the workers of both the Eastern and Western areas into close contact and a joint conference led to the establishment of the new Union in 1888, the first General Secretary being Thomas Phillips. It was the first union for tinplate workers to cover the whole of South Wales, excluding puddlers and rollers of tinplate bar. It was set up solely as a militant organisation with no friendly society benefits payable, with the declared objectives of re-establishing and maintaining the 1874 list of prices throughout the area and the restriction of output of tinplate to 36 boxes each 8-hour shift. It was successful in establishing the 1874 list at certain of the works and in establishing the 36-box rule throughout the trade. In 1889 a dispute in the Swansea Valley led to a settlement negotiated by a joint committee of the Union and the employers, the settlement marking the first recorded recognition of a union in the South Wales tinplate industry. The Union published *The Industrial World*, a journal which ceased publication in October 1898. By 1895 hardly any of the works were still paying wages based on the 1874 list, some having made reductions of 25 per cent. The Union called a general strike of all tinplate works to force the reimposition of the list, which was temporarily successful. But wages were again reduced and in 1896 the Union called another strike and for a few weeks the list price was paid, but union funds were exhausted and membership was falling. It was in serious financial difficulties, having borrowed £1,000 to finance the strike. In addition it was faced increasingly with problems arising from mechanical developments in the trade. The climax in the Union's affairs came with the passing of the McKinley Tariff Act in 1890 with its disastrous effect on the Welsh tinplate trade. The Union lingered on with diminishing support and seems to have ceased at some indefinite date, probably about 1898, many of its members joining the **Tin and Sheet Millmen's Association** when it was formed in 1899.

Sources: Pugh; Carr and Taplin; J.H. Jones, *The Tinplate Industry*, P.S. King and Son, 1914; Clegg, Fox and Thompson; Cole, *British Trade Unionism Today*; C. Wilkins, *The History of Iron, Steel, Tinplate and Other Industries of Wales*, Merthyr Tydfil, Joseph Williams, 1903.

STEEL WORKERS ASSOCIATION AND UNITED LABOUR LEAGUE OF BRITAIN

Formed in 1888, the Association was dissolved in 1892.

Source: Certification Office.

TIN AND SHEET MILLMEN'S ASSOCIATION

The Association (1899) came into being at a delegate conference held in 1898 attended by many of the members of the defunct **Independent Association of Tinplate Makers** at which the decision was taken to form a new organisation for millmen which was to have over 1,000 members. The Independent Association had covered both millmen and tinhousemen, and the proposal to form separate unions for each type of worker was carried by a large majority. In point of fact no separate body was set up for the tinhousemen, most of whom joined general unions. The separation of the two sections had already been started by the creation in some lodges of two separate branches. Ivor Gwynne became President of the new Association and Thomas Phillips (who had previously been Secretary of the **South Wales, Monmouth and Gloucester Tinplate Workers Union**) became Secretary. The membership was drawn chiefly from the tinplate and sheet mills of the Briton Ferry area. The Association pursued an independent line, keeping the other unions in the industry at arm's length, and resisting repeated attempts by the **British Steel Smelters Association** to amalgamate with it. Accusations of poaching were repeatedly made against the Steel Smelters, so much so that following a dispute in October 1911 a demarcation agreement was agreed upon by the two organisations, a clause in the agreement pledging them to endeavour to arrive at an arrangement for amalgamation in the future. In 1912 at a specially convened meeting of all unions connected with the industry which was called by the TUC to discuss amalgamation, a majority of those present voted instead for a form of federation and in 1913 formed the **Iron and Steel Trades Federation**. In 1921 the Association joined the **British Iron, Steel and Kindred Trades Association**.

Sources: Carr and Taplin; Pugh; Clegg, Fox and Thompson; Cole, *British Trade Unionism Today*.

UNION OF PUDDLERS AND FORGEMEN OF GREAT BRITAIN
A Worcestershire union formed in 1912 with 230 members, the Union continued to function until November 1934 when, with 60 members remaining, it ceased to exist.

Sources: Bain and Price; Certification Office.

WELSH ARTISANS UNITED ASSOCIATION
The Association was formed in 1890 to cover maintenance workers and craftsmen such as fitters, roll turners and the like. Although its membership was only numbered in hundreds, the skills of its members put them in a very strong position and enabled them to secure higher wages by independent strikes or threats of strike action, sometimes at the expense of production workers in other unions who at times were laid off because of these tactics. In 1908 the Association joined the Tinplate and Sheet Metal Workers' Wages and Disputes Board, which then became representative of all the unions in the tinplate industry. The Secretary of the Association was J.H. John. In 1936 the Association merged with the **National Union of General and Municipal Workers** (see Vol. 3).

Sources: BoT Reports; Carr and Taplin; Cole, *British Trade Unionism Today*.

Part Three

Agriculture, Fishing and Chemicals

Agriculture and Fishing

AGRICULTURE

E.G. Wakefield, MP, in a pamphlet entitled *Swing Unmasked* (1830), thought fit to note: 'An English agricultural labourer and an English pauper – these words are synonymous.'[1] Such was the general condition of farm labourers when the first effort at forming a union was made. Wages had been reduced to 7s a week and the men were told that shortly they would have to accept 6s. And this at a time when the Grand National Consolidated Trades Union was opening branches all over the country and seemed to be headed for success. The farm labourers, knowing they could hardly survive on so low a wage, agreed after taking advice from various trade societies to form the Agricultural Labourers Union at a small Dorset village called Tolpuddle in 1833. The impact of the founding of the Union was extraordinary. All the trade unions at that time administered an oath of secrecy and possessed some sort of regalia – the Tolpuddle branch had a figure of 'Death painted six feet high' with which to perform the rites of initiation.[2] On 21 February 1834 notices were posted in public places warning that membership of the Union was a crime punishable by 7 years' transportation, and within 3 days of this proclamation its 6 leaders were imprisoned – regardless of the fact that the laws against combination had been repealed 10 years earlier – and were prosecuted under the terms of the Unlawful Oaths Act of 1797. It is an interesting fact that this act of 1797 was not itself repealed until 1981, almost 150 years after the Tolpuddle Martyrs suffered under its provisions.

The men were sent to Botany Bay, but were later pardoned and brought home after two years of unprecedented public agitation for their release. Agricultural trade unionism suffered a severe setback which lasted for many years. Wages remained very low and whole families had to work on the land, including the children. Many were compelled to live in the master's cottages and to offend meant to be turned out. During the next 30 years labourers' unions were formed in isolated areas for the purpose of raising wages, but usually failed in their objectives.[3]

It was not until 1866 that an organised attempt was made again to combine and an Agricultural Labourers Protection Association was formed in Kent. As labour was scarce at the time, wages were raised without much difficulty, and further unions were formed in Buckinghamshire, Herefordshire and Hertfordshire for the purpose of gaining higher wages. The Herefordshire union was formed in 1871, its motto being 'Emigration, Migration, but not Strikes'. In less than a year it had spread to 6 counties and had 30,000 members, and wages rose by 2s a week. The Lincolnshire Labour League was formed in May 1871. In March 1872 a meeting was held in Wellesbourne, Warwickshire, and the decision was taken to form a union. The men chose as their leader Joseph Arch, a farm labourer and lay preacher, and well-attended mass meetings were held at which hundreds joined the union.[4] Some of the farmers and landowners victimized the union men, and a strike was declared. Public sympathy was on their side, and an inaugural meeting was held in Leamington to launch the Warwickshire Agricultural Labourers Union with 64 branches and a membership of 5,000. Encouraged by this success farm labourers all over the country attempted to combine and the time seemed opportune to form a national body. In May 1872 the National Agricultural Labourers Union was established, though the Lincolnshire Labour League preferred to remain independent. In less than 3 months the National Union had a membership of nearly 50,000, and the *Labourers' Union Chronicle* was published. Under the leadership of Joseph Arch the Union preached moderation in all its activities. Persecution and attempts at suppression appeared at first to bind the men together in closer unity. Setbacks were regarded as temporary only. Industrial unions contributed generously to the farm labourers' union funds, as did many middle-class philanthropists, like Charles Bradlaugh and Sir Charles Dilke. Within 4 months of its formation, emigration became an important part of its policy and in 1873–4 over £6,000 was spent out of union funds for this purpose. Although the Union succeeded at times in raising wages its efforts lacked co-ordination and real leadership, and in 1874, following a wage demand and the limitation of hours to 54 a week, some 10,000 labourers were locked out, farmers in various counties not waiting for the men's claims but locking out all union men willy-nilly. The strain on union funds was tremendous and in July 1874 it collapsed, having practically run to the end of its financial resources. Disunity grew, and efforts were made to form rival unions like the National Farm Labourers Union, having for its object the acquisition of land which was to be purchased out of weekly subs and let out to members. It accomplished nothing and soon faded away.[5] The National Union gradually declined until in 1889 it had only 4,254 members scattered in the Midland and Eastern Counties in what were virtually only sick and funeral clubs.

After the successful Dock Strike of 1889 efforts were made yet again to organise farm workers. In May 1890 the Eastern Counties Labour Federation was formed based on Ipswich. In the same year the Norfolk and Norwich Amalgamated Labour Union was established. In 1891 the Kent and Sussex Agricultural and General Labourers Union became the London and Home Counties Labour League. One of the many reasons for the success of the Great Dock Strike of 1889 was, it was said, that it took place at harvest time and farm labourers could not be recruited to do blackleg labour on the docks. The need to organise farm labourers was raised at the 1889 Trades Union Congress, the Dockers' Union making the decision to recruit in Oxfordshire and Lincolnshire.

According to Dr W. Hasbach in his *History of the English Agricultural Labourer*, there were in existence in 1894 the old National Agricultural Labourers Union based on Leamington; the London and Home Counties Labour League; the Warwickshire Agricultural and General Workers Association, the Wiltshire Agricultural and General Labourers Union based on Devizes; the Berkshire Agricultural and General Workers Union at Reading; the Hertfordshire and Bedfordshire Land and Labour League with a headquarters at Hitchin; the Eastern Counties Labour Federation; the Norfolk and Norwich Amalgamated Labour Union; and the Herefordshire Workers Union.[6] By 1900 all these unions had ceased to exist.

In 1899 the Workers' Union (see Vol. 3) which organised semi-skilled and unskilled labour of every kind, began recruiting farm labourers in 4 counties: Staffordshire, North Shropshire, South Cheshire and Norfolk, and claimed some success in raising wages by between 1s and 3s a week. But it was not until 1906 that a further attempt was made at a specifically agricultural organisation. This resulted in the formation of the Eastern Counties Agricultural Labourers and Small Holders Union under the leadership of George Edwards, who had earlier been the Secretary of the now defunct Norfolk and Norwich Amalgamated Labour Union. The Eastern Counties Union laid the basis for the present union, changing its name to the National Agricultural Labourers and Rural Workers Union in 1909; becoming the National Union of Agricultural Workers in 1920; and assuming the title of the National Union of Agricultural and Allied Workers in 1966, thus recognising its membership in ancillary industries in addition to those employed directly on the land.

Ernest Selley writing in 1919 reported that the Workers' Union had over 100,000 farm workers as members and that farm workers were also to be found in the Dockers' Union, the Municipal Employees' Association, the National Union of Gasworkers and even in the Union of Co-operative Employees. By 1924 the agricultural membership of the Workers' Union was no more than 5,000, and other unions suffered similarly, growing only in the more favourable climate during and after the Second World War.

This mixture of membership in industry-based and general unions persisted until the merger of the National Union of Agricultural and Allied Workers into the Transport and General Workers Union in 1981. Some three quarters of hired farmworkers were in membership of the NUAAW, but the Transport and General Workers' Union, through the Workers' Union and the other organisations it had absorbed over the years, has retained a considerable interest and held continuous representation on the Agricultural Wages Boards. Indeed, on the Scottish Board, all employee representatives come from that union.

Notes

1. Ernest Selley, *Village Trade Unionism in Two Centuries*, London, George Allen and Unwin, 1919.
2. *Ibid.*, p. 15.
3. S. and B. Webb's *History of Trade Unionism*, pp. 144–6; 328.
4. Reg Groves, *Seed Time and Harvest*, NU of Agricultural and Allied Workers 1972.
5. Selley, *op. cit.*, p. 73.
6. Dr W. Hasbach, *A History of the English Agricultural Labourer*, London, P.S. King and Son Ltd, 1920.

FISHING

In the fishing industry there appear to have been only a few centres for organisation, Grimsby, Milford Haven and Hull being the most important; the unions concerned had only a small membership. A National Federation of Fishermen came into existence in 1890 and although it lasted only 4 years it managed to win some concessions from the fish companies. With the beginning of steam-trawling, additional local unions came into being on the East Coast, and at the end of the 1890s collective agreements were coming into effect; for example, in Hull, where the fishermen were able to negotiate a settlement with the employers which covered wages and bonuses for all grades with the exception of captains and mates. At that stage only about 4,000 of the 62,000 workers in the industry were organised. Some unions like the Humber Steam Trawler Engineers and Firemen's Association maintained a continuous existence for 45 years, being formed in 1893 and dissolved in 1938. Others such as the Mercantile Marine Trawlermen's Association could only manage to function for 4 years with a gradually dwindling membership. Fishermen and general fish workers of Milford Haven had two attempts at keeping some sort of organisation alive first by means of the Milford Haven and District Fishermen, Fish Workers and General Labourers Union which was formed in 1916, apparently ceasing to exist in 1917, and re-emerging in 1921 as the Milford Haven Fishermen's Amalgamated Society, only to cease functioning in 1928. Grimsby was a seaport which made three attempts to form a lasting union without success. Two further attempts to unionise the industry were made in the form firstly of the National Union of British Fishermen, established in 1917, which merged with the Transport and General Workers Union in 1922; the last effort was the United Fishermen's Union, formed in 1962, which merged with the Transport and General Workers Union in 1966.

ABERDEEN FISHERMEN'S ASSOCIATION
The Association was set up in 1914 with 90 members, and in 1916, with 82 members, it merged with the National Union of Sailors and Firemen (later to become the **National Union of Seamen** (see Vol. 3).

Source: Bain and Price.

ABERDEEN STEAM FISHING VESSELS ENGINEMEN AND FIRE-MEN'S UNION
See **Scottish Sea Fishers' Union**

AGRICULTURAL FARM LABOURERS' LEAGUE OF DORSET
Established in 1890, the League had 281 members in 1892 and nearly 600 in 1895. By 1906 the membership level had been reduced to 101, after which date nothing further appears to be known of its existence.

Source: BoT Reports.

AGRICULTURAL LABOURERS PROTECTION ASSOCIATION
The Association was formed in 1866 with some 200 members and was based in Kent. Its object was to 'organise the agricultural labourers with a view to the amelioration of their social conditions and moral elevation, and to endeavour to mitigate the evils of their serfdom.' As labour was scarce at this time, higher wages were obtained without too much difficulty. But the higher wages paid encouraged a greater influx of labour, and this led to an eventual reduction in wages. A weekly local journal was started but this did not last long. The Association, with a very reduced membership, joined with the **Sussex Agricultural Workers Union** and became the **Kent and Sussex Agricultural Workers Union**, and although most of the small local unions became extinct it was said that Kent and Sussex still had over 10,000 members in 1889. In 1891 it changed its name to the **London and Home Counties Labour League** and extended its activities throughout the South East. In 1892 it claimed to have some 11,000 members but in the following years its membership fell drastically and it ceased to exist as an independent organisation in 1895, the remaining membership joining the **National Amalgamated Union of Labour** (see Vol. 3).

Sources: Selley; Arthur H.D. Acland, 'Land, Labourers and Association', *Contemporary Review*, Vol. L, July 1886; J. Pointing, 'Trade Unionism in Agriculture,' *in* Cole, *British Trade Unionism Today*; Groves, 'The Long Journey Home'; Horn, 'Agricultural Labourers' Trade Unionism'; Groves, *Sharpen the Sickle!*; Green, *History of the English Agricultural Labourer*.

AMALGAMATED AGRICULTURAL AND GENERAL LABOURERS' UNION
Formed in 1874, the Union was dissolved in 1875.

Source: Certification Office.

AMALGAMATED LABOUR LEAGUE (NORFOLK)
Established in 1872, the League had 104 members in 1892, but this number had fallen to 14 members by 1914, when it ceased to exist.

Source: Bain and Price.

AMALGAMATED LABOUR LEAGUE OF LINCOLN AND NEIGH-BOURING COUNTIES
Formed in 1872, the League had its headquarters at Boston. It grew rapidly, achieving a membership of 10,000 in 31 branches with an income of £3,167 and expenditure of £2,861. There was an alteration of the rules in 1890. By 1892 membership was falling steadily and by 1889 the League had only 30 members remaining. It ceased to exist in 1916.

Sources: Wearmouth; BoT Reports; Certification Office.

AMALGAMATED SOCIETY OF GENERAL AND FARM LABOURERS OF GREAT BRITAIN AND IRELAND
Established in 1885, the Society was dissolved in 1887.

Source: Certification Office.

BEDFORDSHIRE AND HERTFORDSHIRE AGRICULTURAL LABOURERS' UNION
Formed in 1872, the Union merged with the **National Agricultural Labourers Union** in 1873.

Source: Wearmouth.

BERKSHIRE AGRICULTURAL AND GENERAL WORKERS UNION
The Union was formed in 1892 and had 245 members in 1893. It remained in existence for 4 years when it was dissolved in 1896 with a membership which had dwindled to 21.

Sources: Selley; Certification Office; BoT Reports.

BIRKENHEAD OPERATIVE GARDENERS' ASSOCIATION
Formed with 40 members in 1900, the Association ceased to exist in 1902.

Source: BoT Reports.

BOTESDALE AGRICULTURAL LABOURERS UNION (SUFFOLK)
Formed in 1872, the Union was dissolved in 1893.

Source: Certification Office.

BRITISH GARDENERS' ASSOCIATION
See **National Agricultural Workers Union**

BUCKINGHAMSHIRE AGRICULTURAL LABOURERS' UNION
This was a local union formed in 1866 for the purpose of trying to raise the wage levels of its members and, as labour was scarce at that time, the Union at first succeeded in its efforts; but when more labour became available, the farmers began to reduce wages. The Union had only a brief independent existence, becoming a branch of the **National Agricultural Labourers Union** upon the formation of that body in 1872.

Source: Selley.

BUCKLE HIRED FISHERMEN'S ASSOCIATION
Established in 1913 with 500 members, the Association had ceased to exist by 1914.

Source: Bain and Price.

CAITHNESS FARM SERVANTS AND PLOUGHMEN'S ASSOCIATION
Formed in 1913 with 700 members, in 1920 with 1,000 members the Union joined the **Scottish Farm Servants Union**.

Sources: Selley; Groves, *Seed Time and Harvest*; Wearmouth; Marwick.

DAIRY WORKERS AND RURAL WORKERS' UNION
The Union was set up in 1914 by the Lancashire branches of the **National Agricultural Labourers Union**, not because of any dissatisfaction with the activities of that union but simply because the members in the Lancashire area felt that organisation and cohesion was becoming increasingly difficult as the National Union grew in size and strength, and that a local organisation would be better able to deal with local issues. In 1918 the Union merged with the **Workers Union** (see Vol. 3) which included rural and town workers amongst its membership.

Source: Cole, *British Trade Unionism Today*.

EASTERN COUNTIES AGRICULTURAL LABOURERS AND SMALL-HOLDERS UNION
See **National Union of Agricultural and Allied Workers**

EASTERN COUNTIES LABOUR FEDERATION
The Federation was established in May 1890 in the aftermath of the 1889 Dock strike. It was centred on Ipswich and had recruited 3,000 members by the end of the year. By 1892 it claimed to have a membership of nearly 17,000, but had to admit that the great majority of this number were in

arrears with their subscriptions, thereby causing great problems for the efficient functioning of the organisation and undermining its effectiveness. The Federation retained an independent existence until 1896 when it was dissolved with a recorded membership of only 4 remaining.

Sources: S. and B. Webb, *History of Trade Unionism*; G. Edwards, *From Crow Scaring to Westminster*, Labour Publishing Co, London, 1922; Selley; Groves, *Sharpen the Sickle!*; F.D. Mills, 'The National Union of Agricultural Workers', *Journal of Agricultural Economics*, Vol. XVI, No. 2, December 1964, pp. 230–53; M. Madden, 'National Union of Agricultural Workers', B. Litt. thesis, University of Oxford, 1957; Green, *History of the English Agricultural Labourer*.

EDINBURGH AND DISTRICT SEED AND NURSERY EMPLOYEES' ASSOCIATION

The Association was set up in 1920 with 105 members, which had fallen to 20 members by 1925. After this date it apparently ceased to function.

Source: Bain and Price.

FEDERAL UNION OF AGRICULTURAL AND TOWN LABOURERS

Formed in 1873, the Union was a rival organisation to the **National Agricultural Labourers Union**. It covered most of the small independent organisations existing at that time and had a membership of 49,344 covering 8 independent district unions, among which was the **Peterborough District Labourers' Union** and the **Lincolnshire Labour League**. The Union was ostracised by Joseph Arch, the leader of the NALU, because of the personal attacks it made upon him. Such differences of opinion only served to weaken the efforts of both organisations. By 1875 the Federal Union had come to the end of its existence.

Sources: Horn, *Joseph Arch*; Report of the Federal Union of Agricultural and Town Labourers, 1874; George Howell Collection, Bishopsgate Institute, London.

FLEETWOOD STEAM TRAWLERS ENGINEMEN AND FIREMEN'S UNION

The Union was formed in 1907 with 140 members, but the numbers gradually dwindled until it ceased to exist in 1911 when its membership was down to 15.

Source: Bain and Price.

FLEETWOOD TRAWLER OFFICERS' GUILD

The Guild was set up in 1949 with 201 members and remained a functioning organisation until 1958, when, with a remaining membership of 186, it was dissolved.

Source: Bain and Price.

FRIENDLY SOCIETY OF AGRICULTURAL LABOURERS

Established in Tolpuddle in Dorset in 1834, the Friendly Society was intended to be a lodge of the **Grand National Consolidated Trades Union** (Vol. 3) which at that time seemed to be breaking new ground in trade union organisation. All unions at that time administered an oath of secrecy and the Tolpuddle lodge was no exception, but its lawful intention is contained in Rule 23 which read 'that the object of this Society can never be promoted by any act or acts of violence, but on the contrary, all such proceedings must tend to injure and destroy the Society itself. This Lodge therefore will not countenance any violation of the laws.' Lodge meetings were run on business lines, one of the rules directing that no member should be 'allowed to eat, read, sleep, swear, bet wagers or use any absurd language during Lodge hours.' Nevertheless, 4 months after its formation, the leaders of the Society were charged with 'administering unlawful oaths' and sentenced to 7 years' penal servitude at Botany Bay. It took two years of unceasing work by a special committee of supporters of these men to obtain a pardon and their return home. The event is celebrated by an annual pilgrimage of trade unionists and friends to the village of Tolpuddle.

Sources: Selley; TUC, *The Book of the Martyrs of Tolpuddle*, TUC, 1934; Joyce Marlow, *The Tolpuddle Martyrs*, Andre Deutsch, 1972; S. and B. Webb, *History of Trade Unionism*; Clegg, Fox and Thompson; Groves, *Sharpen the Sickle!*

GRANTON AND DISTRICT TRAWL FISHERMEN'S ASSOCIATION

Established in 1911 with 286 members, the Association remained in existence until 1919 when, with a membership of 290, it was dissolved.

Source: Bain and Price.

GREAT YARMOUTH AND GORLESTON FISHERMEN'S ASSOCIATION

Formed in 1887, the Union was dissolved in 1899.

Source: Certification Office.

GRIMSBY FISHERMEN'S ASSOCIATION

The Association was first established in 1878 and by 1892 had 359 members, which had dwindled to 136 members when it ceased to exist in 1924.

Source: Bain and Price.

GRIMSBY FISHERMEN'S TRADE UNION
Formed in 1890, the Union merged with the **National Federation of Fishermen of Great Britain and Ireland** in 1891.

Source: Certification Office.

GRIMSBY STEAM AND DIESEL FISHING VESSELS ENGINEERS AND FIREMEN'S UNION
The Union was formed by 14 engineers in 1896 and consisted of engineers and firemen on Grimsby trawlers. At one point in its existence (before the First World War) it had 1,200 members but this number gradually declined. The Union transferred its engagements to the **Transport and General Workers Union** (Vol. 3) in 1976.

Source: Marsh, *Concise Encyclopedia.*

HERTFORDSHIRE AGRICULTURAL AND GENERAL WORKERS UNION
Registered in 1893, the Union withdrew the registration in 1896 when many of the small county unions formed during a brief revival of agricultural trade unionism collapsed.

Source: Certification Office.

HERTFORDSHIRE AGRICULTURAL LABOURERS UNION
This was a local union formed in 1866 for the purpose of trying to raise the wage levels of its members, and as labour was hard to come by at that time the Union at first succeeded in its efforts. When more labour became available the farmers began to reduce wages, which the men had to accept. The Union had only a brief independent existence, becoming a branch of the **National Agricultural Labourers Union** upon the formation of that organisation in 1872.

Source: Selley.

HERTFORDSHIRE AND BEDFORDSHIRE LAND AND LABOUR LEAGUE
The League was formed in 1893 and registration was cancelled in 1896.

Source: Certification Office.

HIGHLAND FISHERMEN'S ASSOCIATION
The Association was established in 1912 with a membership of 4,000, and retained this membership in 1913. There is no trace of it after 1914.

Source: Bain and Price.

HULL TRAWLER OFFICERS' GUILD

The Guild was formed in 1931 with 402 members. It suspended its activities during the Second World War, and restarted as a functioning body in 1945 with 133 members. It held a certificate of independence but now no longer appears to exist.

Sources: Bain and Price; Certification Office.

HUMBER STEAM TRAWLER ENGINEERS AND FIREMEN'S ASSOCIATION

Established in 1893, the Association had 900 members in two branches in 1910. It was dissolved in 1938.

Sources: BoT Reports; Certification Office.

KENT AND SUSSEX AGRICULTURAL AND GENERAL LABOURERS UNION

See **Kent and Sussex Agricultural Workers Union**

KENT AND SUSSEX AGRICULTURAL WORKERS UNION

The Union was formed in 1872 by an amalgamation of the **Agricultural Labourers Protection Association** and the **Sussex Agricultural Workers Union**. Its headquarters was at Maidstone and it soon had 251 branches with 13,300 members and an income of £11,355 in 1876. The name was changed to the **Kent and Sussex Agricultural and General Labourers Union** and in 1889 it claimed to have over 10,000 members and an income of some £10,000 a year, most of which was disbursed in sick and funeral benefits. It ceased to exist as an independent organisation and joined the **National Amalgamated Union of Labour** (Vol. 3).

Sources: Selley; Groves, 'The Long Journey Home'; Groves, *Sharpen the Sickle!*; Horn, 'Agricultural Labourers' Trade Unionism'; J.Pointing, 'Trade Unionism in Agriculture', *in* Cole, *British Trade Unionism Today*; Green, *History of the English Agricultural Labourer*.

LEICESTER AGRICULTURAL LABOURERS ASSOCIATION

Previous to the formation of the **National Agricultural Labourers Union** in 1872, a local organisation was formed in 1866 in the village of Great Glen, Leicester. The labourers of this and nearby villages formed the Association and demanded an increase of 2s in their basic weekly wage of 10s. The landowners responded by evicting all the strikers living in tied cottages, and in the face of this severe opposition the organisation seems to have come to an end.

Sources: Horn, *Joseph Arch*; P.L.R. Horn, 'The Leicester and Leicestershire Agricultural Labourers Society, 1872–3', *The Leicester Historian*, Vol. 1, No. 5, 1969.

LEITH AND GRANTON TRAWLER SKIPPERS AND MATES PROTECTION SOCIETY

Formed in 1938 with 142 members, the Society continued to function for 25 years until it was forced out of existence in 1963 when its membership had dwindled to 42.

Source: Bain and Price.

LINCOLNSHIRE LABOUR LEAGUE

Established in 1871 under the leadership of William Banks, in 1872 the League refused the overtures of Joseph Arch to join in the formation of the **National Agricultural Labourers Union.** For a short period it published a journal, the *Labourers' Union Chronicle*, and Banks consistently used the publication to attack the policies of the NALU and of Arch in particular. In 1873 the League became a founder member of the **Federal Union of Agricultural and Town Labourers.**

Sources: Clegg, Fox and Thompson; Horn, 'Agricultural Labourers' Trade Unionism'; Green, *History of the English Agricultural Labourer.*

LONDON AND HOME COUNTIES LABOUR LEAGUE

See **Agricultural Labourers Protection Association**

MERCANTILE MARINE TRAWLERMEN'S ASSOCIATION

The Association was set up in 1919 with 336 members. This number gradually dwindled until in 1923 the Association ceased to exist when its membership stood at 81.

Source: Bain and Price.

MILFORD HAVEN AMALGAMATED DECK HANDS' UNION

Established in 1924 with 220 members, the Union remained in existence until 1931 when, with a membership numbering 494, it was dissolved.

Source: Bain and Price.

MILFORD HAVEN AND DISTRICT FISHERMEN, FISH WORKERS AND GENERAL LABOURERS UNION

Formed in 1916 with 101 members, the Union apparently ceased to exist in 1917. It re-emerged in 1921 as the **Milford Haven Fishermen's Amalgamated Society** and continued to function until 1928 when, with 197 members, it was dissolved.

Source: Bain and Price.

MILFORD HAVEN FISHERMEN'S AMALGAMATED SOCIETY
See **Milford Haven and District Fishermen, Fish Workers and General Labourers Union**

MILTON AGRICULTURAL LABOURERS UNION (OXFORDSHIRE)
Formed after the successful strike conducted by Joseph Arch in 1872, the Union later became the basis of the Oxford district of the **National Agricultural Labourers Union**.

Sources: Horn, 'Agricultural Labourers' Trade Unionism'; Meeting of 7 May 1872, Minute Book of the Milton Union, Cole Collection, Nuffield College, Oxford.

NATIONAL AGRICULTURAL LABOURERS AND RURAL WORKERS UNION
See **National Union of Agricultural and Allied Workers**

NATIONAL AGRICULTURAL LABOURERS UNION
The Union was established on Good Friday, 29 March 1872, at Wellesbourne, as the **Warwickshire Agricultural Labourers Union**, and was composed of a few hundred farm labourers, shepherds, carters, cowmen and others from several Warwickshire villages. Their spokesman was Joseph Arch. Immediately upon its formation the Union had a series of small strikes and lockouts on its hands, the members involved being supported financially by workpeople in the towns. The strikes lasted 3 months until one by one the farmers agreed to recognise the Union and reinstate their dismissed labourers. By then the Union had 60 branches in the county and local and district unions were being formed elsewhere. In May 1872 delegates from some 20 counties met at Leamington. As well as the union members a number of Liberal personages were present to illustrate their support for the labourers, and after hearing a report of the Union's progress a resolution was passed to form a 'National Union of Agricultural Labourers'. Joseph Arch was elected President, Henry Taylor, a Leamington carpenter active in his own union, was appointed paid Secretary, and a local newspaper editor, Matthew Vincent, became Honorary Treasurer. The entrance fee was 6d and subscriptions were 2d a week. The objects of the Union were to improve the general conditions of agricultural labourers in the United Kingdom, to encourage the formation of branch and district unions, and to promote co-operation and communication between unions already in existence. Its immediate aims were to secure a 9½-hour day and a minimum weekly wage of 16s. It published a weekly journal called the *Labourers' Union Chronicle*. By 1873 wages had risen from between 20 to 25 per cent and the Union was reporting that it had 982 branches, 23 districts and 71,835 members, rising to 86,214 members by 1874. But during the course of this period the farmers themselves were banding together, pledging not to employ union men and offering wages of 2s for a 12-hour day. By the early summer of 1874 10,000 men had been locked out, and between March and August of that

year the Union had paid out £24,423. In July it admitted defeat, many of the members returning to work but secretly retaining union membership. In the following years the Union was affected drastically by bad harvests, the import of cheap food from abroad and farmers leaving the land; by 1887 the membership was below 10,000 and by 1888 less than 5,000. By this time the Union had become a political rather than purely a trade union and the gaining of the franchise became its foremost demand. In January 1890, after the successful Dock Strike of 1889, Joseph Arch began a recruiting campaign and the Union's membership rose to 15,000, 12,000 of them in Norfolk. But again drought and bad harvest brought wage reductions which the union members resisted unavailingly, being again defeated and forced back to work. In 1895 the Union had little more than 1,000 members and it was dissolved in 1896.

Sources: Selley; Groves, *Sharpen the Sickle!*; Groves, *Seed Time and Harvest*; Clegg, Fox and Thompson; Suthers, 'National Union of Agricultural Workers'; J.Pointing, 'Trade Unionism in Agriculture', *in* Cole, *British Trade Unionism Today*; M.Madden, 'The National Union of Agricultural Workers', B. Litt. thesis, University of Oxford, 1957; F.D. Mills, 'The National Union of Agricultural Workers', *Journal of Agricultural Economics*, Vol. XVI, No. 2, December 1964; Horn, 'Agricultural Labourers' Trade Unionism'; *Warwick Advertiser*, 6 January 1872; Wearmouth; *English Labourers Chronicle*, 31 May, 1890, 5 March, 1892; Green, *History of the English Agricultural Labourer*.

NATIONAL AGRICULTURAL WORKERS UNION
The Union appears to have been formed in the 1880s as the **British Gardeners' Association,** the title being changed at the turn of the century. It had 988 members in 1906. In 1920 with a membership which had grown to 5,499, it merged with the **Eastern Counties Agricultural Labourers and Smallholders Union**.

Source: Bain and Price.

NATIONAL ASSOCIATION OF HAYCUTTERS, PARTNERS AND BALERS
The Association had a very brief existence, being formed in 1920 with 100 members and dissolved in 1921.

Source: Bain and Price.

NATIONAL FARM AND DAIRY WORKERS' UNION
The Union was formed in 1914 at the beginning of the First World War with 10,335 members, and continued in existence until the end of the war. In 1918, with 6,800 members, it merged with the **Workers' Union** (Vol. 3).

Source: Modern Records Centre, Warwick University.

NATIONAL FARM LABOURERS UNION
The Union was formed in 1875 under the leadership of Matthew Vincent who, until that time, had been the Honorary Treasurer of the **National Agricultural Labourers Union** and proprietor of its publication, the *Labourers' Union Chronicle*, which was the Union's organ from its formation in 1872. Matthew Vincent had had various differences of opinion with other executive members of NALU (including its leader, Joseph Arch) over union policy and over the question of the heavy expenses incurred at its central office, and decided to break away and form his own organisation which had as its prime purpose the acquisition of land for distribution among members in the form of allotments or smallholdings. In NALU circles the new union was dubbed 'the bogus union' because of the impossibility of its achieving its aims. Through the columns of the *Labourers' Union Chronicle* Vincent attacked Joseph Arch, doing everything possible to undermine confidence in NALU, which inevitably led to splits over the issue in the ranks of Vincent's own union. The Union's membership at this time was between 300 and 400, decreasing all the time, and Vincent was forced to sell the publishing rights of the *Labourers' Union Chronicle* in 1875 and retired through ill-health. The Union was finally wound up in 1881. It had succeeded only in creating disunity before it was finally dissolved.

Sources: Selley; Wearmouth; Horn, *Joseph Arch.*

NATIONAL FEDERATION OF FISHERMEN OF GREAT BRITAIN AND IRELAND
Founded in 1890, the Federation was able to win some concessions from the ship owners before it ceased to exist in 1894. With the introduction of steam trawling, a crop of local organisations for fishermen appeared on the North East coast, and the 1890s saw the beginnings of collective bargaining. In 1899 Hull fishermen negotiated a settlement with the Employers' Association which covered wages and bonuses for all grades except Captain and Mate. At this time, some 4,000 out of the 62,000 workers engaged in the industry were organised.

Sources: 'Report on Changes in Rates of Wages and Hours of Labour in 1899', Cmnd. 309, 1900, p.218; Clegg, Fox and Thompson.

NATIONAL FISHING INDUSTRIES PROTECTION SOCIETY
The Society was formed with 253 members in 1911 but collapsed the next year.

Source: Bain and Price.

NATIONAL UNION OF AGRICULTURAL AND ALLIED WORKERS
The Union was formed in 1906 as the **Eastern Counties Agricultural Labourers and Smallholders Union**. George Edwards, who had hitherto been the leader of the **Norfolk and Norwich Amalgamated Labour**

Union which had ceased to function in 1897, was appointed General Secretary, and George Nicholls, a Liberal MP, became President. Its objects at that time were to 'enable the agricultural labourer to secure proper representation on all local bodies and in Imperial Parliament, protection from political persecution and better conditions of living'. Until 1909 it concerned itself with small individual disputes, accident and victimisation cases and the provision of legal assistance, and by 1910 it had 4,000 members. In that year a strike took place among farm workers at St Faith's Village, Norfolk, without the approval of the Executive Committee of the Union, which lasted until December when the men were ordered back to work by the Executive Committee. The strike achieved nothing and many of the strikers failed to gain reinstatement, causing a good many to leave the Union and leading to criticism of the Executive Committee for its lack of support. In 1912 the name was changed to the **National Agricultural Labourers and Rural Workers Union**, which brought in as members not only farm workers but also carters, roadmen, gardeners, navvies and so on, and women were admitted for the first time. The Union affiliated to the TUC with over 4,000 members. It had 180,000 members in 1920 and the name was changed yet again to the **National Union of Agricultural Workers**. The present title was adopted in 1968 in recognition of its interest in industries ancillary to agriculture. In 1981 the NUAAW amalgamated with the **Transport and General Workers Union** (Vol. 3) which also had interests in this industry through its original absorption of the **Workers' Union** (Vol. 3).

Sources: Selley; S. and B. Webb, *History of Trade Unionism*; Clegg, Fox and Thompson; Barou; M.Madden, 'The National Union of Agricultural Workers', B. Litt. thesis, Oxford University, 1957; G. Edwards, *From Crow Scaring to Westminster*, Labour Publishing Co, London, 1922; Groves, *Seed Time and Harvest*; Green, *History of the English Agricultural Labourer*.

NATIONAL UNION OF AGRICULTURAL WORKERS
See **National Union of Agricultural and Allied Workers**

NATIONAL UNION OF BRITISH FISHERMEN
Formed in 1917 with 450 members, the Union had 1,350 members by 1918 and 4,500 by 1919. In 1922, with 4,209 members, it merged with the newly created **Transport and General Workers Union** (see Vol. 3).

Source: Bain and Price.

NATIONAL UNION OF LAND WORKERS
The Union was established in 1922 with 2,130 members but remained in existence for only 3 years, being dissolved in 1925 with a membership which had dwindled to 30.

Source: Bain and Price.

NORFOLK AND NORWICH AMALGAMATED LABOUR UNION
The Union was founded in 1890 by George Edwards, later to become the General Secretary of the **Eastern Counties Agricultural Labourers and Smallholders Union**. Edwards received a good deal of support from the Liberal Party which at that time saw trade unionism on the land as an instrument for organising the agricultural vote. The Union was dissolved in 1897 when it had only 20 members.

Sources: Certification Office; BoT Reports; Selley; Groves, *Sharpen the Sickle!*

NORFOLK FEDERATED UNION, HARLESTON DISTRICT
Formed in 1890, the Union had a brief success in recruiting more than 100 farm workers in the district. By 1895 this number had fallen to 10, and the Union collapsed in 1896.

Source: BoT Reports.

NORTH HEREFORDSHIRE AND SOUTH SHROPSHIRE AGRICULTU-RAL LABOURERS IMPROVEMENT SOCIETY
Formed in 1871, the Society was established largely through the efforts of a Methodist school teacher, Thomas Strange of Leintwardine, in which village the first meeting was held. It gained considerable support and recruited members in 6 counties covering an estimated membership of about 30,000. It was essentially a peaceful organisation, its stated aim being 'Emigration, Migration but not Strikes'. One of its main achievements was the sending of surplus labour from Herefordshire to work in Yorkshire, Lancashire and Staffordshire where wages averaging 16s to 17s a week were being paid against the 10s or 11s a week being paid in Herefordshire. Some men emigrated to America and even to Queensland with the help of the Society, and although it did not last very long, the work which had been done helped to consolidate the efforts of Joseph Arch in setting up the **National Agricultural Labourers Union**.

Sources: Horn, *Joseph Arch*; *Loughborough Advertiser*, 14 December 1871.

NURSERY AND HORTICULTURAL EMPLOYEES' ASSOCIATION
Established in 1907 with 395 members, the Association ceased to function in 1909 when its membership was 176.

Source: Bain and Price.

PETERBOROUGH DISTRICT LABOURERS' UNION
Formed in 1872, the Union was one of the many district organisations which grew up at that time. The Union was under the leadership of Benjamin Taylor, a high bailiff of the County Court. It refused amalgamation with the newly formed **National Agricultural Labourers Union** in 1872. It ceased to exist in 1893.

Sources: Horn, *Joseph Arch*; Certification Office.

PLOUGHMEN, CARTERS AND LABOURERS' UNION (SCOTLAND)

The Union was established in 1895 and had 1,541 members in 1896. With a gradually dwindling membership it was dissolved in 1901 when it had 807 members.

Sources: BoT Reports; Certification Office.

PORT OF GRIMSBY ASSOCIATION OF SHORE FISHERMEN

The Association was in existence for 3 years, being established in 1901 with 768 members and dissolved in 1904 when the membership had dropped to 168.

Source: BoT Reports.

PORT OF GRIMSBY COD FISHERMEN'S PROTECTIVE SOCIETY

The Society had a very limited existence, being formed in 1872 and ceasing to function in 1875.

Source: Certification Office.

PORT OF GRIMSBY FISHERMEN'S ASSOCIATION

Formed in 1878, the Association had 400 members in 1910. No other information seems to be available as to its further existence.

Source: BoT Reports.

PORT OF GRIMSBY SHARE FISHERMEN'S PROTECTIVE SOCIETY

Formed in 1901, the Society only remained in existence until 1904.

Source: Certification Office.

PORT OF GRIMSBY TRAWL FISHERMEN'S PROTECTIVE SOCIETY

The Society was very shortlived, being formed in 1873 and ceasing to exist in 1874.

Source: Certification Office.

PORT OF HULL TRAWL FISHERMEN'S ASSOCIATION

Established in 1879, the Association had 1,200 members in 4 branches in 1910. No further information is available as to its history.

Source: BoT Reports.

SCOTTISH FARM SERVANTS, CARTERS, AND GENERAL LABOURERS UNION

The Union, formed in 1886, was in its day a remarkable achievement. Besides the obvious difficulties of forming a union of farm workers anywhere, there was the added difficulty in Scotland in that farm servants were engaged for 6-monthly or annual periods of hiring, with the consequent breaking up of union branches. Its immediate aims were the securing of monthly payment of wages for engagements of indefinite periods, a weekly half holiday and the abolition of the bothy system. These objectives were eventually realised and the Union remained in existence until 1895 with a membership varying between 150 and 250. In that year it affiliated to the **Scottish Ploughmen's Federal Union**, a more powerful body based on the Southern and Midland areas of Scotland, but this affiliation did not prevent further decline and by 1900 farm labourers were being catered for mainly by the Aberdeen branch of the Federal Union.

Sources: Kenneth D. Buckley, *Trade Unionism in Aberdeen, 1878–1900*, Oliver and Boyd, Edinburgh, 1955; Wearmouth; Trades Council Minutes, 27 May 1891; Marwick.

SCOTTISH FARM SERVANTS UNION

The Union was founded in 1912 by Joseph F. Duncan, who was then Secretary of the **Scottish Steam Fishing Vessels Enginemen and Firemen's Union**, and through his prominence in the trade union movement in Scotland the Scottish Farm Servants gained some repute and for a number of years issued a monthly journal of high quality. It merged with the **Transport and General Workers Union** (Vol. 3) in 1933 with a membership of just over 2,000, and still retained a measure of autonomy within that union until 1943.

Sources: S. and B. Webb, *History of Trade Unionism*; Wearmouth; Clegg, Fox and Thompson; Cole, *British Trade Unionism Today*; Marwick.

SCOTTISH PLOUGHMEN, CARTERS AND LABOURERS UNION

Formed in 1895, the Union had almost 2,400 members in 1897, but this figure gradually dwindled until the Union ceased to exist in 1900.

Sources: Clegg, Fox and Thompson; Cole, *Trade Unionism Today*; Royal Commission on Labour, C-6894, XV, 1893.

SCOTTISH PLOUGHMEN'S FEDERAL UNION

See **Scottish Farm Servants, Carters, and General Labourers Union**

SCOTTISH SEA FISHERS' UNION

Founded in 1899 as the **Aberdeen Steam Fishing Vessels Enginemen and Firemen's Union,** within a few months of its formation the Union had 400 members, and by 1910 it had 425 members in 3 branches. It was not an organisation of unskilled workers since it deliberately excluded from membership deckhands and cooks. The title was changed to the Scottish Sea Fishers' Union and it merged with the **Transport and General Workers Union** (Vol. 3) in 1937.

Sources: Kenneth D. Buckley, *Trade Unionism in Aberdeen, 1878–1900*, Oliver and Boyd, Edinburgh, 1955; Marwick; Certification Office; BoT Reports.

SCOTTISH STEAM FISHING VESSELS ENGINEMEN AND FIREMEN'S UNION

The Union was set up in 1899 with 420 members. With 720 members it merged with the **Transport and General Workers Union** (Vol. 3) in 1937.

Sources: Certification Office; BoT Reports.

SKIPPERS AND SECOND HANDS' GUILD

The Guild was formed in 1921 with 240 members and continued to function for two years until, with 300 members, it was dissolved in 1923.

Source: Bain and Price.

SOUTH LINCOLNSHIRE LABOURERS' PROTECTION ASSOCIATION

Formed in 1872, the Association was dissolved in 1874.

Source: Certification Office.

SOUTH SHIELDS FISHERMEN'S ASSOCIATION

Formed in 1894 with 148 members, the Association ceased to exist in 1903 when it had 91 members.

Source: BoT Reports.

SOUTHERN COUNTIES AGRICULTURAL AND GENERAL WORKERS UNION

Formed in 1928 with 290 members, the Union merged in 1935 with the **Transport and General Workers Union** (Vol. 3).

Source: Marwick.

STAFFORDSHIRE AGRICULTURAL LABOURERS PROTECTION SOCIETY

Formed in January 1872 at the Fox Tavern, Perry Bar, at about the same time as the Warwickshire agricultural labourers were discussing the formation of their own union, the Society immediately made a demand for higher wages which was refused. It became a part of the **National**

Agricultural Labourers Union when that union was formed in March 1872.

Source: Horn, *Joseph Arch*.

SUSSEX AGRICULTURAL WORKERS UNION
The formation of the Union in the 1860/70s was one of the early attempts at combination by farm workers. In the late 1870s it joined with the **Agricultural Labourers Protection Association** and became the **Kent and Sussex Agricultural Workers Union**, which claimed to have over 10,000 members in 1889.

Sources: Selley; Arthur H.D. Acland, 'Land, Labourers and Association', *Contemporary Review*, Vol. L, July 1886; J. Pointing, 'Trade Unionism in Agriculture,' *in* Cole, *British Trade Unionism Today*; Groves, 'The Long Journey Home'; Horn, 'Agricultural Labourers' Trade Unionism'.

UNION OF AGRICULTURAL AND OTHER LABOURERS
Formed in 1834, the Union was established in the wake of the enthusiasm aroused by the foundation of the Grand National Consolidated Trades Union. Its members were employed in the Kensington, Walkham Green, Fulham and Hammersmith areas of London. It did not long remain in existence.

Source: S. and B. Webb, *History of Trade Unionism*.

UNITED FISHERMEN'S UNION
The Union was established in 1962 with 2,000 members. With 700 members it merged with the **Transport and General Workers Union** (Vol. 3) in December 1966.

Source: Bain and Price.

WARWICKSHIRE AGRICULTURAL AND GENERAL WORKERS ASSOCIATION
The Association was founded in 1893 and registration was cancelled in 1896. It came into existence as a result of a revival of agricultural trade unionism at the beginning of the 1890s, but which later collapsed following a drastic fall in grain prices. In 1897 some 200 of the union's former members joined the **Gasworkers Union** (Vol. 3).

Sources: Clegg, Fox and Thompson; Certification Office; Green, *History of the English Agricultural Labourer*.

WARWICKSHIRE AGRICULTURAL LABOURERS UNION
See **National Agricultural Labourers Union**

WEST DEREHAM DISTRICT UNION (NORFOLK)

The decision was made in October 1875 by the men working in the village of West Dereham to break away from the **National Agricultural Labourers Union** and form their own organisation. The local leader was a lay preacher named George Rix who had earlier been a farm worker, although in 1875 he was a shopkeeper. The breakaway came as the result of severe criticisms of the NALU and of Joseph Arch, in particular including accusations of the wasteful spending of union funds. This small union struggled to remain in existence until 1890 when it merged with the newly formed **Norfolk and Norwich Amalgamated Labour Union** (1890).

Sources: Horn, 'Agricultural Labourers' Trade Unionism'; Selley.

WEST SURREY AMALGAMATED LABOURERS UNION

Formed in 1874, the Union went out of existence in 1876.

Source: Certification Office.

WILTSHIRE AGRICULTURAL AND GENERAL LABOURERS UNION

The Union claimed to have been formed in the 1870s but the Board of Trade Reports give the date as December 1892. It was based mainly on Devizes. It had some success in negotiating wage rises in its early days due to a scarcity of agricultural labour, but the higher wages had the effect of checking migration from the land, thus increasing the supply of labour with the seemingly inevitable result that farmers began reducing wages. Membership was originally of the order of 1,500, but with a fall in grain prices and a consequent reduction in the number employed, the union was faced with a falling membership and ceased to function as an effective body about 1894. In 1897 the 110 members remaining in the union transferred their membership to the **Gasworkers Union** (Vol. 3).

Sources: Clegg, Fox and Thompson; BoT Reports; Selley; Green, *History of the English Agricultural Labourer.*

Chemicals

For industrial relations purposes, the chemical industry today comprises the areas covered by three joint industrial councils, the Chemical and Allied Industries JIC, the Drug and Fine Chemicals Joint Conference and the Gelatine and Glue JIC, with the addition of Imperial Chemical Industries. None of the unions presently concerned in these councils or with ICI has membership wholly confined to the chemical industry – for production workers they are the General and Municipal Workers' Union, the Transport and General Workers Union and the Union of Shop, Distributive and Allied Workers, and for the engineering craftsmen the Amalgamated Union of Engineering Workers, the Boilermakers' Society, the National Union of Sheet Metal Workers, Coppersmiths, Heating and Domestic Engineers, and the Electrical, Electronic, Telecommunication and Plumbing Union. For non-manual employees, recognition is on a company or plant basis only, but the same situation applies, there being membership in AUEW (TASS), in the Association of Scientific, Technical and Managerial Staffs, EESA (being the staff section of the EEPTU) and in the Association of Management and Professional Staffs. Of all these unions, only two, the TGWU and the AMPS, could claim to have had historical connections with employees' organisations which were, in their time, unique to the chemical industry. The former, in 1971, took in the Chemical Workers Union; the latter (being the 1978 title of the Association of Professional Scientists and Technologists formed in 1972) was substantially created under the auspices of the Royal Institute of Chemistry which incorporated within itself the British Association of Chemists originally formed in 1917.

Relatively little is known about early trade union developments in the industry. With the exception of salt making, in which one local union, the Winsford Saltmakers, was founded in 1853, no continuous organisation seems to have existed for production workers until the period of general unionism stimulated by the Great Dock Strike of 1889. A Northwich Salt Workers' Union had been established in the previous year[1] and three more followed for Droitwich, South Durham and Stoke Prior.[2] Thereafter it seems that, in the heavy chemical section of the trade, and therefore in the areas outside London and the Home Counties, where most heavy chemicals were located, such workers were sought out and recruited almost exclusively by those unions which were later amalgamated into the Transport and General Workers Union, the General and Municipal Workers' Union and the Union of Shop, Distributive and Allied Workers, the latter also dating from the 1890s through the National Amalgamated Union of Shop Assistants, Warehousemen and Clerks (established in 1891), having members in the drug and fine chemical sector.[3] It was thus understandable that when, during the First World War, the chemical industry became deeply involved in the execution of the munitions policy under the Munitions of War Act, both government and the employers should relate to the predecessors of these unions for national negotiations. In 1918 the recently formed Chemical Employers Federation initially turned to the Dockers' Union with a view to forming a Joint Industrial Council under the proposals for post-war management–union relations put forward by the Whitley Committee[4] and eventually included all three unions, while a Drug and Fine Chemical Manufacturers' Association developed its relationships with a Drug and Fine Chemical Joint Trade Union Committee with similar union representation.[5]

The establishment of national bargaining in the drug and fine chemicals sector of the industry produced an inter-union dispute which was to linger on for more than half a century. In 1913 the Shop Assistants had created a special drug workers' branch, based on Cripplegate in the City of London, which by the end of the war had more than three thousand members, mainly among wholesale, distributive and production workers. The branch, believing that it understood the needs of such workers better than the head office of the union, resented interference by a National Executive Council composed of 'grocers and hairdressers' in its negotiations with local employers. So much so that when the Drug and Fine Chemicals Joint Trade Union Committee made it inevitable that negotiations would be even more remote and nationally based, the Cripplegate branch determined that since it favoured industrial unionism, its members should transfer as individuals to the Amalgamated Society of Pharmacists, Drug and Chemical Workers, an organisation newly registered as a trade union in August 1918 but having its origin in a Retail Chemists' Association which had been founded by pharmacists 6 years earlier, mainly out of concern for professional standards in the trade. It seems that the militants from the Shop Assistants quickly took control of the Society, ousting the 'professionals' from overall control of the organisation and merging in 1920 with a more working class union, the National Association of Chemists' Assistants, to form a National Union of Drug and Chemical Workers, the title of which was simplified in 1936 into the Chemical Workers Union. The amalgamation also had the effect of extending the membership of the National Union outside London to the Midlands and the North, bringing it to a substantial figure of about 5,000.

It was no doubt partly for this reason that the Union was allowed, in 1920, to join the Drug and Fine Chemicals Joint Trade Union Committee and that, 3 years later, it was accepted as an affiliate by the Trades Union Congress. The Shop Assistants had not, however, forgotten the way in which it had received an injection of new life from dissident SA members in circumstances which, to say the very least, could be considered to be suspicious. Within a few months both that union and the National Union of General Workers complained to the TUC's Disputes Committee that the Chemical Union was a breakaway and poaching their members. The Committee dismissed the first of these claims, but found the second established and asked the parties to the dispute to accept some method of transfer of members between themselves which would serve to avoid such problems in future. Asked to hand back members acquired from the other unions, a general meeting of the Chemical Union instructed its Executive to disaffiliate from the TUC and this was done in 1924. At about the same time membership disapproval of certain decisions of the Drug and Fine Chemicals Joint Committee led it to sign a separate agreement with the Drug and Fine Chemicals Employers' Federation and, as a result, to be expelled from that committee.

Having put itself beyond the trade union pale, both in relation to the TUC and in respect of representation for the purposes of national negotiation, the Chemical Workers Union appears to have fallen prey to left-wing political fashions. Until 1936 it followed the Communist Party line through the National Minority Movement, denouncing the General Council of the TUC as 'labour lieutenants of capitalism'. After the outbreak of the Spanish Civil War it supported the Party's campaign for a

Popular Front against Fascism, arguing from this the necessity for it to rejoin the TUC and for an amalgamation of all unions with membership in the chemical industry. Such tactics could hardly have been calculated more effectively to alarm the general unions in the industry or to ensure that it was not reaccepted into the trade.union fold. Even during the Second World War it continued to behave 'as though the struggle to secure greater gains for workers took precedence over the demands of war'.[6] This hardly endeared it to the general unions which were strongly committed to the policies of the wartime coalition, but eventually brought some sympathy from smaller organisations who may have regarded the increasing power of large organisations with some apprehension. In 1943 the CWU was readmitted to the TUC on what, by that organisation's standards, was a narrow card vote – 3,258,000 to 2,451,000. Readmittance did not, however, gain it membership of the chemical industry's national negotiating machinery and in July 1971 the Union's 15,000 members voted overwhelmingly in favour of merger with the Transport and General Workers Union, which took place in September of that year.

In the 1960s the salt and chemical unions established in the Cheshire area in the late nineteenth century merged with the National Union of General and Municipal Workers.[7]

Notes

1. The Northwich Amalgamated Society of Salt Workers, Rock Salt Miners, Alkali Workers, Mechanics and General Labourers, which had 439 members in 1910.
2. The Droitwich Salt Makers, Mechanics and General Labourers (1889), the South Durham and North Yorkshire Salt Makers (1889) and the Stoke Prior Salt Makers, Mechanics and General Labourers (1889).
3. Shirley Lerner, *Breakaway Unions and the Small Trade Union*, Allen and Unwin, 1961, p.15. Drug worker recruitment appears to have begun in 1913. There were unions specifically designed for chemical workers whose life was very short, e.g. the Oldbury and District Chemical and General Workers' Union registered in 1895 and dissolved in February of the following year; the Fleetwood Salt Makers Union 1892–1898; and the Cheshire United Chemical Labour Union 1893–1897.
4. Roger Charles, *The Development of Industrial Relations in Britain, 1911–1939*, Hutchinson, 1973, p. 134.
5. Lerner, *op. cit.*, p. 17.
6. Lerner, *op. cit.*, p. 30.
7. The Federation of Trade Unions of Salt Workers, Alkali Workers, Mechanics and General Labourers was dissolved in November 1964; the Stoke Prior Salt Makers and the Union of Salt, Chemical and Industrial General Workers transferred their engagements to the GMWU in April 1965 and June 1969 respectively.

AMALGAMATED SOCIETY OF PHARMACISTS, DRUG AND CHEMICAL WORKERS
See **Chemical Workers Union**

BLACKING WORKERS UNION (MANCHESTER)
The Union was set up in 1892 with 150 members but was dissolved in 1909 when its membership was 136.

Source: BoT Reports.

CHEMICAL AND COPPER WORKERS' UNION
The Union was in existence for 6 years, being established in 1890, achieving a membership of 166 by 1892, and ceasing to exist in 1896 when the membership figure was 106.

Source: BoT Reports.

CHEMICAL, COPPER AND GENERAL WORKERS' UNION
Established in 1890 in order to represent workers in the heavy chemical trades in South West Lancashire, the Union was formed as a counter to the employers who had united to found the United Alkali Trust and had created unemployment through the rationalisation of production methods as well as reducing wages. Although the founder of the Union, P.J.King of St Helens, claimed in 1892 that most of the chemical workers in Lancashire were members, the Union had no bargaining power. It continued in existence until 1918 when it transferred its engagements to the **Process and General Workers' Union** with a membership of 240.

Sources: Cole, *Trade Unionism Today*; Modern Records Centre, University of Warwick.

CHEMICAL WORKERS UNION
The Union originated in a professional association, the **Retail Chemists' Association**, which was founded in 1912 primarily to raise the standards of the trade. The Retail Chemists' Association did not originally register as a trade union, but finally did so in 1918, after changing its name to the **Amalgamated Society of Pharmacists, Drug and Chemical Workers**. At that time it had 447 members. Two years later it amalgamated with the **National Association of Chemists' Assistants** (which had been formed in 1913) to form the **National Union of Drug and Chemical Workers** with Herbert Nightingale as its General Secretary. In 1936 the title was shortened to the above. The Union is best remembered for its long fight in the chemical industry as an *industrial* union against the general unions, the struggle being conducted under the leadership of its General Secretary, Bob

Edwards. As a result of this dispute the Union was accused of poaching members, withdrew from the Trades Union Congress in 1924 and was not readmitted until 1943. It was also successfully prevented by the general unions from obtaining national bargaining rights in the industry. It merged with the **Transport and General Workers Union** (Vol. 3) in 1971.

Sources: Shirley Lerner, *Breakaway Unions and the Small Trades Union*, Allen and Unwin, 1961; Certification Office.

CHESHIRE UNITED CHEMICAL LABOUR UNION
Established in 1893, the Union had a very brief existence, with one recorded membership figure of 108 for 1896. It was dissolved in 1897.

Sources: BoT Reports; Certification Office.

COPPER, SPELTER AND ALKALI WORKERS' TRADE UNION OF GREAT BRITAIN AND IRELAND
The Union was established in 1893 with 131 members and ceased to exist in 1896 when the membership had dwindled to only 5.

Sources: Certification Office; BoT Reports.

DROITWICH SALT MAKERS, MECHANICS AND GENERAL LABOURERS' UNION
Formed in 1889, the Union had 106 members in 1892 but only 59 in 1910. It remained in existence for over 50 years and, with 35 members, ceased to function in 1947.

Source: Bain and Price.

FEDERATION OF SALT WORKERS, ALKALI WORKERS, MECHANICS AND GENERAL LABOURERS
See **Federation of Trade Unions of Salt Workers, Alkali Workers, Mechanics and General Labourers**

FEDERATION OF TRADE UNIONS OF SALT WORKERS, ALKALI WORKERS, MECHANICS AND GENERAL LABOURERS
First established in 1890 as the **Federation of Salt Workers, Alkali Workers, Mechanics and General Labourers**, the enlarged title was adopted in 1906. Registration was cancelled in November 1964.

Source: Certification Office.

FLEETWOOD SALT MAKERS UNION
This was a very small local union established in 1892, having a membership of 20 in 1896 which had fallen to 11 in the following year. It ceased to exist in 1898.

Source: BoT Reports.

INDIA RUBBER, CABLE AND ASBESTOS WORKERS UNION
See **Rubber, Plastic and Allied Workers Union**

NATIONAL AMALGAMATED FOREMEN'S SOCIETY
The Society was established in 1918 with 501 members, the majority of whom were employed at chemical works. The membership level slowly dwindled over the years until, with 15 members, the Society ceased to exist in 1948.

Source: Bain and Price.

NATIONAL ASSOCIATION OF CHEMISTS' ASSISTANTS
See **Chemical Workers Union**

NATIONAL ASSOCIATION OF INDUSTRIAL CHEMISTS
The Association was formed in 1917 with 292 members and ceased to exist in 1922, although the membership had by this time risen to 1,013.

Source: Bain and Price.

NATIONAL UNION OF DRUG AND CHEMICAL WORKERS
See **Chemical Workers Union**

NORTHWICH AMALGAMATED SOCIETY OF SALT WORKERS, ROCK SALT MINERS, ALKALI WORKERS, MECHANICS AND GENERAL LABOURERS
Formed in 1888, the Society had 439 members in 1910. There are references to it in Board of Trade and Ministry of Labour records up to 1925, after which there seems to be no further information available.

OLDBURY AND DISTRICT CHEMICAL AND GENERAL WORKERS' UNION
Established in 1895 with 60 members, the Union remained in existence for one year until it was dissolved in 1896.

Source: BoT Reports.

PROCESS AND GENERAL WORKERS' UNION
The Union was formed in 1888, its membership working in the chemical industry. In 1968, with 2,051 members, it merged with the **Transport and General Workers Union** (Vol. 3).

Source: Bain and Price.

RETAIL CHEMISTS' ASSOCIATION
See **Chemical Workers Union**

ROYAL GUNPOWDER FACTORY EMPLOYEES' UNION (WALTHAM ABBEY)
Formed in 1897 with 380 members, the Union appeared to have ceased to exist in 1900 when its membership stood at 40. It emerged again in 1906 when it had a membership of 450. By 1916 it had 540 members and transferred its engagements to the **Workers' Union** (Vol. 3).

Source: Bain and Price

RUBBER, PLASTIC AND ALLIED WORKERS UNION
The Union was formed in 1889 as the **Waterproof Trade Union**. As techniques changed in the industry, it went through a series of name changes. In 1891 it was called the **India Rubber, Cable and Asbestos Workers Union**, the title later being changed to the **United Rubber Workers of Great Britain**. In the 1920s it almost went out of existence as a result of the trade depression and had only 312 members in 1936. During and after the Second World War the Union began recruiting again and reached a membership of over 4,000, the title being changed again to the above. It merged with the **National Union of General and Municipal Workers** (Vol. 3) in 1974.

Sources: H.A. Clegg, *General Union*, Basil Blackwell, Oxford, 1954; Certification Office; Marsh, *Concise Encyclopedia*.

SALT MAKERS' UNION
Formed in 1886, the Union had 1,226 members in 1892. In 1914, with 1,897 members, it amalgamated with the **National Union of Quarrymen** in order to form the **Amalgamated National Quarry Workers and Salt Makers' Union**.

Source: Bain and Price.

SOUTH DURHAM AND NORTH YORKSHIRE SALT MAKERS' UNION
The Union was formed in 1889, and had 308 members in 1892 and 184 in 1910. It remained in existence as an independent organisation until 1955 when with 131 members, it merged with the **National Union of General and Municipal Workers** (Vol. 3).

Source: Bain and Price.

STOKE PRIOR SALT MAKERS, MECHANICS AND GENERAL LABOURERS UNION
Formed in 1889, the Union had 245 members in 1892, which had fallen to 158 in 1900. In April 1965, with a membership of 117, it merged with the **National Union of General and Municipal Workers** (Vol. 3).

Source: Certification Office.

UNION OF SALT, CHEMICAL AND INDUSTRIAL GENERAL WORKERS (CHESHIRE)
This is a union of very limited membership which has had recognition by ICI for many years. It transferred engagements to the **National Union of General and Municipal Workers** (Vol. 3) in 1969.

Sources: D.R. Elsworth, 'Industrial Relations in the West German and British Chemical Industries', D. Phil. thesis, Surrey University, October 1980; Certification Office.

UNITED ALKALI AND COPPER WORKERS PROTECTION SOCIETY OF GREAT BRITAIN AND IRELAND
Formed in 1891, the Society was dissolved in 1893.

Source: Certification Office.

UNITED RUBBER WORKERS OF GREAT BRITAIN
See **Rubber, Plastic and Allied Workers Union**

WATERPROOF TRADE UNION
See **Rubber, Plastic and Allied Workers Union**

WINSFORD SALTMAKERS ASSOCIATION

Founded in 1853, the Association had 1,544 members in 1892, 1,340 in 1900 and 1,361 in 1910. It survived as an independent body until 1969 when it merged with the **General and Municipal Workers Union** (Vol. 3) when it had some 1,500 members.

Sources: C. Gill, R. Morris and J. Eaton, *Industrial Relations in the Chemical Industry*, Gower, 1978; BoT Reports.

Farriers

How many societies of journeymen farriers existed during the age of horse transport it is probably impossible to say. By the time the Board of Trade began to list such organisations, there were probably about twenty which were readily identifiable and consolidation had already begun into two main societies, the Permanent Amalgamated Farriers, whose membership reached a peak of more than 1,600 in 1896, and the National Amalgamated Farriers. An amalgamation of these two unions in 1902 into the Amalgamated Society of Farriers and Blacksmiths brought more than 80 per cent of the organised workers in these trades into a single union which was later known as the Amalgamated Society of Blacksmiths, Farriers and Agricultural Engineers (1951). This union was dissolved in 1964.

ABERDEEN AND DISTRICT HORSE SHOERS SOCIETY

This was a local journeymen farriers' organisation formed in 1895. It seldom had more thàn 30 members and was dissolved in 1910.

Source: BoT Reports.

AMALGAMATED FARRIERS SOCIETY

Established in 1879, the Society was apparently broken up in 1893.

Source: Certification Office.

AMALGAMATED SOCIETY OF BLACKSMITHS, FARRIERS AND AGRICULTURAL ENGINEERS

The Society was established in 1892 as the **Manchester and District Farriers Trade Protection Society**, the name being changed in 1893 to the **National Amalgamated Farriers Society**, and in 1899 to the **National Society of Farriers**. The **Permanent Amalgamated Farriers Protection Society** merged with the union in 1902 and the **City of Liverpool Farriers Society** joined it in 1903. The above title was adopted in 1930. It was dissolved in 1964.

Sources: Certification Office; Marsh, *Industrial Relations*.

AMALGAMATED SOCIETY OF FARRIERS AND BLACKSMITHS

See **National Amalgamated Farriers Society**

AMALGAMATED SOCIETY OF HORSE NAIL FORGERS

Formed in 1882, the Society went out of existence in 1893.

Source: Certification Office.

BIRMINGHAM AND DISTRICT AMALGAMATED FARRIERS SOCIETY

Formed in 1896 with 153 members, the Society combined with three others in the following year to form the **Midland Counties Amalgamated Farriers Society**.

Source: BoT Reports.

CITY OF LIVERPOOL FARRIERS SOCIETY

This was formed in 1886 as the **City of Liverpool Horse Shoers Friendly Society**, the name being changed to the above in 1899. The Society merged with the **National Amalgamated Farriers Society** in 1903.

Source: Certification Office.

CITY OF LIVERPOOL HORSE SHOERS FRIENDLY SOCIETY
See **City of Liverpool Farriers Society**

DERBY AND DISTRICT FARRIERS SOCIETY
A local organisation of journeymen farriers formed in 1895. It had no more than 30 members and in 1897 combined with three other local societies to form the **Midland Counties Amalgamated Farriers Society**.

Source: BoT Reports.

LEEDS AND DISTRICT FARRIERS PROTECTION SOCIETY
Formed in 1892, registration was cancelled in 1900.

Source: Certification Office.

LEICESTER FARRIERS PROTECTION AND BENEFIT SOCIETY
This was a journeymen farriers' society formed in 1891. In 1897, with about 60 members, it joined other local societies in the area to form the **Midland Counties Amalgamated Farriers Society** which in the following year joined the **National Amalgamated Farriers Society**.

Source: BoT Reports.

LIVERPOOL FARRIERS CENTRAL FRIENDLY SOCIETY
Formed in 1876, the Society was dissolved in 1890.

Source: Certification Office.

LONDON OPERATIVE FARRIERS TRADE SOCIETY
The Society claimed to have been founded in 1808. In 1893, with rather more than 500 members, it amalgamated with the **Permanent Amalgamated Farriers Protection Society**.

Source: Certification Office.

LONDON WEST END FARRIERS TRADE SOCIETY
Formed in 1894 and claiming origins from 1840, the Society merged with the **Permanent Amalgamated Farriers Protection Society** in 1894 when it had some 450 members.

Source: Certification Office.

LONDON WEST END FARRIERS TRADE UNION
Established in 1894, the Union merged with the **Permanent Amalgamated Farriers Protection Society** in the same year.

MANCHESTER AND DISTRICT FARRIERS TRADE PROTECTION SOCIETY

See **Amalgamated Society of Blacksmiths, Farriers and Agricultural Engineers**

MIDLAND COUNTIES AMALGAMATED FARRIERS SOCIETY

This was formed by the amalgamation in 1897 of four local journeymen farriers' societies representing Birmingham, Leicester, Nottingham and Derby, of which the first, with 153 members, was by far the largest. It joined the **National Amalgamated Farriers Society** in the following year.

Source: BoT Reports.

NATIONAL AMALGAMATED FARRIERS SOCIETY

Formed in 1891 as the **Manchester and District Farriers Trade Protection Society** and taking the above title in 1893, the Society was by the end of the century, with some 1,200 members, larger than its main rival, the **Permanent Amalgamated Farriers,** having also absorbed the **Yorkshire Farriers Protection Society.** These two principal unions came together in 1902, and the resulting **Amalgamated Society of Farriers and Blacksmiths** dominated the trade with 62 branches and almost 2,000 members in the early twentieth century. In 1903 the **City of Liverpool Farriers Society** also joined. In 1951 the union changed its name to the **Amalgamated Society of Blacksmiths, Farriers and Agricultural Engineers**.

Source: BoT Reports.

NATIONAL ASSOCIATION OF HORSE SHOE MAKERS

Formed in 1897 with 114 members, the Association gradually fell in membership and was dissolved in 1904.

Source: BoT Reports.

NATIONAL SOCIETY OF FARRIERS

See **Amalgamated Society of Blacksmiths, Farriers and Agricultural Engineers**

NEWCASTLE TOWN JOINT OPERATIVE HORSE SHOERS TRADE AND BENEFIT SOCIETY

Founded in 1872, the Society was dissolved in 1895.

Source: Certification Office.

NOTTINGHAM AND DISTRICT FARRIERS SOCIETY

This was a local journeymen farriers' society formed in 1892 which had 60 members in 1896. It combined with other local societies in 1897 to form the **Midland Counties Amalgamated Farriers Society**.

Source: BoT Reports.

OLD WEST END FARRIERS TRADE SOCIETY

Formed in 1897, the Society appears to have had no direct connection with the **London West End Farriers Trade Union**. It had 212 members in 1910 and was dissolved in 1917.

Source: BoT Reports.

PERMANENT AMALGAMATED FARRIERS PROTECTION SOCIETY

There is no record of the Permanent Amalgamated Farriers before 1870. It had 10 branches at the end of the nineteenth century and some 600 members, which rose to a peak of 1,646 in 1896. The Society amalgamated with the **National Amalgamated Farriers Society** in 1902.

Source: Certification Office.

YORKSHIRE FARRIERS PROTECTION SOCIETY

Founded in 1894, the Society amalgamated with the **National Amalgamated Farriers Society** in 1896.

Source: Certification Office.

Pottery and Glass

POTTERY

Not until the latter part of the nineteenth century were there successful attempts to form trade unions in the potteries, although an item of news in the *London Star* of 26 November 1792 read as follows: 'Country News, Staffordshire: workmen employed in the potteries here have combined to obtain an increase of wages; hitherto the masters have denied their demands and the men remained inactive, except in punishing some of their comrades who attempted to work at the usual price.' Failure of efforts at organisation in the early part of the nineteenth century were numerous.

Between 1824 and 1831 two unions were established, the Union of Clay Potters covering the craftsmen handling clay in its earliest stages of manufacture, that is, throwers, turners, handlers and hollow-ware pressers, and the Pottery Printers Union, whose membership comprised the workers who decorated the finished products by transfers printed from copper plates. Both unions had a very limited membership but in 1825 they called the first official trade union strike in the potteries in support of a wage increase. The strike was defeated and its leaders were victimised. In 1830, under the auspices of the National Association for the Protection of Labour, a conference was held in the potteries and a third organisation, the China and Earthenware Turners Society, was formed which was in substance a revival of the purely craft and local union of clay potters which had been destroyed in the strike in 1825. This met the same fate as the earlier union. A further effort was made in 1831 with the establishment of the National Union of Operative Potters, again under the encouragement and auspices of the National Association for the Protection of Labour. The new union recruited all pottery workers including those from the 'out-potteries', so that including members from outside the Five Towns its membership rose at one point to 8,000. In 1834 and 1836 the two most bitter strikes in the history of the industry were fought and lost. Again the union was defeated and ceased to function. A fresh effort at organisation was made in 1843 under the leadership of William Evans, who had been one of the victimised leaders of the 1825 strike. The United Branches of Operative Potters was non-militant, advocating no strikes, but only local turnouts at separate factories. Evans was the instigator of the *Pottery Examiner and Workmen's Advocate*, a well written and well thought-of publication in its day. In 1850, when the *Pottery Examiner* became defunct, the union's affairs were reduced to a very low and purely local level.

In the 1870s there was a period of trade revival which gave encouragement to a comparable revival of trade unionism, and to a reorganisation of unions which had become weakened by a long period of adversity. The membership of the Hollow-Ware Pressers Society, for example, rose from 500 in 1868 to 1,400 in 1873. In 1872 the Flat Pressers, the Crate-makers and the Printers reorganised their weak organisations, and the Hollow-Ware Pressers and Flat Pressers demanded high subscriptions from their members in return for improved benefits. The Printers and Transferrers Trade Protection Society established in 1871 had a low subscription rate and paid purely trade benefits, mainly because the membership comprised a large number of women earning very low wages who were unable to afford a high subscription. Little is known of the Cratemakers Society formed in 1872. Its membership was fairly good until the trade depression of 1879 when it collapsed and ceased to exist. Trade union organisation continued nevertheless, in the formation of unions like the Packers' Association which catered for pottery ware packers, the United Ovenmen's Society for ovenmen, kilnmen, dippers and saggar makers, and the National Amalgamated Society of Male and Female Pottery Workers.

In 1883 the National Order of Potters was set up and for some years had 1,000 and more members. By 1898 it had lost over half this number and in 1899 it merged with the larger Hollow-Ware Pressers under the title of the Amalgamated Society of Hollow-Ware Pressers and Clay Potters, which soon became the only organisation for mould-makers and earthenware clay potters, the Throwers, Turners and Handlers Society being dissolved in that year. The Operative Sanitary Pressers Society ended its independent existence in 1900; the Jet and Rockingham Workmen's Society and the Mouldmakers Society merged in 1902. In 1906 the Amalgamated Society of Hollow-Ware Pressers, the China Potters Federation, and the Printers and Transferrers Society united to form the National Amalgamated Society of Male and Female Pottery Workers, and by 1914, with the exception of the United Ovenmen and the Packers' Association, all organised potters in North Staffordshire were in the National Society, the China and Earthenware Gilders Union having been dissolved in 1894 and the Potteries China and Earthenware Decorators' Union in 1907. The China Furniture and Electrical Appliance Throwers and Turners Society joined the National Society in 1907 and the Society of Operative Pottery Engravers in 1908. In 1919 the union changed its name to the National Society of Pottery Workers, absorbing into its ranks the Packers and United Ovenmen's Societies, and for the first time all the craft unions were in one national organisation. The Society became the Ceramic and Allied Trades Union in 1970.

GLASS

Our knowledge of the history of trade unionism in the glass industry is slight. For almost the whole of the nineteenth century the industry was heavily dependent in all its aspects on craftsmen, often with close family ties, and enjoyed, despite highly unpleasant working conditions in many cases, a high degree of independence and high earnings. In bottle making and in the flat glass trade mechanisation made relatively small progress until the 1890s; specialised and decorated glassware remain a traditional skilled trade to this day.

In 1983 two unions only, the National Union of Flint Glass Workers, based on Stourbridge and the Pressed Glass Makers Friendly Society of Great Britain, remained of the 50 or more known to have existed in the industry. The antecedent of the first of these unions, the United Flint Glass Makers Society, was founded in 1844 or 1845.[1] This was not the earliest known organisation. An earlier union had been formed in Stourbridge in 1836,[2] and the Yorkshire Glass Bottle Makers, which continued in existence until 1941 started, almost contemporaneously with the bottle trade in Castleford, in 1827.[3] The Yorkshire Society was, without doubt, the largest which ever existed in the industry. In the 1890s it reached a peak of about 2,500 members in 14 branches, somewhat ahead of the Flint Glass Makers with about 2,200 in the same period.

At that time these two organisations could claim almost one-half of the organised glass workers of the day. Other glass bottle unions, about 10 in number, were widely scattered over the country and mostly small. A notable exception was the Lancashire and District Society, formed in 1853, and having over 800 members at that time. This society survived until about 1950, with a membership of about 150 at the end. What happened to the rest is far from clear, since not all were registered under the Trade Union Act 1871 in membership of the Trades Union Congress, or left any records.

Bottlemaking and decorated glassware seem to have been more readily organised in the last century than flat glass. Plate glass making for mirrors and carriage windows was a luxury trade akin to that of flint glass and overlapping with it. Possibly it had early unions in common. Crown glass, an entirely different product, though still associated with highly skilled family craft, benefited especially from the removal of excise duties on glass in 1845. The apparently short-lived British Crown Glass Makers Society formed at St Helens in 1846 is noted by Barker as 'the first trade union in the industry of which we have any evidence.[4] There was then, it seems, a gap in attempts at organisation until the 1870s. In 1870 a Sheet Glass Makers Society was formed at St Helens and lasted for a number of years. It seems to have failed to survive an unsuccessful strike in 1879.[5] A Pressed Glass Makers Society, formed in 1872 and based in the North East, in which a strong section of the flat glass industry had become established as early as the beginning of the seventeenth century,[6] grew to eight branches and some 500 members in the 1890s and has survived to the present day.

Outside the glass bottle trade, Lancashire seems to have been a difficult area for organisation. In St Helens employers such as Pilkingtons seem to have been determined and cost conscious, so much so that Pilkingtons men were tempted in the early 1880s to leave for America where their skills were in demand. American unions in the industry became concerned about the effects of this influx of foreign labour and in 1884 St Helens became the centre of determined efforts by the Knights of Labor to organise British glassmakers, setting up a local assembly based on Sunderland with a branch at St Helens, where they apparently made little progress.[7] Nor did a United Plate Glass Workers Society set up in 1889 have much better fortune. After a strike which dragged on from 21 June to 5 November 1890, the union lasted barely more than two years. When trade unionism revived this was apparently the result of the activities of the National Amalgamated Union of Labour under the encouragement of the local mineworkers union and its leader Thomas Glover who, with union assistance, was returned to Parliament at the election of January 1906.[8] In 1924 the NAUL became part of the amalgamation which produced the National Union of General and Municipal Workers, but not before it had been recognised in their factories by Pilkington Bros. in 1917.[9]

In 1925 there were some 17 unions catering for workers in the industry. G.D.H. Cole,[10] writing before the Second World War, records that at that time there were some 46,000 workers in the glass trade, including some 20,000 making glass bottles, the bulk of the trade union membership being in six primary local unions, the National Glass Workers Trade Protection Association (600), the London Glass Bottle Workers Trade Society (400), the National Flint Glass Makers Sick and Friendly Society of Great Britain and Ireland (500), the Lancashire District Glass Bottle Makers (300), the Pressed Glass Makers (300), and the Midland Glass Bevellers and Kindred Trade Society (300). Of these only the National Flint Glass Makers and the Pressed Glass Makers have survived to the present day.

Notes

1. H. Jack Haden, *The Stourbridge Glass Industry*, Black Country Society, 1971, p. 26, gives 1844; the Board of Trade Reports give 1845.
2. Haden, *op. cit.*
3. Board of Trade, *Statistical Tables and Report on Trade Unions*, Fourth Report, Cd. 6475, 1891, p. 228.
4. T.C. Barker, *The Glassmakers: Pilkingtons; the rise of an international company*, George Allen and Unwin, 1977, p. 82.
5. Barker, *op. cit.* pp. 175, 178.
6. T.C. Barker, *Pilkington Brothers and the Glass Industry*, George Allen and Unwin, 1960, p. 37.
7. Barker, *The Glassmakers*, p. 180.
8. Alan Wild, 'The Origins of the National Union of General and Municipal Workers at Pilkington Brothers, St. Helens', University of Warwick, MA Thesis, 1974.
9. Barker, *The Glassmakers (op. cit.)*, p. 396.
10. G.D.H. Cole, *British Trade Unionism Today*, 1939, p. 511.

ALLOA GLASS BOTTLE MAKERS SOCIETY
The Society was formed in 1894, the membership having seceded from the **Glasgow and District Glass Bottle Makers Trade Protection Society**. The Society had 49 members in 1910. There is evidence of its existence in the middle 1920s; thereafter no information seems to be available.

Source: BoT Reports.

AMALGAMATED CLAY WORKERS' SOCIETY
Founded in 1893 as the **Amalgamated Society of Pottery Moulders and Finishers**, the Society had 39 members in 1900 and ceased to exist in 1902.

Source: Certification Office.

AMALGAMATED PLATE GLASS WORKERS ASSOCIATION
The Association came into existence in 1893 as the result of an amalgamation between the **National Plate Glass Bevellers Trade Union** and the **National Society of Plate Glass Silverers, Siders and Fitters**. The partnership between the two organisations lasted only until 1895 when they agreed to separate and resume their former independent existence, thus bringing to a close the Amalgamated Plate Glass Workers Association.

Source: BoT Reports.

AMALGAMATED POTTERY MOULDERS AND FINISHERS
See **Amalgamated Clay Workers' Society**

AMALGAMATED PRINTERS AND TRANSFERRERS SOCIETY
Formed in 1871, the Society had 282 members in 1897 and was dissolved in the following year.

Source: BoT Reports.

AMALGAMATED SOCIETY OF GLASS MOULD MAKERS AND SMITHS
See **Amalgamated Society of Glass Works Engineers**

AMALGAMATED SOCIETY OF GLASS PAINTERS, EMBOSSERS, FRET, LEAD GLAZIERS AND CUTTERS OF THE UNITED KINGDOM
See **National Amalgamated Society of Glassworkers of the United Kingdom**

AMALGAMATED SOCIETY OF GLASS WORKS ENGINEERS
This was a Yorkshire based Society formed in 1893 under the title of the **Amalgamated Society of Glass Mould Makers and Smiths**. It had 119

members in 8 branches in 1910. The Society was one of the sectional organisations which joined the **Federation of Engineering and Shipbuilding Trades**. It had 111 members in 1900 and 119 in 1910. It declined to amalgamate with the **Amalgamated Engineering Union** in 1920 when that union was newly formed, but it eventually did so in 1944.

Sources: Jefferys; BoT Reports; Certification Office.

AMALGAMATED SOCIETY OF HOLLOW-WARE PRESSERS AND CLAY POTTERS

The Society was formed in 1868 with 500 members, which had risen to 1,400 by 1873 but fell again to 800 in 1874. It was not until 1891 that the Society again reached a figure in excess of 800, and the 1873 level was not surpassed until 1900. It adopted a policy of high subscriptions and substantial benefits; the subscription rate was 1s per week, and sick, funeral, no-situation, out-of-work, victimisation, lockout, and strike benefits were paid. The rules emphasised the importance of settling disputes by conciliation but also recognised that strikes might be necessary at times, and the decision to call a strike was in the hands of the Executive Committee. It became the only organisation for mould makers and earthenware clay potters when the **Amalgamated Society of Throwers, Turners and Handlers** was dissolved in 1899. In 1906 the Society amalgamated with the **China Potters Federation** and the **Printers and Transferrers Trade Protection Society** to form the **National Amalgamated Society of Male and Female Pottery Workers**.

Sources: Warburton, *History of Trade Union Organisation*; Cole, *Organised Labour*; E.J.Smith, *The New Trades Combination Movement*, London, Revingtons 1899; Twelfth Report of Trade Unions, 1899 (1900), pp. 100–1.

AMALGAMATED SOCIETY OF MEDICAL GLASS BOTTLE MAKERS

1900 is given as the date of foundation of the Society, reorganisation having taken place in 1905. It was based in Glasgow and the Secretary for many years was J. Heenan of Kirkpatrick Street. There is no further reference to the Society under this title after 1919.

Sources: BoT Reports; MoL Reports.

AMALGAMATED SOCIETY OF POTTERY MOULDERS AND FINISHERS

The Society was first formed under this title in 1893. The name was changed to **Amalgamated Clay Workers' Society** in 1900 and the union dissolved in 1902.

Source: Certification Office.

AMALGAMATED SOCIETY OF THROWERS, TURNERS AND HAND-LERS

The Society was formed in 1888 and had 100 members in 1896, but this fell to 36 in 1898 and the Society was dissolved in the following year.

Source: BoT Reports.

ASSOCIATED STONEWARE THROWERS

This was a Scottish union formed in 1877 which joined the **National Amalgamated Society of Male and Female Pottery Workers** in 1908, when it had 55 members.

Sources: Warburton, *History of Trade Union Organisation*; BoT Reports.

ASSOCIATION OF WHITE HOLLOW-WARE PRESSERS OF SCOT-LAND

Formed in 1886, the Association had 70 members in 1897 when it amalgamated with the **Scottish Potters' Flat-branch Defence Association** in order to form the **National Amalgamated Operative White Potters of Scotland**.

Source: BoT Reports.

BAROMETER, THERMOMETER AND TUBE BLOWERS' SOCIETY

Formed in 1890 and with its membership concentrated in a single branch, the Society had 52 members in 1900 and 31 members in 1910. It ceased to exist in 1915.

Sources: BoT Reports; Certification Office.

BIRMINGHAM AND DISTRICT GLASS BEVELLERS AND KINDRED TRADES SOCIETY

See **Midland Glass Bevellers and Kindred Trades Society**

BIRMINGHAM AND DISTRICT GLASS BOTTLE MAKERS SOCIETY

The first reference to the existence of the Society is in 1919, but after that date nothing further seems to be known of its history.

Source: MoL Reports.

BIRMINGHAM UNITED GLASS BEVELLERS SOCIETY

See **Midland Glass Bevellers and Kindred Trades Society**

BRIERLEY HILL DISTRICT GLASS BOTTLE MAKERS' ASSOCIA-TION

Formed in 1857, the Association was a long established but very small sectional union, its membership only ever reaching between 30 and 40. For reasons unknown it was suspended in 1899. Nothing more is known of its existence.

Source: BoT Reports.

BRISTOL GLASS BOTTLE MAKERS TRADE AND BENEFIT SOCIETY
Formed in 1872 and with its membership in a single Bristol branch, the Society had 86 members in 1900 and 79 members in 1910, after which date nothing further is known of its history.

Source: BoT Reports.

BRISTOL STONE POTTERS SOCIETY
The Society was established in 1891 and had no more than 20 members in the early 1900s. It joined the **National Amalgamated Society of Male and Female Pottery Workers** in 1908.

Source: Warburton, *History of Trade Union Organisation.*

BRITISH CROWN GLASS MAKERS SOCIETY
This was a craft union of crown glass makers formed in 1846 at a meeting of delegates from the St Helens and Birmingham glass factories. It placed special emphasis on restricting entry to the trade and on preserving the rights of the sons of existing glassmakers to enter the trade.No records have survived which would illustrate its subsequent history.

Source: T.C. Barker, *The Glassmakers: Pilkingtons; the rise of an international company*, George Allen and Unwin, 1977, p. 82.

CERAMIC AND ALLIED TRADES UNION
The Union was formed in 1906 as the **National Amalgamated Society of Male and Female Pottery Workers**, and it came into being as the result of an amalgamation between the **Printers and Transferrers Trade Protection Society**, the **China Potters Federation**, and the **Amalgamated Society of Hollow-ware Pressers and Clay Potters**. The new organisation grew quite rapidly after its formation, taking over the members of several small unions which had been on the point of dissolution. By 1914, with the exception of the **United Potters Packers Labour Protection Association** and the **United Ovenmen, Kilnmen and Saggarmakers Union**, all organised potters in North Staffordshire were members of the Society. Soon after its establishment in 1906 the Society began to extend its influence to the out-pottery districts and in that year the **National Amalgamated Operative White Potters of Scotland** merged with it. In 1907 a branch of the Society was formed in London, and in that year the **Insulator,**

China Furniture and Electrical Appliance Throwers and Turners Union
transferred its engagements to the National Amalgamated. In 1908 the
Associated Stoneware Throwers, the **Bristol Stone Potters Society**, and the
Operative Pottery Engravers merged with it. Contributions were 4d per
week. In 1911 the Society drew up its first scale of minimum piece rates,
and in 1919 it was able to reach agreement to abolish the custom of
payment for 'good from oven' and replacing it with 'good from hand'.
Under the latter system the potter was paid for all the work he made that
was good when it left his hands. Under the former system he had been
paid only for the goods which successfully withstood the test of 'firing' or
baking. Also in 1919 the Society became the **National Society of Pottery
Workers**, with a membership of 48,000. In 1921 the Packers' Society and
the United Ovenmen's Society merged with it. The Union changed its title
to the above in 1970.

Sources: Sixteenth Report on Trade Unions, 1905–7 (1909); Seventeenth Report on Trade Unions, 1908–10 (1912–13); Warburton, *History
of Trade Union Organisation*; D.I. Gregory and R.L. Smyth, *The Worker
and the Pottery Industry*, Department of Economics, University of Keele,
1964; Marsh, *Trade Union Handbook*; *Pottery Gazette*, September 1911,
November 1911, December 1911, March 1912, March 1914.

CHESTERFIELD AND DISTRICT POTTERS TRADE SOCIETY
The Society had the briefest of existences, being formed in 1899 with 58
members and dissolved at about the end of 1900.

Source: BoT Reports.

CHINA AND EARTHENWARE DECORATORS' UNION (HANLEY)
It is not known when the Union was formed, but it registered in 1903 and
was dissolved in 1907.

Sources: Warburton, *History of Trade Union Organisation*; Certification Office.

CHINA AND EARTHENWARE GILDERS UNION
The Union was formed in 1891. Nothing is known of its history except that
it was dissolved in 1894.

Source: Certification Office.

CHINA AND EARTHENWARE TURNERS SOCIETY
Formed in 1830, the Society came into existence after the defeat of the
Union of Clay Potters by the pottery manufacturers in 1825. A
conference was held under the auspices of the **National Association for
the Protection of Labour** (Vol. 3) and this led to the formation of the new
craft union. In 1831 the Society merged with the **National Union of
Operative Potters**.

Sources: *Voice of the People*, 5 March, 1831; Warburton, *History of Trade Union Organisation*.

CHINA POTTERS FEDERATION

Formed in the 1870s, the Federation amalgamated in 1906 with the **Amalgamated Society of Hollow-ware Pressers and Clay Potters** and the **Printers and Transferrers Trade Protection Society** to form the **National Amalgamated Society of Male and Female Pottery Workers**.

Sources: BoT Reports; Warburton, *History of Trade Union Organisation*.

CRATEMAKERS SOCIETY

The Society came into existence in 1872 following a successful strike of pottery workers in 1871. Membership increased rapidly until 1879 when with the advent of a trade depression and consequent unemployment, it lost members and the Society was dissolved. Pottery workers were very much affected by the growth of machinery and mass production methods at that time.

Sources: *The Beehive*, 16 September 1871, 23 September 1871; *Pottery Examiner*, 30 September 1871; Warburton, *History of Trade Union Organisation*.

EMPLOYEES OF MOORE, NETTLEFORD & CO. (WOOLWICH)

This was a factory-based union formed in 1903 with 120 members rising to 167 in 1904. It was dissolved in 1906 with a membership totalling 172.

Source: BoT Reports.

FRET, LEAD GLAZIERS AND CUTTERS TRADE UNION

Established in 1890, the Union merged with the **National Society of Decorative Glassworkers of the United Kingdom** in 1921.

Source: BoT Reports.

GLASGOW AND DISTRICT GLASS BOTTLE MAKERS TRADE PROTECTION SOCIETY

Formed in 1848 and always with a single Glasgow branch, the Society had 120 members in 1900 and 230 members in 1910. After this date no further details are known of its history, though it continued to exist in the 1920s.

Sources: BoT Reports; MoL Reports.

GLASS BOTTLE MAKERS AMALGAMATED TRADE ASSOCIATION OF GREAT BRITAIN AND IRELAND

Founded in 1877, the Association went out of existence in 1879.

Source: Certification Office.

GLASS BOTTLE MAKERS TRADE ASSOCIATION

Based on Brierley Hill, the Association was formed in 1882 and dissolved in October 1893.

Source: Certification Office.

INSULATOR, CHINA FURNITURE AND ELECTRICAL APPLIANCE THROWERS AND TURNERS UNION

The Union was a short-lived organisation formed in 1905 with 45 members, which merged with the **National Amalgamated Society of Male and Female Pottery Workers** in 1907.

Source: BoT Reports.

INTERNATIONAL UNION OF GLASS BOTTLE MAKERS

The Union was based on the Brierley Hill district and was established about 1857. It appears to have been a very small body with a membership ranging between 27 and 37. It is reported as having been suspended in 1899.

Source: BoT Reports.

JET AND ROCKINGHAM WORKMEN'S SOCIETY

This was a single branch society formed in 1899. It had 160 members in 1900, but was dissolved two years later.

Sources: Warburton, *History of Trade Union Organisation*; BoT Reports.

JUNIOR FLINT GLASS CHIMNEY AND BOTTLE MAKERS SOCIETY

Formed in 1883, the Society went out of existence in 1895.

Source: Certification Office.

LANCASHIRE DISTRICT GLASS BOTTLE MAKERS TRADE PROTECTION ASSOCIATION

Formed as early as 1853 as the **Lancashire Glass Bottle Makers Association**, this union had 900 members in two branches in 1900 and 953 members in 1910. It was based on St Helens and continued to exist, with little more than 150 members, until about 1950.

Sources: BoT Reports; MoL Reports.

LANCASHIRE GLASS BOTTLE MAKERS ASSOCIATION
See **Lancashire District Glass Bottle Makers Trade Protection Association**

LANCASHIRE MEDICAL GLASS BOTTLE MAKERS SOCIETY
Formed in 1909 the Society was based in Manchester. It had 48 members in 1910 and seems to have gone out of existence at some time during the course of the First World War.

Sources: BoT Reports; Certification Office.

LEEDS TERRA COTTA MODEL MAKERS SOCIETY
The Society existed briefly between 1897 and 1900 and never had more than 40 members.

Source: BoT Reports.

LIVERPOOL AND DISTRICT GLASS WORKERS INDUSTRIAL UNION
There is a reference to the Union's existence in 1919, the secretary then being F.W. Griffin of Rupert Street. It appears to have been still in existence in 1925 when the secretary was J. McHiggins of Elm Street, Bootle, after which date no more appears to be known of its history.

Source: MoL Reports.

LONDON AND COUNTRY UNITED POTTERY KILN BURNERS UNION
Formed in 1890, the Union was dissolved in 1892.

Source: Certification Office.

LONDON GLASS BLOWERS TRADE SOCIETY
Formed in 1873, the Society had 380 members in a single branch in 1900 and 422 members in 1910. It seems to have become the **London Glass Bottle Workers Trade Society** between 1918 and 1924. Under that title the union continued until about 1963. Whether it was dissolved or amalgamated is not clear, but its membership was about 150 at the time.

Sources: BoT Reports; MoL Reports; Cole, *British Trade Unionism Today*.

LONDON GLASS BOTTLE STOPPERERS AND CUTTERS TRADE SOCIETY
There is one reference to the Society in the Ministry of Labour Report of 1919 when the secretary was J. Ware of High Street, Homerton. Nothing further seems to be known of its existence.

Source: MoL Reports.

LONDON GLASS BOTTLE WORKERS TRADE SOCIETY
See **London Glass Blowers Trade Society**

MACHINE SECTION OF THE GLASS BOTTLE MAKERS OF YORK-SHIRE TRADE PROTECTION SOCIETY
See **Yorkshire Glass Bottle Makers United Trade Protection Society**

MIDLAND FLINT GLASS MAKERS UNION
Although the actual date of foundation of the Union is unknown, it was in existence in 1892, and all Midland workers in the industry were members of the Union. It became part of the **National Flint Glass Makers Sick and Friendly Society of Great Britain and Ireland**, which merged with the **National Union of Glass Cutters and Decorators** in order to form the **National Union of Flint Glass Workers**.

Source: S. and B. Webb, *History of Trade Unionism.*

MIDLAND GLASS BEVELLERS AND KINDRED TRADES SOCIETY
The Society was formed in 1900 by members who had broken away from the **National Plate Glass Bevellers Trade Union** in order to form their own independent organisation, originally under the title of the **Birmingham United Glass Bevellers Society**, the name later being changed to the **Birmingham and District Glass Bevellers and Kindred Trades Society** and later to the above. It transferred its engagements to the **National Union of Furniture Trade Operatives** (Vol. 3) in 1970.

Sources: BoT Reports; Certification Office.

NATIONAL AMALGAMATED OPERATIVE WHITE POTTERS OF SCOTLAND
The Union came into being in 1897 by the amalgamation of the **Scottish Potters' Flat-branch Defence Association** and the **Association of White Hollow-ware Pressers of Scotland**. In 1906 it merged with the **National Amalgamated Society of Male and Female Pottery Workers**.

Sources: BoT Reports; Certification Office.

NATIONAL AMALGAMATED SOCIETY OF GLASSWORKERS OF THE UNITED KINGDOM
The Society was formed in 1894 as the **Amalgamated Society of Glass Painters, Embossers, Fret, Lead Glaziers and Cutters of the United Kingdom**, the title being changed in 1898 to the National Society of Decorative Glassworkers of the United Kingdom and then at a later date to

the **National Society of Glassworkers of the United Kingdom**. It merged with the **Sign and Display Trades Union** in 1950.

Source: BoT Reports.

NATIONAL AMALGAMATED SOCIETY OF MALE AND FEMALE POTTERY WORKERS
See **Ceramic and Allied Trades Union**

NATIONAL FLINT GLASS MAKERS SICK AND FRIENDLY SOCIETY OF GREAT BRITAIN AND IRELAND

The year of formation of the Society is given as 1849. From 1850 it published its own journal called the *Flint Glass Makers' Magazine* which was still in existence in 1919. The Magazine had 96 pages of news and advocated 'the education of every man in our trade'. The policy of the Society was the repudiation of the strike weapon, and in 1854 it abolished the allowance of strike benefit by a vote of the entire membership. It was a powerful union in its day. For the next 10 years an emigration fund became a constant feature of many societies, including the Flint Glass Makers, the view being taken that 'if you remove surplus labour, oppression will soon be a thing of the past' (*Flint Glass Makers' Magazine*, August 1854). The Flint Glass Makers were always notorious for their strict limitation of the number of apprentices (*Flint Glass Makers' Magazine*, September 1857). In 1948 the Society amalgamated with the **National Union of Glass Cutters and Decorators** in order to form the **National Union of Flint Glass Workers**. The Union is mainly based on the Stourbridge area where the manufacture of crystal glass is centred, but it also has members in other parts of the country.

Sources: BoT Reports; Marsh, *Concise Encyclopedia*; Cole, *British Working-Class Movements*; H.J. Haden, *The Stourbridge Glass Industry*, Black-Country Society, 1971, p.26.

NATIONAL GLASS BOTTLE MAKERS SOCIETY OF GREAT BRITAIN AND IRELAND

This was a Leeds-based organisation. Formed in 1903 the members of the Society had seceded from the **National Flint Glass Makers Sick and Friendly Society of Great Britain and Ireland**. In 1910 the Society had 951 members in 13 branches. It disappeared some time between 1919 and 1925.

Sources: BoT Reports; MoL Reports.

NATIONAL GLASS WORKERS TRADE PROTECTION ASSOCIATION
See **Yorkshire Glass Bottle Makers United Trade Protection Society**

NATIONAL ORDER OF POTTERS
This society was set up in 1883 in the aftermath of the failure of previous

attempts to form a national union for pottery workers. Among the previous organisations had been the **Union of Clay Potters** and the **China and Earthenware Turners Society**, the first remaining in existence from 1825 to 1830 and the second for only one year. In 1831, under the guidance of the National Association for the Protection of Labour, a **National Union of Operative Potters** had been formed which lasted until 1836, and a fresh effort was made again in 1843 under the title of the **United Branches of Operative Potters**. For some years the National Order of Potters kept a record membership of about 1,000, but by 1898 this number had fallen to 550 and fell again in the following year, when it merged with the **Amalgamated Society of Hollow-ware Pressers and Clay Potters**.

Sources: Warburton, *History of Trade Union Organisation*; Cole, *British Trade Unionism Today*.

NATIONAL PLATE GLASS BEVELLERS TRADE UNION

TheUnion was founded in 1877 and appears to have had 650 members in 1892. In 1893 it amalgamated with the **National Society of Plate Glass Silverers, Siders and Fitters** in order to form the **Amalgamated Plate Glass Workers Association**. The partnership between the two organisations lasted only until 1895 when it broke up and the National Plate Glass Bevellers resumed their previous title. It had 640 members in 1900 and 449 and 489 in 1901 and 1902 respectively. It was dissolved in 1903.

Sources: BoT Reports.

NATIONAL SOCIETY OF GLASSWORKERS OF THE UNITED KING-DOM

See **National Amalgamated Society of Glassworkers of the United Kingdom**

NATIONAL SOCIETY OF PLATE GLASS SILVERERS, SIDERS AND FITTERS

Established in 1891 the Society had 236 members in 1892. In 1893 it amalgamated with the **National Plate Glass Bevellers Trade Union** in order to form the **Amalgamated Plate Glass Workers Association**, but the agreement between the two bodies broke down in 1895 and they agreed to separate. The union resumed its independent existence with 313 members which fell to 224 in 1899. In 1900, 1901 and 1902 the membership numbered 210, 213 and 201 respectively. The organisation was dissolved in 1903.

Source: BoT Reports.

NATIONAL SOCIETY OF POTTERY WORKERS

See **Ceramic and Allied Trades Union**

NATIONAL UNION OF FLINT GLASS WORKERS

Formed in 1948 by an amalgamation of the **National Flint Glass Makers Sick and Friendly Society of Great Britain and Ireland** and the **National Union of Glass Cutters and Decorators**, the Union is mainly based on the Stourbridge area where the manufacture of crystal glass is centred, but it also has members in other parts of the country.

Source: Marsh, *Trade Union Handbook.*

NATIONAL UNION OF GLASS CUTTERS AND DECORATORS

See **United Flint Glass Cutters Mutual Assistance and Protective Society**

NATIONAL UNION OF OPERATIVE POTTERS

The Union was formed in 1831 under the auspices of the **National Association for the Protection of Labour** (Vol. 3) and catered for all pottery workers, including those from the 'out-potteries' as they were then called – that is, outside the Five Towns. During its first years the Union's activities were mainly confined to the redressing of 'truck' and 'good from oven' grievances, a worker at that time being paid only for the pottery ware which had successfully withstood the test of 'firing' or baking. In 1833 the Union held its second annual conference with delegates representing lodges in North Staffordshire and from potteries in Bristol, Swansea, Newcastle upon Tyne and different parts of Worcester, Derby and Yorkshire. The membership at that time numbered 6,000 in North Staffordshire and 2,000 in the out-potteries. In 1834 the master potters announced that they would discontinue paying the union rates, which the Union refused to accept, and negotiations between masters and men broke down. The ensuing strike resulted in a defeat for the Union and a return to work on the masters' terms. In 1836 the employers issued a statement that hirings for the coming year would be made only if the men signed an agreement renouncing the Union. The Union replied by offering to put the matter before a conciliation board, but the masters refused. By this time Martinmas, the time of hiring, had arrived and as neither masters nor men could agree on the form of hiring agreement, the whole industry came to a standstill. The suffering of the potters was considerable as their union funds only allowed for the payment of a few shillings strike money each week, but the strike continued and resulted in some success. The new hiring agreement guaranteed the potter 16 days' work per month; the 'good from oven' system was retained but with certain advantageous alterations; and the men were allowed to draw weekly on account a sum equal to two thirds of the value of the unfired pottery ware. But the financial strain of the strike forced the Union out of existence, and its leader, William Evans, was victimised and lost his job. In 1843 a new union called the **United Branches of Operative Potters** was set up (again under the leadership of Evans) which published its own journal, the *Pottery Examiner and Workman's Advocate*, later called the *Pottery Examiner and Emigrant's Advocate*. It ceased publication in 1851. After the failure of a national body the pottery workers had fallen back on small sectional societies, but in 1883 a fresh effort was made with the establishment of the **National Order of Potters** which survived until 1890.

Sources: *Staffordshire Mercury*, 17 August 1833; *Crisis*, 19 October 1833; Warburton, *History of Trade Union Organisation*; *Pottery Examiner*, 28 December 1844; *The Times*, 29 November 1836, 13 December 1836; Cole, *British Trade Unionism Today*; J. Boyle, 'An Account of the Strikes in the Potteries, 1834–1836', *Journal of the Statistical Society*, Vol. 1, 1839.

NATIONAL UNION OF SIGN, GLASS AND TICKET WRITERS AND KINDRED TRADES
See **Sign and Display Trades Union**

NEW UNION OF GLASS WORKERS AND KINDRED TRADES
There is one reference to the existence of the Union in the Ministry of Labour Report of 1925. It seems to have been based on the Brierley Hill area and the secretary was J. Wilson, Church Street, Brierley Hill. No further information appears to be available as to its history.

Source: MoL Reports.

NORTH OF ENGLAND GLASS BOTTLE MAKERS SOCIETY
The Society came into existence in 1873 and was based in Sunderland. It had 263 members in 2 branches in 1910. There is no further reference to it after 1925. There was, however, an organisation called the **Northern Glass Workers Employees Association** which may have been the same organisation. This union merged with the **Sign and Display Trades Union** in 1950.

Sources: BoT Reports; MoL Reports.

NORTHERN GLASS WORKERS EMPLOYEES ASSOCIATION
See **North of England Glass Bottle Makers Society**

OPERATIVE POTTERY ENGRAVERS
See **Ceramic and Allied Trades Union**

OPERATIVE SANITARY PRESSERS SOCIETY
The Society was a shortlived potters' union formed in 1894. Initially it had about 100 members, but these dwindled to 40 and it was dissolved in 1900.

Sources: Warburton, *History of Trade Union Organisation*; BoT Reports.

PORTOBELLO GLASS BOTTLE MAKERS TRADE PROTECTION ASSOCIATION

Formed in 1895 the Association had 215 members in 1910. There is no further reference to its existence after 1925. It was apparently an unregistered union.

Sources: BoT Reports; MoL Reports.

POTTERS PAINTERS UNION

The Union was an early craft society in the pottery industry. There is evidence of its existence in 1831, but it is unlikely that it lasted long. Possibly it amalgamated with the **National Union of Operative Potters**.

Sources: Warburton, *History of Trade Union Organisation; Voice of the People*, 10 September 1831.

POTTERS UNION

The Union was founded in 1830 under the leadership of John Docherty, who was then Secretary of the **Manchester Cotton Spinners Society** (Vol. 3), and who became Secretary and founder of the **National Association for the Protection of Labour** in 1831. The Union had a membership of 8,000 in 1833, of whom 6,000 were in Staffordshire and the remainder in lodges at Newcastle upon Tyne, Derby, Bristol and Swinton. The Union went from strength to strength and in 1835 gained a notable victory with the employers by the agreement to the 'Green Book of Prices' which formed the basis for wage negotiations in the pottery trade for many years. But the employers formed a Chamber of Commerce to put up joint resistance to the potters' demands, and when the 'yearly bond' was rigidly adhered to by the workers, a strike ensued which ended in 1837 with the virtual collapse of the Union. It was re-established in 1843 under the title of the **United Branches of Operative Potters**, later called the **National Union of Operative Potters**.

Sources: S. and B. Webb, *History of Trade Unionism; Crisis*, 19 October, 1833; *Pottery Examiner*, September, 1843; Warburton, *History of Trade Union Organisation*; Cole, *British Working-Class Movements*; J. Boyle, 'An Account of the Strikes in the Potteries, 1834–1836', *Journal of the Statistical Society*, Vol. 1, 1839.

POTTERY PRINTERS UNION

This was an early established craft union in the industry organising those workers who decorated the finished pottery by means of transfers from copper plates. In 1825 the Union, together with the **Union of Clay Potters** engaged in the first official strike in this industry and were beaten by the Pottery Manufacturers.

Sources: Cole, *British Trade Unionism Today*; Warburton, *History of Trade Union Organisation; Potters Mercury*, 20 April 1825, 22 June 1825; J. Boyle, 'An Account of the Strikes in the Potteries, 1834–1836', *Journal of the Statistical Society*, Vol. 1, 1839.

PRESSED GLASS MAKERS FRIENDLY SOCIETY OF GREAT BRITAIN

Formed in 1872, the Society had 7 branches with 526 members in 1900 and 6 branches with 453 members in 1910. It was based on Co. Durham. The entry of trade union registration was removed by request in 1973, but the Society was still in existence in 1983 with 40 members.

Sources: BoT Reports; Certification Office; T.C. Barker, *Pilkington Brothers and the Glass Industry*, George Allen and Unwin, 1960, p. 37; Cole, *British Trade Unionism Today*.

PRINTERS AND TRANSFERRERS TRADE PROTECTION SOCIETY

The Society was established in 1871 (although the Board of Trade gives the date as 1898), and the members paid a low subscription rate and received purely trade benefits. The low subscription was based on the fact that the membership was a mixed one and women were paid very poor wages. As a result men paid 4d a week and women 2d, benefits being granted proportionately. Apprentices had to serve for 5 years, and not more than one apprentice was allowed for 5 journeymen. In 1900 it had 1,739 members in 5 branches. The Society amalgamated in 1906 with the **China Potters Federation** and the **Amalgamated Society of Hollow-ware Pressers and Clay Potters** to form the **National Amalgamated Society of Male and Female Pottery Workers,** male and female members carrying out the work of printers and transferrers respectively.

Sources: Warburton, *History of Trade Union Organisation*; BoT Reports.

ST. HELENS SHEET GLASS FLATTENERS TRADE PROTECTION SOCIETY

Established in 1891, the Society had 140 members in 1900 and 131 members in 1910. It seems to have gone out of existence during the First World War. The BoT gives the foundation date as 1892.

Source: *St Helens Newspaper*, 26 September 1891; BoT Reports.

ST. HELENS SHEET GLASS MAKERS ASSOCIATION

A rule book of the Association dated 1874 refers to its having been founded in 1870. At that time it had three branches (St. Helens, Smethwick and Sunderland) and an accumulated fund of £1,000 for investment. Thereafter its history is obscure. Such evidence as there is suggests it may have become inoperative after an unsuccessful strike in 1879. Whether it had any connection with the **Sheet Glass Makers Society of St. Helens** or the **St. Helens United Plate Glass Workers Society** is not clear.

Sources: T.C. Barker, *The Glassmakers: Pilkingtons; The rise of an international company*, 1977, George Allen and Unwin, p. 82.

ST. HELENS UNITED PLATE GLASS WORKERS SOCIETY

There is a reference to the Society in 1889 and 1890 having 1,246 and 800 members respectively, but in the Board of Trade Reports for the years 1892 to 1910 there is no reference to such a body being in existence in 1889 and having such a membership level.

Sources: Board of Trade, *Statistical Tables and Report on Trade Unions. Fourth Report*, Years 1889 to 1890 Cd-6475, 1891; T.C. Barker, *The Glassmakers: Pilkingtons; The rise of an international company*, George Allen and Unwin, 1977, p. 82.

SCOTTISH POTTERS' FLAT-BRANCH DEFENCE ASSOCIATION

Formed in 1889, the Association had a membership of 30 in 1897 when it amalgamated with the **Association of White Hollow-ware Pressers of Scotland** in order to form the **National Amalgamated Operative White Potters of Scotland**.

Source: BoT Reports.

SHEET GLASS MAKERS SOCIETY OF ST. HELENS

Formed in 1894, the Society was a single branch organisation and had 295 members in 1900. It merged with the **National Amalgamated Union of Labour** (Vol. 3) in 1904. It appears that glasscutters and other St Helens glass workers began to join the NAUL in 1892 and were much enthused by the campaign of the Labour Representation Committee. The Committee ultimately returned its candidate, Thomas Glover, to Parliament in January 1906.

Sources: Certification Office; Alan Wild, 'The Origins of the National Union of General and Municipal Workers at Pilkington Brothers, St Helens', University of Warwick MA Thesis, 1974.

SIGN AND DISPLAY TRADES UNION

The Union was founded in 1918 as the **National Union of Sign, Glass and Ticket Writers and Kindred Trades** and later as the **National Union of Sign, Glass and Ticket Writers**. The above title was adopted in 1945. The Union organised sign and glass sign writers, ticket writers, cinema and poster writers, etc. The **National Society of Glassworkers of the United Kingdom** and the **Northern Glass Workers Employees Association** transferred their engagements to the SDTU in 1950. The Union has now merged with the **National Society of Operative Printers, Graphical and Media Personnel** (Vol. 4).

Source: Arthur Marsh, *Concise Encyclopedia*.

SOCIETY OF OPERATIVE POTTERY ENGRAVERS

The Society was a small sectional organisation formed about the 1880s.

Always weak, it struggled to remain independent until, in 1908, it merged with the **National Amalgamated Society of Male and Female Pottery Workers**.

Source: Warburton, *History of Trade Union Organisation.*

STAFFORDSHIRE POTTERIES CHINA JIGGERERS SOCIETY
Founded in 1878, the Society went out of existence in 1879.

Source: Certification Office.

STAFFORDSHIRE POTTERIES MOULD MAKERS TRADE ASSO-CIATION
Established in 1874, the Association was dissolved in 1875.

Source: Certification Office.

STAFFORDSHIRE POTTERIES OPERATIVE CRATEMAKERS' SOCI-ETY
The Society existed briefly between 1901 and 1903. Nothing further seems to be known about it.

Source: Certification Office.

STAFFORDSHIRE POTTERIES OPERATIVE FLAT PRESSERS SOCI-ETY
Established in 1873, the Society ceased to exist after 1895.

Source: Certification Office.

STAFFORDSHIRE POTTERIES TRADE PROTECTION SOCIETY OF THE ENGRAVERS, CHINA AND EARTHENWARE MANUFACTUR-ERS
Formed in 1873, the Society went out of existence in 1876.

Source: Certification Office.

UNION OF CLAY POTTERS
The Union was formed in 1824, and its membership included hollow-ware pressers, saucer and plate makers, turners, throwers, handlers, and all workers handling clay in its earliest stages of manufacture. In 1825, together with the **Pottery Printers Union**, it engaged in the first official trade union strike of pottery workers, but was defeated by the Pottery

Manufacturers' Association. From 1825–31 the leadership, although victimised, maintained contact with the national organisations which were attempting to unify the trade union movement generally. In 1830 a conference was held for the potteries under the auspices of the **National Association for the Protection of Labour** (Vol. 3), and this led to the formation of a local **China and Earthenware Turners Society**. This was really a revival of a type of purely craft and local union like those smashed in 1825 and consequently it did not survive.

Sources: *Potters Mercury*, 30 March 1825; Cole, *British Trade Unionism Today*; Warburton, *History of Trade Union Organisation*.

UNITED BRANCHES OF OPERATIVE POTTERS
See **National Union of Operative Potters** and **National Order of Potters**

UNITED FLINT GLASS CUTTERS MUTUAL ASSISTANCE AND PROTECTIVE SOCIETY
The Society is recorded as having been formed in 1844. It had 830 members in 1892 and 822 in 1899. It retained a steady membership of between 600 and 800 members until 1910. J. Hewitt of Cavendish Road, Birmingham was secretary of the Society from 1913 until 1925 by which time the title had been changed to the **National Union of Glass Cutters and Decorators**. In 1948 it amalgamated with the **National Flint Glass Makers Sick and Friendly Society of Great Britain and Ireland** in order to form the **National Union of Flint Glass Workers**.

Sources: BoT Reports; MoL Reports; Arthur Marsh, *Concise Encyclopedia*.

UNITED FLINT GLASS MAKERS SOCIETY
See **National Flint Glass Makers Sick and Friendly Society of Great Britain and Ireland**

UNITED (MACHINE) GLASS BOTTLE MAKERS SOCIETY
In about 1918 the **Yorkshire Glass Bottle Makers United Trade Protection Society** added a Machine Section into the organisation of the union. A. Greenwood of Wesley Street, Castleford is listed as being secretary of the main Yorkshire Society and of the new Machine Section. In addition, in the same period a body called the United (Machine) Glass Bottle Makers Society with J. Smith of Leeds Road, Castleford is also listed as a functioning organisation, and continued to be registered up to 1925, after which date nothing further appears to be known of its subsequent existence.

Sources: BoT Reports; MoL Reports.

UNITED OVENMEN, KILNMEN AND SAGGARMAKERS UNION
Formed in 1860, the Union had 5 branches in 1900 catering for ovenmen,

kilnmen, dippers and saggar makers, and was later known as the United Ovenmen's Society. It had 6 branches and 915 members in 1900 and 420 members in 1910. In 1921 it merged with the **National Society of Pottery Workers**, now known as the **Ceramic and Allied Trades Union**.

Source: Warburton, *History of Trade Union Organisation.*

UNITED PLATE GLASS WORKERS SOCIETY

Established in 1889, as part of the spread of the new unionism, the Society claimed a membership of 800 in June of that year, most of them men. In 1890 it organised a strike which lasted for 20 weeks at three St Helens glass factories. This was completely unsuccessful and the Society went out of existence in 1892.

Sources: Certification Office; T.C. Barker, *The Glassmakers: Pilkingtons; the rise of an international company,* George Allen and Unwin, 1977, p. 82.

UNITED POTTERS PACKERS LABOUR PROTECTION ASSOCIATION

This was a small out-district Association formed in 1887 for pottery ware packers. It had 60 members in 1900 and 105 in 1910. It merged with the **National Society of Pottery Workers** in 1921.

Sources: BoT Reports; Warburton, *History of Trade Union Organisation.*

YORKSHIRE GLASS BOTTLE MAKERS UNITED TRADE PROTECTION SOCIETY

This Society, it has been claimed, started at almost the same time as the bottle trade was established at Castleford in 1827. It became an important body, having 692 members in 1867 organised in 17 branches with an annual income of £2,213. By 1890 it was registering a membership of 1,889 and an annual income of £6,321. The method of payment in the trade was stated to be 'somewhat peculiar' in as much as the men worked in sets and although there was a standard wage, there was also a fixed standard equivalent of so many dozens of bottles which had to be made, which were paid for at a fixed rate per gross. The trade also included blowers whose wages were 2s less than the bottle makers, gatherers and blowers paid at 4s 6d less, and gatherers paid 7s a week less, so that in 1890 the rates of wages were finishers £1.10s a week, blowers £1.8s a week and gatherers £1.3s a week, these rates being identical with those paid in 1854. The workmen were paid one-half the rate for bottles, whether melted, cracked or not properly annealed. From 1892 to 1910 the Society registered a membership which ranged between 2,300 and 2,800. By 1925 it had become the **National Glass Workers Trade Protection Association** and in about 1938 it had about 600 members. In 1941 registration was cancelled.

Sources: BoT Reports; Board of Trade, *Statistical Tables and Report on Trade Unions. Fourth Report,* Years 1889 and 1890 Cd. 6475, 1891, p. 228; MoL Reports; Certification Office; Cole, *British Trade Unionism Today.*

Index